Communication and Human Behavior

THIRD EDITION

Brent D. Ruben

Rutgers University

PRENTICE HALL, *Englewood Cliffs, New Jersey* 07632

Library of Congress Cataloging-in-Publication Data

Ruben, Brent D.
Communication and human behavior / Brent D. Ruben. — 3rd ed.
p. cm.
Includes bibliographical references and indexes.
ISBN 0-13-155847-1
1. Communication. 2. Human behavior. I. Title.
P90.R78 1992
302.2—dc20 91-35908
CIP

Acquisitions Editor: Stephen Dalphin
Production Editor: Marianne Peters
Interior Designer: Andrew Zutis
Cover Designer: Lydia Guershey
Cover Art: Computer Illustration/The Image Bank
Prepress Buyer: Kelly Behr
Manufacturing Buyer: Mary Ann Gloriande
Supplements Editor: Sharon Chambliss
Editorial Assistant: Caffie Risher

Printed in the United States of America
10 9 8 7 6 5 4 3 2 1

ISBN 0-13-155847-1

Prentice-Hall International (UK) Limited, *London*
Prentice-Hall of Australia Pty. Limited, *Sydney*
Prentice-Hall Canada Inc., *Toronto*
Prentice-Hall Hispanoamericana, S.A., *Mexico*
Prentice-Hall of India Private Limited, *New Delhi*
Prentice-Hall of Japan, Inc., *Tokyo*
Simon & Schuster Asia Pte. Ltd., *Singapore*
Editora Prentice-Hall do Brasil, Ltda., *Rio de Janeiro*

For Jann, Robbi, and Marc
family, friends, teachers

Contents

PART 1 HISTORICAL AND THEORETICAL PERSPECTIVES

Preface

Each generation faces a number of problems and prospects. For us there are the challenges of poverty and homelessness, drug and substance abuse, evolving concepts of marriage and family, changing gender roles, regional conflicts, an aging population, high crime rates, economic pressures, and fast-paced technological change.

We also face a host of smaller, but no less significant challenges on a daily basis: a relationship that doesn't work out, the low grade we receive, a job that doesn't come through, a friend who no longer seems to care, the prejudice or discrimination that inflicts pain, a parent who doesn't understand, a marital conflict that can't be reconciled, or a child who disappoints loved ones.

Whether approached from the perspective of psychology or communication, political science or art, literature or sociology, a knowledge of human behavior can be of great value in our efforts to comprehend and deal with the circumstances we encounter. And, it can also help us understand ourselves, our actions, our motives, our feelings, and our aspirations.

Perhaps the greatest value comes from approaches which draw upon a number of disciplinary perspectives. *Communication and Human Behavior, Third Edition,* aims to provide this kind of framework. The contributions of general system theory have been particularly helpful in developing the perspective presented in the book. The general systems approach directs attention to the various disciplines in which communication has been studied, and provides the encouragement and means necessary for unifying these often divergent points of view. Systems theory encourages the exploration of the role of communication not only in human life, but also in the essential activities of all living things. Further, the systems approach underscores the importance of examining communication at various levels—biological, psychological, social, organizational, cultural, societal, international, and technological. And finally, systems theory provides a way of characterizing the structures and relationships within and among these levels of human activity. Symbolic interaction, general semantics, sociology of knowledge, cultural studies, and cognitive science have also contributed importantly to the approach taken.

About the Third Edition

The First and Second Edition of *Communication and Human Behavior* have been well received by students and instructors at the many colleges and universities where it has been adopted. This response has been very gratifying, personally. It has also meant that a number of helpful comments and suggestions on the book have been provided, and as a result this Third Edition improves on its predecessors in a number of respects.

The basic approach—viewing communication as a fundamental life process that is necessary to our lives as individuals, and to our relationships, groups, organizations, cultures, and societies—remains the same. However, in this Third Edition, new and expanded chapters and refinements in content and organization further clarify the meaning, importance, and implications of this perspective.

The result is a book that is appropriate for an even broader range of audiences than the First and Second Editions. Among the changes in this edition are:

- Chapter 1—**Introduction**: a new chapter focusing on the intrinsic value (academic, professional, and personal) of communication theory/study, the nature of personal and scholarly theory, and issues and dimensions in defining communication.
- Chapter 2—**History of Communication Study**: includes extensive discussion of developments in communication study in the 1980s and 1990s—"the information age."
- Chapter 4—**Complexities of Human Communication**: focuses on the "communication iceberg—"the concept that much of what makes communication work is invisible to those who have not studied communication theory.
- Chapter 6—**Verbal Codes:** stresses conversation and conversational rules, including a section on gender differences in language use.

- Chapter 8—**Mediated Communication**: an extensively revised chapter examining the impact of information age media on human communication, including a section on mass communication.
- Chapter 11—**Groups**: includes new sections on types of groups, decision making, and problem solving.
- Chapter 13—**Cultures and Societies**: expands coverage of culture and intercultural communication.
- **Implications and Applications** sections conclude each chapter to help readers identify and explore the everyday uses of the theoretical material discussed.

Organization of the Book

Communication and Human Behavior is organized into parts and chapters that focus on elements of the communication process. Chapter 1 presents an **Introduction** to the study of human communication. Part I provides **HISTORICAL AND THEORETICAL PERSPECTIVES**. Included in this section are three chapters. Chapter 2, **History of Communication Study**, provides an overview of the more than 2,500-year evolution of the concept and discipline of communication. Chapter 3, **Communication—A Basic Life Process**, examines the essential role communication systems play for humans and other animals. Chapter 4 focuses on **Complexities of Human Communication**, and introduces the idea of the "communication iceberg."

Part 2 of the book is **PROCESS, MESSAGES, AND MEDIA** and includes four chapters. Chapter 5 focuses on **Message Reception**, and Chapters 6 and 7, **Verbal Codes** and **Nonverbal Codes. Mediated communication**, which includes a discussion of mass communication, is the topic of Chapter 8.

Part 3 is entitled **CONTEXTS AND CONSEQUENCES**. Chapter 9 focuses on communication and **Individuals**, and examines the role of communication in decision making, cognitive development, self-development, self-expression, and self-awareness. Chapter 10 examines **Relationships** including their characteristics, functions, evolution, and dynamics. Chapter 11 considers **Groups**—types, stages, processes, and roles. Chapter 12 explores **Organizations**, including culture, climate, networks, and control mechanisms. Chapter 13 focuses on **Cultures and Societies**. Among the topics considered are culture, the communication-culture relationship, cultural adaptation, intercultural communication, international communication, and information societies.

Acknowledgments

A number of people have contributed to the formation of the ideas presented in this book. In some cases the contributions have been in written form, as with the work of Gregory Bateson, Peter Berger, Ludwig von Bertalanffy, Herbert Blumer, Kenneth Boulding, Hugh Duncan, Erving Goffman, Thomas Kuhn, Desmond Morris, and Jack Prince. In other instances, valued assistance has come through personal contact over the years. In this regard, I want especially to thank Julie Billingsley, Dick Budd, Michael Cheney, Frank Dance, Stan Deetz, Dick Hixson, Irving Louis Horowitz, Todd Hunt, Dan Kealey, Mark Knapp, Bob Kubey, Linda Lederman, Valerie Manusov, Harty Mokros, C. David Mortensen, Ron Rice, Jorge Schement, Alfred Smith, Lea Stewart, and Lee Thayer. My sincere thanks to each of these individuals, and to the many other colleagues, friends, and students who have contributed to this book and to my thinking about communication and human behavior over the years.

Several colleagues have assisted in the development of this edition. I wish to thank Professor Julie Yingling of Humboldt State University, Dr. Larry Samovar of San Diego State University, and Dr. Ferald J. Bryan of Northern Illinois University for reviewing this edition and providing me with helpful comments.

I also want to express my appreciation to Jim Anderson, Nurit Guttman, Maureen McCreadie, Jeff Pierson, Jann Ruben, Marc Ruben, Robbi Ruben, Heather Corbley, Hyesun Hwang, and Joan Chabrak who provided invaluable assistance at various stages in the processing of manuscript and index for this book. Thanks also to Patrick Carter for the original work, *Images We Hold in Common,* which appears on the title page of Chapter 4, and for permission to reproduce an earlier work, entitled *Ad Infinitum,* on the title page of Chapter 9.

I remain grateful to Chris Kilyk, Nat Clymer, Hong Ha, Jon Jacobson, Bill Gilhooly, Robert Convoy, Rick Budd, and Bill Gudykunst, who provided photos and/or processed photos taken by me.

Special thanks to Lloyd Chilton whose early support and encouragement was essential to launching the *Communication and Human Behavior* project, and to Steve Dalphin, Prentice Hall Speech/Communication Editor, for his guidance in the preparation of this edition. Appreciation is also expressed to production editor Marianne Peters and other members of the Prentice Hall staff.

Lastly, I want to express my appreciation to my parents, Nate and Ruth Ruben, whose long-standing support and encouragement have always been important to these endeavors.

Brent D. Ruben

com·mu·ni·ca·tion (kə-mū′nə-kā′shən), *n.* [Fr.; L. *communicatio;* see COMMUNICATE], 1. a transmitting. 2. a giving, or giving and receiving, of information, signals, or messages by talk, gestures, writing, etc. 3. the information, message, etc. 4. a means of communicating; specifically, *a)* *pl.* a system for sending and receiving messages, as by telephone, telegraph, radio, etc. *b)* *pl.* a system for moving troops and matériel. *c)* a passage or way for getting from one place to another. 5. the science and art of communicating as a branch of study. Abbreviated **com., comm.**

1

Introduction

Why Study Communication?
Academic Value
Professional Value
Personal Value
Theories: Guides for Analysis
Personal Theories
Scholarly Theories
Personal and Scholarly Theories of Communication
Understanding Communication
Level of Observation
The Question of Intent
Point of View
The Issue of Outcome
Fundamentals of Communication
Communication Is a Process
Communication Is Essential to Individuals, Relationships, Groups, Organizations, and Societies
Communication Involves Responding to and Creating Messages
Communication Involves Relating to the Environment and Other People
Communication: A Definition
Goals of *Communication and Human Behavior*

Why Study Communication?

It is difficult to get through a conversation with a friend or a colleague, a speech by a business or community leader, or the pages of a newspaper or magazine, without being reminded that communication is a very fundamental and important aspect of life. Communication is a central theme in discussions about topics as seemingly diverse as public speaking, international relations, marriage and divorce, group dynamics, labor negotiations, teaching, management, computer networking, child rearing, marketing, and sales. And phrases like "trying to send a message," "breakdown in communication," "good communicator," "communication problem," "information age," and "communication technology," are familiar expressions in contemporary speech.

Not surprisingly, communication is also a very popular discipline on campuses across the country. One reason is that the field offers students an opportunity to combine academic, professional, and personal values.

ACADEMIC VALUE

As we shall explore in some detail in Chapter 2, the discipline of communication has a rich and lengthy heritage. Historians generally trace the beginning of systematic study of communication and human behavior to the early Greeks. Interest in communication study grew primarily out of philosophy, at a time when that field was the single discipline concerned with the pursuit of knowledge.

Greek concepts of knowledge dominated thinking in Europe until the scientific revolution in the seventeenth century. The emergence of science and a growing trend toward specialization in the pursuit of knowledge led to the development of separate disciplines for the study of behavior, and communication was among these. August Comte (1798–1857) gave the name *sociology* to the study of society and social existence, whose founders include Emile Durkheim, Max Weber, and Karl Marx. A decade later the psychological laboratories of Wilhelm Wundt and William James were established. The origins of anthropology also date to the middle of the nineteenth century and the work of British scholars Maine, Tylor, and Frazer. In the 1900s, political science and communication, two other fields with an ancient heritage, took on contemporary identities as disciplines in their own right. Political science, of course, focuses on political facets of human activity; whereas *communication* focuses on the study of message-related behavior.

Thus, from its early beginnings, communication has had much in common with other behavioral and social science disciplines, each of which approaches the study of human behavior from a particular vantage point.

As a discipline, communication has also maintained intellectual ties with the humanities—especially philosophy, literature, religion, cultural studies, and art. For example, some scholars in philosophy study speech or language, and a number of communication researchers are particularly concerned with the philosophy of communication. Some approaches to cultural studies emphasize the role of communication, and many communication scholars examine the impact of culture on communication.

There are also significant connections between communication and professional fields such as law, medicine, business, information science, social work, education, computer science, and library science. In medicine, for instance, there is a long-standing interest in communication between doctors and patients, and a significant number of communication researchers see medicine as a very fruitful area in which to examine a wide array of communication concepts. Information scientists concerned with the storage, retrieval, and dissemination of knowledge regard communication as important; and information storage and retrieval are increasingly important topics to many who study communication.

Today, the field of communication is both a behavioral/social science and an applied liberal art. The communication discipline shares with psychology, sociology, anthropology, and political science the pursuit of knowledge about human individuals and social activity. The field also draws on the traditions of the humanities and the professions. Thus, another of the attractions of the field of communication is the opportunity to study a single discipline that combines the liberal arts and professional tradition.

PROFESSIONAL VALUE

Regardless of the career one selects, the ability to understand the nature of communication, to communicate competently, and to work effectively with others is of prime importance. In the United States, Japan, Sweden, England, and a number of other countries, at least half of the work force is engaged in communication or information-related work, and this number has increased steadily over the past 100 years.[1] Communication is the primary focus of careers in speech communication, mass communication, organizational communication, political communication, health communication, public relations, advertising, information services, marketing, and others. See Table 1–1.

In many other occupations, technical disciplinary expertise goes hand-in-hand with communication knowledge and ability. This is the case in fields like teaching, management, health care, international business, personnel, counseling, politics, sales, computer applications, library and information science, and speech pathology. To perform competently, a teacher, a counselor, or a politician needs *technical* ability plus *communication* ability.

The results of a recent study conducted by AT&T underscore the importance of communication in organizational life. The goal was to determine the skills and behaviors that will be important for leaders of the future. The following areas were identified as vital:[2]

Managing Interpersonal Relationships
- Energizing and empowering others
- Building and managing teams
- Interpersonal flexibility

Gaining Influence and Managing Information Flow within Organizations
- Influencing others
- Building information networks

Achieving Results for the Organization
- Planning and implementing
- Decision making
- Strategic thinking
- Technical knowledge
- Results orientation

Communication knowledge and skill is basic to many of these suggested leadership qualities. It is fundamental to interpersonal relationships, influence, and information flow within organizations. Communication also plays an important supporting role in planning, implementing, decision making, strategic thinking, acquiring technical knowledge, and assessing results.

PERSONAL VALUE

Communication also has practical value in understanding and coping with events around us—international events such as the Gulf crisis or the impact of the Information Age on the world community—and with

TABLE 1–1 Selected Communication Careers

Managing Communication (Integrating communication operations, programs, and services with the mission of an organization)	
Corporate Communication	Internal Communication
Publishing	Information Management
Media Management	Communication Centers
Employee Communication	Advertising Management
Public Affairs	Technical Information
Communication and Information Policy	International Communication
Telecommunication Management	Information Services

Preparing Communication Products and Services (Preparing, packaging, or repackaging communication products or services for use by others)	
Editing	Advertising Production
Science and Technical Writing	Community Outreach
Speech Writing	Reporting
Marketing Communication	Abstracting
Video Production	Consumer Advocacy
Computer Information Services	Broadcast Journalism
Public Relations	Documentary Film Writing
Conference and Special Events Coordination	Public Information
Customer Relations	Information Retrieval

Analyzing Communication (Studying the foundations and theories related to communication systems, processes, programs, and services, and/or assessing their functioning)	
Communication Research	Individual Interviewing
Market Research	Focus Group Interviewing
Public Opinion Research	Academic Research
Audience Analysis	Customer Satisfaction Analysis

Communication Education and Training (Providing instruction or training in communication)	
Communication Education	Organizational Development
College and University Teaching	Staff Development
Communication Training	Human Resource Development

far more local events like dynamics between roommates, friends, lovers, colleagues, and family members. Consider the following:

- You have been asked to prepare a ten-minute presentation for Thursday afternoon. You have limited background on the topic, are unclear as to the purpose of the speech, and have little knowledge of the audience. Where do you begin?
- You have had a really bad week. A family member has health problems, you are extremely frustrated with your job, and things generally look pretty bleak. An acquaintance asks you, "How are things going?" Do you respond with the routine, "Fine, how are things with you?" or do you answer honestly?
- You find you are increasingly annoyed at your roommate. She is messy, constantly borrows your clothes, and is generally inconsiderate. You've tried to use sarcasm to let her know you're annoyed, but it hasn't worked. When you find a favorite sweater gone, you've had enough and explode. Your roommate looks puzzled and claims she has no idea what you're talking about. Can she be for real?
- At work you are assigned to participate in a culturally- and racially-diverse group. As much as you hate to admit it, you find yourself uneasy in this situation. You can't seem to put your finger on any specifics; you just feel uncomfortable. What's going on here? And what, if anything, can you do to put yourself at ease?

Occurrences like these are familiar to most of us. In these kinds of situations, communication plays a very central role, and the study of communication provides a very useful perspective on them. It helps us to understand the dynamics of individual behavior, relationships, groups, organizations, cultures, and societies. Just as important, it also offers new insights about our own behavior and our impact on others in occupational and social situations. The more we understand the nature of communication, the better able we are to assess and deal competently with the communication situations we encounter.

Theories: Guides for Analysis and Action

Communication and Human Behavior is a book about thinking—thinking about communication. That makes it a book which emphasizes *theory*—and not how to give speeches or write essays.

Most basically, theories are ways of understanding something. More specifically, theories allow us to *describe, explain, predict,* and sometimes *control* phenomena and circumstances we encounter.

PERSONAL THEORIES

We all have *personal theories* about a range of things—theories about relationships, doors, friends, and weather, for instance. Our personal theories, which are termed *native theories* by some social scientists, allow us to describe how to get from one place to another, or how to determine who our friends are. They also allow us to explain how to develop close relationships, to predict the weather, or to control the volume of a television set using a remote control. If we didn't have these theories, we would have to regard each situation we encounter as completely new. We would be unable to think about new situations in more general terms and would be unable to draw upon previous experiences in our efforts to understand them.

These natural, taken-for-granted theories can be termed personal theories. They are theories about people, objects, and events that we operate on as we go about our daily activities, usually with little conscious thought about their nature, how they were developed, or how we are using them.

Personal theories are based on everyday experience. They are taken-for-granted, private, and tend to be stable.

Based on Everyday Experience. Personal theories are developed over time as we cope with the situations and people we encounter. For example, our "theories about relationships" are based on personal experiences with acquaintances, friends, colleagues, and family members over the course of our lifetime.

Taken-for-Granted. Most of us do not think very much about our personal theories, the manner in which they are formed, or the way we use them. Once developed, we tend to accept them on faith. For instance, we each have our own "theories about doors," and we take these theories for granted. We don't think about how we formed these theories and give little conscious attention to our theories when we turn a door knob. We push or pull to open a door, with full confidence that it will open.

Private. Personal theories are based on experiences which are to some extent unique for each of us. We often do not discuss our theories or the experiences on which they were developed. Our "theories about friends" are based on our personal experiences, for example, and we generally discuss them only in a limited range of circumstances.

Stable. Once formed, personal theories are generally quite resistant to change. Our personal theories tend to guide us to see and interpret what we observe in particular ways. Often we ignore or unintentionally distort observations that don't fit in with our personal theories. We are likely to cling to our "theories about friends" even after we have encountered evidence which seems to contradict our theories. For instance, if a friend has told us something that we know to be untrue, we are likely to tell ourselves he or she probably believed it was true or else altered the facts for a very good reason. Most likely, this kind of event could occur any number of times before we would conclude that someone is a liar and thus no longer worthy of being thought of as a friend.

SCHOLARLY THEORIES

Theories of a scholarly or scientific nature are similar to personal theories in terms of their basic functions: they, too, are used to describe, explain, predict, and sometimes control objects, people, and events. However, in contrast to personal theories, they are based on systematic observation and testing. They are also questioned, public, and subject to modification.

Based on Systematic Observation and Testing. Scholarly theories are developed as a result of research involving systematic observation, information gathering, and analysis. Studies may be conducted in experimental laboratories or in natural settings. Data is gathered purposefully by means of interviews, questionnaires, or careful observations; and the results are methodically analyzed. For example, a theory about relationships may be based on the analysis of information derived from direct observations. Or a theory could result from interviews with a cross-section of individuals in varying types of relationships.

Questioned. Unlike personal theories which tend to be accepted on faith once they are formed, scholarly theories are continually questioned. Scientific theories are regarded as tentative, and are reexamined through follow-up studies and analyses. Consider the example of doors and door knobs: We have personal theories that allow us to predict that when we turn the door knob, and push or pull, a door will open. Rather than be satisfied with a personal theory that door knobs open doors, a scientific theory would be continually and methodically tested to ensure predictability. Thus, engineers in a corporation that manufactures door entry and lock systems would test and retest their products to determine precisely how likely it is that the door knob mechanism will operate as intended. They might want to determine the average number of uses a sample of door entry mechanisms can tolerate before they fail to function. And then they would want to further study how and why breakdowns occur.

Public. The methods and results of scholarly and scientific theories are generally made public through publication. The goal is to allow others to further evaluate theories in terms of at least three standards:

- validity—accuracy;
- reliability—consistency and dependability; and
- utility—usefulness and applicability.

A scholarly theory about friendship will be reported at conferences and in journals, book chapters, and books so that other scholars and students can test and apply the ideas. (Exceptions to the public nature of research occur in the case of research done within a context of secrecy, where findings are purposely not shared with competitors.)

Subject to Modification. Because scholarly and scientific theories are published, they are available, accessible, and subject to being refuted or modified based on new information. For instance, a scientific theory about weather prediction can be modified as findings from new research are published.

PERSONAL AND SCHOLARLY THEORIES OF COMMUNICATION

We all have personal theories of communication and human behavior. Like other such theories, our views of communication are based on a lifetime of experience. They are personal. We take them for granted, and they tend to be stable. There are also many scholarly and scientific theories regarding communication and human behavior.

We will be examining a number of communication theories in this book. A familiarity with these theories has great value in its own right in helping us to become more aware of the nature and dynamics of communication. Exploring these theories can have additional value: this process can encourage us in—and give us tools for—a more critical evaluation of our own personal theories. We can begin to subject our own theories to more rigorous standards. Do our personal theories hold up in light of more systematic observation and testing? Do we continually question their validity, reliability, and utility? Can we benefit from discussing our personal theories with other people to see where they converge and where they differ? Are we able to modify our personal theories when evidence warrants? By comparing our personal theories and scholarly theories, we can better understand each and narrow the gap between them. Through this process, we also enrich our understanding of human behavior.

Understanding Communication

Few words are used in as many different ways, by as many different people, as the word *communication.* To some, communication brings to mind an image of a speaker addressing an audience from behind a lectern, the lively discussion among colleagues at a meeting, or an exchange of glances between lovers. Others associate the term primarily with mass media—newspapers, television, books, radio, or film. For still others, communication has to do with computers, telephones, satellites, or military command and control.

Communication can be a debate, a sermon, a memorable night at the theater, the efforts of a child striving to conquer stuttering, Morse code, a roadside sign, or a thoughtful walk on the beach. Communication is what we think of when we see a Patriot missile colliding with a SCUD, a tear, an outstretched arm, a knowing smile, the sign language of a deaf-mute, a kiss, a four-letter word scrawled on a rest room wall, even silence.

The multiple uses of the term communication can be confusing. People who are unfamiliar with the field may wonder whether the term has any limits. Is everything communication? How does being interested in communication differ from being interested in life?

To address the issue, it is important to understand that

- *Communication* is the name of a discipline, as well as the label for a phenomenon. It is the name of an academic field and a focus of study.
- *Communication* has popular, professional, as well as technical mean-

ings. It is used broadly by the general public, in a more focused occupational framework in professional circumstances, and in more specialized ways in technical and academic settings.

There are obviously a number of different meanings of the word *communication.* In one classic study, communication scholars Frank Dance and Carl Larson identified 126 published definitions.[3] The 1989 *Oxford English Dictionary* alone lists twelve definitions.[4] Let's look briefly at a sampling of definitions:

"Communication means that information is passed from one place to another."[5]

"Communication . . . include(s) all the procedures by which one mind may affect another."[6]

"The transmission of information, ideas, emotions, skills, etc. by the use of symbols—words, pictures, figures, graphs, etc."[7]

"In the main, communication has as its central interest those behavioral situations in which a source transmits a message to a receiver(s) with conscious intent to affect the latter's behavior."[8]

"The process of taking something into account."[9]

"The imparting, conveying, or exchange of ideas, knowledge, or information whether by speech, writing, or signs."[10]

Not surprisingly, these definitions of communication, and others, have elements in common; they also have a number of differences in terms of the level of observation, the question of intent, the point of view, and the issue of outcome.[11]

LEVEL OF OBSERVATION

One can study communication on the level of ants or bees, the level of individuals, the level of groups, the level of a particular culture or society, or the international level. Definitions may focus on any one or several of these levels.

THE QUESTION OF INTENT

In some descriptions, communication is seen as something that is done purposefully to send a specific message, such as when we give a speech or engage in a conversation. Other definitions also include communication which is unintended (such as a nervous gesture or an unintentional frown).

POINT OF VIEW

Communication can be defined in a way that emphasizes the perspective of a message source (for example, a public speaker or writer). Definitions can also emphasize the perspective of the receiver (for instance, a listener or reader). Or definitions may focus on the messages (the content of a speech, letter, or conversation), or communication media (such as telephone or television).

THE ISSUE OF OUTCOME

Some definitions of communication include only situations where a sender is successful in getting a receiver to understand, accept, and agree with his or her ideas—when the result of communication is positive. Others emphasize the need for definitions also to include situations where misunderstanding, disagreement, or other negative outcomes occur.

Fundamentals of Communication

To make sense of these many distinctions, to explain the field to others, and to organize our study of the field, we need a comprehensive and unifying definition of communication. To serve these goals, a definition should include and integrate the following fundamentals of communication.

COMMUNICATION IS A PROCESS

A *process* is an activity that has many separate but interrelated steps that occur over time. When we prepare for and deliver a public presentation, for instance, we are not engaged in a single, static act. We move, instead, through a sequence of interrelated activities as we plan, gather materials, rehearse, present the speech, and perhaps adjust the presentation as we're giving it, based on the audience's reaction.

The communication that occurs in a conversation is, similarly, an activity composed of a number of interrelated steps occurring over time. Consider the following:

"Hi, how are you?"

"Fine, and you?"

Even in such a simple exchange, a number of steps are involved as messages are created, sent, received, interpreted, and responded to.

COMMUNICATION IS ESSENTIAL FOR INDIVIDUALS, RELATIONSHIPS, GROUPS, ORGANIZATIONS, AND SOCIETIES

For us as individuals, communication is our link to the world, our means of making impressions, expressing ourselves, influencing others, and giving of ourselves. It is also our means of learning about the world and other people, becoming who we are, being entertained, persuaded, humored, deceived, or informed.

It is through communication that we form relationships of all kinds—from the casual exchanges that take place between a customer and a hot dog vendor or between strangers waiting in line at a movie theater, to the intimate conversations between lovers or members of a family. For friends, acquaintances, family, or colleagues at school or work, communication is the means of pursuing joint activities, relating, sharing, and exchanging ideas.

In groups, organizations, and societies, communication is the means through which we coordinate our own needs and goals with those of others. Within larger organizations, societies, and the world community, communication provides the web of connections that allows for collective action, the establishment of a common identity, and the development of leadership.

COMMUNICATION INVOLVES RESPONDING TO AND CREATING MESSAGES

It is through the processing of messages that we interact with our surroundings and one another. A *message* is any symbol or collection of symbols which has meaning or utility. Messages may involve verbal codes—such as spoken or written language—or nonverbal codes, involving appearance, gestures, touch, or other means. Examples include a speech, letter, wink, flag, poem, advertisement, or painting.

Responding to messages, or *message reception* as it can be more generally termed, refers to the process of interpretation. This has to do with the way we attend to, attach significance to, and use messages—as individuals and in relationships, groups, organizations, or societies. Message reception is a complex process. Our interpretations are not a tangible commodity that can simply be transported from one individual, organization or society to another. Rather, they are transformed and changed in various ways as messages are transferred from one person or location to the next, through a process we will examine in some detail later.

We are engaged in message creation through verbal and nonverbal behavior. For example, we create messages when we introduce ourselves to someone, since we are in the process of constructing a meaningful message—at least, it is meaningful to us. And, of course, the person who we are meeting is engaged in message reception when he or she notices, attaches meaning to, and makes use of our introductory comments.

In face-to-face settings, messages are conveyed from person-to-person or place-to-place verbally and nonverbally. In other situations, communication *media* play an important role by extending our "natural" capabilities for communication. In these instances, communication between the individuals, groups, organizations, or societies is *mediated.*

COMMUNICATION INVOLVES RELATING TO THE ENVIRONMENT AND OTHER PEOPLE

We create and interpret messages—as individuals, and in relationships, groups, organizations, and societies—to relate to the environment and to the people around us. In some cases, the process consists primarily of adjusting to the circumstances in which we find ourselves. More often, communication involves actively creating situations and coordinating our actions with others. As we shall see, the same basic dynamics occur in groups, organizations, and societies, but on a progressively larger scale.

Communication: A Definition

We can combine these fundamentals to derive the following definition of communication:

> *Human communication is the process through which individuals—in relationships, groups, organizations, and societies—respond to and create messages to relate to the environment and one another.*

This definition is helpful for thinking about the nature of communication and for explaining it in fairly straightforward terms to others. Moreover, it also provides a useful framework for organizing the ideas presented in this book.

Goals of *Communication and Human Behavior*

Communication and Human Behavior, Third Edition, is a book aimed at helping you think cogently and systematically about communication and its relationship to human behavior. It is based on the assumption that the way we think about communication makes an important difference in the way we understand what is going on around us and in the way we conduct our lives.

The book has three goals:

1. To introduce communication as an area of study. *Communication and Human Behavior* provides an overview and explanation of communication theories, basic concepts, key scholars, issues, and applications.
2. To provide a framework that helps make connections between communication theory and communication processes in action. The objective is to help you develop a communication-oriented perspective on events taking place around you—personally, socially, in work situations, nationally, and internationally.
3. To provide tools to help you use this communication-oriented perspective to analyze, better understand, and be more competent in your own communication behavior.

Notes

1. Jorge R. Schement, "Porat, Bell, and the Information Society Reconsidered: The Growth of Information Work in the Early Twentieth Century," *Information Processing and Management,* Vol. 26, No. 4, 1990, pp. 449–465; Katz, Raul, *The Information Society* (New York: Praeger, 1988); Marc U. Porat, *The Information Economy: Definition and Measurement (OT Special Publication*

77-12), Volumes 1–9 (Washington, DC: Department of Commerce/Office of Telecommunication, Government Printing Office, 1977), pp. 1–3. Also see discussion by Anthony Debons, *The Information Professional: Survey of an Emerging Field* (New York: Marcel Dekker, 1981).

2. Based on Deborah Stahl, "Managing in the 1990s: Versatility, flexibility and a wide range of skills. A New Study Outlines the Requirements for Managerial Success in a Complex and Fast-Changing Business World," *AT&T Journal,* March, 1989, pp. 8–10.

3. Frank E. X. Dance and Carl Larson, *The Functions of Human Communication: A Theoretical Approach* (New York: Holt, Rinehart, Winston, 1976).

4. J. A. Simpson and E. S. C. Weiner, Eds., *The Oxford English Dictionary,* Second Ed. Vol. III (Oxford: Clarendon Press, 1989), pp. 578–579.

5. George A. Miller, *Language and Communication* (New York: McGraw-Hill, 1951), p. 6.

6. Gerald R. Miller, "On Defining Communication: Another Stab," *Journal of Communication,* Vol. 16, No. 2, June, 1966, p. 92.

7. Claude Shannon and Warren Weaver, *The Mathematical Theory of Communication* (Champaign, IL: University of Illinois Press, 1963), p. 96.

8. Bernard Berelson and Gary Steiner, *Human Behavior* (New York: Harcourt Brace Javonovich, 1964), p. 527.

9. Lee Thayer, *Communication and Communication Systems* (Homewood, IL: Richard Irwin, 1968).

10. Simpson and Weiner, 1989, p. 578.

11. The discussion of levels of analysis, the question of intent, and normative judgement is based on Dance and Larson, 1976, pp. 27–28.

References and Suggested Readings

DANCE, FRANK E. X. and CARL LARSON. *The Functions of Human Communication: A Theoretical Approach.* New York: Holt, Rinehart, Winston, 1976.

FISKE, JOHN. *Introduction to Communication Studies.* Second Ed. London: Routledge, 1990.

GUMPERT, GARY and ROBERT CATHCART. *Inter/Media: Interpersonal Communication in a Media World.* New York: Oxford University Press, 1986.

HUNT, TODD and BRENT D. RUBEN. *Mass Communication: Producers and Consumers.* Harper Collins, 1992.

INFANTE, DOMINIC A., ANDREW S. RANCER, and DEANNA F. WOMACK. *Building Communication Theory.* Prospect Heights, IL: Waveland, 1990.

The Information Economy: Volumes 1–9. Washington, DC: Office of Telecommunication, Government Printing Office, 1977. See discussion by Anthony Debons. *The Information Professional: Survey of an Emerging Field.* New York: Marcel Dekker, 1981.

KATZ, RAUL. *The Information Society.* New York: Praeger, 1988.

LITTLEJOHN, STEPHEN W. *Theories of Human Communication.* Third Ed. Belmont, CA: Wadsworth, 1989.

MILLER, GERALD R. "On Defining Communication: Another Stab." *Journal of Communication,* June, Vol. 16, No. 2, 1966.

PEARCE, W. BARNETT. *Communication and the Human Condition.* Carbondale, IL: Southern Illinois University Press, 1989.

Porat, Marc U. *The Information Economy: Definition and Measurement. (OT Special Publication 77-12), Volumes 1–9.* Washington, DC: Department of Commerce/Office of Telecommunication, Government Printing Office, 1977.

SALVAGGIO, JERRY L. "The Telecommunications Revolution: Are We Up to the Challenge." In *Telecommunications: Issues and Choices for Society.* Ed. by Jerry L. Salvaggio. New York: Oxford University Press, 1983, 148–153.

SCHEMENT, JORGE R. "Porat, Bell, and the Information Society Reconsidered: The Growth of Information Work in the Early Twentieth Century." *Information Processing and Management,* Vol. 26, No. 4, 1990, 449–465.

SCHEMENT, JORGE R., and LEAH LIEVROUW. *Competing Visions, Complex Realities: Social Aspects of the Information Society.* Norwood, NJ: Ablex, 1987.

SIMPSON, J. A. and E. S. C. WEINER, eds., *The Oxford English Dictionary.* Second Ed. Vol. III. Oxford: Clarendon Press, 1989, 578–579.

THAYER, LEE. *Communication and Communication Systems.* Homewood, IL: Richard Irwin, 1968.

X1
X2
X3
A
X'
C
X''
B
S
M
R
1
2
3
4
5
6
7
8
9
S — M — C — R
Who says what
to whom in what
channel with
what effect

2

History of Communication Study

Early Communication Study

It is difficult to determine precisely when and how communication first came to be regarded as a significant factor in human life. According to historians, considerable concern about communication and its role in human affairs was expressed prior to the fifth century B.C., in classical Babylonian and Egyptian writings and in Homer's *Iliad.*[1]

One of the most familiar historic statements on the importance of communication appears in the *Bible.* In the opening passage of the Old Testament the spoken word is described as the incredibly powerful force through which God created the world—God said, "Let there be light; and there was light."

As with other disciplines that have sought to explain human behavior, the beginning of systematic theory development in communication can be traced to the Greeks. Their initial interest sprang from the practical concerns of day-to-day life. Greece had a democratic form of government, and virtually all facets of business, government, law, and education were carried on orally. Greek citizens also had to be their own lawyers. Accused and accuser alike presented their cases before a jury of several hundred persons who would have to be convinced of the rightness of a position. Lawsuits were common in Athens, and, as a result, legal public speaking became a preoccupation.

RHETORIC AND SPEECH

What might be considered as the first theory of communication was developed in Greece by Corax and later refined by his student Tisias. The theory dealt with courtroom speaking, which was considered the craft of persuasion. Tisias became convinced that persuasion could be taught as an art and provided encouragement for instructors of what was called *rhetoric.*

Aristotle (385–322 B.C.) and his teacher Plato (427–347 B.C.) were central figures in early communication study. Both regarded communication as an art or craft to be practiced on one hand, and as an area of study on the other. As Aristotle noted in the opening paragraph of his classic work on rhetoric:

> To a certain extent all men attempt to discuss statements and to maintain them, at random or through practice and from acquired habit. Both ways being possible, the subject can plainly be handled systematically, for it is possible to inquire the reason why some speakers succeed through prac-

> tice and others spontaneously; and everyone will at once agree that such inquiry is the function of science.[2]

Aristotle saw communication as the means through which citizens participated in democracy. He described communication in terms of an *orator* or *speaker* constructing an *argument* to be presented in a *speech* to *hearers*—an *audience.* The speaker's goal was to inspire a positive image of himself or herself and to encourage the members of the audience to be receptive to the message:

> rhetoric exists to affect the giving of decisions . . . the *orator* must not only try to make the argument of his *speech* demonstrative and worthy of belief; he must also make his own character look right and put his *hearers,* who are to decide, in the right frame of mind.[3] (Italics added)

For Aristotle, communication was primarily a verbal activity in which a speaker tried to persuade—to achieve his or her own purposes with a listener through skillful construction of an argument and delivery of a speech.

In his writings, Plato outlined what he thought would be necessary for the study of rhetoric to contribute to a broader explanation of human behavior. He believed that the field would need to include the study of the nature of words, the study of the nature of human beings and their ways of approaching life, the study of the nature of order, and the study of the instruments by which human beings are affected.[4] Thus, although the earliest interest in communication focused on public speaking, it was recognized that in order to understand fully how persuasion operated it would be necessary to develop a broader and more comprehensive theory.

The writings of two other scholars—Cicero (106–43 B.C.) and Quintilian (35–95 A.D.)—also contributed to the broadening theory of communication. Like Plato and Aristotle, Cicero saw communication as both an academic and practical matter. His view of communication was so comprehensive as to include all of what is now considered the domain of the social sciences. Quintilian is remembered primarily as an educator and synthesizer, bringing together in his writing the previous five hundred years' thinking about communication.[5]

The view that communication was critical to virtually all aspects of human life was widely held during the Classical period. However, the comprehensive perspective that characterized communication during

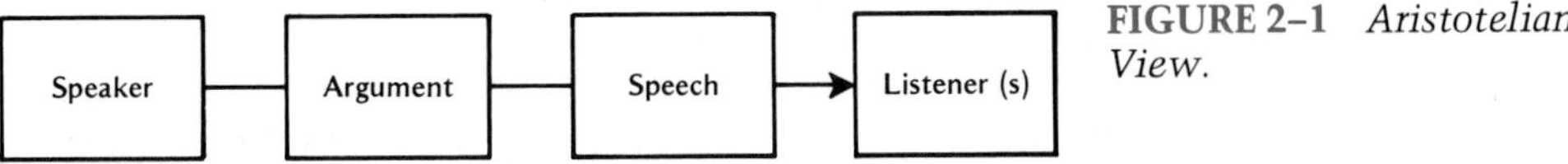

FIGURE 2–1 *Aristotelian View.*

this era was largely reversed in the Medieval and Renaissance periods. With the decline of the oral tradition and democracy, much of the interest in communication also waned, and the study of rhetoric was dispersed among several different fields. By the end of the fourteenth century, most of the communication theory that had originally been developed in rhetoric was now being studied in religion.

Eventually, the work of Augustine led to a rediscovery of classical Greek theory. His writings applied communication to the interpretation of the *Bible* and other religious writings, and to the art of preaching. In so doing, Augustine united the *practical* and *theoretical* aspects of communication study.

During the eighteenth and nineteenth centuries, emphasis in communication study was placed on written argument and literature. There was also great interest in speaking style, articulation, and gesture, leading to the formation of the National Association of Elocutionists in 1892.

By the end of the nineteenth century, most colleges and universities were organized into departments, and rhetoric and speech were often within departments of English.

JOURNALISM

The other field that contributed to the heritage of communication study is *journalism*. Like rhetoric and speech, journalism also dates back several thousand years. The practice of journalism began some 3,700 years ago in Egypt, when a record of the events of the time was transcribed on the tomb of an Egyptian king. Years later, Julius Caesar had an official record of the news of the day posted in a public place, and copies of it were made and sold.[6]

Early newspapers were a mixture of newsletters, ballads, proclamations, political tracts, and pamphlets describing various events. Like speech and rhetoric, they were forms of public communication. The mid-1600s saw the emergence of the newspaper in its modern form; and the first paper published in the United States, *Publick Occurrences Both Forreign and Domestick,* appeared in 1690 in Boston.

The 1900s–1930s: Development of Speech and Journalism

In the early twentieth century, speech emerged as a discipline in its own right. In 1909, the Eastern States Speech Association—now the Eastern

Communication Association—was formed, and in 1910, held its first annual conference. The National Association of Teachers of Public Speaking, which became the Speech Association of America and more recently the Speech Communication Association, was formed in 1914. In 1915, the *Quarterly Journal of Public Speaking* was first published, followed soon after by the *Quarterly Journal of Speech. Communication Monographs* began publication in 1934. Unlike previous publications which emphasized speech practices, the new journal stressed research. Most of the studies published in the early volumes dealt with speech phonetics and phonology, physiology and pathology.[7] By 1935, the speech association had 1700 members, and speech was well established as a field.

Although the practice of journalism dates back many years, formalized study in the area did not progress rapidly until the early 1900s. In 1905, the University of Wisconsin offered what were perhaps the first courses in journalism, at a time when there were few, if any, books on the topic. By 1910, there were half a dozen volumes available, and between 1910 and 1920, some twenty-five works on journalism and newspaper work were compiled, signaling a pattern of continued growth.[8]

The advent of radio in the 1920s and television in the early 1940s resulted in the wider application of journalistic concepts. These new media gave impetus to the development of a broadened view of the nature of journalism.

Interest in communication was not limited to speech and journalism. In philosophy scholars wrote about the nature of communication and its role in human life. Anthropologists, psychologists, and sociologists focused on communication and its role in individual and social process; and writers in the area of language also contributed to the advancement of communication study.

The 1940s and 1950s: Interdisciplinary Growth

In the 1940s and early 1950s, the scope of the field of communication broadened substantially. A number of scholars from the various behavioral and social science disciplines began to develop theories of communication which extended beyond the boundaries of their own fields. In anthropology, for example, research concerned with body positioning and gestures in particular cultures laid the groundwork for more general studies of nonverbal communication. In psychology, interest focused on persuasion, social influence, and, specifically, attitudes—how they form, how they change, their impact on behavior, and the role of communication in these dynamics.

Sociologists and political scientists studied the nature of mass media in various political and social activities, such as voting behavior, and other facets of life. In zoology, communication among animals began to receive considerable attention among researchers. During these same years, scholars in linguistics, general semantics, and semiotics, fields that focused on the nature of language and its role in human activity, also contributed to the advancement of communication study.

Studies in rhetoric and speech in the late 1940s and 1950s broadened to include oral interpretation, voice and diction, debate, theater, physiology of speech, and speech pathology. In journalism and mass media studies, growth and development were even more dramatic, spurred on in no small way by the popularity of television and efforts to understand its impact. In a number of classic works in the 1950s, the focus on specific media—newspapers, magazines, radio, and television—began to be replaced by a more general concern with the nature and effects of *mass media* and *mass communication.*

By the end of the 1950s a number of writings had appeared that paved the way for the development of more integrated views of communication. It was during these years that the National Society for the Study of Communication (now the International Communication Association) was established with the stated goal of bringing greater unity to the study of communication by exploring the relationships among speech, language, and media.[9] These developments set the stage for the rapid growth of communication as an independent discipline.

LASSWELL'S VIEW OF COMMUNICATION

During this period a number of scholars sought to describe the nature of the communication process. One of the most often cited characterizations of communication was advanced by political scientist Harold Lasswell in 1948 as an outgrowth of his work in the area of political propaganda. Lasswell provided a general view of communication that extended well beyond the boundaries of political science. He said that the communication process could best be explained by the simple statement:

> "Who says what to whom in what channel with what effect."[10]

Lasswell's view of communication, as had Aristotle's some two thousand years earlier, focused primarily on verbal messages. It also em-

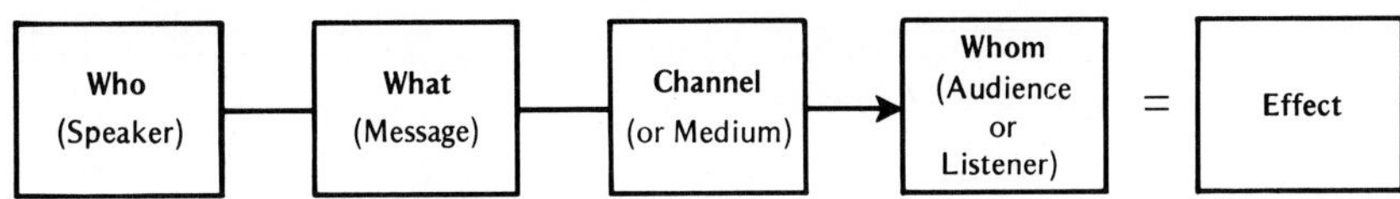

FIGURE 2–2 *Lasswell Model.*

phasized the elements of *speaker, message,* and *audience,* but used different terminology. Both men viewed communication as a one-way process in which one individual influenced others through messages.

Lasswell offered a broadened definition of *channel* to include mass media along with speech as part of the communication process. His approach also provided a more generalized view of the *goal* or *effect* of communication than did the Aristotelian perspective. Lasswell's work suggested that there could be a variety of outcomes or effects of communication, such as to inform, to entertain, to aggravate, as well as to persuade.

SHANNON AND WEAVER'S MODEL

About a year after the introduction of the Lasswell perspective, Claude Shannon published the results of research he had undertaken for Bell Telephone to study the engineering problems of signal transmission. The results of his study provided the basis for what came to be known as the Shannon and Weaver model of communication.

The authors described the communication process in this way:

> Communication include(s) all the procedures by which one mind may affect another. This, of course, involves not only written and oral speech,

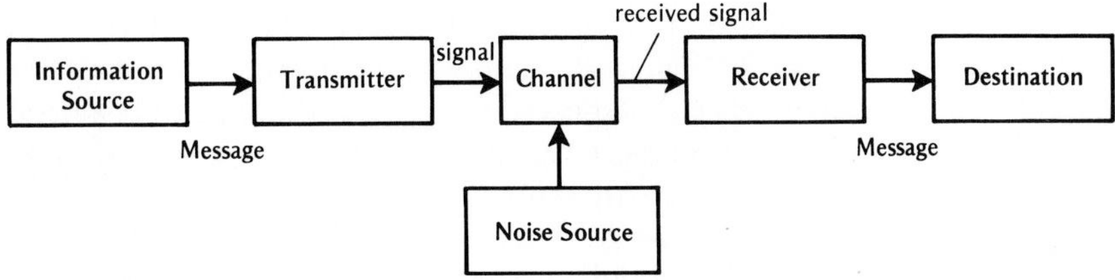

FIGURE 2–3 *Shannon and Weaver Model.*

Source: The Mathematical Theory of Communication, Claude E. Shannon and Warren Weaver. Copyright © 1949 by the University of Illinois. Renewed 1977. By permission.

> but also music, the pictorial arts, the theatre, the ballet, and in fact all human behavior.[11]

The Shannon and Weaver concept represented an important expansion of the idea of communication from the act of speaking or writing in a public setting or through mass media, to activities such as music, art, ballet and the theater—in fact, all human behavior.

Like Lasswell, Shannon and Weaver saw communication in terms of a one-way process by which a message was sent from a source through a channel to a receiver. Their model was somewhat more detailed, however, because Shannon and Weaver made several distinctions that the other models had not. Specifically, they differentiated between a *signal* and a *message*, an *information source* and a *transmitter*, and a *receiver* and *destination*. They described the workings of the model as follows:

> The *information source* selects a desired message out of a set of possible messages. . . . The selected message may consist of written or spoken words, or of pictures, music, etc. . . . The *transmitter* changes the *message* into the signal which is actually sent over the *communication channel* from the transmitter to the *receiver*.[12]

If one considers the example of a dramatic production carried by cable television, the *channel* is the cable, the *signal* is the varying electrical current carried by the cable; the *information source* is the performers, their backdrop, and so on; the *transmitter* is the set of devices (camera, audio and video amplification system, and so on) that converts the visual and vocal images of the performers into electrical current.

In our example, the *receiver* is the television set and cable converter equipment. The receiver's purpose is to change the signal back into a *message* that can be received and interpreted at the *destination* (a cable viewer, in the case of our example).

Shannon and Weaver introduced the term *noise* as the label for any distortion that interferes with the transmission of a signal from the source to the destination. In our example, an illustration of noise would be electrical interference, leading to audio or video distortion, in the cable line. They also advanced the concept of *correction channel*, which they regarded as a means of overcoming problems created by noise. The correction channel was operated by an observer who compared the initial signal that was sent with that received; when the two didn't match, additional signals would be transmitted to correct the error.[13]

SCHRAMM'S MODELS

In an article published in 1954 entitled, "How Communication Works," Wilbur Schramm provided several additional models of communication. The first, shown in Figure 2–4, was essentially an elaboration of the Shannon and Weaver model.

Describing this model, Schramm said:

> A *source* may be an individual (speaking, writing, drawing, gesturing) or a communication organization (like a newspaper, publishing house, television station or motion picture studio). The *message* may be in the form of ink on paper, sound waves in the air, impulses in electric current, a wave of the hand, a flag in the air, or any other signal capable of being interpreted meaningfully. The *destination* may be an *individual* listening, watching, or reading; a member of a *group*, such as a discussion group, a lecture audience, a football crowd, or a mob; or an individual member of a particular group we call the mass audience, such as the reader of a newspaper or a viewer of television.[14]

Schramm saw communication as a purposeful effort to establish a *commonness* between a source and receiver, noting that the word *communication* comes from the Latin *communis,* which means *common:*

> What happens when the source tries to build up this commonness with his intended receiver? First, the source encodes his message. That is, he takes the information or feeling he wants to share and puts it into a form that can be transmitted. The pictures in our heads can't be transmitted until they are coded. . . . Once coded and sent, a message is quite free of its sender. . . . And there is good reason . . . for the sender to wonder whether his receiver will really be in tune with him, whether the message will be interpreted without distortion, whether the picture in the head of the receiver will bear any resemblance to that in the head of the sender.[15]

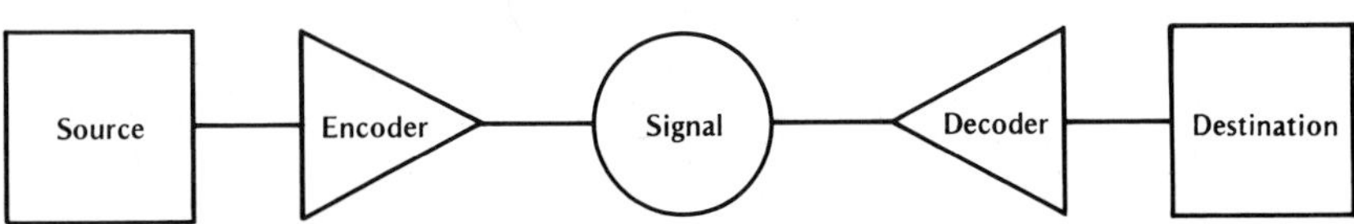

FIGURE 2–4

Source: The Process and Effects of Mass Communication. Ed. by Wilbur Schramm. Copyright © 1965 by the University of Illinois Press. By permission.

Schramm introduced the concept of *field of experience,* which he thought to be essential to determining whether or not a message would be received at the destination in the manner intended by the source. See Figure 2–5. He contended that without common fields of experience—a common language, common backgrounds, a common culture, and so forth—there was little chance for a message to be interpreted correctly. In this respect his work significantly expanded the thinking of Shannon and Weaver.

Schramm suggested the importance of *feedback* as a means of overcoming the problem of noise. He said that feedback "tells us how our messages are being interpreted. . . . An experienced communicator is attentive to feedback and constantly modifying his messages in light of what he observes in or hears from his audience."[16]

As shown in Figure 2–6, Schramm believed that when a receiver provided feedback he or she became a source, thus eliminating the need for a distinction between the source and receiver. Each individual was viewed as both source and recipient of messages, and communication was viewed as circular, rather than one-way, as with earlier models.

The Schramm view of communication was more elaborate than many others developed during this period and added new elements in describing the process. In addition to reemphasizing the elements of source, message, and destination, it suggested the importance of interpretation and the role of field of experience. Whereas other models had acknowledged that the receiver might be either a single person or a large audience, this model suggested that a source could also be one individual or many, and that in actual operation, source and receiver were often indistinguishable.

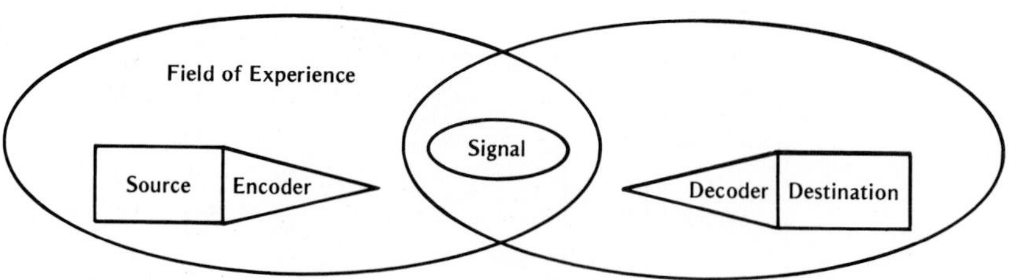

FIGURE 2–5

Source: The Process and Effects of Mass Communication. Ed. by Wilbur Schramm. Copyright © 1965 by the University of Illinois Press. By permission.

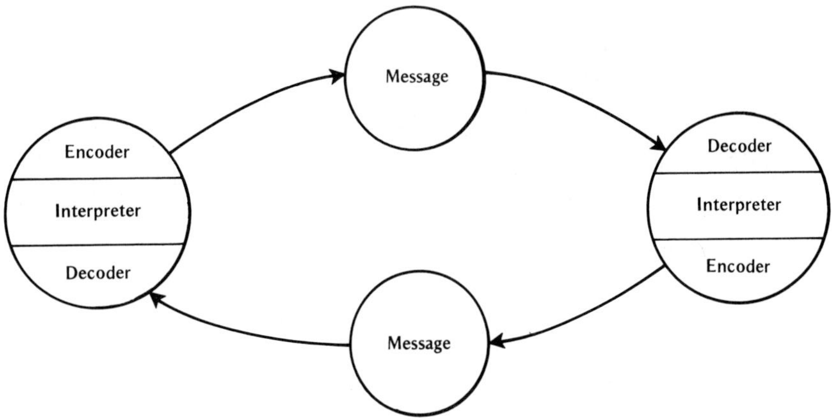

FIGURE 2–6
Source: The Process and Effects of Mass Communication Ed. by Wilbur Schramm. Copyright © 1965 by the University of Illinois Press. By permission.

KATZ AND LAZARSFELD'S MODEL

In 1955, political scientists Elihu Katz and Paul Lazarsfeld presented a *two-step flow* concept of communication in their book *Personal Influence.* The model was based on earlier research in which they found that information presented in the mass media did not reach and have an impact upon receivers as previous views of communication seemed to suggest it would. Specifically, their research found that political radio and print messages had a negligible effect on individuals' voting decisions.

In searching for an explanation for this lack of effect, they developed a view that linked interpersonal dynamics to mass communication. They determined that undecided voters were influenced more by people around them than by information provided by the mass media; husbands and wives were influenced by their spouses, club members by other club members, workers by their colleagues, children by their parents, and so on. Their research also indicated that some people were consistently more influential than others, leading them to conclude that "ideas often seem to *flow* from radio and print *to* opinion leaders and *from them* to the less active sections of the population"—in a two-step flow.[17] (See Figure 2–7.)

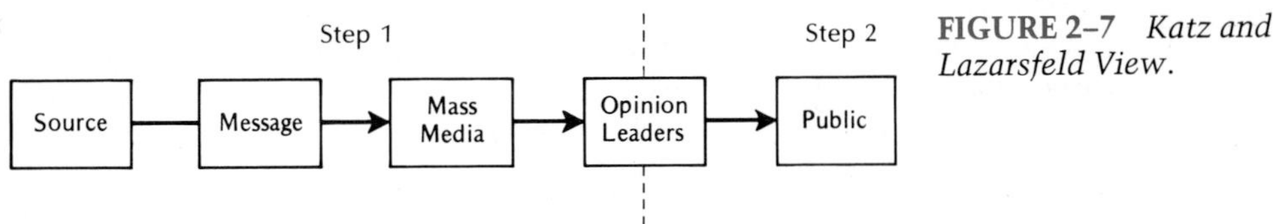

FIGURE 2–7 *Katz and Lazarsfeld View.*

In some respects, the two-step flow concept was quite similar to earlier views of communication. Although research has since suggested that the two-step concept is only applicable in some situations, the formulation has been very influential over the years. It served to link face-to-face and mass communication and to introduce the idea of opinion leaders. It has also served as the basis for the development of *diffusion theory*, which describes how information and innovations are introduced and adopted within a group, organization, or community.

WESTLEY AND MACLEAN'S MODEL

A somewhat different approach to communication was developed by Bruce Westley and Malcolm S. MacLean, Jr. They suggested that the communication process begins with *receiving* messages, rather than *sending* them. To be more precise, Westley and MacLean's view indicates that the process actually begins with a series of *signals* or potential messages. There are a large number of signals—potential messages—in a communicator's environment, which they referred to as "*X*s" in their model.

The model suggests that signals may involve a single sense modality such as sight or sound (X). Or they may involve a combination of several modalities, for instance, sight, sound and touch. The designation for such a signal would be X_{3m}— the "*3m*" indicating that three modalities are involved.

The model indicates that in a given situation only some of the many signals (Xs) in one's environment at any point in time are attended to by an individual (A). When individual A processes these signals and interprets them, what is, in effect, a new message (X^{I}) results. It is this new message—A's personal representation of the sum of all the Xs—that is passed along when individual A describes what he or she saw or heard to a second individual (C).

As an illustration, consider that A is a reporter who goes to the scene of a major tragedy to gather facts and write a story for his or her editor, who in turn may modify the story before including it in the script of the evening newscast. In this example, the reporter is A. The "facts" he or she gathers are Xs. The story that is written based on the facts is X^{I}. The editor to whom the story is submitted is C. The final version of the story included in the script for the newscast is X^{II}, and members of the viewing audience are Bs.

Two other parts of the model require explanation: First, note the arrow in the model from X_3 to C. This would describe a situation where individual B had direct exposure to the same signal—X—as did individual *A*. In our illustration, suppose, for instance, that the editor drives by the scene of the tragedy and sees the same three dead bodies that reporter *A* notices.

Next, note the dotted arrows from *B* to *C*, *B* to *A*, and *C* to *A*. These represent feedback—response signals sent from *B* to *C*, *B* to *A*, and *C* to *A*, respectively. Let's refer, once again, to the illustration. A letter from an audience member to the editor is an example of fb_{BC}. A phone call from the audience member to the reporter would be designated fb_{BA}. Questions posed by the editor to the reporter or a letter of commendation for a fine article would be classified as fb_{CA}.

Obviously, the Westley-MacLean model is considerably more complicated than others; and the additional elements, lines, and arrows result in a view of communication that is broadened in several significant ways. The model accounts for the relationship between interpersonal communication and communication involving mass media. It also suggests that communication begins with an individual receiving messages rather than sending them. This change emphasizes that many of the signals that are important to the communication process may not be intentionally sent. The three dead bodies in the example above came to be

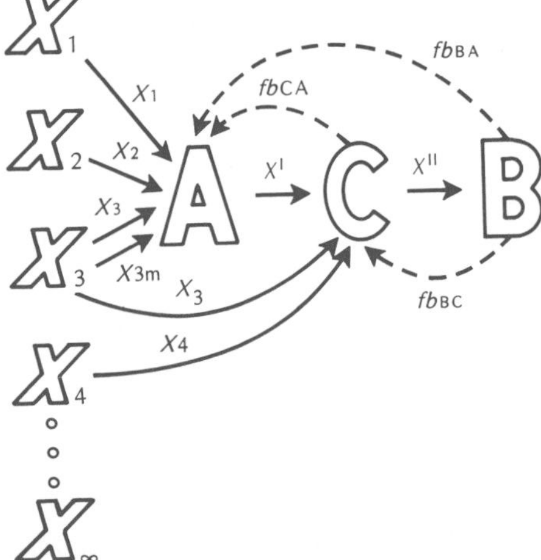

FIGURE 2–8 *Westley-MacLean Model.*

Source: Bruce Westley and Malcolm S. MacLean, Jr., "A Conceptual Model for Communication Research," *Audio-Visual Communication Review*, Winter, 1955. Reprinted by permission of the Association for Educational Communications and Technology. Copyright 1955 by AECT.

significant to the communication experiences of the reporter and editor despite the fact that this message was not intentionally sent by anyone. Additionally, the model emphasizes the changes messages undergo as they are passed along from one person to another.

The 1960s: Integration

In the 1960s, scholars synthesized thinking from rhetoric and speech, journalism and mass media, and the other social science disciplines. Among the noteworthy contributions to this integration were landmark books such as *The Process of Communication* (1960), *The Effects of Mass Communication* (1960), *On Human Communication* (1961), *Diffusion of Innovations* (1962), *The Science of Human Communication* (1963), *Understanding Media* (1964), and *Theories of Mass Communication* (1966).

The generalized views of communication reflected in these volumes were applied beginning in the middle of the decade. The term *communication* was linked to *speech* and *rhetoric* in basic books on the field during these years. In 1966, *Speech Communication: A Behavioral Approach* appeared, and two years later, *An Introduction to Rhetorical Communication* was published. In the mid-1960s, major volumes also linked *communication* with *culture* and *persuasion*. Additionally, the first books with *interpersonal communication* in their titles were published during this decade.

Communication was of interest in many disciplines during the 1960s. Sociologists focused on group dynamics, social relations, and the social origins of knowledge. Political scientists wrote about the role of communication in governments, governance, public opinion, propaganda, and political image building, providing the foundation for the development of the area of political communication that was to blossom a decade later.

In administrative studies, writings on organization, management, leadership, and information networks provided the basis for the growth of *organizational communication*, an area of study that also emerged in the 1970s. Writings in anthropology and linguistics, together with those in communication, set the stage for the emergence of intercultural communication as an area of study. Advances by zoologists during the 1960s encouraged the study of animal communication.

BERLO'S MODEL

In 1960 David Berlo advanced a new model in his book *The Process of Communication.* The model looked a good deal like the original Aristotelian view of communication, including the traditional elements of source, message, channel, and receiver. However, for each of these elements, controlling factors were listed. The skills, attitudes, knowledge, culture, and social system of the source were all seen as important to understanding the way communication operates, as were the content, treatment, and code of the message. The model acknowledged all five senses as potential information channels and indicated that the same factors influenced receivers as well as sources (Figure 2–9).

In his discussions of the model, Berlo, more than others before, emphasized the idea that communication was a *process.*[18] He also stressed the idea that "meanings are in people, not in words"—another way of saying that the interpretation of a message depends mainly on the meaning of the words or gestures to the sender and receiver, rather than on the message itself.[19] In emphasizing the importance of the meaning attached to a message by a source and receiver, the Berlo framework reinforced a shift away from views of communication that emphasized solely the *transmission* of information to perspectives that focused also on the *interpretation* of information.

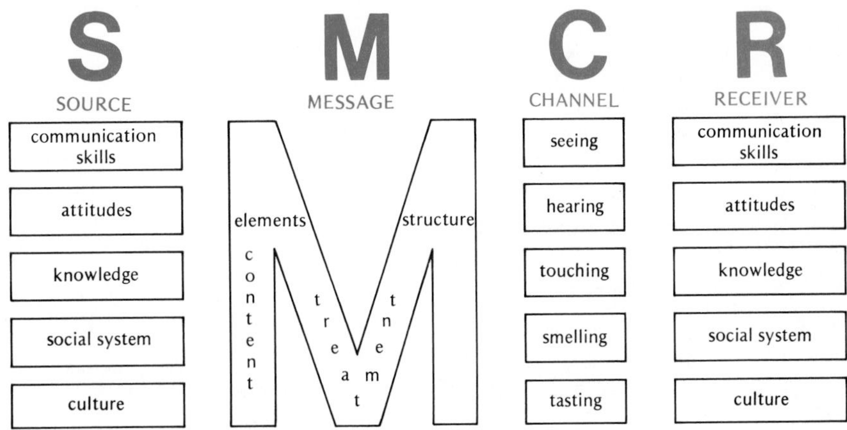

FIGURE 2–9 *Berlo Model.*

Source: The Process of Communication: An Introduction to Theory and Practice, by David Berlo. Copyright © 1960 by Holt, Rinehart and Winston. Reprinted by permission of Holt, Rinehart, and Winston, CBS College Publishing.

DANCE'S MODEL

In 1967, Frank Dance developed a helical-spiral view of communication. The Dance model was substantially different in appearance from others it postdated. The choice of this visual form was intended to convey the idea that communication is a complex and evolutionary process.

> If communication is viewed as a process, we are forced to adapt our examination and our examining instruments to the challenge of something in motion, something that is changing while we are in the very act of examining it.[20]

The helix, shown in Figure 2–10, was a way of combining the desirable features of the straight-line models with those of the circle, while avoiding the weaknesses of each.[21] To the circular feedback models, the Dance perspective added a concern with the dimension of *time*, suggesting that each communicative act builds upon the previous communication experiences of all parties involved. For instance, an exchange between two friends could be represented as a particular point on the helix. The history of the relationship is represented by previous points on the line, the future by subsequent points.

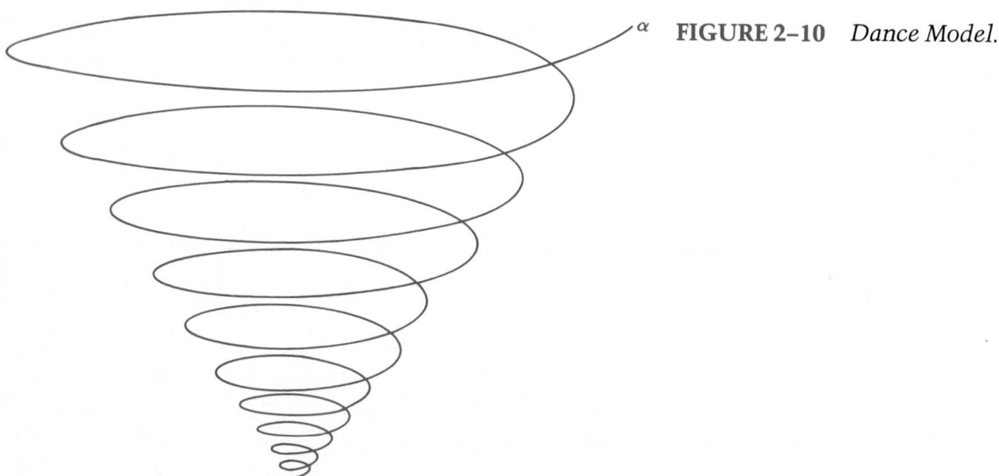

FIGURE 2–10 *Dance Model.*

Source: "Toward A Theory of Human Communication," in *Human Communication Theory: Original Essays.* Ed. by Frank E. X. Dance. Copyright © 1967. By permission.

WATZLAWICK, BEAVIN, AND JACKSON'S MODEL

In that same year, Paul Watzlawick, Janet Beavin, and Don Jackson wrote *Pragmatics of Human Communication,* which provided a general view of communication on the basis of psychiatric study and therapy. Their approach and many of the concepts and propositions they advanced have become influential in communication thinking.

The Watzlawick-Beavin-Jackson view, presented in a general form in Figure 2–11, portrayed communication as a process involving a give-and-take of messages between individuals.[22] The perspective stressed the view that communication is not something that occurs only when a source intentionally chooses to send messages. Rather, they asserted that because we are always behaving, "one cannot not communicate."[23]

Communication was characterized as an ongoing, cumulative activity between individuals who function alternatively as sources and receivers, as shown in Figure 2–11. Their writings suggested that in order to understand how communication worked, one needed to look beyond the messages and channels to the meanings that the individuals involved attach to the words and actions they create.

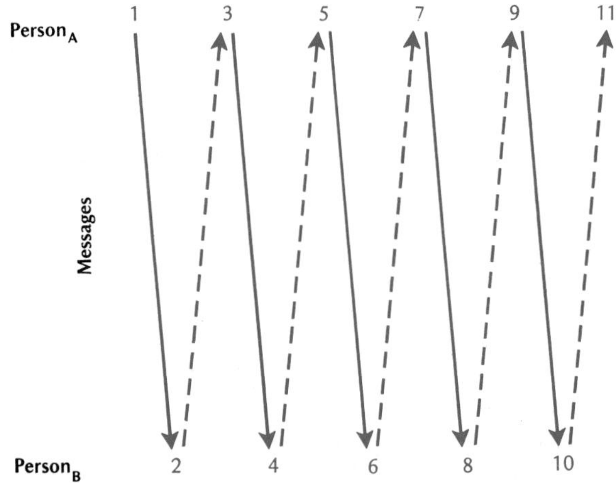

FIGURE 2–11 *Watzlawick-Beavin-Jackson Model.*

Source: Adapted from *Pragmatics of Human Communication,* Paul Watzlawick, Janet H. Beavin and Don D. Jackson. Copyright © 1967 by W. W. Norton. By permission.

THE 1970S: GROWTH AND SPECIALIZATION

The expansion and specialization that began in the late 1960s reached new heights in the early 1970s. *Interpersonal communication* became an increasingly popular area, as did the study of nonverbal interaction. Information science, information theory, and information and communication systems were other topics of increasing interest. During these same years, *group, organizational, political, international,* and *intercultural communication* emerged as distinct areas of study.

Rhetoric, public speaking, debate, theater, speech pathology, journalism, mass media, photography, advertising, and public relations continued to grow and prosper alongside communication, speech communication, and mass communication. New areas such as instructional, therapeutic, and developmental communication also became attractive to researchers and practitioners.

Increased research activity led to a remarkable increase in the publication of books and periodicals. In addition to the many books appearing in interpersonal, group, organizational, cross-cultural, political, speech, and mass communication, other volumes dealt with animal communication, audiovisual techniques, communication in education, and communication in business and personnel. Specialized books focused on communication and children, intimate communication, dyadic communication, satellite communication, communication and ethics, classroom communication, cable communication, and communication and sex differences. Some books sought to provide summaries and overviews of the expanding field. See Figure 2–12.

Increased interest in communication study during the 1970s was also evident in periodicals and scholarly journals. The first publications with the term *communication* in their titles were published in the mid-1930s, and during the 1950s four more appeared. Eight new periodicals appeared during the 1960s, and the 1970s brought the arrival of seventeen new publications bearing *communication* in their titles. A number of new academic journals were introduced, and several other journals of speech and journalism added the word *communication* to their titles to reflect a broadened focus. By the end of the decade, *Ulrich's International Periodical Dictionary* listed one hundred thirty-seven publications on communication.

The expansion and diversification of communication study was reflected in college and university curricula. A number of new departments of communication were formed throughout the 1970s, and some

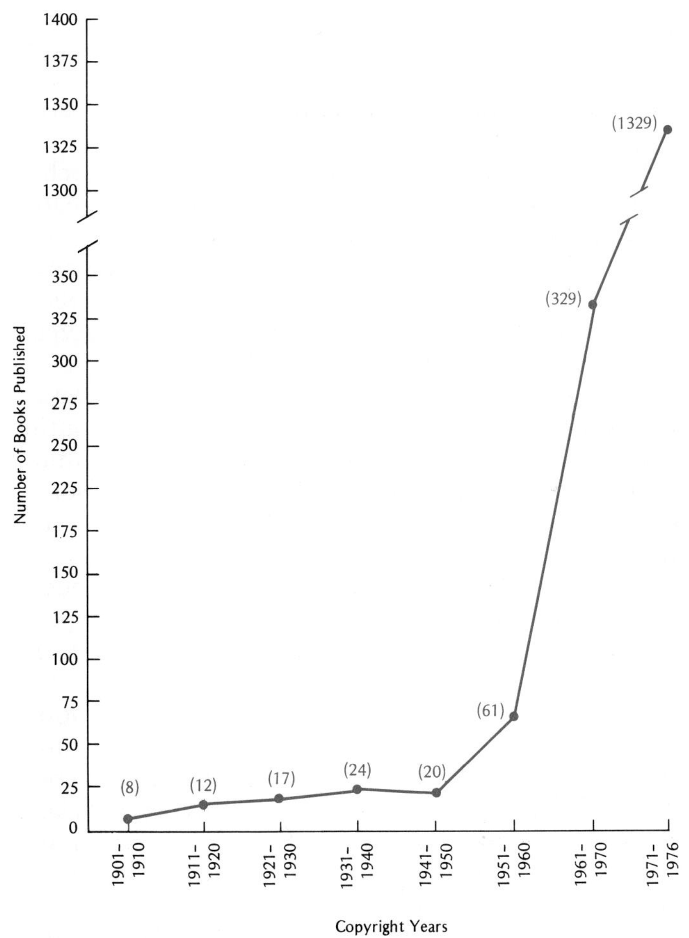

Source: *Books in Print*, 1979.

FIGURE 2–12 *Communication and Communication Related Books Currently in Print.*

programs in speech changed their names to speech communication or communication. The same was true in some journalism departments, where the shift was from journalism to mass communication, communication, or communications.

POPULARITY: A MIXED BLESSING

Interest in communication was apparent in the popular, as well as the academic, realm. In 1975, the *Harper Dictionary of Contemporary*

Usage listed communication as a "vogue word—a word . . . that suddenly or inexplicably crops up . . . in speeches of bureaucrats, comments of columnists . . . and in radio and television broadcasts." This notoriety was very much a mixed blessing. It focused attention on the importance and relevance of communication and brought individuals with various perspectives and backgrounds to the field. However, it also resulted in wholesale and often uncritical usage of the term communication, which detracted from efforts of scholars who were working to clarify definitions of concept.

Discipline, Activity, and Profession. One factor that contributed to the ambiguity of the term during this period of increasing popularity was the use of a single term to refer to a field of study, a set of activities, and a profession. People study communication, people communicate (or more accurately, engage in communication), and people earn their livelihood creating communication products and services. This potential source of confusion does not occur in most other disciplines. For example, scholars study psychology and English, but they do not "psychologize" or "Englishicate." They study English and write. Or they study psychology and engage in therapy or counseling. In these fields, as in most others, different terms are used to differentiate the discipline from the phenomenon itself and from its professional practice. With communication one word refers to the discipline, the activity, and the profession.

In an attempt to clarify the distinction, some writers suggested the terms *communicology, communication science,* or *communication studies* to refer to the discipline, and *communicologist* and *communication scientist* or *communication researcher* to refer to those within it. The phrase, *communication professional,* was sometimes used to refer to individuals who earned their livelihoods engaged in communication activities. These terms were not widely adopted, leaving a source of confusion that continues to the present day.

Communication and Communications. Another factor adding to the confusion was the use of communication and communications. Traditionally, communications had been used to refer to media or to specific messages being transmitted through these media. Communication has generally been used to refer to the activity of sending and receiving messages (through media or face-to-face) and to the discipline as a whole. With the increasing interest in communication media in the 1970s, the term communications began to be used interchangeably with communication in popular—and sometimes academic—contexts, blurring what had originally been a useful technical distinction.

The 1980s and 1990s: The Information Age

"Information Age" is an apt description of the present and previous decade in communication study. The phrase underscores the increasingly pervasive role communication, information, and media play in our personal and professional lives.

INFORMATION AS A COMMODITY

During the 1980s and 1990s, there has been an increasing interest in information (messages) as an economic good or commodity—something that can be bought and sold—and in the technology by which this commodity is created, distributed, stored, retrieved, and used. Today's information companies have emerged as some of North America's largest. The most obvious example is AT&T. Other notable information and communication companies are IBM, ITT, MCI, Dow Jones, McGraw-Hill, Capitol Cities/ABC, Dun & Bradstreet, *Reader's Digest,* Xerox, RCA, and Northern Telecom. Communication and information are central in the telecommunication, publishing, and computer industries, as well as in banking, insurance, leisure and travel, and research. People in these fields spend their time packaging information into products and services that can be sold in domestic and foreign markets.

Current estimates suggest that what is called the *information sector* of the economy accounts for approximately 50 percent of the United States' Gross National Product.[24] In the United States, Japan, Sweden, England, and a number of other countries at least half of the society's labor force is engaged in communication and information-related work; and the number of workers whose jobs involve information, compared to those working in noninformation jobs, has increased steadily over the past 100 years.[25]

NEW AND CONVERGING MEDIA

New and converging media have been a fundamental feature of the landscape of the period. Certainly the most important new technology during this age has been the computer. So significant is its impact, that some have used terms like "commputication" (communication + computers) or "telecomputerenergetics" to signal the blending of once-distinct technologies.

During these years, media have been brought together to form hybrid technologies that permit communication sources and receivers to carry out functions that were once difficult, time-consuming, or even impossible. In earlier periods, specific technologies had more or less specific uses. Television, for example, was a medium for viewing mass produced and distributed programs which reached the set via the airwaves. Today, television is not only a medium for the mass distribution of standardized programs but also a device for use with interactive video games, cable systems, and a display for print as well as visual computer output. The telephone has undergone a similar transformation. Designed for one-to-one conversation, telephones and telephone lines are now used not only in this way, but also in conjunction with computers and facsimile machines for information transmission. Typewriters, once used exclusively for print correspondence and report preparation, combine with the telephone and television screen to form new, hybrid telecommunication systems.

ECONOMIC AND MARKETPLACE INFLUENCES

Since the times of Aristotle, developments in the communication discipline and communication theory have been influenced by the events of the day. As the demands of an oral culture shaped communication thinking in the Classical period, so the challenges of technology are very influential today. The impetus is the infamous "Information Age," with its new labels, new and hybrid media, extended concepts of communication and information, changing economic realities, and new jobs for an increasing number of communication and information workers.

COMMUNICATION AS A PROCESS

Developments of the period have reemphasized the fundamental role of communication as a process through which messages are sent and received. If information is seen as a commodity in the Information Age, communication is popularly viewed as the process by which the commodity is transported from one person, group, organization, or society to another.

The Information Age has also emphasized the role increasingly played by media in a wide range of communication situations. By means of new media, messages may be organized, moved, stored, or retrieved with greater ease than previously. Answering machines and cellular phones bring new flexibility to interpersonal and organizational communication. Portable cassette players, CDs, and VCRs add flexibility to mass communication. Computers create possibilities for greatly increased capacities for the storage, retrieval, reorganization, and reformatting of messages.

The increased capacities and flexibility afforded by the new media have not lessened the need for understanding the underlying communication processes. In fact, the expanded message transmission capacities of today's technology actually give greater urgency to the need to understand the processes through which humans create, interpret, and use information.

STRENGTHENING INTERDISCIPLINARY CONNECTIONS

Many of the challenges we face today require approaches that extend beyond the boundaries of the communication discipline, giving rise to a new era of interdisciplinary study. This is the case, for instance, with goals like anticipating and meeting individuals' information needs; appreciating racial, ethnic, and gender differences; heightening the efficiency and effectiveness of our organizations; identifying the most appropriate personal and professional applications of new media; and improving international relations.

In communication studies, we approach issues such as these from the perspective of the creation, transmission, interpretation, and use of messages by individuals in relationships, groups, organizations, cultures, and societies. The value of integrating our efforts with the works of scholars in other disciplines has become increasingly apparent. Potential connections exist with a number of areas, including:

- Cognitive Psychology: Focus on perception, interpretation, storage, and use of information.
- Cultural and Critical Studies: Focus on the historical, social, and cultural influences on message creation, transmission, interpretation, and use.
- Economics: Focus on the production and consumption of information as an economic resource.
- Computer Science and Electrical Engineering: Focus on the storage, retrieval, manipulation, and transmission of information.

- Information Science: Focus on information classification, management, and storage.
- Journalism: Focus on information sources, content, public communication, and media.
- Literature: Focus on the creation and reader interpretations of textual material.
- Marketing: Focus on user needs and preferences in relation to adoption and use of messages, products, and services.

Reflections on the Evolution of Communication Theory

A number of models of communication have been advanced over the nearly 2,500-year history of the field. This chapter has examined the evolution of communication by reviewing some of the significant models of the process. Models are often a useful way to examine the nature of a phenomenon such as communication, because they miniaturize, simplify, and highlight major facets of a theory. Through an analysis of these models, many changes are apparent.

PARADIGMS AND ANOMALIES

The earliest perspectives on communication were concerned with public speaking to a listener or listeners with persuasion as the goal. Gradually, concern broadened to private as well as public speaking, nonverbal and mediated as well as verbal channels, multiple speakers and listeners as well as individual sources and receivers, and outcomes such as entertainment along with persuasion.

Amidst all the obvious change, certain patterns remained fairly constant. Throughout much of the history of communication study, the process has been described in terms of a source constructing messages to be transmitted to a receiver in order to bring about a particular effect. In this way of thinking, as depicted in Figure 2–13, communication is a one-way transfer of information from source to receiver. The S→M→R = E view of communication has been so pervasive in the thinking of the

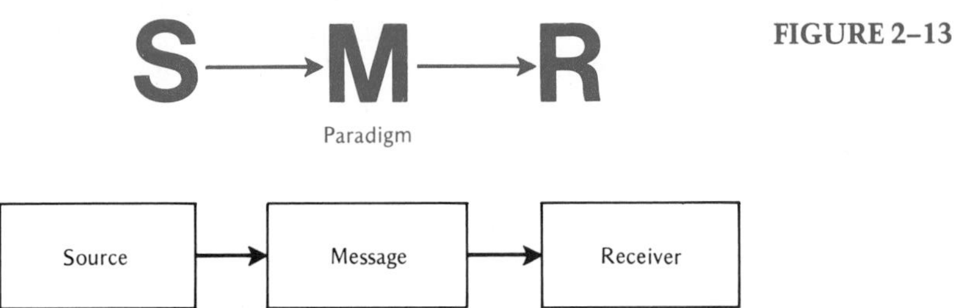

FIGURE 2–13

field that it represents what philosopher Thomas Kuhn and others refer to as a *paradigm*—a broad framework that guides the work of scholars over a long period of time as they conduct research and develop specific theories.[26]

In communication, as in other fields, paradigms do not endure forever. Often they change in response to *anomalies*—research findings, observations, or events that cannot be explained by, or are inconsistent with, existing paradigms.[27] When one reviews the recent history of the field, it is evident that this kind of change has been occurring in communication. Further examination reveals that the anomaly that has given impetus to this transition is relatively simple: *Message sent is not equal to message received—MS ≠ MR.*

Even as Aristotle advanced his orator-to-listener view of communication, he and his contemporaries acknowledged that the persuasive efforts of the speaker were not always successful. It was presumed, however, that the match between the message sent and that received could be made more predictable if sources learned more about how to construct and deliver messages effectively.

The models and writings of Shannon and Weaver, and most especially Schramm, provide evidence of a recognition of the MS ≠ MR anomaly and the beginning of a changing view of communication. Shannon and Weaver's concept of *noise* represented the first formal acknowledgement in a basic communication model that the *message sent by a source,* and the *message received by a receiver* often do not correspond. At the same time the concept of *noise,* as they explained it, offered an explanation as to why the two often may not coincide. The notion of a *correction channel* or *feedback,* suggested by Shannon and Weaver and elaborated upon by Schramm and others went one step beyond acknowledging that the message sent and the message received often do not match, by providing a mechanism for remedying the "problem."

The work of Westley and MacLean dealt head on with the MS ≠ MR anomaly by creating a model that did not begin with the sending of messages, but rather with an individual surrounded by *Xs*—cues—some of which were intentionally provided by others and some not. This way of thinking provided a logical and broadened explanation as to why the message as interpreted by a receiver often had little in common with the message as intended by the source.

The *field of experience* concept, introduced by Schramm, represented yet another means of explaining why the "picture in the head" of the source was not duplicated in the head of the receiver following the transmission of a message. The idea of *opinion leaders* and *the two-step flow,* first suggested in the work of Katz and Lazarsfeld, again reflected an awareness of the fundamental anomaly. Like *feedback,* the two-step concept provided an explanation for the lack of predictive value of the classical paradigm.

Other changes in the ways scholars described the communication process occurred as a consequence of the recognition that the message as received often did not correspond well to the message that was sent. The Katz and Lazarsfeld model, for instance, presented the view that sender-to-receiver effects are more often *mediated* than *direct.* Schramm's perspective indicated that communication was *circular* rather than *unidirectional.* Berlo's writings stressed the role of *meaning* rather than *messages.* Berlo also characterized communication as *process,* not *single event,* a point of view that was carried forward by Dance.

COMMUNICATION THEORY TODAY

Our review of communication models suggests that whereas the S→M→R = E paradigm predominated during much of the history of the field, the past thirty-five years have brought the beginnings of fundamental change to this perspective. The evolution of the concept has been dramatic:

- From source- and message-centered to receiver- and meaning-centered;
- From one-way to circular or spiraling;
- From static to process-oriented;
- From an exclusive emphasis on information transmission to an emphasis on interpretation, as well as information transmission;
- From public speaking to a framework that takes account of communication in a variety of contexts including the individual, relationship, group, organization, society, and media.

The more recent models and theories have substantially broadened our understanding of the nature of communication. They have also provided a foundation for the development of more comprehensive explanations of the role of communication and human behavior of the type presented in Chapters 3 and 4.

The Evolution of the Discipline

In addition to looking at the evolution of communication theory, this chapter has also traced the development of the discipline from its early beginnings, through periods marked by interdisciplinary development, through its emergence and growth as a discipline in its own right, to its present status. From this overview, one can draw a number of conclusions that are helpful in understanding communication study today.

TABLE 2–1 Model of Communication: An Overview

Model	How Communication Works	Major Factors Stressed in Explaining Communication Outcomes	Directional Flow
Aristotle	Speaker constructs messages that bring about persuasive effects among listeners.	source and message	one-way
Lasswell	Speaker constructs messages, selects a channel, and thereby bring about a range of effects among listeners.	source, message and channel	one-way
Shannon-Weaver	Source encodes message and transmits through channel to receiver.	source, message, noise	one-way with feedback
Schramm[1]	Source encodes message and transmits through channel to receiver.	source and message	one-way
Schramm[2]	Source encodes message and transmits information through channel to receiver, if they have shared field of experience.	source, message, receiver	one-way

TABLE 2–1 **(continued)**

Model	How Communication Works	Major Factors Stressed in Explaining Communication Outcomes	Directional Flow
Schramm[3]	An individual encodes message and transmits information through channel to another person who in turn transmits message to source, etc., providing feedback to enable both persons to improve communication fidelity.	source, message, receiver, feedback	circular (through feedback)
Katz-Lazarsfeld	Source encodes messages and transmits information through mass media to opinion leaders who relay it to public.	channel, message, receiver, opinion leader	one-way (mediated)
Westley-MacLean	Source selectively encodes messages and transmits information in modified form to receiver who decodes, encodes, and transmits information in modified form to other individual(s) with feedback at every step.	receiver, meaning, feedback	circular (through feedback)
Berlo	Source encodes messages and transmits to receiver whose interpretation of the message depends on his/her meanings	source, receiver meanings, process	one-way
Dance	Individuals encode and decode messages based on previous communication experiences	process, time	helical-spiral
Watzlawick-Beavin-Jackson	Individuals exchange messages through behavior, the meaning of which varies with each person depending largely upon the communicative relationship between them	receiver, meaning, process, metacommunication	two-way

ANCIENT AND NEWLY EMERGENT

The core of modern communication study has its origins in the work of the early Greek philosophers. The 1900s, however, brought a number of changes to the discipline, including a new name. Within the last thirty-five years, the scope of the field has broadened, its structure has changed, and every facet of it has grown substantially. In this respect, communication can be viewed as a newly emergent field, the newest of the disciplines concerned with the study of human behavior.

INTERDISCIPLINARY HERITAGE

Throughout its history, communication has been greatly influenced by, and has contributed to, a wide range of diverse intellectual disciplines and points of view. Although communication is a distinctive field in its own right, the communication process continues to be of interest to scholars in a number of other fields. This is not unique to communication but is characteristic of nearly all disciplines concerned with the study of human behavior. Social processes are of interest in psychology, political science, and anthropology, as well as in sociology. The individual is a topic of concern in sociology, history, and literature, as well as in psychology. Similarly, information processes play a significant role in psychology, sociology, and political science, as well as in the field of communication.

FIELD OF STUDY, ACTIVITY, AND PROFESSION

From its early beginnings, communication has been the subject of scholarly thought, as well as the label for a range of everyday activities such as speaking and writing. This duality has led to a good deal of confusion about both the term and the discipline; yet the dual meaning has not been without benefit. Perhaps in part because of a broad range of meanings of the term, theorists, researchers, and professionals have been drawn to this single field of study. The consequences have been a generally productive stress among those with different orientations and the formulation of more comprehensive ways of thinking than would be likely to be formulated by any group in isolation.

This duality has had yet another consequence. Because the term *communication* is used to refer to everyday activities such as speaking and listening, as well as to a scholarly field, the word has popular, as well as academic and technical, meanings. This has further contributed to both the richness and relevance of the field, on the one hand, and the diversity of meaning and potential ambiguities associated with the term, on the other.

TRADITIONS OF SCIENCE, ARTS, AND HUMANITIES

Communication has been studied in a variety of ways over the years. Early on, the field developed primarily in the tradition of the humanities. Interest in the critical and qualitative examination of communication events continues to be very strong today. The influence of the scientific tradition has been great in the past forty years, resulting in a commitment to systematic testing and quantitative measurement.

THE ROLE OF MEDIA

Owing to its journalistic heritage, a concern for media and technology has long been a part of the tradition of communication study. Initially, interest was focused on specific forms, such as newspapers, radio, or television. More recently the perspective has broadened to include the nature and function of communication technology in general along with particular media. The Information Age has greatly heightened attention to the pervasive role of media in our lives and its impact on human communication processes.

Implications and Applications for the 1990s

- Communication has long been regarded as important to the practice and understanding of human affairs.
- In the past several decades, communication study has become an increasingly popular academic subject.
- Communication study offers students the richness and diversity of the liberal arts tradition, blended with the applied focus of a professional field.
- Models of communication are useful ways of thinking about the communication processes that occur everyday. Any model highlights certain aspects of communication and obscures others.

• When we use phrases like: "John made me angry," "Beards and long hair are a turn off," or "Video violence and explicit sexuality are responsible for the increase in violence among cable and film viewers," we are applying the $S \rightarrow M \rightarrow R = E$ communication paradigm. Such phrases suggest that receivers are directly controlled by sources and messages.

• Phrases like: "I found myself getting angry at what John said," "I turn off to beards and long hair," or "Video violence may contribute to an increase in these behaviors among viewers," are more consistent with contemporary views of communication. They emphasize the complexity of the process, and the importance of meaning and receiver interpretation in communication outcomes.

Summary

Communication has a rich and lengthy history, which can be traced back to Babylonian and Egyptian writings prior to the fifth century B.C. The initial contributions to communication study came from scholars in what was termed *rhetoric.* They viewed communication as the practical art of persuasion. Aristotle and Plato, who were particularly significant to early communication study, saw rhetoric and the practice of public speaking not only as an art, but also as a legitimate area of study. From its early beginnings, communication was seen as a process in which a speaker constructed messages to bring about desired responses in his or her receiver—the classical $S \rightarrow M \rightarrow R = E$ perspective.

Along with rhetoric and speech, journalism also contributed to the heritage of communication study. As with rhetoric, journalism initially was concerned primarily with practical rather than theoretical matters. By the beginning of the twentieth century, rhetoric and speech were clearly established as disciplines in their own right; and journalism began to take shape as a field as well.

During the early twentieth century, interest in communication continued in rhetoric and speech, and the advent of radio and later television led to the wider application of journalistic concepts and the development of more theories of the overall process. The 1940s and 1950s were years of interdisciplinary growth, as scholars from various disciplines advanced theories of communication that extended beyond the boundaries of their own fields. Among those to provide such descriptions of communication were Lasswell, Shannon and Weaver, Schramm, Katz and Lazarsfeld, and Westley and MacLean.

The 1960s was a period of integration. A good deal was done to synthesize the writings of rhetoric and speech, journalism and mass media, as well as other disciplines. A number of landmark books appeared within the field.

During this most recent period of history, additional models of the communication process were advanced, extending the work of earlier scholars. Among these new models were the writings of Berlo, Dance, and Watzlawick, Beavin, and Jackson.

The decade of the 1970s was a time of unprecedented growth within the field. It was also a period in which much specialization occurred, giving rise to progress in our understanding of interpersonal, group, organizational, political, international, and intercultural communication.

Continuing growth and interdisciplinary advancement have distinguished the communication field in the 1980s and 1990s. Developments of the Information Age have been important influences. Converging media, along with economic and marketplace developments, have underscored the pervasive impact of communication and communication media on our lives.

The overview of the history of communication reveals a number of changes during the 2,500-year heritage of the field—changes both in the theory of the communication process and in the discipline in which it is studied. The earliest perspectives on communication emphasized public speaking with persuasion as the goal. With increasing evidence that the message sent and the message received seldom equalled one another, movement away from the $S \rightarrow M \rightarrow R = E$ paradigm has taken place. Replacing it is a broadened view emphasizing meanings, interpretation, and over-time processes.

We have seen that the communication field is both ancient as well as a product of the twentieth century, interdisciplinary in heritage, the home of scholars and professionals, a discipline which benefits from the approaches of both the humanities and behavioral sciences, and an area in which media are of continuing concern.

Notes

1. For a detailed summary of the early history of speech and rhetorical communication study overviewed here, see *Human Communication Theory: His-*

tory of a Paradigm by Nancy L. Harper (Rochelle Park, NJ: Hayden, 1979), pp. 16–68.

2. Aristotle, *Rhetoric and Poetics,* translated by W. Rhys Roberts (New York: Random House, Modern Library, 1954), in Harper, 1979, p. 20.

3. W. Rhys Roberts, *Works of Aristotle* (Oxford: Clarendon Press, 1924), p. 1377b.

4. Harper, 1979, p. 22.

5. Harper, 1979, p. 27–30.

6. J. F. Frank, *The Beginnings of the English Newspaper 1620–1660* (Cambridge, MA: Harvard University Press, 1961), p. 2.

7. E. G. Bormann, *Theory and Research in the Communicative Arts* (New York: Holt, 1965), pp. 16–17. See also Penny Demo, "Celebrating our 75th Anniversary and our Early Publications," in *Spectra,* May, 1989, p. 4.

8. Grant M. Hyde, "Forward," in *Survey of Journalism.* Ed. by G. F. Mott (New York: Barnes & Noble, 1937), p. viii.

9. Carl H. Weaver, "A History of the International Communication Association," in *Communication Yearbook 1.* Ed. by Brent D. Ruben (New Brunswick, NJ: Transaction-International Communication Association, 1977), pp. 607–609.

10. Harold D. Lasswell, "The Structure and Function of Communication in Society," in *Mass Communications.* Ed. by Wilbur Schramm (Urbana, IL: University of Illinois Press, 1960), p. 117.

11. Claude E. Shannon and Warren Weaver, *The Mathematical Theory of Communication* (Urbana, IL: University of Illinois Press, 1949), p. 3.

12. Shannon and Weaver, 1949, p. 7.

13. Shannon and Weaver, 1949, p. 68.

14. Wilbur Schramm, "How Communication Works," in *The Process and Effects of Mass Communication.* Ed. by Wilbur Schramm (Urbana, IL: University of Illinois Press, 1954), pp. 3–4.

15. Schramm, 1954, p. 4.

16. Schramm, 1954, p. 9; See also, Norbert Wiener, *The Human Use of Human Beings: Cybernetics and Society* (New York: Avon Books, 1967), pp. 47–81, who advanced a similar view of feedback.

17. Elihu Katz and Paul F. Lazarsfeld, *Personal Influence: The Part Played by People in the Flow of Mass Communications* (New York: Free Press, 1956), p. 32.

18. David K. Berlo, *The Process of Communication.* (New York: Holt, 1960), pp. 23–28.

19. Berlo, 1960, p. 175.

20. Frank E. X. Dance, "Toward a Theory of Human Communication," in *Human Communication Theory: Original Essays.* Ed. by Frank E. X. Dance (New York: Holt, 1967), pp. 293–294.

21. Dance, 1967, pp. 294–295.

22. Paul Watzlawick, Janet H. Beavin, and Don D. Jackson, *Pragmatics of Human Communication: A Study of Interactional Patterns, Pathologies, and Paradoxes* (New York: Norton, 1967), pp. 48–51.

23. Watzlawick, Beavin, and Jackson, 1967, pp. 51–54.

24. *The Information Economy: Volumes 1–9* (Washington, DC: Office of Telecommunication, Government Printing Office, 1977), pp. 1–3. See discussion by Wilson P. Dizard, Jr., *The Coming Information Age: An Overview of Technology, Economics, and Politics* (New York: Longman, 1989), p. 101.

25. Jerry L. Salvaggio, "The Telecommunications Revolution: Are We Up to the Challenge." In *Telecommunications: Issues and Choices for Society.* Ed. by Jerry L. Salvaggio (New York: Oxford University Press, 1983), p. 148–153; and *The Information Economy: Volumes 1–9,* pp. 1–3. See discussion by Dizard, Jr., 1989, pp. 101–103.

26. See Thomas S. Kuhn, *The Structure of Scientific Revolutions,* Second Ed. (Chicago: University of Chicago Press, 1970), pp. 1–42.

27. Kuhn, 1970, pp. 52–65.

References and Suggested Readings

ARISTOTLE. *Rhetoric and Poetics.* Translated by W. R. Roberts. New York: Modern Library, 1954.

AUER, J. JEFFERY, CAROLYN CALLOWAY-THOMAS, PATTI P. GILLESPIE, ROBERT C. JEFFREY, GERALD R. MILLER, and LAURENCE L. ZUCKERMAN. *Communication 1940–1989.* New York: Time, Inc/Scott, Foresman and Company, 1989.

BARNLUND, DEAN. *Interpersonal Communication.* Boston: Houghton Mifflin, 1968.

BELL, DANIEL. *The Coming of Post-industrial Society.* New York: Basic Books, 1973.

BENIGER, JAMES. *The Control Revolution.* Cambridge, MA: Harvard University Press, 1986.

———. "Identifying the Important Theorists of Communication: Uses of Latent Measures to Test Manifest Assumptions in Scholarly Communication." In *Scholarly Communication and Bibliometrics.* Ed. by Christine L. Borgman. Newbury Park, CA: Sage, 1990, 254–280.

BERLO, DAVID K. *The Process of Communication: An Introduction to Theory and Practice.* New York: Holt, 1960.

BETTINGHAUS, ERWIN P. *Persuasive Communication.* New York: Holt, 1968.

BINEHAM, JEFFEREY L. "A Historical Account of the Hypodermic Model in Mass Communication." *Communication Monographs.* Vol. 55, No. 3, Sept. 1988, 230–249.

BORMANN, E. G. *Theory and Research in the Communicative Arts.* New York: Holt, 1965.

BROWN, W. R., and M. J. SCHAEFERMEYER. "Progress in Communication as a Social Science." In *Communication Yearbook 4.* Ed. by Dan Nimmo. New Brunswick, NJ: Transaction-International Communication Association, 1980, 37–48.

BUDD, RICHARD W. "Perspectives on a Discipline: Review and Commentary." In *Communication Yearbook 1.* Ed., by Brent D. Ruben. New Brunswick, NJ: Transaction-International Communication Association, 1977, 29–36.

BUDD, RICHARD W. and BRENT D. RUBEN, eds. *Approaches to Human Communication.* Rochelle Park, NJ: Spartan-Hayden, 1972.

———. *Beyond Media: New Approaches to Mass Communication.* New Brunswick, NJ: Transaction Books, 1988.

BURKE, KENNETH. *Language as Symbolic Action.* Berkeley, CA: University of California Press, 1968.

CARROLL, JOHN B. *The Study of Language.* Cambridge, England: Cambridge University Press, 1953.

CHAFFEE, STEVEN H. and JOHN L. HOCHHEIMER. "The Beginnings of Political Communication Research in the United States: Origins of the 'Limited Effects' Model." In *The Media Revolution in American and Western Europe.* Ed. by E. M. Rogers and F. Balle. Norwood, NJ: Ablex, 1985, 267–296.

CHERRY, COLIN. *On Human Communication.* New York: Science Editions, 1961.

CHOMSKY, NOAM. *Aspects of the Theory of Syntax.* Cambridge, MA: M.I.T. Press, 1965.

———. *Syntactic Structures.* The Hague, Netherlands: Mouton, 1957.

COCHRAN, BARBARA D. "The Evolution of Journalism." In *Survey of Journalism.* Ed. by G. F. Mott. New York: Barnes & Noble, 1937, 16–31.

DANCE, FRANK E. X., ed. *Human Communication Theory: Original Essays.* New York: Holt, 1967.

———. "Toward a Theory of Human Communication." In *Human Communication Theory: Original Essays.* Ed. by Frank E. X. Dance. New York: Holt, 1967, 228–309.

DEFLEUR, MELVIN. *Theories of Mass Communication.* New York: McKay, 1966.

DELIA JESS G., *"Communication Research: A History"* In *Handbook of Communication Science.* Ed. by Charles R. Berger and Steven H. Chaffee. Newbury Park, CA: Sage, 1987, 20–98.

DIDSBURY, H. F., JR. *Communication and the Future: Prospects, Promises, and Problems.* Bethesda, MD: World Future Society, 1982.

DIXON, P. D. *Rhetoric.* London: Methuen, 1971.

DIZARD, WILSON P., JR. *The Coming Information Age: An Overview of Technology, Economics, and Politics.* New York: Longman, 1989.

ERIKSON, K. V., ed. *Aristotle: The Classical Heritage of Rhetoric.* Metuchen, NJ: Scarecrow, 1974.

FRANK, J. F. *The Beginnings of the English Newspaper 1620–1660.* Cambridge, MA: Harvard University Press, 1961.

FRINGS, HUBERT, and MABLE FRINGS. *Animal Communication.* New York: Wiley, 1964.

GARDNER, HOWARD. *The Mind's New Science: A History of the Cognitive Revolution.* New York: Basic Books, 1985.

GUMPERT, GARY and ROBERT CATHCART. *Inter/Media: Interpersonal Communication in a Media World.* New York: Oxford University Press, 1986.

HAMMER, D. P. *The Information Age: Its Development and Impact.* Metuchen, NJ: Scarecrow Press, 1976.

HARDT, HANNO. "Philosophy: An Approach to Human Communication." In *Approaches to Human Communication.* Ed. by Richard W. Budd and Brent D. Ruben. New York: Spartan-Hayden, 1972, 290–312.

HARPER NANCY L. *Human Communication Theory: History of a Paradigm.* Rochelle Park, NJ: Hayden, 1979.

HOVLAND, CARL I., IRVING, JANIS, and HAROLD KELLY. *Communication and Persuasion.* New Haven: Yale University Press, 1953.

HUNT, TODD, and BRENT D. RUBEN. *Mass Communication.* New York: Harper Collins, 1991.

HYDE, GRANT M. "Foreward." In *Survey of Journalism.* Ed. by G. F. Mott. New York: Barnes and Noble, 1937, vii–viii.

KATZ, ELIHU. "The Two-Step Flow of Communication." In *Mass Communications.* Ed. by Wilbur Schramm. Urbana, IL: University of Illinois Press, 1960, 346–365.

KATZ, ELIHU and PAUL F. LAZARSFELD. *Personal Influence: The Part Played by People in the Flow of Mass Communications.* New York: Free Press, 1955.

KLAPPER, JOSEPH. *The Effects of Mass Communication.* New York: Free Press, 1960.

KUHN, THOMAS S. *The Structure of Scientific Revolutions.* Second Ed. Chicago: University of Chicago Press, 1970.

LASSWELL, HAROLD D. "The Structure and Function of Communication in Society." In *The Communication of Ideas.* Ed. by Bryson Lyman. Institute for Religion and Social Studies, 1948. Reprinted in *Mass Communications.* Ed. by Wilbur Schramm. Urbana, IL: University of Illinois Press, 1960, 117–130.

LAZARSFELD, PAUL F., BERNARD BERELSON, and HAZEL GAUDET. *The People's Choice.* New York: Columbia University Press, 1944.

LIPPMAN, WALTER. *Public Opinion.* New York: Free Press, 1922.

LITTLEJOHN, STEPHEN W. *Theories of Human Communication,* Third Ed. Columbus, OH: Merrill, 1989.

LOWERY, SHEARON and MELVIN L. DEFLEUR. *Milestones in Mass Communication Research.* New York: Longman, 1983.

MACHLUP, FRITZ and UNA MANSFIELD, eds. *The Study of Information: Interdisciplinary Messages.* New York: Wiley-Interscience, 1983.

MANCA, LUIGI D. "Seven Notes on MacLean." *The Journal of Communication Inquiry.* Spring 1976, 36–60.

MANDLER, GEORGE. *Cognitive Psychology: An Essay in Cognitive Science.* Hillsdale, NJ: Lawrence Erlbaum, 1985.

MASUDA, YONEJI. *The Information Society as Post-industrial Society.* Washington, DC: World Future Society, 1980.

MCCROSKEY, JAMES. *An Introduction to Rhetorical Communication.* Englewood Cliffs, NJ: Prentice-Hall, 1968.

MCLUHAN, MARSHALL. *The Mechanical Bride.* New York: Vanguard, 1951.

———. *Understanding Media.* New York: McGraw-Hill, 1964.

MILLER, GERALD R. *Speech-Communication: A Behavioral Approach.* New York: Bobbs-Merrill, 1966.

MIRABITO, MICHAEL M., and BARBARA L. MORGENSTERN. *The New Communications Technologies.* Boston: Focal, 1990.

MOTT, FRANK LUTHER. *American Journalism—A History 1690–1960.* New York: Macmillan, 1962.

MOWLANA, HAMID. *Global information and World Communication: New Frontiers in International Relations.* New York: Longman, 1986.

NIMMO, DAN. "Political Communication Theory and Research: An Overview." In *Communication Yearbook 1.* Ed. by Brent D. Ruben. New Brunswick, NJ: Transaction-International Communication Association, 1977, 441–452.

OGDEN, C. K., and I. A. RICHARDS. *The Meaning of Meaning.* London: Kegan Paul, 1923.

PALMGREEN, PHILIP. "Uses and Gratifications: A Theoretical Perspective." In *Communication Yearbook 8.* Ed. by Robert N. Bostrom. Beverly Hills: Sage, 1984, 20–55.

POOL, ITHIEL DE SOLA. *Technologies of Freedom.* Cambridge, MA: Belknap, 1983.

PORAT, MARC. *Information economy: Definition and measurement.* Washington, DC: U.S. Department of Commerce, Office of Telecommunications, May, 1977.

REDDING, W. CHARLES. "Organization Communication Theory and Ideology: An Overview." In *Communication Yearbook 3.* Ed. by Dan Nimmo. New Brunswick, NJ: Transaction-International Communication Association, 1979, 309–342.

RICE, RONALD. *The New Media: Communication, Research, and Technology.* Beverly Hills, CA: Sage, 1984.

RICHETTO, GARY M. "Organizational Communication Theory and Research: An Overview." In *Communication Yearbook 1.* Ed. by Brent D. Ruben. New Brunswick, NJ: Transaction-International Communication Association, 1977, 331–346.

ROGERS, EVERETT M. *Communication Technology.* New York: Free Press, 1986.

ROGERS EVERETT M., and D. LAWRENCE KINCAID. *Communication Networks.* New York: Free Press, 1981.

RUBIN M. R. and M. T. HUBER. *The Knowledge Industry in the United States: 1960–1980.* Princeton, NJ: University Press, 1986.

SCHEMENT, JORGE R. and LEAH LIEVROUW. *Competing Visions, Complex Realities: Social Aspects of the Information Society.* Norwood, NJ: Ablex, 1987.

SCHRAMM, WILBUR. "The Beginnings of Communication Study in the United States." In *Communication Yearbook 4.* Ed. by Dan Nimmo. New Brunswick, NJ: Transaction-International Communication Association, 1980, 73–82.

———. "How Communication Works." In *The Process and Effects of Mass Communication.* Ed. by Wilbur Schramm. Urbana, IL: University of Illinois Press, 1954, 3–26.

———. *Mass Communications.* Champaign, IL: University of Illinois Press, 1960.

———. *The Science of Human Communication.* New York: Basic, 1963.

———. ed. *The Process and Effects of Mass Communication.* Urbana, IL: University of Illinois Press, 1954.

SHANNON, CLAUDE E. and WARREN WEAVER. The Mathematical Theory of Communication. Urbana, IL: University of Illinois Press, 1949.

SKINNER, B. F. *Verbal Behavior.* New York: Appleton-Century-Crofts, 1957.

SMITH, ALFRED G. "Taxonomy of Communication: Review and Commentary." In *Communication Yearbook 1.* Ed. by Brent D. Ruben. New Brunswick, NJ: Transaction-International Communication Association, 1977, 79–88.

———, ed. *Communication and Culture.* New York: Holt, 1966.

SMITH, ANTHONY. *Goodbye Gutenberg.* New York: Oxford University Press, 1980.

SMITH, DAVID H. "Communication Research and the Idea of Process." *Speech Monographs,* 39 (1972), 175–182.

SMITH, RONALD L. "General Models of Communication." Paper presented at the Summer Conference of the National Society for the Study of Communication, 1962.

STEWART, CHARLES J., "Historical Survey: Rhetorical Criticism in Twentieth Century America." In *Explorations in Rhetorical Criticism.* Ed. by Charles J. Stewart, Donovan J. Oches and Gerald P. Mohrmann. University Park, PA: Pennsylvania State University Press, 1973, 1–31.

STEWART, CHARLES J., DONOVAN J., OCHS, and GERALD P. MOHRMANN, eds. *Explorations in Rhetorical Criticism.* University Park, PA: Pennsylvania State University Press, 1973.

THAYER, LEE. "Communication—Sine Qua Non of the Behavioral Sciences." In *Vistas in Science.* Ed. by D. L. Arm. Albuquerque, NM: University of New Mexico Press, 1968. Reprinted in *Interdisciplinary Approaches to Human Communication.* Second Ed. Ed. by Richard W. Budd and Brent D. Ruben. New Brunswick, NJ: Transaction, 1988, 7–32.

———. *Communication: Theory and Research.* Springfield, KL: Thomas, 1967.

——— ed. *Communication: Concepts and Perspectives.* New York: Spartan, 1967.

———. *Communication and Communication Systems.* Homewood, IL: Irwin, 1968.

———. "On Theory-Building in Communication: Some Conceptual Problems." *Journal of Communication,* 13 (1963) 217–235.

WATZLAWICK, PAUL, JANET H. BEAVIN, and DON D. JACKSON. *Pragmatics of Human Communication: A Study of Interactional Patterns, Pathologies, and Paradoxes.* New York: Norton, 1967.

WEAVER, CARL H. "A History of the International Communication Association." In *Communication Yearbook 1.* Ed. by Brent D. Ruben. New Brunswick, NJ: Transaction-International Communication Association, 1977, 607–609.

WESTLEY, BRUCE H., and MALCOLM S. MACLEAN, JR. "A Conceptual Model for

Communication Research." *Audio-Visual Communication,* 3 (Winter, 1955), 4. Reprinted in *Journalism Quarterly,* 34 (1957), 31–38.

WIENER, NORBERT. *The Human Use of Human Beings: Cybernetics and Society.* Boston: Houghton Mifflin, 1950. Reprinted in New York: Avon Books, 1967.

———. *Cybernetics or Control and Communication in the Animal and the Machine.* Cambridge, MA: M.I.T. Press, 1948.

WILLIAMS, FREDERICK. *Technology and Communication Behavior.* Belmont, CA: Wadsworth, 1987.

WRIGHT, CHARLES R. *Mass Communication.* Third Ed. New York: Random House, 1986.

SPECIES CONTINUITY • MATING • REPRODUCTION • PARENT-OFF SPRING RELATIONS • FEEDING • LEARNING • IDENTITY IMPRINTING • DEVELOPMENT OF COMMUNICATION CAPABILITIES • ADAPTATION • LOCOMOTION • SELF-DEFENSE • TERRITORIALITY • COOPERATION • COMPETITION • DIVISION OF LABOR • MOBILIZING FOR GROUP ACT-TION • DOMINANCE-SUBMISSION • STATUS CONFERRAL • SOCIAL ORGANIZATION •
SPECIES CONTINUITY • MATING • REPRODUCTION • PARENT-OFF SPRING RELATIONS • FEEDING • LEARNING • IDENTITY IMPRINTING • DEVELOPMENT OF COMMUNICATION CAPABILITIES • ADAPTATION • LOCOMOTION • SELF-DEFENSE • TERRITORIALITY • COOPERATION • COMPETITION • DIVISION OF LABOR • MOBILIZING FOR GROUP ACT-TION • DOMINANCE-SUBMISSION • STATUS CONFERRAL • SOCIAL ORGANIZATION •
SPECIES CONTINUITY • MATING • REPRODUCTION • PARENT-OFF SPRING RELATIONS • FEEDING • LEARNING • IDENTITY IMPRINTING • DEVELOPMENT OF COMMUNICATION CAPABILITIES • ADAPTATION • LOCOMOTION • SELF-DEFENSE • TERRITORIALITY • COOPERATION • COMPETITION • DIVISION OF LABOR • MOBILIZING FOR GROUP ACT-TION • DOMINANCE-SUBMISSION • STATUS CONFERRAL • SOCIAL ORGANIZATION •
SPECIES CONTINUITY • MATING • REPRODUCTION • PARENT-OFF SPRING RELATIONS • FEEDING • LEARNING • IDENTITY IMPRINTING • DEVELOPMENT OF COMMUNICATION CAPABILITIES • ADAPTATION • LOCOMOTION • SELF-DEFENSE • TERRITORIALITY • COOPERATION • COMPETITION • DIVISION OF LABOR • MOBILIZING FOR GROUP ACT-TION • DOMINANCE-SUBMISSION • STATUS CONFERRAL • SOCIAL ORGANIZATION •
SPECIES CONTINUITY • MATING • REPRODUCTION • PARENT-OFF SPRING RELATIONS • FEEDING • LEARNING • IDENTITY IMPRINTING • DEVELOPMENT OF COMMUNICATION CAPABILITIES • ADAPTATION • LOCOMOTION • SELF-DEFENSE • TERRITORIALITY • COOPERATION • COMPETITION • DIVISION OF LABOR • MOBILIZING FOR GROUP ACT-TION • DOMINANCE-SUBMISSION • STATUS CONFERRAL • SOCIAL ORGANIZATION •
SPECIES CONTINUITY • MATING • REPRODUCTION • PARENT-OFF SPRING RELATIONS • FEEDING • LEARNING • IDENTITY IMPRINTING • DEVELOPMENT OF COMMUNICATION CAPABILITIES • ADAPTATION • LOCOMOTION • SELF-DEFENSE • TERRITORIALITY • COOPERATION • COMPETITION • DIVISION OF LABOR • MOBILIZING FOR GROUP ACT-TION • DOMINANCE-SUBMISSION • STATUS CONFERRAL • SOCIAL ORGANIZATION •
SPECIES CONTINUITY • MATING • REPRODUCTION • PARENT-OFF SPRING RELATIONS • FEEDING • LEARNING • IDENTITY IMPRINTING • DEVELOPMENT OF COMMUNICATION CAPABILITIES • ADAPTATION • LOCOMOTION • SELF-DEFENSE • TERRITORIALITY • COOPERATION • COMPETITION • DIVISION OF LABOR • MOBILIZING FOR GROUP ACT-TION • DOMINANCE-SUBMISSION • STATUS CONFERRAL • SOCIAL ORGANIZATION •
SPECIES CONTINUITY • MATING • REPRODUCTION • PARENT-OFF SPRING RELATIONS • FEEDING • LEARNING • IDENTITY IMPRINTING • DEVELOPMENT OF COMMUNICATION CAPABILITIES • ADAPTATION • LOCOMOTION • SELF-DEFENSE • TERRITORIALITY • COOPERATION • COMPETITION • DIVISION OF LABOR • MOBILIZING FOR GROUP ACT-TION • DOMINANCE-SUBMISSION • STATUS CONFERRAL • SOCIAL ORGANIZATION •

3

Communication - A Basic Life Process

The Value of Systems Thinking for Communication Study

Basic Systems Concepts
Systems
Boundaries
Environment
Closed and Open Systems
Living Systems

Communication Processes in Animal and Human Systems

Communication Modes
Visual Messages
Tactile Messages
Olfactory and Gustatory Messages
Auditory Messages

Basic Functions of Communication
Courtship and Mating
Reproduction
Parent-Offspring Relations and Socialization
Navigation
Self-Defense
Territoriality

The Adaptation Perspective

Implications and Applications: Systems, Animals, and People

The Value of Systems Thinking for Communication Study

Even a cursory examination of the history of communication study reveals the richness and complexity of the field and the phenomenon. Contributions to our understanding come from scholars in communication and a number of other fields who bring a variety of perspectives and methods.

Developing a comprehensive view of the role of communication processes in human affairs requires us to draw together wide-ranging theory and research. *Systems Theory* provides a framework that assists in meeting this goal. The basic approach involves conceiving of the universe as a collection of interrelated structures organized *hierarchically*—from complex units like societies, to "simple" entities like cells. The biological and social world is viewed in broad terms as being composed of societies, which in turn are composed of cultures, which are composed of subcultures, of communities, and so on, as shown in Figure 3–1.

As we shall see in the pages ahead, the systems approach highlights the fundamental functions communication serves at each of these levels and in relationships that exist between them.

Basic Systems Concepts

SYSTEMS

A *system* is any entity or whole that is composed of interdependent elements. Systems have characteristics and capabilities that are distinct from those of the separate parts. A simple example of a system is a cake. The ingredients of a typical cake are sugar, flour, salt, eggs, butter, vanilla, and baking powder and/or soda. When these are combined and baked, the result is an entity that is much different than any of the individual ingredients.

The organs of the body are also systems in that the cells, blood, and tissues all operate together to make the organ a unique, functioning unit that is capable of performing operations none of its parts could accomplish independently. An automobile—composed of tires, radiator, alternator, engine, drive train, and a variety of other parts—is yet another example of a system. Societies, organizations, groups, relation-

FIGURE 3–1 *Systems View of the Biosocial Universe.*

ships, and individuals are also systems. Each has interconnected component parts and, as a whole, has attributes and performs functions that would be impossible for any one part alone.

Most systems have physical properties, as, for example, the solar system, a society, a transportation system, a neurological system, a skeletal system, a stereo system, an exhaust system, an animal, or a cell. The nature of these properties varies greatly and, depending on the particular system, may consist of such ingredients as atoms, stars, individuals, bones, machines, neurons, genes, muscles, or gases.

BOUNDARIES

Boundaries define the edges of a system and hold the parts together as indicated in Figure 3–2. They protect the system from the environment

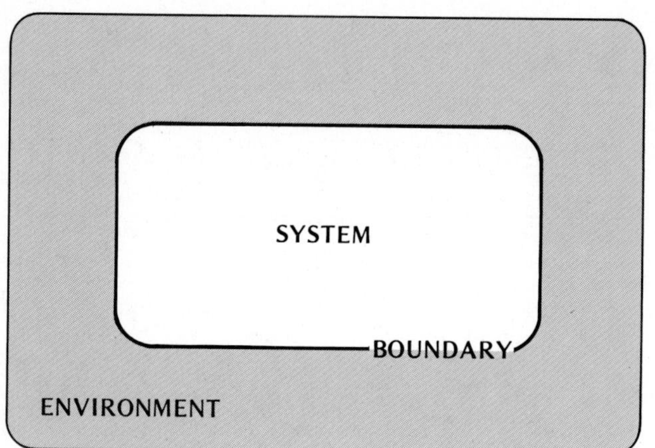

FIGURE 3–2

and exclude or admit substances to ensure the system's continued functioning. For a cake, the pan in which the ingredients are baked serves as a boundary. It holds together the components and allows for the exchange of heat and air. The boundaries of cells are walls. Organs have membranes. Animals have skin, shells, fur, or external skeletons that bind the parts together and protect the system.

ENVIRONMENT

Beyond the boundaries of a system is the *environment* in which it exists and upon which it depends. The immediate environment of a cake being baked is the inside of the oven and the heated air contained within. In a broader sense, the environment is everything beyond the edges of the pan. Generally, one can think of the environment as the physical surroundings and influences separated from a system by its boundary.

CLOSED AND OPEN SYSTEMS

Some systems engage in a give-and-take exchange with their environments; others do not. *Closed systems* are so named because they operate in isolation of their environment. An example of a closed system is the reaction of several chemicals mixed together in a sealed container. The action of the ingredients that defines such a system is totally a consequence of the dynamics that occur among the chemicals, without influence from the environment outside the test bottle.

Open systems are engaged in a continual give-and-take exchange with their environment. Such systems influence and are influenced by their environment. Because they *interact* with their environment, the dynamics of open systems are usually less predictable than those in closed systems, in which the outcome depends only on the isolated exchange among parts of the system.

LIVING SYSTEMS

Of all those systems that influence and are influenced by their environment, our particular concern is with *living systems*—open systems that go through a life cycle. For all living things, that cycle begins with birth or initial emergence, moves through various stages of growth and development, and eventually leads to deterioration, decay, and death.

As with other open systems, the dynamics of living systems involves an ongoing interaction between the entity and its environment. The basic process is one in which a living system takes in certain materials that are necessary to its life functioning through openings in its boundary and gives off into the environment other materials as wastes.

With plants, the critical environmental exchange involves a give-and-take of chemicals and other substances necessary to growth. The process through which this development occurs is photosynthesis. Necessary to this process are the presence of a number of environmental inputs, including sunlight, heat, water, and carbon dioxide. As a by-product of photosynthesis, plants give off oxygen into the environment.

Animals, on the other hand, require the intake of oxygen, and they give off carbon dioxide. Animal metabolism also requires the intake of food substances. The food is transformed into living tissue and energy by the animal, and organic wastes are returned to the environment.

Communication Processes in Animal and Human Systems

As one moves from plants to animals, the nature of the system-environment interaction becomes increasingly complex. Animals not only depend for their survival upon chemical and physical exchanges but also upon the exchange of messages. This latter process—communication—enables animals to create, gather, and use information to interact with and adapt to their environment and its inhabitants.

Just as animal and human systems take in oxygen and foodstuffs and transform them into materials necessary to their functioning, they also take in and use information.[1] In this most basic sense, communication is the essential life process through which animal and human systems create, acquire, transform, and use information to carry out the activities of their lives. See Figure 3–3.

Communication Modes

The information used as the basis for behavior is derived by producing and responding to messages in the environment. The world in which living systems exist is filled with a vast array of such messages. Some of these, such as the words exchanged between friends, or the mating call of a bird, are purposefully created by another living system. Other cues, such as the flash of lightning or the sound of a falling tree are not. Both purposeful and nonpurposeful cues are vital as potential sources of the information necessary to behavior, as illustrated in Figure 3–4.

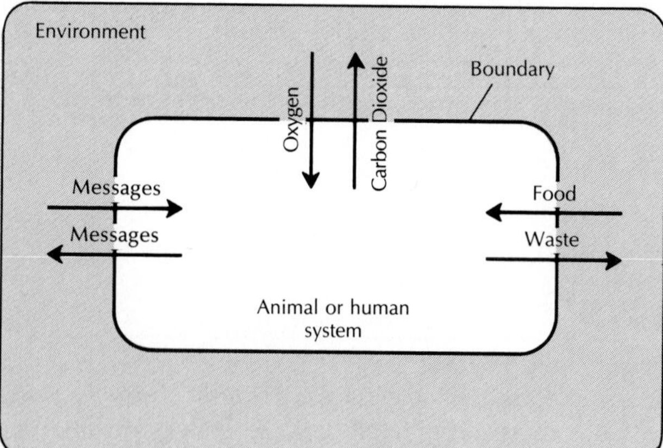

FIGURE 3–3 *Basic Processes of Animal and Human Systems.* In order to survive, higher-order living systems must interact with the environment. These exchanges take place through the boundary of the system. In this manner, animal or human systems exchange oxygen for carbon dioxide, food inputs for organic wastes, and information.

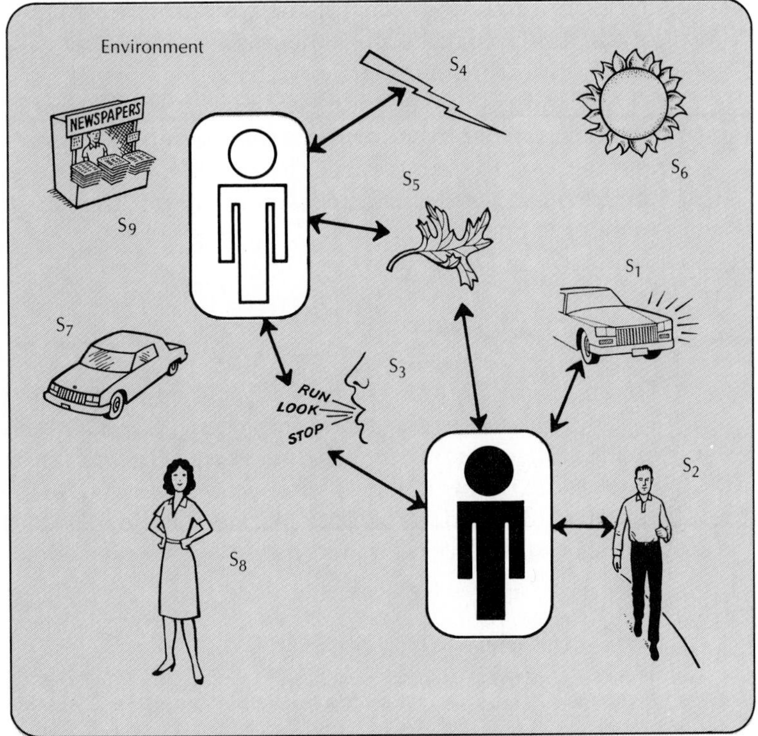

FIGURE 3–4 *Communication Sources and Modes.* Within an environment there are a number of potential message sources to which a living system may attend and react, represented by S_1 through S_9 in the illustration above. Some of these messages may be produced by inanimate sources, such as the sound of a horn, the visible flash of lightning, or the touch of a leaf blowing past in the wind—S_1, S_4, and S_5. Other messages, S_2 and S_3, taking the form of a smell, taste, sound or sight, are produced by other living systems. These messages may be unintended, like the sound created by a person walking down the street (S_2), or they may be more purposeful, such as spoken words (S_3). At any instant, many potential messages are not taken account of at all—S_6, S_7, S_8, and S_9.

VISUAL MESSAGES

For humans, visual messages are particularly important; a wave and a smile from a friend, a blush of embarrassment, a tear, a new dress or a new car, and the headlines of a newspaper are all potential sources of information that can hold great significance for us. Some animals also make substantial use of visual cues. The color and acrobatics of male birds, the luring colored wings of the male butterfly, the rhythmic light of the firefly, and the movement of head, ears, or tail by primates all serve as valuable information sources.

As significant as sight is for humans and some animals, it is generally not as crucial as other communication modes in most species. Many animals lack the visual capacities necessary for processing light and depend instead on touch, sound, smell, or taste to relate to their environment or to one another.

TACTILE MESSAGES

For animal and human systems, touch, bumping, vibration, and other types of tactile messages are important. See Table 3–1. From before birth through the first months and years of life, physical contact plays a critical role in the biological and social development of human infants, as well as of the young of other species. Tactile messages remain crucial throughout the lives of many animals, in parent-young relations, court-

TABLE 3–1 Communication Modes

Modality	Form of Message
Visual	. . . *Sight* —facial displays —movement of body parts —distance and spacing —position —dress —other symbols, adornment, and emblems
Tactile	. . . *Touch* —vibration —stroking —rubbing —pressure —pain —temperature
Olfactory and Gustatory	. . . *Smell and Taste (Pheromones)* —body odors —special chemicals —food sources, fragrances, and taste
Auditory	. . . *Sound* —incidental sounds —vibrations —whistling —drumming —rubbing —vocalization

ship and intimate relations, social greetings, play, and aggression and combat. These cues also play a vital role in self-defense and self-preservation. Receptors in the skin and other locations throughout the body detect heat, cold, pressure, and pain and serve as signals that the safety of the system is threatened. For humans, tactile signals are the major source of the symptoms, such as fatigue, nausea, dizziness, muscular strain, or apprehension that are used to determine if one is ill and to identify the problem and its location.

OLFACTORY AND GUSTATORY MESSAGES

Many living systems also use olfactory and gustatory information to relate to their environment and to one another. *Pheromones* is the technical term used to refer to these chemical messages. Some of the chemically-based messages are produced by other animals; others, such as the smell of rain, have inanimate sources. Pheromones are carried through water or air to the specialized receptor at the boundary of the living system. Vertebrates receive these messages through a nose, fish through a nose or odor-sensitive cells on the body, and insects by means of sensors located in their antennae.

As Jack Prince explains:

> [The odor-sensitive cells] are situated so air or water passes over them and allows them to absorb the odor particles it carries. In air these cells pick up more particles with each sniff or breath, so the odor builds up in the receptor cells and becomes stronger. Each cell is connected by a nerve fiber with the brain . . . which is more developed in animals that use smell as the dominant sense than in animals that rely on vision or hearing.[2]

As with other modes, the brain and/or nervous system filters out irrelevant cues and guides the system to respond only to those signals to which the system is attuned or to which it has learned to attend. Although humans have the set of organs thought necessary for chemical message production and reception, olfactory information plays a much less substantial role in the activities of humans than in the lives of many other animals.

AUDITORY MESSAGES

For humans and many animal systems, auditory messages provide critical links to the environment and to one another. Some sounds—thunder, an earthquake, or the surf splashing against the shore—have inanimate sources. Other auditory messages are produced by living things through speaking, whistling, drumming, or striking a part of the body against an object, the ground, or another part of the body. Additional messages are created as an extension of human activity, such as those which result from the firing of a rifle or operating an engine. Actions of this kind produce vibrations that are transported through air or water. See Figure 3–5.

In order for auditory signals to be useful to a living system, the vibrations must be detected, received, and processed by means of a special organ which converts the data into electrical impulses that can be utilized by the brain. Lower-order animals generally respond to sound either by approaching or moving away from the source; most higher-order systems are able to act upon auditory messages in any number of ways due to prior learning. Auditory messages are important in the lives of a wide range of species, including birds, insects, and primates in addition to humans, all of which depend upon these cues in caring for the young, learning, courtship and mating, and language acquisition and use.

Basic Functions of Communication

The significance of communication and the various information-processing modes of human and animal systems is perhaps clearest

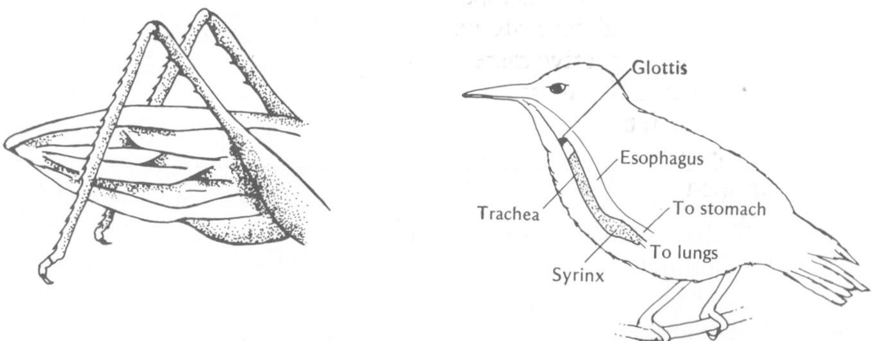

FIGURE 3–5 *Insect and Bird Sound Production.* Many insects produce a sound called *stridulation* by rubbing their hind legs against their bodies. The inner thigh of the hind legs contains a saw-like ridge of teeth (a *file*) that produces a range of sounds when pulled across a wing vein (or *scraper*). Birds, which lack the larynx associated with sounds of most mammals, produce sounds by means of a *syrinx.*

Source: Languages of the Animal World, J. H. Prince (Nashville: Nelson), 1975.

when one considers some of the basic biological functions they serve. See Table 3–2.

COURTSHIP AND MATING

Although differences exist in the specific courtship and mating practices of various species, all of these involve communication. Humans and other animals must be able to identify other individuals of their own species and determine gender relative to their own. Also, individuals must attract and sometimes persuade one another, and the mating activity must be synchronized.

As with other species, human courtship involves the identification and attraction of mates. These processes occur primarily through visual, auditory, and tactile modes, although some studies suggest that chemical cues may also play a role. See Figure 3–6. Human courtship and mating involves persuasion and negotiation. Humans arrange the terms, timing, and implications of their intimate relations, and in these interactions communication plays an indispensable role.

Members of animal species identify, locate, and attract one another by emitting and responding to cues of one kind or another. The songs of grasshoppers and crickets serve this purpose, as does the odor of moths and the light flashing of fireflies. See Figure 3–7. With birds, mating involves the creation and reception of auditory messages ranging from a simple, repetitive, and not necessarily musical call to complex song-and-dance presentations, acrobatics, and rituals. In some species the male birds build and decorate nests, which they use to advertise their availability to prospective mates.

For many animals, mating involves not only identifying and attracting an individual but also synchronizing the timing of sexual activities in order for fertilization to occur. The oyster and certain other marine animals apparently acquire the information needed for the proper timing of fertilization from the ocean tides. Reproduction begins in the spring, following a migration toward a breeding ground. The increased

TABLE 3–2 Basic Functions of Communication

Courtship and Mating
Reproduction
Parent-offspring Relations and Socialization
Navigation
Self-defense
Territoriality

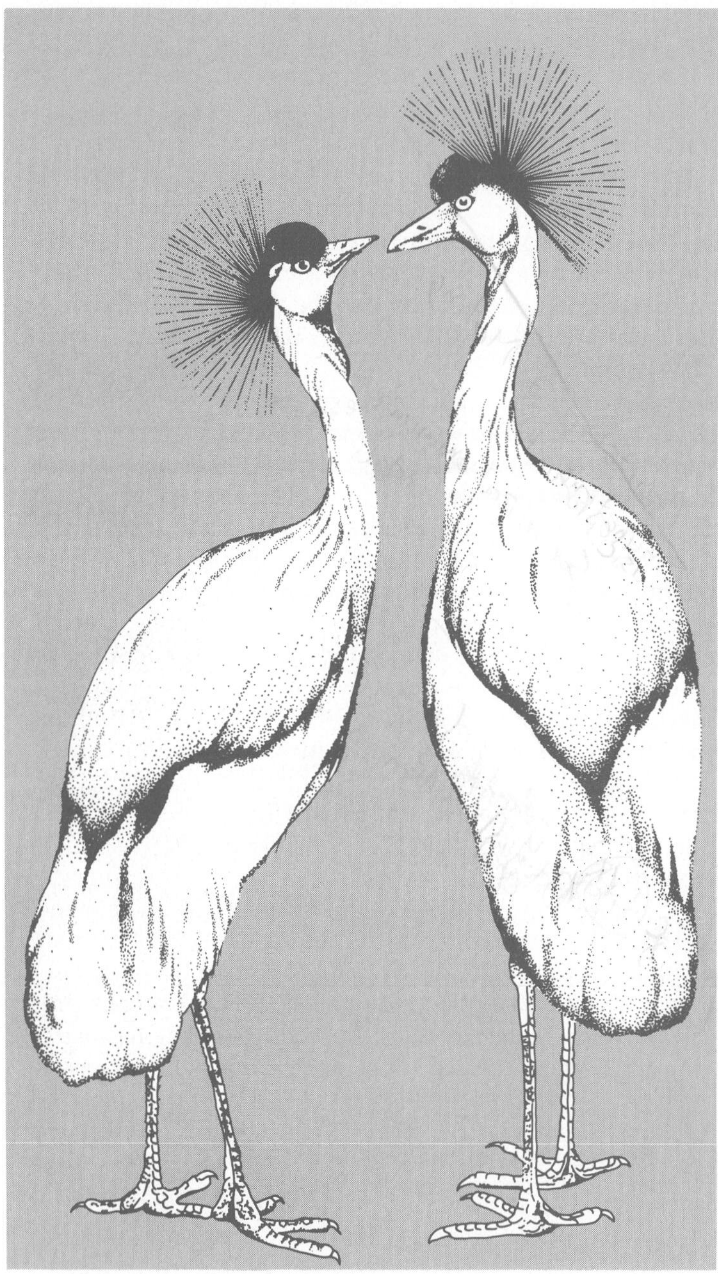

Crowned Cranes

FIGURE 3–6 Communication plays a basic, and in many ways similar, role in the courtship and mating practices of humans and animals.

FIGURE 3–6 (continued)

FIGURE 3–7 *Visual Signal Patterns of Firefly Messages.* Male lightning bugs begin their flight during early evening hours of the spring or summer, flashing the luminescent light on the abdomen to attract a mate. In many species, the female does not fly, but rather signals the male from the grass, guiding him to her location. Because there are often a number of different varieties of fireflies in any one area, different codes are necessary in order for individuals to identify and attract members of their own species. These codes consist of distinctive flash and flight patterns—dots, swoops, curves, lines, zigzags and the timing of flashes.

Source: Margaret Cosgrove, *Messages and Voices*. Copyright © 1974 by Margaret Cosgrove. Reprinted with permission.

daylight in this season triggers the change in hormonal functions through which reproductive cycles are coordinated.[3]

For some insects, recognition, attraction, synchronization, and coordination occur as a result of messages provided by chemicals. With moths, for example, the female sex pheromone triggers a sequence of activities in the male, starting with the activation of the animal, followed by its movement toward the chemical source, and culminating in courtship and copulation. The pheromone is so vital an information source in the mating process that the female's body need not even be present. If a small quantity of the chemical is placed on some nonliving object, nearby male moths exhibit the entire sequence of mating and copulation actions toward the object that are normally associated with the presence of the female moth.[4]

REPRODUCTION

It is almost too obvious to note that offspring of any species as they reach adulthood bear strong physical resemblance to their parents. A bear cub grows up to look and act like a bear, not a cat or a dog. Physiologically, structurally, in general appearance, and in a number of behavioral patterns, the young of any species replicate or reproduce their parents. This reproduction comes about through a biological communication process in which the sperm cell of the male parent and female egg cell merge to provide a blueprint for the growth and development of the offspring.[5]

DNA, located within cells, is the molecular basis of heredity in many organisms. Living systems, their subsystems, and their subsubsystems are composed of cells. The general pattern of growth of living things is through division of cells. A single cell divides to produce two, each of which divides to produce two more, and so on. In some organisms, this continues until thousands, millions, or billions of cells are produced. Division, growth, and development proceed according to the blueprint, as the cells form into layers and masses that fold together and intermesh to form more complex systems—tissues, bones, and organs.

Reproduction of human offspring by their parents begins at the moment of conception as the male sperm and the female egg join. The egg cell, most of which is filled with food, is about one two-hundredth of an inch across. In this space are all the instructions that represent the mother's contribution to the inherited characteristics of the child. The sperm cell, which is only about 1/80,000 the size of the egg, carries only the messages necessary to the father's contribution to the developmental blueprint.[6] Through the union of these two cells, all the information needed for the continuity of the species is transmitted in what is undoubtedly life's most fundamental communication process.

PARENT-OFFSPRING RELATIONS AND SOCIALIZATION

Humans are among those animals whose survival depends directly upon relations with adults. The human infant, in fact, is dependent on others of his or her species longer than are other creatures. In lower-order animals, the survival of a species and the communication capabilities necessary to this end are largely assured through inheritance. For this reason, among amphibians, reptiles, and fish, little or no contact between adults and their offspring is necessary. However, with social insects, birds, and mammals early parent-offspring relations are essential to survival. Even before baby ducklings are born, for example, sounds in the egg may help the parents prepare for the tasks ahead. Visual, auditory, tactile, gustatory, and olfactory signals are also necessary to the feeding process—often in ways that one might not predict. Adult birds, for instance, seem to react to auditory cues from their babies, rather than to visual messages, in determining how many offspring are present and, therefore, how much food to bring.[7]

With many social animals, extended contact between parent and young is required. When this contact does not occur, the important role of communication in the survival of a species is underscored. Some birds that are raised without interaction with others of their kind become totally confused about their identity. Konrad Lorenz was the first to study the processes by which birds and other animals learn or imprint their identity in early social interaction. He observed:

> One of the most striking as well as pathetically comical instances . . . concerned an albino peacock in an Australian zoo, the lone survivor of a brood that had succumbed to a spell of bad weather. The peafowl chick was placed in the only warm room available during the meagerly funded postwar years. The room just happened to be the one in which the giant tortoises were housed. Although the young peacock flourished in these surroundings, the peculiar effect of its reptilian roommates on the bird became apparent not long after it had attained sexual maturity and grown its first train: Beginning then and forever after, the peacock displayed his magnificent plumes in the famous "wheel" position *only* to giant tortoises, eagerly if vainly courting these reptiles while ignoring even the most handsome peahens with which the zoo supplied him. . . . In the case of the albino peacock, (imprinting) condemned the unfortunate bird to a life in involuntary celibacy.[8]

NAVIGATION

The term *navigation* refers to the purposeful movement of a living system through space, from one location to another. Goal-directed movement of this kind is necessary for nearly all of life's activities, including mating, food location, and self-defense.

Anyone who, as a child, experimented with ants or other insects by placing sticks or rocks in their path probably remembers well how skilled they were at determining the presence of an obstacle and adjusting their course accordingly. Even in a simple example of this kind the role of communication is apparent. In order to move systematically from one position to another, a substantial amount of information must be processed. A living system must use various cues—sound, sight, odor, temperature, or other sources—to determine its present location. It must also process information relative to the direction it wants to proceed and its progress toward a desired endpoint. Adjusting for impediments, cracks in a sidewalk, or rocks and sticks requires the acquisition and processing of still more information. See Figure 3–8.

Many animals have highly developed navigation capabilities and can travel great distances with precision. The skills of cats, horses, and homing pigeons are well known in this regard, as are those of ducks and geese, who maintain two seasonal homes several hundred miles apart. Apparently, some animals that travel great distances orient themselves by processing data about landmarks, the sun, or stars. Other animals use a sonarlike system of sounds and echoes to find their way about. The echolocation skills of bats are so well developed that in total darkness they can pass between two black silk threads placed less than a foot apart without touching. And, the dolphin's echo system has such sensitivity that the animal can distinguish two different fish at a distance of fifteen to eighteen feet.[9] See Figure 3–9.

One of the most elaborate navigation processes is that used by social bees in locating and securing food. Karl von Frish found that when a worker bee locates a desirable source of food, it announces the find to

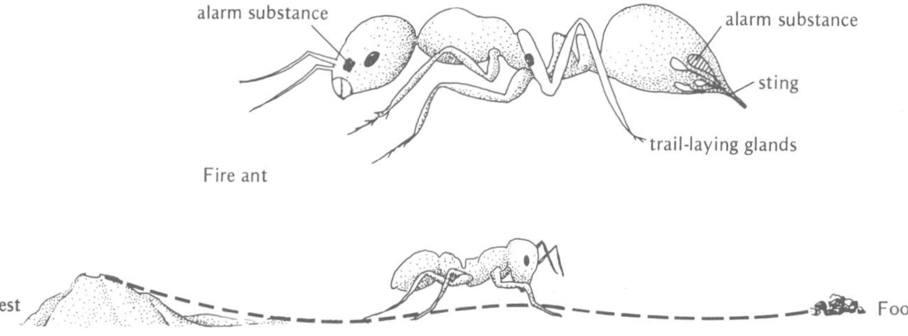

FIGURE 3–8 *The Ant's Olfactory Message Making.* The extended sting at the rear of the ant's body lays an odor trail between the nest and the food source that lasts about 100 seconds, and that other ants can easily follow.

Source: The Insect Societies, Edward O. Wilson (Cambridge, MA: Belknap Press-Harvard University Press), 1971.

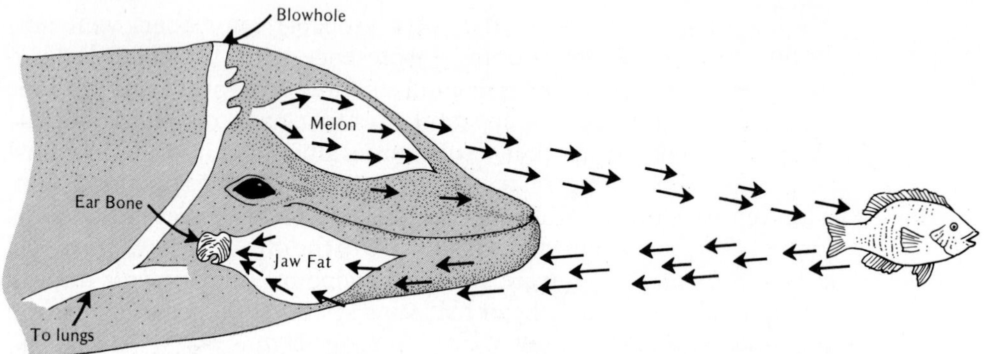

Echolocation Technique of Dolphins. Dolphins send out click-like echolocation signals through the forehead and receive returning messages through the jaw and throat. Whistles are apparently created by forcing air back and forth between the lungs and air sacks connecting to the channel leading to the blowhole. The clicks are transmitted through the water, striking any object in the area. The time it takes the echo to return to the dolphin indicates the distance of the object.

other bees in the hive by either a "round dance" or a "tail-wagging dance."[10] If the food is located closer than fifty or sixty meters, the bee dances in circles in the hive, indicating to others that the food is located nearby. As shown in Figure 3–10, if the food is farther away, the scout bee performs a tail-wagging dance. The closer the food, the more the tail wags back and forth. The direction of the bee's flight while carrying out the dance indicates the direction in which the food is located.

Navigation processes are also essential for humans, although the form and communication modes involved differ. Walking across a room to turn on a stereo set, for instance, requires the processing of information relative to one's present location, destination, and progress toward it. When the task is completed, the return trip requires another series of information-processing steps. In a basic sense, the man or woman scurrying along a busy sidewalk at rush hour or driving on a crowded multilane highway has a great deal in common with the navigation activities of the ant, bat, dolphin, or songbird. Each must analyze an immense quantity of information in order to arrive safely at the intended destination.

SELF-DEFENSE

Communication plays an important role in the processes through which living systems identify and respond to potential threats to their

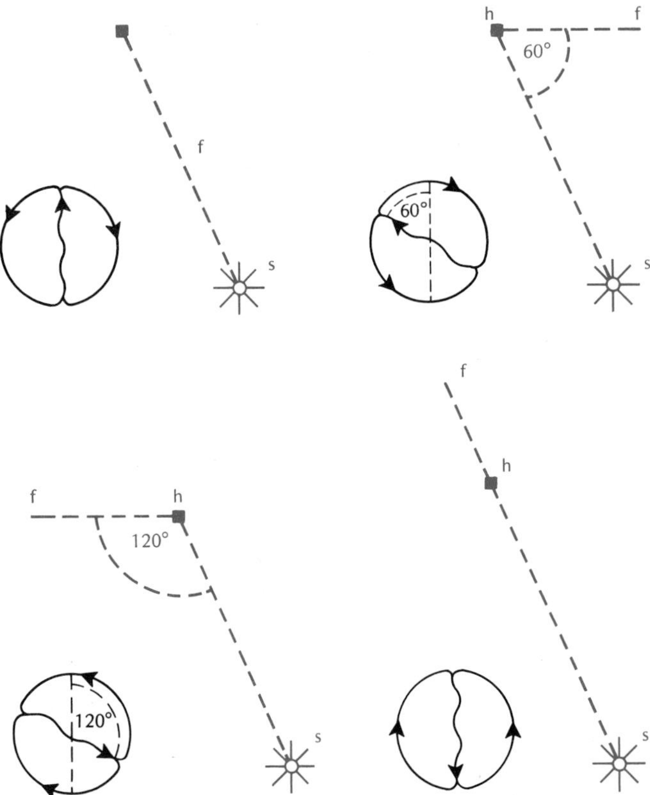

FIGURE 3–10 *Bee Navigation and Food Finding*. The scout bee conveys the *distance* of the food by rhythmic tail wagging. The closer the food, the more the tail wags back and forth. The *direction* of the food is indicated by the path traveled by the bee. The direction of movement of the bee while it dances indicates the relationship of the hive (h), the food source (f), and the sun (s). If the tail-wagging dance points straight upward, the food lies in the direction of the sun. If the dance runs 60° left of straight up, the food is 60° to the left of the sun; if the dance is straight down, the food is in the opposite direction (180° away from the sun), and so on.

Source: Reprinted from Karl von Frisch, *Bees: Their Vision, Chemical Senses, and Language, Revised Edition.* Copyright © 1950, 1971, by Cornell University. Used by permission of the publisher, Cornell University Press.

safety and well-being. If a human or animal system notes the presence of a danger—a predator, a falling tree, the headlights of an auto, and so on—it prepares instinctively to defend itself or to flee. As a part of what has been termed the *stress response,* hormonal and muscular systems are activated, readying the animal for maximum physical output.[11]

The outlet for this stress energy—the act of fighting or retreating—is often the basis for information used by others. Other animals may use messages generated by fight or flight as a signal that their safety is also threatened. This is so, for instance, when the alarm response of one bird evokes a reaction in others who in turn produce their own distress calls. Similarly, as a part of the fight-or-flight response, injured or disturbed fish give off chemical signals that serve to alert other fish of impending danger. To the predator, for example, such cues are useful in anticipating, countering, and overpowering the actions of its prey.

Thus, for living systems, communication is necessary for identifying and reacting to environmental stressors and for signaling others of the need to mobilize for action or dispersal. Among humans, the natural fight-or-flight response is often constrained or channeled into other culturally sanctioned actions. When this occurs, communication also plays a central role in ways that will become clear in later discussion.

TERRITORIALITY

The establishment and maintenance of a home or territory is another activity in which communication plays a vital role. Humans and most other animals become attached to particular places, often to those locations where they were born, spent their youth, or mated; and many living creatures mark and even defend these territories. See Figure 3–11.

Perhaps the best examples of animal territoriality are provided by birds. In the spring, male birds take possession of an area, hedge, or por-

FIGURE 3–11 Some birds, such as wrens, construct a number of nests and conduct the female on a guided tour of the construction sites. She selects the one she likes best for their home. Typically, of the various nests the male builds, one is more carefully constructed and frequently the female selects this nest. Occasionally the male bird takes other females on a tour of the remaining nests; if one is reasonably well-made, he may end up with a second companion in a "downtown apartment."

tion of a meadow. Thereafter, they make an effort to keep out other males by singing. Some birds create songs with two distinct forms, one by which they maintain contact with their partners, and another by which they define and display their territory. Because each male has a unique song pattern, it is not difficult for other birds to determine when a song belongs to a "neighbor" and a "familiar face," and when it is that of a "stranger."[12] The neighbor whose home is already established represents no threat to the territory; the foreigner may, and his presence therefore evokes a much different reaction.

Territories also play an important role in the lives of social insects. Many species go to great lengths to construct their dwellings and to compete for prime housing sites. Often insects can determine the presence of a foreigner and will often attack if an individual violates the territory.[13]Animals also establish and maintain what might be thought of as *mobile* or *transitory territories,* and these, too, involve communication. Some fish and birds, for example, travel or rest in groups, and a stranger that violates the boundary may well meet with considerable resistance.

Territoriality is as important to human life as it is to the lives of many other animals, although often less obviously so. In many situations, humans maintain *personal space*—portable or transitory territories—in a manner similar to other animals, as shown in Figure 3–12. In face-to-face discussions, for example, a certain amount of space usually is maintained between individuals. When this space is violated, substantial discomfort often occurs. A coat or briefcase on an empty seat in a bus, or a towel or umbrella on the beach may also serve to mark transitory territories, in much the same way as the bird's song claims a section of a grove.

Humans also use communication to mark geographic territories. Over the years a great deal of human effort has been directed toward acquiring, dividing, and maintaining nontransitory territories of one kind or another—countries, states, counties, municipalities, and personal properties. The use of fences as territorial boundary markers is common, as illustrated in Figure 3–13.

People also spend a considerable amount of time selecting, allocating, and decorating homes, offices, and apartments. The human tendency to create and construct elaborate dwellings would seem to be unsurpassed in the animal world. Whether a garden apartment, condo, brownstone, or home in the suburbs, the acquisition, maintenance and decoration of home territories becomes an important life activity of many humans. In addition to providing shelter from the elements, territories serve other communicative functions, including the establish-

FIGURE 3–12 Through various forms of communication, individuals of various species define and maintain personal space.

FIGURE 3–13 Territorial boundary markers play a role in human life.

ment and display of personal, social, economic, and occupational identity and status. Our territories are extensions of ourselves, defined and maintained through communication. See Figure 3–14.

The Adaptation Perspective

In this chapter our focus has been on the role communication plays in the fundamental life activities of animals and humans. We have pre-

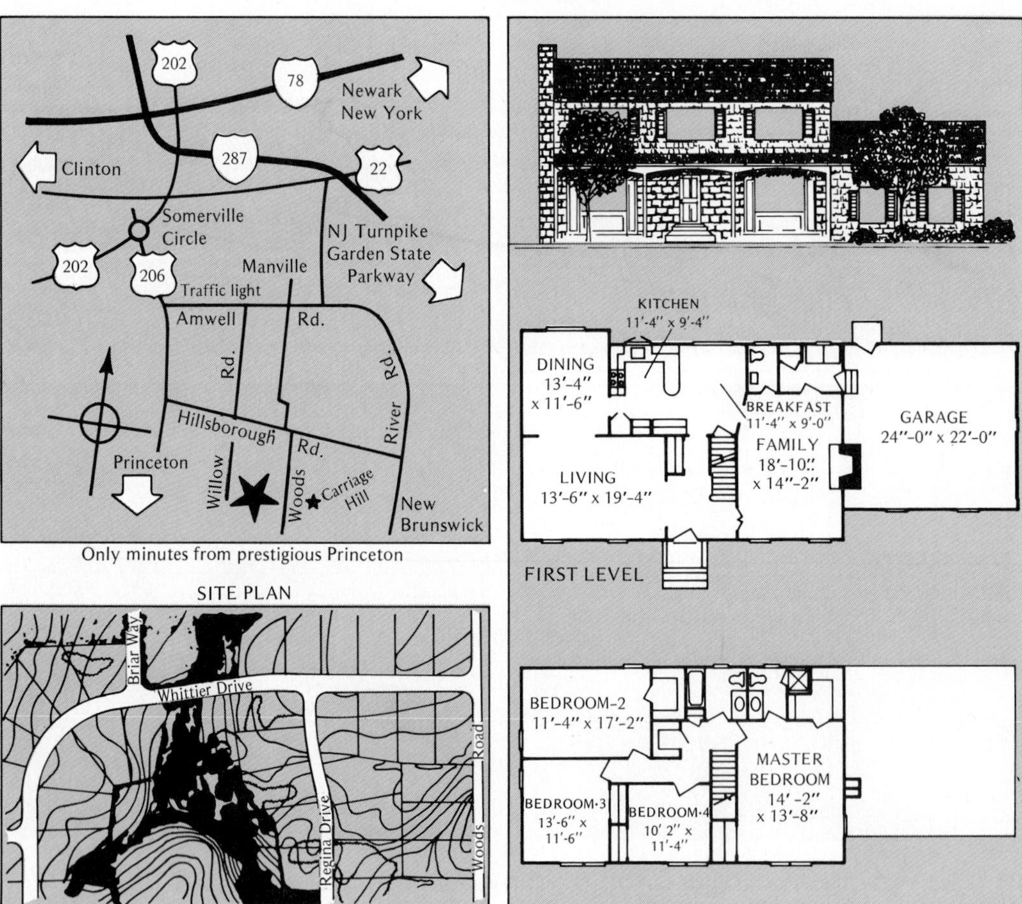

FIGURE 3–14 *Human Territories.*

sented a perspective in which communication is viewed as the process through which living systems create and use messages in order to relate to their environment and one another.

The S→M→R= E approach viewed communication primarily from the perspective of information transmission, where the goal is presumed to be establishing a commonness between source and receiver. The framework presented in this chapter envisions communication more broadly as the process whereby humans and animals process messages in order to adapt—to cope with and shape the demands and challenges that present themselves. The effort is to interpret, use, create, and transmit messages to establish an accommodation, or a commonness, with the environment and its inhabitants. Sometimes this involves recognizing and adjusting to the circumstances in which we find ourselves. Often, adaptation involves actively creating messages and situations, and a mutual adjustment and coordination by all individuals involved. This perspective can be represented visually as *L*iving *S*ystem↔*M*essages↔*E*nvironment = *A*daptation, or:

$$LS \leftrightarrow M \leftrightarrow E = A$$

Implications and Applications: Systems, Animals, and People

• Systems thinking provides a way of approaching any complex situation. We begin by identifying structures—like cells, individuals, families, organizations, or societies—and their parts, looking next for processes—such as communication, chemical exchange, or monetary transactions—by which the parts and the whole relate to each other and their environment.

• Communication is far more than speaking and listening, reading and writing. It is a basic life process.

• We tend to assume that *human* communication is far more complex than communication among other animals, and in some respects it is. However, the dance of bees and the echolocation systems of bats and dolphins are examples of elaborate communication systems which operate in the animal world.

• Humans have a good deal in common with other animals. As an illustration, one might point to numerous similarities between the courtship and territorial practices of some birds and the courtship rituals and territorial practices of humans that take place on campuses and in communities.

• Like other animals, we engage in communication in order to adapt to and coordinate our actions with the environment and one another.

Summary

As special as human communication seems to us, it is important to understand that our ability and need to engage in communication is not wholly unique. We share much in common with many other living systems. In this chapter we have considered the role of communication in the basic life processes of living systems, as a foundation for better, more comprehensive understanding of the nature of human communication.

A *system* is any entity or whole that is composed of interdependent parts. Other basic systems concepts which were discussed include boundaries, environment, closed and open systems, and living systems. Animal and human systems must interact with and adapt to their environment and its inhabitants. Communication is the essential life process through which animals and humans create, transform, and use messages to carry out the activities of their lives.

Five communication modes are used by animals and humans: visual, tactile, olfactory, gustatory, and auditory. Communication serves a number of basic functions in life activities, including courtship and mating, reproduction, parent-offspring relations, socialization, navigation, self-defense, and the establishment and maintenance of territories.

Notes

1. See James G. Miller, "Living Systems," *Behavioral Science,* Vol.10, pp. 193–237, 1965, and Lee Thayer, *Communication and Communication Systems* (Homewood, IL: Irwin, 1968), p. 17.

2. Jack H. Prince, *Languages of the Animal World* (Nashville, TN: Nelson, 1975), p. 33.

3. Niko Tinbergen, *Social Behaviour in Animals with Special Reference to Vertebrates* (London: Methuen, 1965), p. 25.

4. H. H. Shorey, *Animal Communications by Pheromones* (New York: Academic Press, 1976), p. 99.

5. A fascinating discussion of this complex topic is provided by Isaac Asimov in *The Genetic Code* (New York: New American Library, 1962), and Chester Lawson in "Language, Communication, and Biological Organization," in *General Systems Theory and Human Communication*. Ed. by Brent D. Ruben and John Y. Kim (Rochelle Park, NJ: Hayden, 1975), p. 88. A related discussion is presented in *The Selfish Gene* by Richard Dawkins (New York: Oxford University Press, 1976).

6. Isaac Asimov, 1962, p. 19.

7. Gerhard A. Thielcke, *Bird Sounds* (Ann Arbor, MI: University of Michigan Press, 1970), pp. 65–66.

8. Hilda Simon, *The Courtship of Birds* (New York: Dodd, Mead, 1977), p. 23. Parentheses added

9. Fernand Méry, *Animal Languages*. Translated by Michael Ross (Westmead, England: Saxon House, 1975), p. 3; For further discussion of echolocation, see Prince, 1975, p. 23; and Forrest G. Wood, *Marine Mammals and Man: The Navy's Porpoises and Sea Lions* (Washington, D.C.: Robert Luce, 1973), pp. 70–83.

10. Martin Lindauer, *Communication among Social Bees* (Cambridge, MA: Harvard University Press, 1961), p. 33. A more detailed discussion of dance and communication among social bees of which this is a summary is provided on pp. 32–58. See also *The Insect Societies*, by Edward O. Wilson (Cambridge, MA: Belknap Press, 1971).

11. See Hans Selye, *The Stress of Life* (New York: McGraw-Hill, 1956). The notion of stress and its relationship to communication will be discussed in more detail in subsequent chapters.

12. See Thielcke, 1970, pp. 43–47.

13. Shorey, 1976, pp. 81–82.

References and Suggested Readings

AMON, ALINE. *Reading, Writing, Chattering Chimps.* New York: Atheneum, 1975.

ASIMOV, ISSAC. *The Genetic Code.* New York: New American Library, 1962.

BARASH, DAVID P. *Sociobiology and Behavior.* New York: American Elsevier, 1977.

BOULDING, KENNETH E. "General Systems Theory—Skeleton of Science." *Management Science.* Vol. 2 1956, 11–17.

BRIGHT, MICHAEL. *Animal Language.* Ithaca: Cornell University Press, 1984.

CANNON, WALTER B. *The Wisdom of the Body.* New York: Norton, 1932.

CHURCHMAN, C. WEST. *The Systems Approach.* New York: Delacorte, 1968.

COSGROVE, MARGARET. *Messages and Voices.* New York: Dodd, Mead, 1974.

COUSTEAU, JACQUES-YVES, and PHILIPPE DIOLÉ. *Dolphins.* Translated by J. F. Bernard. Garden City, NY: Doubleday, 1975.

DAWKINS, RICHARD. *The Selfish Gene.* New York: Oxford University Press, 1976.

DIMOND, STUART J. *The Social Behavior of Animals.* London: Batsford, 1970.

EDELSON, EDWARD. "Conduits for Cell/Cell Communication." *National Science Foundation Mosaic.* Vol. 21, No. 2, Summer, 1990, 50–56.

ENGLE, GEORGE L. "The Biopsychosocial Model and the Education of Health Professionals." *General Hospital Psychiatry,* 1979, 156–165.

FRANKLIN, JON, LEWIS DONAHEW, and VIKRANT DHOUNDIYAL. "Attention and Our Ancient Past: The Scaly Thumb of the Reptile." *American Behavioral Scientist,* 1989.

FRINGS, HUBERT. "Zoology." In *Interdisciplinary Approaches to Human Communication.* Second Ed. Ed. by Richard W. Budd and Brent D. Ruben. New Brunswick, NJ: Transaction, 1988, 33–35.

——— and MABLE FRINGS. *Animal Communication.* Second Ed. Norman, OK: University of Oklahoma, 1975.

GELDART, FRANK A. *The Human Senses.* New York: Wiley, 1972.

GRINKER, R. R., SR., ed. *Toward a Unified Theory of Human Behavior.* New York: Basic Books, 1967.

HALL, A. D., and R. W. FAGEN. "Definition of System." *General Systems.* Vol.1 1956, 18–28. Reprinted in *General Systems Theory and Human Communication.* Ed. by Brent D. Ruben and John Y. Kim. Rochelle Park, NJ: Hayden, 1975, 52–65.

HANCOCKS, DAVID. *Master Builders of the Animal World.* New York: Harper, 1973.

HARTSHORNE, CHARLES. *Born to Sing: An Interpretation and World Survey of Bird Song.* Bloomington, IN: Indiana University Press, 1973.

HINDE, ROBERT A. *Biological Bases of Human Social Behavior.* New York: McGraw-Hill, 1974.

LASZLO, ERVIN, ed. *The Systems View of the World.* New York: Braziller, 1972.

LAWSON, CHESTER A. "Language, Communication and Biological Organization." *General Systems,* Vol.8 1963. Reprinted in *General Systems Theory and Human Communication.* Ed. by Brent D. Ruben and John Y. Kim. Rochelle Park, NJ: Hayden, 1975, 80–95.

LINDAUER, MARTIN. *Communication among Social Bees.* Cambridge, MA: Harvard University Press, 1961.

LITTLEJOHN, STEPHEN W., *Theories of Human Communication.* Third Ed. Belmont, CA: Wadsworth, 1989. See especially Chapter 3, "System Theory," 34–51.

MACHLUP, FRITZ, and UNA MANSFIELD. *The Study of Information.* New York: Wiley, 1983.

MÉRY, FERNAND. *Animal Language.* Translated by Michael Ross. Westmead, England: Saxon House, 1975.

MILLER, JAMES G. "Living Systems" *Behavioral Science.* Vol.10, 1965, 193–237.

PRINCE, JACK H. *Languages of the Animal World.* Nashville, TN: Nelson, 1975.

RUBEN, BRENT D. "Communication and Conflict: A System-Theoretic Perspective." *Quarterly Journal of Speech*, Vol.64, No.2, 1978, 202–210.

———. "General Systems Theory." In *Interdisciplinary Approaches to Human Communication.* Second Ed. Ed. by Richard W. Budd and Brent D. Ruben. New Brunswick, NJ: Transaction, 1988, 95–118.

——— and JOHN Y. KIM, eds. *General Systems Theory and Human Communication.* Rochelle Park, NJ: Hayden, 1975.

SEBEOK, THOMAS A. *Animal Communication: Techniques of Study and Results of Research.* Bloomington, IN: Indiana University Press, 1968.

———, ed. *How Animals Communicate.* Bloomington, IN: Indiana University Press, 1977.

SELYE, HANS. *The Stress of Life.* Rev. ed. New York: McGraw-Hill, 1976.

SHOREY, H. H. *Animal Communication by Pheromones.* New York: Academic Press, 1976.

SIMON, HILDA. *The Courtship of Birds.* New York: Dodd, Mead, 1977.

THAYER, LEE. *Communication and Communication Systems.* Homewood, IL: Irwin, 1968.

THIELCKE, GERHARD A. *Bird Sounds.* Ann Arbor, MI: University of Michigan Press, 1970.

VON BERTALANFFY, LUDWIG. *General Systems Theory.* New York: Braziller, 1968.

———. "General System Theory." *General Systems.* Vol. 1, 1956, 1–10.

VON FIRSCH, KARL. *Bees: Their Vision, Chemical Senses and Language.* Ithaca, NY: Cornell University Press, 1950.

———. *The Dance Language and Orientation of Bees.* Cambridge, MA: Belknap Press-Harvard University Press, 1967.

WILSON, EDWARD O. *The Insect Societies.* Cambridge, MA: Belknap Press–Harvard University Press, 1971.

WOOD, FORREST G. *Marine Mammals and Man: The Navy's Porpoises and Sea Lions.* Washington, D.C.: Robert Luce, 1973.

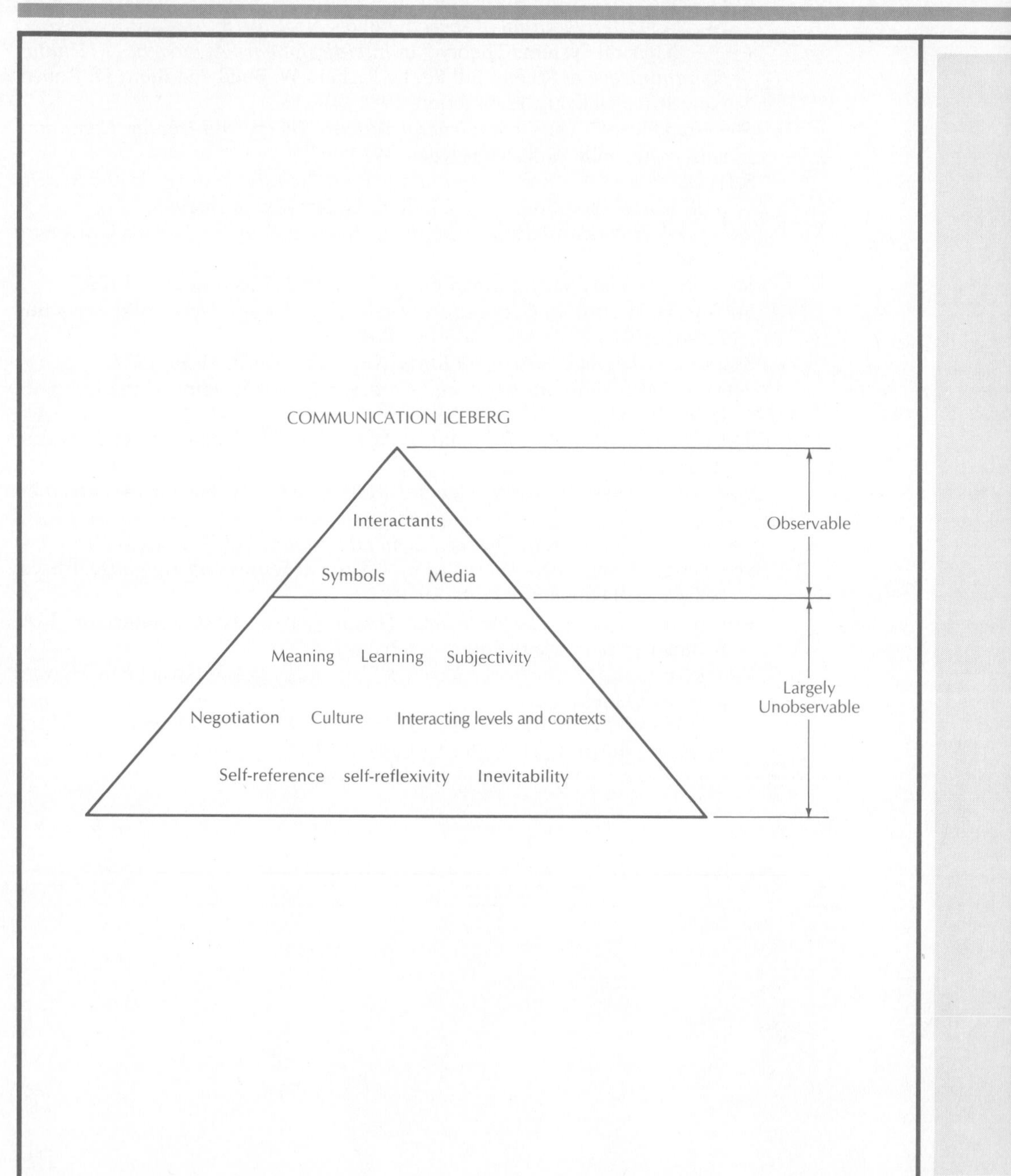
COMMUNICATION ICEBERG
Interactants
Symbols Media
Observable
Meaning Learning Subjectivity
Negotiation Culture Interacting levels and contexts
Self-reference self-reflexivity Inevitability
Largely Unobservable

Complexities of Human Communication

As we know, humans have a good deal in common with a number of other living systems in terms of the basics of communication. However, our communication is also unique in many respects. In this chapter we examine the characteristics and complexities of human communication.

The Communication Iceberg

THE VISIBILITY AND INVISIBILITY OF HUMAN COMMUNICATION

When a person without a background in communication theory listens to two people engaged in conversation, watches a group standing to salute a flag, observes a small group decision-making session, or orders products over the telephone, the communication process appears to be rather simple and straightforward. Messages are sent, messages are received, people behave accordingly, and that's that.

Or so it seems. Actually, in the case of human communication, the aspects of the process that can be easily observed are really only the tip of the communication iceberg, as suggested by Figure 4–1. Most of the

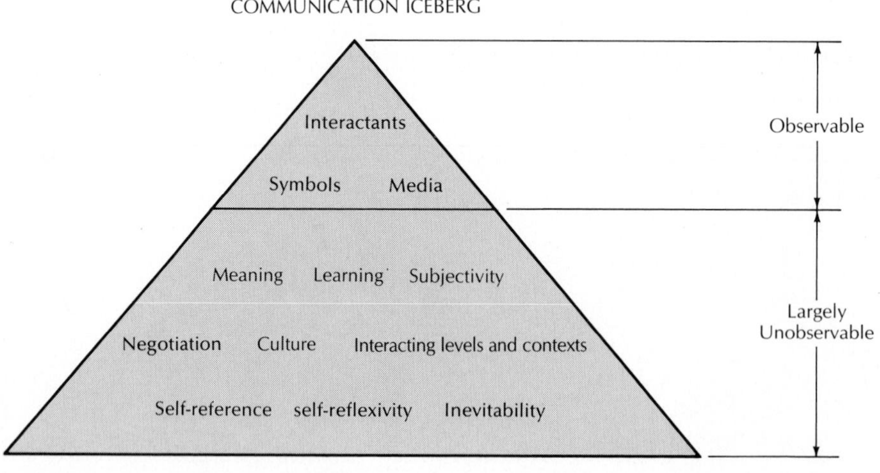

FIGURE 4–1 *Communication Iceberg.*

operations and functions that are necessary to make the communication process "work" are invisible to the untrained eye. Consider the following situation. Bill says: "Jane, please pass the salt." Jane picks up a salt shaker and passes it to Bill. In this circumstance as in others, it seems that meaning has been transferred from Bill to Jane through his verbalized message. However, even in a simple situation like that involving the passing of the salt, the communication process is far more complex than it appears. And most of that process is invisible.

Even in this simple example, as we shall see in greater detail in the pages ahead, a number of elements are involved in the communication process; and each affects the outcome. First, Bill must decide to engage in communication. Then, he must create a message that conveys his desire to have the salt. Next, the message must be sent. At this point, Jane has to "decide" to attend to the message, must interpret it appropriately, and must choose to act on it in accordance with Bill's intent.

In order for either party to be able to use language in this way, prior learning is required; "pass" and "salt" are workable symbols only because their meanings have come to be standardized through a complex process of social communication. A simple communication event that begins with a request for salt and ends up with the salt being passed is no small accomplishment.

To appreciate fully the complexities involved in even simple acts of communication, it is necessary to have an understanding of both the "visible" and "invisible" characteristics of human communication.

Visible Aspects of Communication

When we observe communication taking place we can see interactants, symbols, and media.

INTERACTANTS

By *interactants,* we mean people—people engaged in communication either as message senders or receivers. We include in this category public speakers, as well as individuals speaking to one other person, a group, or an organization. Individuals engaged in writing or other forms of message creation and transmission are also included. In our definition of interactant, we also include individuals who are the recipients of messages in a communication situation, either as listeners, readers, or observers.

SYMBOLS

There have been many attempts to identify precisely what it is that makes us different from other living things.[1] A number of writers have pointed to our social nature. However, many animals depend for their survival on other members of their species. Other scholars have suggested that our capacity for communication might be the distinguishing characteristic. As we know, however, the production, transmission, and reception of messages is essential to the social lives of many species; and communication in one form or another is necessary to the adaptation and survival of all animals. As humans, we do have a unique communication capability: We can create and use symbols and symbolic language, and it is this skill and the many consequences of it that perhaps best highlight the special nature of the human animal.

What exactly does it mean to say that humans create and use symbolic language? A *language,* in the most general sense, is a set of characters, or elements, and rules for their use in relation to one another. There are many types of languages. Most familiar are spoken and written languages, such as English, Spanish, or Swahili. The Morse code, Braille, genetic code, BASIC, and other computer languages are less obvious examples. See Figure 4–2.

With language, we code and transmit information from one point to another using one or more communication modes. Oral, spoken, and other acoustically coded languages make use of the auditory mode. Written or light-utilizing languages utilize the visual channel.

Symbols are characters, letters, numbers, words, objects, people, or actions that stand for or represent something beside themselves. While letters and words are the most obvious elements in our symbolic language, there are many others that are important to human life. An illuminated red light located on a pole near an intersection is a symbol, as is George Washington, the Eiffel Tower, or a rectangular piece of cloth with thirteen red and white stripes and fifty white stars on a blue field in the upper corner. See Figure 4–3.

Another fundamental, but easily overlooked, illustration of symbolic language is our monetary system. We think little about the communication process that occurs when we go into a store, pick out an item priced at $15, go to the cashier, hand over a ten- and a five-dollar bill, and leave the store with a "thank you" and the item in a bag. This exchange is very much a communication event, one in which symbolic language

	Morse Code	Manual (Deaf)	Braille	ASCII
A	•–		⠁	01000001
B	–•••		⠃	01000010
C	–•–•		⠉	01000011
D	–••		⠙	01000100
E	•		⠑	01000101
F	••–•		⠋	01000110
G	––•		⠛	01000111
H	••••		⠓	01001000
I	••		⠊	01001001
J	•–––		⠚	01001010
K	–•–		⠅	01001011
L	•–••		⠇	01001100
M	––		⠍	01001101
N	–•		⠝	01001110
O	–––		⠕	01001111
P	•––•		⠏	01010000
Q	––•–		⠟	01010001
R	•–•		⠗	01010010
S	•••		⠎	01010011
T	–		⠞	01010100
U	••–		⠥	01010101
V	•••–		⠧	01010110

FIGURE 4–2 The English alphabet, Morse Code, sign language, braille, and the ASCII (American Standard Code for Information Interchange) computer code are among our most used languages. Each has evolved to meet a specialized set of human needs. The languages differ from one another in their structure, yet in terms of the more basic functions served, they have much in common.

	Morse Code	Manual (Deaf)	Braille	ASCII
W	•−−		⠺	01010111
X	−••−		⠭	01011000
Y	−•−−		⠽	01011001
Z	−−••	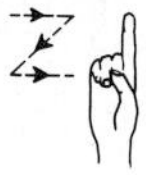	⠵	01010110
1	•−−−−		⠁	00110001
2	••−−−		⠃	00110010
3	•••−−		⠉	00110011
4	••••−		⠙	00110100
5	•••••		⠑	00110101
6	−••••		⠋	00110110
7	−−•••			00110111
8	−−−••		⠓	00111000
9	−−−−•		⠊	00111001
0	−−−−−		⠚	00110000

FIGURE 4–2 (continued)

FIGURE 4–3 "Symbols We Hold in Common" by Patrick Carter.

THE UNITED STATES OF AMERICA
B 13595376 J
B
I ♥ NY
TALKING
MICHELANGELO
5
OTHELLO
STREETCAR
MOBY DICK
CAN FOOL

plays a crucial role. When we give the clerk a ten- and a five-dollar bill, in effect, we are only handing over two pieces of high-quality paper. They have no inherent value, other than the expense of the paper and ink. They are symbols. We live, quite literally, in an environment filled with symbols of various kinds. See Figures 4–4 and 4–5.

Permanence and Portability. A distinguishing characteristic of human symbolic language is its potential for permanence and portability. For most animals, visual, tactile, olfactory, gustatory, and auditory signals are transitory in nature. A sound, a gesture, a touch, a sensation, or an odor may effectively link animals to one another and their environment; each is short-lived, and once the message has served its original informational function, no traces of it remain. In most cases, animals must be within sight or hearing range in order to respond to messages from another individual; even olfactory cues used to mark a territory or provide a trail are generally fleeting.

FIGURE 4–4 As humans we are literally enveloped in a sea of symbols, an understanding of which is essential to even simple activities like traveling from one place to another, shopping for consumer goods, or enjoying a favorite hobby.

McDonald's
OVER 30 BILLION SERVED

7UP

DANGER
HARD HAT
AREA

THE KING'S HIGHWAY
16
ONTARIO
?

Big
Apple
TAXI WILL ARRIVE
RADIO DISPATCHED
24 Hour Service
259-3003

FIGURE 4–5

Because symbols represent something besides themselves, they can have permanence and significance apart from the situation in which they were originally used. Messages provided in a letter sent to a friend, a book, a poem, a scientific formula, the blueprint for a building, or signs along a highway are not transitory in nature. They may have a virtually unending existence and use. In fact, their life is limited only by our human capacity for preserving the physical materials on which they were initially recorded.

The nontransitory nature of symbols makes it possible for us to accumulate and transmit information from one generation to the next. This enables us to "bridge" or "bind" time—to use records of the past, as well as the present, and to create messages today that will be a part of the environment of future generations.

Human communication also has the capacity for "portability"—for bridging space. The objects or persons to which particular symbols refer need not be present in order for the symbol to be useful in communication. Information coded and packaged at one geographic location can be transmitted to persons on another continent.

FIGURE 4–6

MEDIA

There was a time when human communication was exclusively face-to-face. Beginning with the tools used to send smoke signals or scratch drawings on the walls of caves, media began to change the nature of human communication and human culture. Then, as now, communication media extend and provide an alternative to face-to-face communication, as a means of sending and receiving messages.

When one considers the total spectrum of today's uses of media—including telephones, letters and other written documents, for instance—we realize that few aspects of our personal, social, and occupational lives are exclusively conducted through face-to-face communication. Media are playing an increasingly pervasive and visible role in many types of communication situations.

Invisible Aspects of Communication

Aspects of communication which are critical but invisible to the untrained eye include: meaning, learning, subjectivity, negotiation, culture, interacting contexts and levels, self-reference, and inevitability.

MEANING

We invent symbols. In order to use them in communication, we also have to invent their meanings and the responses we make to them. To illustrate the point, consider the word *bird* as an example. *Bird* has no inherent, intrinsic meaning or significance. It is simply a particular pattern of auditory vibrations that comes about by the manipulation of the vocal cords, lips, tongue, and mouth, or a configuration of ink on paper in the case of written language. The characteristics of the words and sounds of their spoken pronunciation comprise a symbolic code that is useful only to those who have learned to decipher it. The word is arbitrary in the sense that it has no relation to the animal to which it refers, other than that which we have invented and accepted. Any word could have been chosen in its place.

As another illustration, let's return to the example of a red light at the intersection. In casual conversation, we may say that the light "means" stop. Actually, however, the light means nothing itself. It is a symbol.

Its meaning was invented. Through custom and habitual use—and, in this case, legislation—people have come to interpret the symbol as an indication to stop. Similarly, the red, white, and blue cloth that we know as the American flag has no meaning other than that which we have created and accepted.

Even in the simplest of activities, such as a race, this important characteristic of human communication is apparent.[2] When an athlete hears a starting gun, his or her initial response to the auditory cue is identical to the response to a gazelle. The heartbeat speeds up, and at top running speed the heart pumps five times more blood than normally. Most of the blood is needed for the muscles. There is also a need for twenty gallons of air per minute to supply oxygen to the blood. For the runner and gazelle alike, most of the energy needed by the muscles is lost as heat. Since chemical burn-up by the muscles is too fast to be complete, waste products remain in the blood, leading to fatigue that can be eliminated only when fresh oxygen is introduced into the blood supply.

In all these respects, the behavior of the runner and that of the gazelle are alike. Both creatures function in a manner that is normal for an animal in flight. But, the key point is that the man or woman in the example is not in flight. Where the gazelle's behavior is directed solely by reflex, the runner's actions are not. The behavior of the gazelle is automatic. It could only occur in response to uncontrolled and uncontrollable fears; the runner's response, on the other hand, is a consequence of meaning he or she attaches to the situation and the symbols that comprise it. The runner's behavior is self-initiated, deliberate, and directed by desire.

As humans, we are not only capable of creating events, but also the significance and meaning those events will have for us. We can invent and organize contests, plan and train to participate in them, voluntarily direct our actions during the activity, experience pride and satisfaction upon receiving a ribbon or trophy, and later reflect upon ourselves and our experience. We do all this because of our capacity for inventing and bestowing meaning upon the people, objects, and circumstances that surround us—and upon ourselves.

Even matters as basic as determining what and how to eat are not solely matters of biology and genetic programming. While many North Americans, for example, look forward with enthusiasm to a juicy barbecued steak, a member of the Hindu faith might well choose the prospect of death by starvation rather than eating the meat of the sacred cow, the holiest of creatures. In a similar sense, decisions as to whether to eat with fingers, fork and knife, or chopsticks, and whether to use one's left hand to eat—as would be acceptable in most countries—or only one's right hand—as is customary in Arab cultures—depend upon the meanings we have invented and attached to life's circumstances. See Figures 4–7 and 4–8.

LEARNING

Birds are born knowing how to build the nest necessary for mating and survival; the instructions are inscribed on the chromosomes of the fertilized egg cell from which it developed.[3] Lightning bugs inherit the knowledge needed to emit and respond to luminescent messages of a potential mate, and bees are apparently born programmed with the information needed to create and interpret the waggle dance. Human beings have to acquire much of the physical and communication skill that is "natural" for other animals. Unlike lightning bugs, we have to learn

FIGURE 4–7 What to eat, what utensils to use, what order to eat this and that, where to place one's hands when they are not in use, and how to signal one's satisfaction with a meal, exemplify the sorts of concern that distinguish human symbolic communication from that of other animals. Humans go to great lengths to invent and standardize symbolic practices even with regard to basic biological activities such as eating. Being familiar and fluent with these symbolic realities is often crucial to assuring one's acceptance by those who have themselves learned and accepted a particular symbolic pattern. Knowing not to ask for a straw with your drink at a $70-per-dinner restaurant, realizing that it's "improper" to rest one's elbow on the table, knowing to use your "salad fork" only for the salad, being able to manage to eat and appear composed with chop sticks when others at the table can, are often the sort of skills that others take as an indication of refinement, proper upbringing, worldliness, and being "cultured."

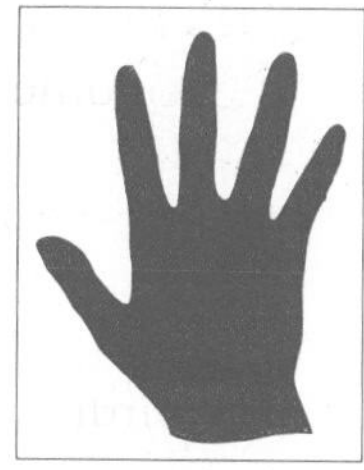

FIGURE 4–8 In addition to performing a number of mechanical functions, hands serve important symbolic functions, as well. For example, it is the right hand we place over our heart and raise to our head in a salute to the flag. It is also the right hand which makes new acquaintances and greets old ones, concludes contracts, presents religious offerings, transmits spiritual messages in benedictions, takes possession, and lends assistance. If the right hand symbolizes *strength, honor, dignity, and cleanliness,* the *left* hand often is symbolic of the opposite qualities. Arabs, for example reserve the right hand for eating, while delegating responsibilities having to do with affairs of the toilet exclusively to the left. And, among certain tribes in lower Niger, women are forbidden from using their left hands in preparing food, presumably because the left hand is an instrument of sorcery and the medium for evil spirits. Similarly, many inhabitants of the Guinea Coast cling to the belief that when having a drink at the dwelling of a local resident, it is necessary to watch their host closely, because even the slightest contact between his or her left hand and the drink to be served might result in poisoning the liquid. Members of many cultures go to great lengths to insure that their young develop a preference for using their right hands rather than their left. In the Netherlands Indies, for example, children have been observed with their left arms completely bound—no doubt a rather effective teaching technique. It is quite likely that the preference for right-handedness over left-handedness apparent in many cultures including our own is reflective of the often subtle symbolic realities which have come to be associated with each hand over the years.

Source: R. Hertz, "The Hands," in *Rules and Meanings,* Mary Douglas, ed., (New York: Penguin), 1973, pp. 118–124.

the communication patterns associated with courtship. Unlike bees, we have to learn the verbal and nonverbal language necessary to give directions to a friend.

We are born with certain message-responding tendencies—reflexes. The touch of a nipple to the mouth of a newborn infant, for example, is a tactile cue which triggers the sucking response necessary for eating. Likewise, if we accidentally place a finger on a hot stove, a signal is sent to the brain, and in an instant we pull our hand away. Responses such as these are automatic. They are nonsymbolic and do not involve symbolic learning. They are what we can term *first-order, information-processing events.*

This kind of automatic, unlearned, nonsymbolic response accounts for a very small percentage of our activities. Most of our experiences require us to process messages based on meanings we have learned. This is evident even in the most fundamental situations. In the case of placing a finger on the hot stove, for example, as soon as we begin to think about the experience of being burned, try to comprehend the reasons for the pain, consider various medical remedies, relate the pain to other sensations in our previous experience, or talk about the event with others, we are involved in a *second-order, information-processing event*—we are using symbols and meanings. For the most part then, our behavior depends not on genetic programs but on the meanings and information value we have learned to attach to particular symbols. Some of the necessary learning—how to read, write, and calculate, for instance—comes from formal schooling. Most of this learning comes from experience. As Geoffrey Vickers has noted:[4]

> Insofar as I can be regarded as human, it is because I was claimed at birth as a member of a communication network, which programmed me for participation in itself.

A moment of reflection will remind us how much effort must be expended on the fundamentals of human communication. Whether we consider interactions between scientists using mathematical equations, the "value" of the money we carry around in our pockets, the significance we attach to our flag, a spoken exchange between acquaintances, or facial expressions and gestures between colleagues at work, the symbols and their meanings have to be created, agreed upon, and learned to be useful for communication. Their significance is created by us, and they are useful for communication only to the extent that we learn and are able to use them appropriately.

SUBJECTIVITY

The symbols we use in human communication will not necessarily mean the same things to those who create and send messages as they do to those who receive them. We relate to messages in a particular way as a product of our experiences. No two of us have precisely the same experiences, and therefore, no two of us attach precisely the same meaning to the messages around us. To put it differently, we do not all encode and decode messages in the same way. As the adage goes, "I know you believe you understand what you think I said, but I am not sure you realize that what you heard is not what I meant." Furthermore, even one individual may not attach exactly the same meaning to a particular message at different points in time or in different circumstances.

The subjective aspect of human communication extends to all types of symbols—art, money, flags, and so on. When two people look at a work of art, for instance, the meanings it will have for them are personal, reflecting their own experience. Consider, again, the illustration in Figure 4–3. Some may see the arch located near the center as the MacDonald's "Golden Arch." For others the symbol may be thought of in terms of a famous landmark in St. Louis. Likewise, the adaptation of Grant Wood's "American Gothic" in the upper left hand corner is likely

FIGURE 4–9

I Know
you believe
you understand
what you think
I said but,
I am not sure you
realize that what
you heard is not
what I meant

to evoke a range of interpretations among viewers. For some the association is with the artist; for others it is likely to be with Kellogg's Corn Flakes. The meanings one attaches to this work as a whole will no doubt provide a further illustration of the subjectivity of communication.

Monetary symbols also illustrate the personal nature of human communication. The value of money is subjective. While a child walking in a crowd may bend down to pick up a penny, an adult is likely not to. To some people, a birthday gift of ten dollars is regarded as generous; for others it may be seen as insignificant.

A recognition that much of communication is subjective and personal has led to the observation that the amazing thing about human communication is not that it sometimes seems to *fail* but, rather, that it ever seems to *succeed*. Is it any wonder how often two lovers, colleagues or countries come away with very different interpretations of who is to blame in a conflict?

NEGOTIATION

As unique as we and our meanings may be, communication between people generally seems to work pretty well. How can this be? In order for symbols to work in our efforts to relate effectively to others, our meanings must mesh with the meanings of others. Each of us has learned to attach significance to the symbols of our experience. When we engage in communication, we take part in a process of negotiation, as we reconcile our meanings with those of others.

Unlike efforts by management and representatives of a labor union to arrive at terms for a contract, this negotiation is not overt. The process is far more subtle. Interactants adjust and readjust the messages they send and the interpretations they attach to messages of others, in an effort to make sense of, cope with, and adapt to the demands and opportunities that present themselves.

CULTURE

The fact that our meanings often seem to mesh reasonably well with other's meanings is no accident. We learn from and with other people. We are influenced through our participation in groups, organizations, and as a participating member of society. Through this participation, we establish a commonness of experience with other people. In this social communication process, our symbols and their meanings become shared and standardized—*intersubjectified.* Though they are subjective in the sense that they are arbitrary, they nonetheless take on an objective quality and seem very real. With continued use, symbols and their meanings become part of the cultural environment we take for granted and to which we must adapt.

Through human communication, we create a common culture and a shared view of reality and come to be able to understand one another—to coordinate the meanings for the symbols we use. The more we develop common meanings for symbols with another person, the better the communication process will seem to "work." Store owners who trade pieces of high-quality green paper for goods or services do so because they have learned to attach a similar meaning to the pieces of paper as customers do. Merchants also operate in the belief that the bank and creditors will attach a similar significance to them.

Artist Ben Shahn makes this point very eloquently:

> It is the images we hold in common, the characteristics of novels and plays, the great buildings, the complex pictorial images and their meanings, and the symbolized concepts, principles, and great ideas of philosophy and religion, that have created the human community. The incidental items of reality remain without value or common recognition until they have been symbolized, recreated, and imbued with value.[5]

INTERACTING CONTEXTS AND LEVELS

Human communication operates in various contexts and at various levels. It is the lifeblood of individuals, relationships, groups, organizations, and societies. Intrapersonal, interpersonal, group, organizational, and societal communication do not operate in isolation of one another. There is interplay between all levels. The relationships in which we are involved, the groups of which we are members, the organizations we work for, and the society and world community in which we live, all have an impact on our individual communication activities. In turn, intrapersonal communication and the way we feel and think about ourselves influence our interactions in relationship, groups, organizations, and society. Human communication is the web that unites and gives mutuality to the various levels of human activity.

SELF-REFERENCE

The meanings we learn to attach to the symbols we use—and the symbols others use—reflect our own experiences. As a result, the things we

TABLE 4–1 Characteristics of Human Communication

1. Interactants
2. Symbols
3. Media
4. Meaning
5. Learning
6. Subjectivity
7. Negotiation
8. Culture
9. Interacting Levels and Contexts
10. Self-Reference
11. Self-Reflexivity
12. Inevitability

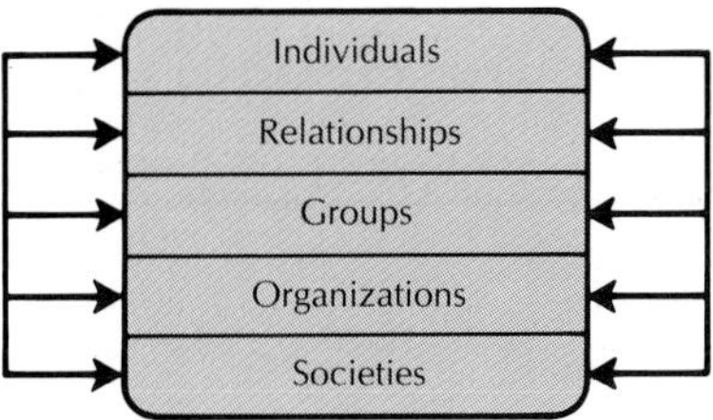

FIGURE 4–10 *Interacting Contexts and Levels.*

say and do and the way we interpret others' words and actions are a reflection of our meanings, experiences, needs, and expectations. When a person says, "It certainly is cold out today," "Mexican food is hot," "That movie is excellent," or "That course is very difficult," he or she is talking as much about his or her own feelings, meanings, and experiences as about the temperature, Mexican food, the movie, or course.

It is in this sense that human communication is self-referencing and autobiographical. What we see in and say about other people, messages, and events in the environment always says as much about us as it does about them.

SELF-REFLEXIVITY

Another related characteristic of human communication is our capacity for self-reflexiveness, or self-consciousness. This human capacity which allows "man to view himself as a 'self,' as a part of and apart from his environment, is the core of the communication process."[6]

Because of *self-reflexiveness,* we are able to think about our encounters and our existence, about communication and human behavior. This capability enables us to set goals and measure our progress toward them, to have expectations of ourselves, and to recognize when we have met them. On the other hand, it is also through self-reflexiveness that we recognize our own failures, the expectations we do not meet, and the qualities we admire but do not possess.

It is our capacity for self-reflexiveness that allows us to theorize about ourselves and our experiences—to "get outside ourselves" in order to look at ourselves. In effect, we enter into a relationship with ourselves that is similar in many ways to the relationships we have with others. We talk to ourselves, think about ourselves in particular ways, and "act" in particular ways toward ourselves. Our patterns of self-reflexive communication have great implications for how we talk to, think about, and act toward others; and these behaviors, in turn, have consequences for how we relate to ourselves.[7]

INEVITABILITY

"We cannot not communicate." This is the phrase coined by Watzlawick, Beavin, and Jackson to emphasize the point that we are inevitably engaged in the process of creating and processing messages during every waking hour of our lives.[8] Our verbal and nonverbal behavior are ongoing sources of information for others, and, in turn, we are continually and unavoidably processing information about the people, circumstances, and objects in our environment, and about ourselves.

From this perspective, we can see the technical inaccuracy of concepts such as "communication breakdown" or "failure to communicate." Communication is always taking place. Messages are inevitably being created and processed. Most often, "breakdowns" and "failures" result not from the lack of message sending and receiving but, instead, from differing interpretations of messages, differing expectations, or differing intentions.

Implications and Applications: What Meets the Eye and What Doesn't

- Very few human activities take place without the use of symbols and symbolic language. Even instinctive behaviors, such as pulling away from a source of pain, involve the use of symbols when we wish to talk or think about them.

- The most common symbolic languages are spoken and written languages; but music, computer, art, and sign languages are also basic to human communication.

- The meanings we attach to the people and events around us grow out of our experiences. Thus, whenever we talk or write about someone or something, we are always saying something about ourselves—about what we noticed or thought was worth mentioning, or about our attitudes, opinions, beliefs, values, or point of view. When you comment on how much you like or dislike a particular person, object, or circumstance, you are saying as much—if not more—about your own tastes, preferences, and meanings as you are about the intended focus of your evaluation.

- Because message sending and message receiving are ongoing and inevitable, there can be no "breakdowns in communication" in the sense of communication stopping. Even silence or the refusal to negotiate are messages. Their impact will depend on factors beneath the surface of easily observable activity.

- To those who have not thought much about human communication, the process appears to be very simple and easy to understand and predict: Send a message and people will behave as intended. From this perspective, "communication problems" are seen as the exception to the rule. When they do occur, it is assumed that the message simply needs to be re-sent or refined: "If they didn't get the message, we'll tell them again, and this time we'll say it louder."

- Those who have studied human communication recognize that it is very complex and is difficult to understand and predict: Send a message and anything can happen! Sometimes we have the impact we intend; often we do not. From this perspective, "communication problems" are no surprise. In fact, we may even take notice when problems don't occur. When they do, we assume very little about the factors involved. The "problem" could be that the message needs to be re-sent or refined. Perhaps our message wasn't heard. More than likely, however, the difficulty can be found in factors that operate below the level of observable experience. It may be that others have different meanings for the words we used, or perhaps cultural barriers are operating. If they didn't get our message—and it is sometimes quite difficult to determine whether they did or not—we want to first determine what may have happened, and then strive to develop strategies that may help to overcome the difficulty.

- We can see symbols, interactants, and media when they are present. These are the observable aspects of a complex process. Most of what makes communication work occurs below the surface of observable experience. It is invisible. We cannot see meaning, learning, subjectivity, negotiation, or culture at work. We don't see interacting levels of analysis, self-reference, self-reflexivity, or inevitability. However, each plays a role in the communication process and its outcomes that is monumental. It is the effort to understand these fundamental but largely invisible characteristics—and their consequences—that makes the study of human communication so intriguing and so vital.

Summary

This chapter has examined visible and invisible characteristics that are fundamental to human communication. Visible characteristics include interactants, symbols, and media. We can create and use symbols and symbolic language. A language, in the most general sense, is a set of characters, or elements, and rules for their use in relation to one another. Symbols are characters, letters, numbers, words, objects, people, or actions that stand for or represent something besides themselves. Symbols have the potential for permanence and portability. For most animals, visual, tactile, olfactory, gustatory, and auditory signals are transitory in nature. Human symbols can have permanence and significance apart from the situation in which they were originally used and may have a virtually unending existence and use. The permanent nature of symbols makes it possible to bridge time and space.

Invisible characteristics include meaning, learning, subjectivity, culture, interacting levels and contexts, negotiation, self-reference, self-reflexivity, and inevitability. Human communication also involves meaning. In order to use symbols in communication, their significance and the responses to them must be created. The characteristics of the words and the sounds of their spoken pronunciation comprise a symbolic code that is useful only to those who have learned to decipher it.

Learning is another characteristic. Animals are born with the knowledge of the meanings to attach to the signals necessary to their survival; humans must learn communication patterns and meanings.

Human communication is subjective. The symbols used in human communication will not necessarily mean the same things to those who create and send messages as they do to those who receive them. People relate to messages in a particular way as a product of their experiences. No two individuals have precisely the same experiences; and, therefore, no people attach precisely the same meaning to the messages in the environment.

Negotiation is another characteristic of human communication. As unique as individuals and their meanings may be, communication between people generally works. Through experience, individuals have learned a set of meanings for the symbols of their experience.

When we engage in communication with others, we negotiate a shared culture. Generally, meanings mesh reasonably well with other's meanings, because others' meanings are learned through social interaction. In this social communication process, symbols and their meanings become shared and standardized—intersubjectified.

Human communication operates in various contexts and at various levels. It is the lifeblood of individuals, relationships, groups, organizations, and societies. There is interplay between contexts and between levels.

Self-reference is another characteristic of human communication. The meanings we learn to attach to the symbols we use reflect our own experiences. As a result, things that we see in or say about other people, messages, and events in the environment are always autobiographical—they say as much about the person offering the description as they do about the objects being described.

Another related characteristic of human communication is our capacity for self-reflexiveness. Because of our symbol-using capacity we are able to reflect upon ourselves and our actions, to set goals and priorities, to have expectations.

Human communication is inevitable. "We cannot not communicate." Our verbal and nonverbal behaviors are ongoing sources of information for others; and, in turn, we are continually and unavoidably processing information about the people, circumstances, and objects in our environment, and about ourselves.

Notes

1. See discussion of human uniqueness and symbols in Anatol Rapoport, "Man, The Symbol User," in *Communication: Ethical and Moral Issues.* Ed. by Lee Thayer (New York: Gordon and Breach, 1973), especially pp. 23–30.
2. The example and discussion of the runner and gazelle is based upon an illustration provided by Jacob Bronowski, *The Ascent of Man* (Boston: Little, Brown, 1973), pp. 3–36.
3. Rapoport, 1973, p. 27.
4. Geoffrey Vickers, "The Multivalued Choice," in *Communication: Concepts and Perspectives.* Ed. by Lee Thayer (New York: Spartan Books, 1967), p. 272.
5. Ben Shahn, *The Shape of Content* (Cambridge, MA: Harvard University Press, 1967), pp. 130–131.
6. Richard W. Budd and Brent D. Ruben, *Beyond Media,* Second Ed. (New Brunswick, NJ: Transaction Books, 1987), p. 109.
7. Linda C. Lederman, "Communication Effectiveness in the Business World: A Preliminary Examination of the Impact of the Self-Self-Relationship of the Meanings Derived in Conversations with Others." Paper presented at the Annual Meetings of the Eastern Communication Association, Atlantic City, NJ, May, 1986.

8. Paul Watzlawick, Janet H. Beavin, and Don D. Jackson, *Pragmatics of Human Communication: A Study of Interactional Patterns, Pathologies, and Paradoxes* (New York: Norton, 1967), pp. 48–49.

References and Suggested Readings

BERGER, PETER L., and THOMAS LUCKMANN. *The Social Construction of Reality.* Garden City, NY: Anchor, 1966.

BLUMER, HERBERT. *Symbolic Interactionism.* Englewood Cliffs, NJ: Prentice-Hall, 1969.

BOULDING, KENNETH. *The Image.* Ann Arbor, MI: University of Michigan Press, 1950.

BRONOWSKI, JACOB. *The Ascent of Man.* Boston: Little, Brown, 1973.

BUDD, RICHARD W. "General Semantics: An Approach to Human Communication." In *Approaches to Human Communication.* Ed. by Richard W. Budd and Brent D. Ruben. New York: Spartan-Hayden, 1972, 97–119; and *Interdisciplinary Approaches to Human Communication.* Second Ed. by Richard W. Budd and Brent D. Ruben. New Brunswick, NJ: Transaction, 1988, 71–93.

BUDD, RICHARD W., and BRENT D. RUBEN. *Beyond Media: New Approaches to Mass Communication.* Second Ed. New Brunswick, NJ: Transaction, 1988.

———, eds. *Interdisciplinary Approaches to Human Communication.* Second Ed. New Brunswick, NJ; Hayden, 1988.

DAHNKE, GORDON L., and GLEN W. CLATTERBUCK. *Human Communication.* Belmont, CA: Wadsworth, 1990.

DEETZ, STANLEY, and SHERYL STEVENSON. *Managing Interpersonal Communication.* New York: Harper and Row, 1986.

DOUGLAS, MARY, ed. *Rules and Meanings.* New York: Penguin, 1973.

DREYFUSS, HENRY. *Symbol Sourcebook.* New York: McGraw-Hill, 1972.

DUNCAN, HUGH D. *Symbols and Social Theory.* New York: Oxford University Press, 1969.

———. *Symbols in Society.* New York: Oxford University Press, 1968.

FISKE, JOHN. *Introduction to Communication.* Second Ed. London: Routledge, 1990.

GOFFMAN, ERVING. *Frame Analysis.* Cambridge, MA: Harvard University Press, 1974.

GUMPERT, GARY, and ROBERT CATHCART. *Intermedia.* Third Ed. New York: Oxford University Press, 1986.

GUMPERT, GARY, and SANDRA L. FISH. *Talking to Strangers.* Norwood, NJ: Ablex, 1990.

HERTZ, R. "The Hands." In *Rulings and Meanings.* Ed. by Mary Douglas. New York: Penguin, 1973.

HOLZNER, BURKHART. *Reality Construction in Society.* Cambridge, MA: Schenkman, 1968.

HUNT, TODD, and BRENT D. RUBEN. *Mass Communication.* New York: Harper Collins, 1992.

JOHNSON, WENDELL. *People in Quandaries.* New York: Harper, 1946.

JUNG, CARL G. *Man and His Symbols.* New York: Doubleday, 1964.

KORZYBSKI, ALFRED. *Selections from Science and Sanity.* Lakeville, CN: International Non-Aristotelian Library, 1948.

LEDERMAN, LINDA. "Communication Effectiveness in the Business World: A Preliminary Examination of the Impact of the Self-Self Relationship on the Meanings derived in Conversations with Others" An unpublished paper presented at the annual meeting of the Eastern Communication Association, Atlantic City, NJ, May, 1986.

LITTLEJOHN, STEPHEN W. *Theories of Human Communication.* Third Ed. Belmont, CA: Wadsworth, 1989.

MCHUGH, PETER. *Defining the Situation.* Indianapolis, IN: Bobbs-Merrill, 1968.

MEAD, GEORGE H. *Mind, Self, and Society.* Chicago: University of Chicago Press, 1934.

MORRIS, CHARLES. *Signification and Significance.* Cambridge, MA: MIT Press, 1964.

MORRIS, DESMOND. *Manwatching.* New York: Abrams, 1977.

PEARCE, W. BARNETT, and VERNON CRONEN. *Communication, Action and Meaning.* New York: Praeger, 1980.

PEARCE, W. BARNETT. *Communication and the Human Condition.* Carbondale, IL: Southern Illinois University Press, 1989.

RAPOPORT, ANATOL. "Man, The Symbol User." In *Communication: Ethical and Moral Issues.* Ed. by Lee Thayer. New York: Gordon and Breach, 1973.

RUBEN, BRENT D. "General Systems Theory: An Approach to Human Communication." In *Approaches to Human Communication.* Ed. by Richard W. Budd and Brent D. Ruben, New York: Spartan-Hayden, 1972, 120–144, and *Interdisciplinary Approaches to Human Communication.* Second Ed. Ed. by Richard W. Budd and Brent D. Ruben, New Brunswick, NJ: Transaction, 1988, 95–118.

SHAHN, BEN. *The Shape of Content.* Cambridge, MA: Harvard University Press, 1967.

THAYER, LEE. *Communication and Communication Systems.* Homewood, IL: Irwin, 1968.

———. "Communication—Sine Qua Non of the Behavioral Sciences." In *Interdisciplinary Approaches to Human Communication.* Second Ed. Ed. by Richard W. Budd and Brent D. Ruben. New Brunswick, NJ: Transaction, 1988, 7–32.

———, ed. *Communication: Concepts and Perspectives.* New York: Spartan-Hayden, 1967.

VICKERS, GEOFFREY "The Multivalued Choice." In *Communication: Concepts and Perspectives.* Ed. by Lee Thayer. New York: Spartan Books, 1967.

WATZLAWICK, PAUL. *How Real Is Real?* New York: Random House, 1969.

WATZLAWICK, PAUL, JANET H. BEAVIN, and DON D. JACKSON. *Pragmatics of Human Communication: A study of Interactional Patterns, Pathologies, and Paradoxes.* New York: Norton, 1967, 48–49.

WHORF, BENJAMIN LEE. *Language, Thought and Reality.* Cambridge, MA: MIT Press, 1956.

5

Message Reception

Selection

Interpretation

Retention—Memory

Short-term and Long-term Memory

Episodic and Semantic Memory

Receiver Influences

Needs

Attitudes, Beliefs, and Values

Goals

Capability

Use

Communication Style

Experience and Habit

Message Influences

Origin

Mode

Physical Character

Organization

Novelty

Source Influences

Proximity

Physical and Social Attraction and Similarity

Credibility and Authoritativeness

Motivation and Intent

Delivery

Status, Power, and Authority

Media and Environmental Influences

The Medium

The Environment

An Active and Complex Process

Implications and Applications: Listening, Observing, Interpreting, and Remembering

Message reception involves attending to and transforming environmental messages into a form that can be used to guide behavior. This process is an active one, consisting of three elements—*information selection, interpretation,* and *retention.* We will discuss each of these in detail in the pages ahead, beginning with an illustration.

Ed awoke this morning at 7:30 to a grey sky and light rain. He noticed the weather almost immediately, because it was a Saturday and he had looked forward all week to a chance to get outside. He chatted with his wife, Jane, about a variety of topics while he dressed and ate breakfast. He began to ponder his options as to how to spend the day, given that he was stuck inside. Ed left the breakfast table and walked down the hallway.

He glanced in the study and saw the piles of typed pages strewn about his desk. "I should work on the year-end report due next month," he thought to himself. "My future depends on how well that's received."

He continued into the family room where he noticed his children, Robert and Ann, sitting in front of the television set watching cartoons. He reflected to himself on how fast time goes by, and decided that he really ought to spend more time with the kids. "Maybe a game or some sort of craft project that we could work on together . . ." He exchanged a few brief words with his children, and it seemed that Woody Woodpecker was of more interest to the kids than he was, and he turned his attention to a stack of newspapers and magazines lying across the room on a table. As he looked at the pile of reading material, he thought about the fact that he had spent only a few minutes with the mail, newspapers, and magazines all week. "I really should go through them today," he noted to himself. "No . . . the report has got to come first!"

He made his way back to the study, turned on the radio, and searched for a station that played the kind of music he liked as "background." Ed situated himself at the desk and began to shuffle through the materials before him. He came across a book he had been using as a primary source in his report, picked it up, and began rereading sections of the text and leafing through the illustrations.

The radio station kept fading in and out, and the news was annoying him. He walked over to a nearby CD rack, and picked several jazz instrumentals, which he thought would be enjoyable, but not distracting.

As he walked back to the desk, Ed happened to glance out the window. Incredible! The grey skies had cleared; the rain had stopped and the sun was shining brightly. Ed heard the distant whine of a neighbor's lawn mower and glanced almost instinctively at his own lawn. "Damn, it really does need to be mowed . . . And the car is dirty," he thought to himself. "I could do both jobs tomorrow, if the weather holds."

He turned the radio on again and scanned for a local station and the weather report. "Clearing this afternoon, highs in the low 80's."

"I'll wash the car today, so it will be clean for the weekend, and put off mowing the lawn until tomorrow," he decided. "This grass is still a bit wet now, anyway . . . But what if the weather report is wrong? If it's wrong? It's always wrong. If I put off mowing until tomorrow, and it rains, I might not be able to mow until next weekend; and by then the grass will be so long it would take most of two days to mow."

"How ridiculous this is!" he concluded. "The lawn is ruling my life. It's amazing how one's priorities evolve by default. That settles it. Back to the report!"

The foregoing summary reveals a good deal about Ed's communication habits, values, orientations, and, at the same time, helps to illustrate how message reception and processing work. For analytic purposes, let's briefly reconstruct the scenario, paying particular attention to the cues Ed attended to, the meanings he attached to them, and the manner in which these meanings guided his behavior.

There are a number of things Ed might think about upon waking on a given day. On this particular day, he was primarily concerned with the day and the weather—*Saturday* and *rain*. That he chose to be interested in these particular things and not others had largely to do with the meanings each had for him. Saturday was a special day, one he had looked forward to all week. Grey clouds and rain meant it would be impossible for him to pursue some of the activities he had hoped and planned for. Together, Saturday and rain signified plans ruined, nothing more, nothing less.

Despite this reality, Ed moved through the information-processing sequence necessary to the activities he had come to think of as essential to the start of each day: taking a shower, shaving, selecting clothes, dressing, making his way to the kitchen, sitting down at the table, talking to his wife Jane, eating breakfast, and so forth.

As he chatted with Jane, new messages were introduced into his purview. These provided an opportunity for him to overcome the "plans ruined" aura, which to that point had been the dominant theme in his information processing.

In talking to his wife—and himself—Ed determined that there was little to be gained by stewing over one set of plans ruined. There were, after all, a number of plans one might have that *Saturday + rain* would not ruin. As he began to attach new meaning to the situation, his attention was directed toward messages and possible interpretations he was unaware of only minutes earlier.

Because Ed was ready to consider options as to how to spend the day, the stack of typed pages from his report was singled out from other potential messages in the environment. At some level of awareness, those pages meant a variety of things to him at that point, including *job unfinished, frustration, guilt,* and *challenge.* None of these meanings were compelling enough to lead him to undertake work on the report at that instant.

In the family room, his children almost instantly became prominent message sources. They triggered a variety of meanings—*affection, enjoyment, responsibility, concern.* As with the significance of the year-end report, these meanings were central to his self-concept and sense of what he was about, and as a result they commanded his interest and receptivity.

In passing, he also attended momentarily to the television show they were watching. He recognized at some slightly-less-than-conscious level that the messages generated by the cartoon were performing very different functions for Robert and Ann than for him. In some sense, Ed was competing with Woody Woodpecker for his children's attention.

The presence of the week's mail, magazines, and newspapers provided the basis for additional messages which were significant to him. In the context of his own life they signified knowledgeability, credibility, enjoyment, and obligation. Ed was also aware of a need to be familiar with the "news" in order to be knowledgeable and current in discussions with his friends and colleagues.

Though these meanings were also important to his definition of himself, they were not, at that instant, as critical as the meanings related to the report. Ed "decided"—again, in a less-than-wholly-aware manner—to reject these and other options in favor of returning to work on the report.

His message processing continued as he selected a particular information source—FM radio—and a particular frequency on the dial with a message set he had learned to associate with that station. His unstated objective in so doing was to control the background cues in the immediate environment.

In looking through the materials on his desk, his eyes fell upon a book that had been significant earlier in his work. It became a primary object of attention for several minutes, as he recalled its contents and his reaction to them. Noise resulting from the fading of the radio station became another unavoidable message source, and he acted to replace the messages from the radio with others from records, which he assumed would better meet his needs.

On glancing out the window, the clearing skies and sun were especially meaningful cues. They signified "original plans O.K.; no need to pursue the present options, unless you want to." As his attention shifted to messages in the environment outside, Ed noted the whine of a lawn mower, which triggered a variety of issues, each of which required attention and resolution—the lawn, the car, and so on.

In examining the alternative meanings called up from memory, he inadvertently began a self-reflexive thought process. As he reflected on his own information processing, this time quite consciously, he decided to execute more control over himself and his surroundings and pursue what he had determined to be the most "logical" alternatives for use of his time.

In returning his attention to work on the report, Ed, in effect, decided to attach less value to messages related to the physical environment external to his study—the lawn, cars, and so on. He chose instead to focus on information sources that were pertinent to his report. This decision was itself reflective of the relative importance he attached to the various message sources available to him at that point. At the same time, the act of selecting the option he did also had the effect of reaffirming his priorities.

Many interesting facets of information reception and processing are illustrated in even a commonplace situation such as the one just described. As simple and automatic as such events may seem, they involve a complex of factors operating in the very active processes of selection, interpretation, and retention.

Selection

At any instant in time we are surrounded in our environment by persons, objects, and circumstances that are sources of the messages that vie for our attention and interest. In the foregoing sequence, Ed's radio, stereo, wife and children, the pages of his report, the outdoors, the lawnmower, and the weather were each potential information sources that were competing for his attention, as illustrated in Figure 5–1.

Predictably, in such circumstances we select certain messages to attend to and disregard others. Even in a simple situation we make a number of elaborate decisions, and we are unaware of many of them. Ed "decided" to give attention to the weather, the day of the week, his children, and the year-end report rather than to other messages in his environment—such as the room that needed painting, the clothes that were to be taken to the cleaners, the unopened package on the table, the expressions on his children's faces when they exchanged words, and so on.

This same message-selection process operates in other situations. Consider a circumstance where we pause in a hallway to chat with an acquaintance. First, the very act of noticing the other person involves the systematic selection of messages. Triggered by the constellation of

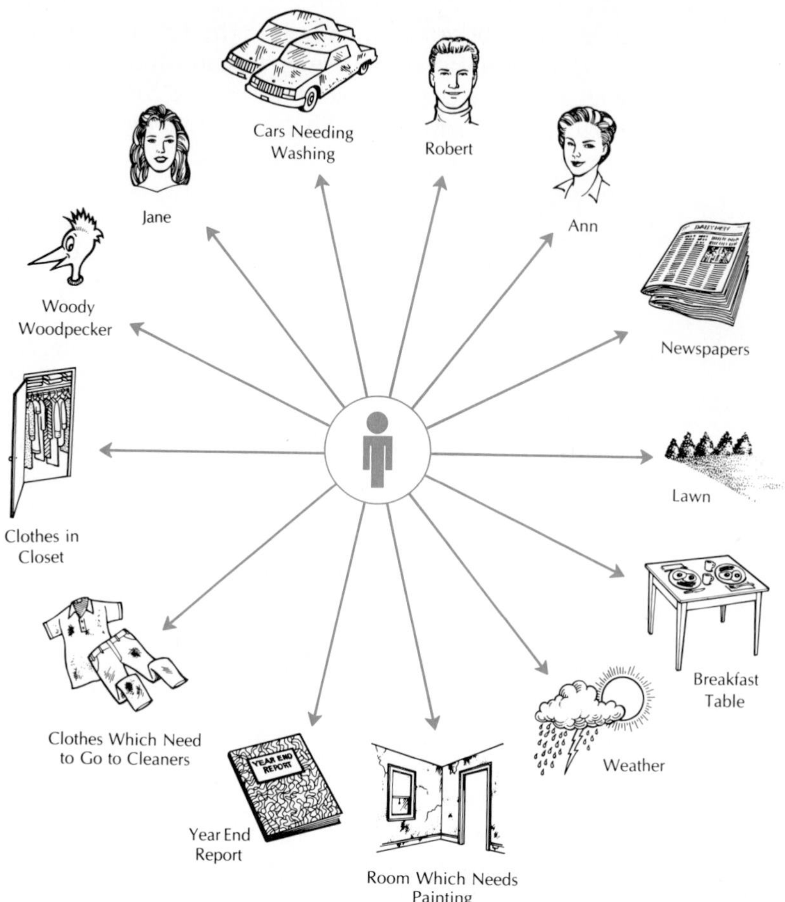

FIGURE 5–1 At any one point in time we are surrounded by a large number of persons, events, objects, and circumstances that are sources of the messages that compete for our attention.

factors associated with the appearance of the other person, and perhaps some verbal cue—"Hi"—we begin focusing ourselves on the other person and on the messages necessary to the interchange that will follow. In so doing, we ignore other potential cues—the temperature, the color of the carpeting, the appearance of other persons who may pass by, the noise of a nearby copy machine, or the thunderstorm outside—through a complex process that has occupied the attention of many scholars over the years.[1]

The classic illustration of *selective attention* is provided by cocktail parties and similar social gatherings. During such affairs, one finds that it is not at all difficult to carry on a series of perfectly intelligible discussions without being overly distracted by other conversations. It is even possible to tune in to an exchange between several other persons a good distance away, without shifting one's position and while appearing to be deeply engrossed in conversation with a person close at hand. In that same setting, we are able to tune out the entire external environment, periodically, in order to concentrate on our own feelings, decide what we ought to be doing, or think about how we are being perceived by others. It is also possible to attend to the gathering as a whole, paying attention to the level, pitch, rhythm, number of interactions, and level of activity, as a basis for making some general assessments of the gathering as a whole—whether it is sedate or wild, winding up or down, and so on.[2]

Given these examples, it may seem as though selection operates much like a filter, letting in some sounds, images, or smells, while screening out others.[3] However, the process is often more complex than this way of thinking implies. For instance, we know that even when we have "tuned in" to a particular information source and "tuned out" others, the selected-out messages may, nonetheless, be taken note of. This is the case, for instance, when a honking horn interrupts our attention in a discussion with a colleague while crossing the street, or when the sound of one's own or a friend's name is heard "through" the otherwise unintelligible din of a party.[4] Additionally, there is evidence to suggest that it is possible to take note of and attach meaning to messages even when one is unaware of doing so.[5] And some studies suggest that under hypnosis we may be able to remember information that we were not fully aware of selecting for attention in the first place.[6]

An understanding of the complexity of the attention process has led to the adoption of a "modified filter model" as a way of thinking about selection.[7] It is thought that we assign priorities to competing information sources and allocate attention among them, while monitoring other messages and perhaps even attending to still other sources that are unknown even to the individual involved.

Interpretation

Interpretation occurs when we determine what meaning or significance to attach to a message—whether to regard it as fiction or nonfiction, serious or humorous, new or old, contradictory or consistent, amusing or alarming.

Depending upon the way we select and interpret messages, very different consequences result. For example, in Figure 5–2, Illustration A, if we define the white area as the object to be looked at, we see a vase. If, on the other hand, we focus our attention on the black area, we see the silhouettes of two persons staring at one another.

If we are drawn first to the large white portion, in Figure 5–2, Illustration D, we see a skull. Attention to subtleties of the drawing in black, however, reveals a lady seated at a dressing table staring into a mirror. In Illustration B, we count either 3 or 5 cubes depending upon which cues we define as pertinent to interpreting the figure.

Again, depending upon message selection and interpretation, Figure 5–2, Illustration C either appears to be a stylish young lady with a feather in her hat or an older, haggard woman with a wart on her nose, staring downward in apparent depression.

At first glance, Illustration E may appear to be a weather satellite photo, a highly magnified bacterial organism, or simply a random, nonsense image. Once our attention is directed to particular elements of the photo, however, the nonsense image becomes the image of a cow. Interestingly, once we see a cow, it becomes virtually impossible to see it any other way.

Even our reaction to a simple, "Hi, how are you?" will depend, among other things, on whether the person is male or female (and the significance we attach to each), whether we regard the individual as attractive or unattractive, whether the person is a family member or a stranger, whether he or she dressed in swimwear or formal dinner attire, whether we are situated on nearby blankets at the beach or next to one another in a doctor's waiting room, whether we interpret the individual's motives as platonic or romantic, and a host of other factors. See Figure 5–3.

Retention—Memory

From the preceding discussion, it should be apparent that memory plays an indispensable role in the interpretative process. We are able to store and actively use an incredible amount of information—at least several billion times more than a large research computer—and yet we can locate and use it with an efficiency and ease of operation that is astounding.[8]

FIGURE 5–2 *Interpretation—The Construction of Meaning.*

A

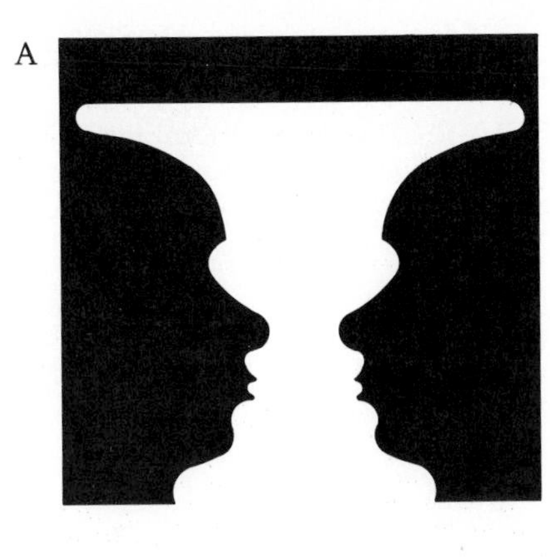

B

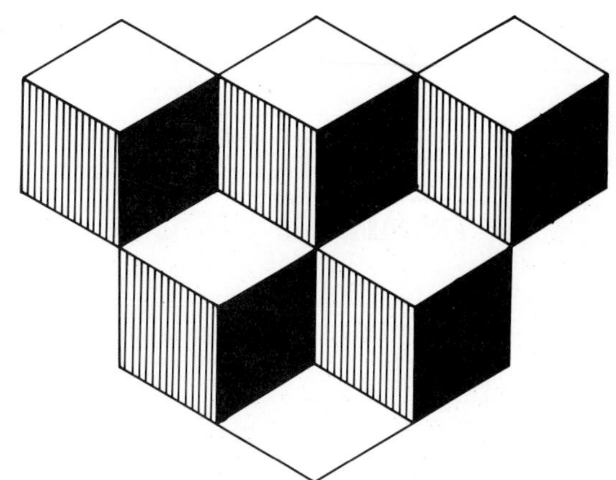

C

D

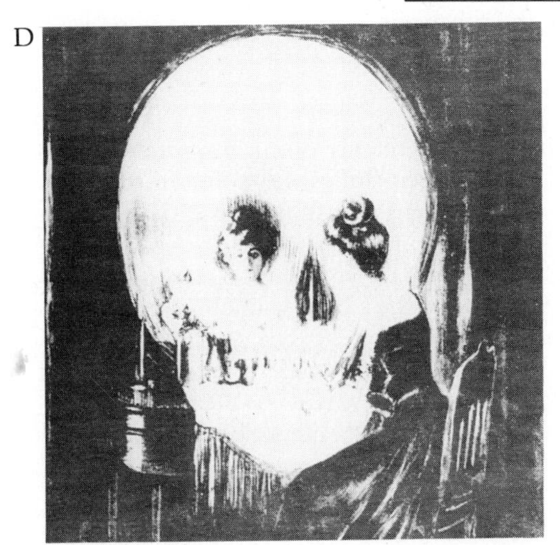

E

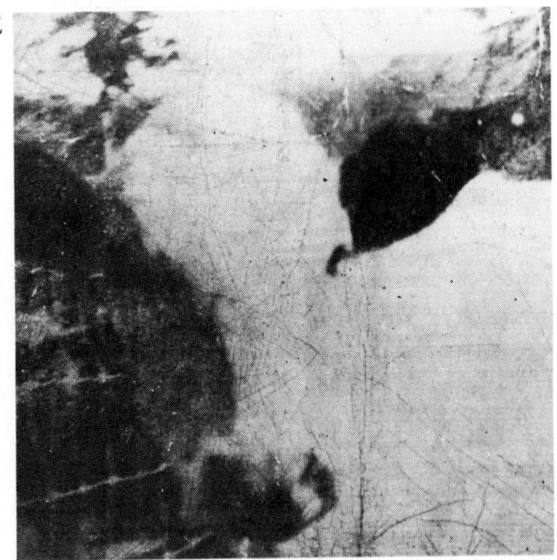

MAN DIES AFTER HEARING WIFE DIED

Linden, NJ (AP)–A Linden man collapsed and died after learning that his wife was killed in a plane crash earlier that day in Poland, police and hospital authorities said yesterday.

Police said that (the man) 61, had suffered an apparent heart attack Friday after learning that his wife. . .was one of 87 people who died in the Warsaw, Poland, plane crash.

Source: Associated Press, March 17, 1980.

FIGURE 5–3 *A Dramatic Example of the Impact of Interpretation.*

We have little difficulty accessing the information we need in order to go about our daily routine—to locate the bathroom, closet, and kitchen; to select appropriate clothing and to dress; to start and operate an automobile; or to find the way to the bus or train. In a split second, and with a high degree of accuracy, we can answer questions like "Who was the first president of the United States?" or "What is the name for the sound frequently heard following lightning?" These certainly seem like "simple" questions. But think how long it would take to answer these questions in a book, library, or electronic database using a table of contents, index, or other search technique.

As Morton Hunt notes:

> Although every act of thinking involves the use of images, sounds, symbols, meanings, and connections between things, all stored in memory, the organization of memory is so efficient that most of the time we are unaware of having to exert any effort to locate and use these materials. Consider the ranges of kinds of information you keep in, and can easily summon forth, from your own memory: the face of your closest friend . . . the words and melody of the national anthem . . . the spelling of almost every word you can think of. . . the exact place where you keep the pliers . . . the name of every object you can see from where you are sitting . . . the way your room looked when you were eight . . . the set of skills you need to drive a car in heavy traffic . . . and enough more to fill many shelves full of books. . . .[9]

These are examples of *recall*—active, deliberate retrieval of information from memory, a capability that may well be unique to humans. We share with other animals the capacity to use information for *recognition*—recognizing objects, places, circumstances, and people when in their presence.[10] See Figure 5–4.

Particularly in recent years, much effort with promising results has been directed to understanding the complex processes by which memory operates.[11] Much of this work has been concerned with identifying stages of information processing.

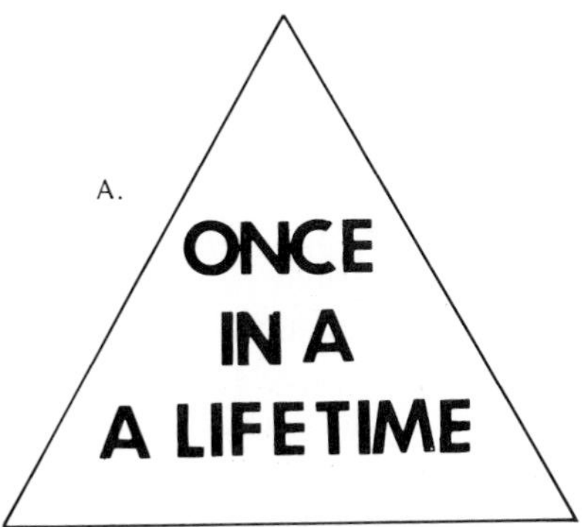

FIGURE 5–4 Memory plays an important role in the processing of information at any point in time. A quick glance at either of the two triangles leads us to conclude that the sentences are "Once in a lifetime" and "Paris in the spring." These two phrases are familiar to most of us and we expect such phrases to follow the normal rules of grammar we have learned. Thus, the repeated "A" and "THE" are easy to miss. Looking at Illustration C, we have little trouble determining that the image is that of a "dog." Actually, very little detail is provided in the illustration. Were it not for substantial previous experience in selecting and interpreting messages relative to "dog," we would have great difficulty making sense of this image.

SHORT-TERM AND LONG-TERM MEMORY

Information enters the system through one or several communication modes. In selecting and attending to particular messages, we begin to attach meaning to those symbols following rules we have learned and frequently used.[12] A good deal of sensory information can be processed within the system at any one time. If, for example, you looked through the newspaper to determine what movie was playing at a particular theater, not only that information but also information relative to other items in the paper, such as other movies and other theaters, would also be processed at some level of awareness. The information other than that being sought would be lost and would decay very rapidly—probably within a second or so.[13]

Information that is to be further used becomes a part of what is termed *short-term memory* and is available for a relatively restricted period of time—perhaps fifteen seconds.[14] Our short-term memory capacity is limited under normal circumstances to a few pieces of information only—a phone number or a string of several letters or words. Most of us have had the experience of looking up a number, only to forget it by the time we walked across the room to the phone. This forgetting illustrates how rapidly information is lost from short-term memory. Through recitation or rehearsal, however, we can extend the time available to use information. Thus, if we repeat a phone number to ourselves several times as we walk across the room, the likelihood of remembering it for the needed time period greatly increases.

Some of the information is further processed and elaborated to become a part of our *long-term memory.* Generally, the longer time information is available to us in short-term memory, the greater the chance it will become a part of our long-term memory. Therefore, a phone number looked up, rehearsed, and dialed several times over the period of an hour because of a busy signal, is far more likely to be remembered than a number successfully reached on the first try. Phone numbers that are dialed often become a part of an individual's long-term memory naturally, or actively, through memorization.

Recall and recognition exemplify the two general classes of human memory: (1) relatively slow retrievals that require conscious processing, and (2) relatively fast retrievals that require no conscious processing. Some of the other characteristics of these two retrieval processes include:[15]

Slow Retrievals	*Fast Retrievals*
Nonautomatic	Automatic
Conscious	Unconscious

Slow Retrievals	*Fast Retrievals*
Controlled	Uncontrolled
Indirect access	Direct access
Voluntary	Involuntary

EPISODIC AND SEMANTIC MEMORY

Our general knowledge of the people, places, and things in the world is termed *semantic memory. Episodic memories* relate to recollections and retrieval of information regarding personal happenings, particular objects, people, and events experienced by an individual at a specific time and place.[16] *Autobiographical memories*—memories of oneself—are considered to be episodic.[17] While this distinction is a useful one, scholars also point out that the two types of memory are related: Semantic knowledge is derived from episodic memory, and episodic memories are organized and categorized based on semantic categories.[18]

In the summary of his book, *Memory in the Real World,* Gillian Cohen provides the following list of characteristics of memory:

- Memory is an overloaded system—there is more to be remembered than can possibly be managed by the brain.
- Memory must be selective—decisions must be made as to what to remember and what to ignore.
- Memory must be dynamic—adjustments must be made to changes in the world around us.
- Memory must link past, present, and future—memory provides for continuity of meaning across time.
- Memory must be able to construct hypothetical representations—imagination, creativity, and consideration of possibilities are necessary characteristics of memory.
- Memory must store both general and specific information—generalized and specialized knowledge are both required in human activity.
- Memory must store information implicitly—information must be easily and automatically stored and organized for retrieval. Often this is done in terms of categories, time periods, and level of generality/specificity.
- Memory processes must be complex—elaborate information sorting and organizing processes are necessary to integrate new information with past experience.

- Memory retrieval strategies are critical—retrieving information becomes more critical and difficult as memories proliferate.
- Memory retrieval must utilize spontaneous and deliberate retrieval—memories must be able to be retrieved spontaneously as well as deliberately.[19]

As useful as the foregoing view of information processing is, it is important to be aware of the limitations of what has been termed the sequential-stage model. Researchers remind us that information processing is an extremely complex operation. It is often difficult to distinguish between its various stages. The distinction between selection, interpretation, and episodic and semantic memory can be fuzzy. Further, a sequential-stage model could imply that the individual plays a passive role in information processing. Clearly this is not the case; complex interactions between the individual and environment are fundamental to the ongoing dynamics of information reception.

Receiver Influences

For each of us, a complex set of influences works together to influence our decisions as to which messages we will attend to and how we will interpret and retain the information that results. Many of these have to do with the nature of the *receiver*.

NEEDS

Among the most crucial factors that play a role in our message reception and decisions are what are commonly termed *needs*. Scholars generally agree that our most basic needs, like those of other animals, have to do with our physiological well-being—food, shelter, physical well-being, and sex.[20] Basic needs can be potent forces in directing our behavior. When needs are not met, our efforts to satisfy them are important guiding forces in information reception. To the individual who hasn't eaten for several days, for example, few message sources are likely to be as noteworthy, or *salient*, as those relating to food. A knowledge that unsatisfied needs often increase the attention and importance attached to particular messages has led popular authors to suggest that a good way to save money and to diet is to shop for groceries after eating rather than before.

The same pattern occurs with regard to our health. A headache or upset stomach, which is readily dismissed by persons who believe themselves to be well, may become the focus of great attention and concern for persons who believe themselves to be ill. Messages about the upcoming football game, a book manuscript, or grass that needs mowing take on far less significance than they would under normal conditions.

Other needs or motives, including social contact, reality exploration and comprehension, socialization, diversion, entertainment, and play, have to do with our spiritual, psychological, social, and communicative well-being.[21] Perhaps the most basic of these needs has to do with maintaining and developing our identity and self-concept.[22] We want to be seen positively, as worthy, desirable, competent, and respectable. There are, of course, differences between us as to the particular qualities for which we wish others to value us. Some of us aspire to be seen as creative, intelligent, professionally competent, and a vocational success. Being seen as religious, honest, honorable, or empathetic may be more important to others. Some of us would prefer to be admired for our leadership capacity; others wish to be respected for their loyalty as followers, and so on.

Personal, social, and communicative needs play an important role in message selection, interpretation, and retention. Their role has begun to be highlighted by scholars who have focused attention on the "uses and gratifications" of mass media.[23] This work helps substantiate the view that there can be a direct relationship between particular unsatisfied, or ungratified, needs and resulting patterns of exposure to mass media programs and other message sources.

Information processing orientations are not rigid. They may change over time as we move through various life stages and circumstances. As children we adapt to a world in which we are highly dependent upon parents and other adults for the satisfaction of our needs, wants, and desires. That dependence carries with it a particular set of information-reception tendencies for most of us, in which our parents, relatives, and, gradually, peer relations are highly significant.

The thrust toward independence which confronts many of us as a crisis, similarly signals a change in the messages and message sources to which we are likely to respond. These changes are accompanied by new ways of interpreting information as well. Dependence on parents, for example, may give way to counterdependence, as a prior step to independence. Where we once "heard and agreed," we come to "hear and disagree," and later learn to "hear sometimes and agree sometimes."

Every stage in our lives—twenties, thirties, forties, fifties, sixties, seventies, and beyond—presents additional problems and challenges. Each stage brings about changes in our needs and in our selection, interpretation, and retention patterns, as we strive to adapt to and act upon the personal, social, and occupational circumstances that beset us.

ATTITUDES, BELIEFS, AND VALUES

The attitudes, preferences, and predispositions one has about particular topics, persons, or situations also play a critical role in information-receiving activities and outcomes. People will generally attend to and be favorably disposed toward new messages, sources, and interpretations that support their views before they consider nonsupportive messages, sources, or conclusions.[24] The person who supports candidate X for a particular elective office is likely to pay far more attention to articles and political ads and sources of new information about that candidate than he or she will to items about candidate Y or Z. And such a person is also likely to spend time talking politics with others who share his or her view.

Values is a term used to refer to basic principles that we live by—our sense of what we ought and ought not do in our relations with the environment and the people in it. As with attitudes and beliefs, values also can substantially influence selection, interpretation, and retention. Individuals who believe that "all able-bodied adults ought to be gainfully employed" are likely to take notice of and react strongly to people who are complacent about receiving welfare checks and who make only superficial attempts to find a job.

There are instances where messages that are likely to be interpreted as inconsistent and nonsupportive of our attitudes, beliefs, or values can lead to *more,* rather than *less,* attention and interest. We may devote considerable attention and effort to converting individuals who cling to beliefs or values that differ from our own. Similarly, we often spend more time reflecting upon people and events that trouble us than on those that reassure and comfort us, simply because we come to take the latter for granted.

GOALS

Most of us are at best only partially aware of our needs, attitudes, beliefs, and values. We consciously set our *goals.*

When an individual decides to pursue a particular plan, career, personal relationship, or personal challenge, that goal serves to direct his or her attention toward certain messages and away from others, as suggested in Figure 5–5.

If a woman has the goal of driving from Princeton, New Jersey, to JFK Airport in New York to catch a specific flight, this objective plays a major role in guiding information selection, interpretation, and retention. On the way to the airport, she must process messages concerning the location, direction, and rate of speed of her car and other vehicles in the vicinity. She must also attend to, interpret, and remember the road markings and signs that provide pertinent information and those that indicate the path to the airport. The gauges, instruments, and other controls of the car must also be monitored. Additionally, the driver must take account of weather conditions, time remaining before arrival at the final destination, location of the long-term parking area, the proper terminal, the flight number, and the seat assignment, and so on. Until the goal is achieved and the individual is comfortably seated aboard the airplane, a substantial amount of the person's information-receiving effort is influenced by the commitment to the self-determined goal of catching a plane. See Figure 5–6.

In a similar manner, a decision to pursue a particular career—to become a medical doctor, for instance—directs one's attention toward certain messages and away from others. The aspiring doctor is influenced by his or her goal toward knowledge based in physiology, anatomy, and chemistry and away from information pertinent to students of engineering, business administration, and journalism. Acquiring appropriate interpretations for these messages is a priority until the goal is met or changed. A change of goals often also involves information processing.

When an individual sets the goal of achieving certain competence in an area such as athletics, this objective shapes not only the messages to which the individual attends but also the interpretations of them that he or she makes. First, the goal increases the likelihood that the individual will expose himself or herself to messages that pertain to athletics in general and his or her sport in particular. Secondly, the goal may well increase the individual's contact with other people interested in a similar activity, and this will have an additional influence on information reception. The demands of physical fitness may also play an important role in determining how information about food, drinking, smoking, health, and drugs will be attended to, interpreted, and remembered.

CAPABILITY

Our level of intelligence, previous experience with a particular topic area, and facility with language have an important impact upon the kinds of messages we attend to and the manner in which we interpret

CIRCUS
A
FUN
BREAKFAST
LIVE GAMES
97.4 % PAY BACK
ALL $ SLOT CAROUSELS
RV
OPEN 6 AM
REGISTRATION
PARKING
ONLY

FIGURE 5–5

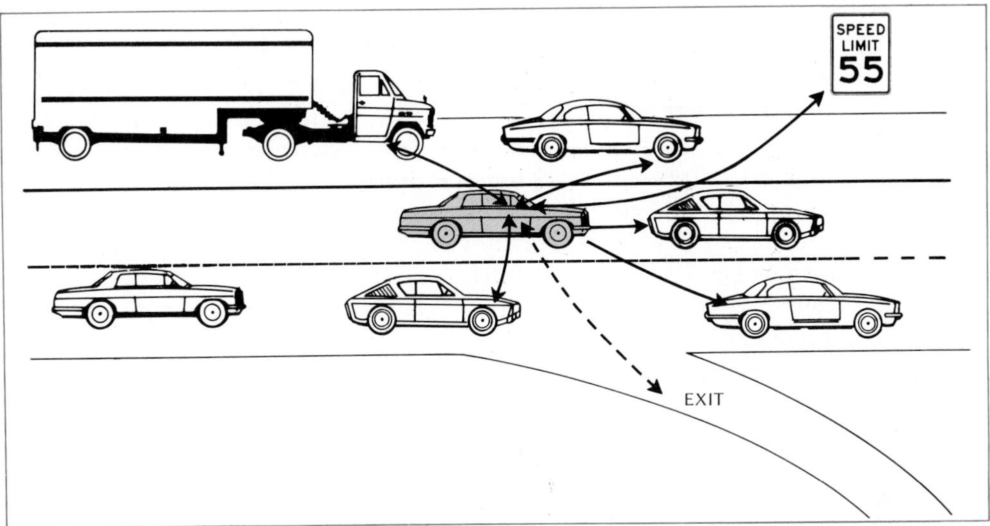

FIGURE 5–6 Even a relatively simple goal, like driving from point A to point B, makes incredible demands on one's message selection, interpretation, and retention skills. Information must be gathered and processed as to the location and rate of speed of other vehicles, and projections must be developed as to where nearby vehicles will be at future points in time. Road signs, gauges in one's own auto, and remembered information as to which exit to take, what lane to be in, and so forth, must also be utilized. In time, this complex information processing task becomes so natural that one can listen to the radio, plan a speech, or replay the day's events while driving.

and retain them. The probability of an English-speaking individual spending much time listening to Spanish radio broadcasts, watching Spanish television programming, or reading Spanish publications is naturally very low, simply because he or she lacks the capability of meaningfully processing the information. By the same token, it is not likely that an individual with no quantitative or research background will be drawn to reading articles in technical or scholarly journals. While the individual may possess the intellectual potential, his or her lack of familiarity with research and with the technical language used in the publication would affect potential interest and comprehension, not to mention retention.

USE

We attend to and devote effort to understand and remember messages we think we will need or be able to use. The learning of language offers an excellent example. It is a virtual certainty that individuals living in a social setting will learn to speak the language of those around them. For the most part, this learning occurs irrespective of whether there are efforts at formal schooling. We attend to, learn to interpret, and retain messages about how to use spoken language because it is necessary to our participation in most human activities.

In school one attends to and retains a large quantity of information on a variety of topics that may have no immediate personal relevance. Were it not for the opportunities and requirements to "rehearse" and "use" this retained knowledge to demonstrate course mastery on exams and quizzes, much less information would be remembered.

The same principle operates in many other domains. To the individual who is thinking about purchasing a new automobile, statistics such as fuel capacity, estimated miles per gallon, wheel base, horsepower, zero-to-sixty acceleration, and price of accessories suddenly become much more salient and far easier to remember than they were prior to the decision to shop for a new car.

COMMUNICATION STYLE

Communication style can influence message-reception dynamics in two ways: First, depending upon our habits and preferences, we may be drawn to or may actively avoid the opportunity to deal with other people. People who are shy or apprehensive about engaging in verbal communication in a group setting, for example, may avoid such circumstances whenever possible.[25] Such an individual might prefer to watch a television show on health or consult a home medical guide guide for information on a particular illness, rather than ask a doctor for information. Even when a person with this style of communication makes an effort to take part in interpersonal situations, he or she may be uncomfortable. This discomfort may affect the way he or she attends to, interprets, and retains information.

A less direct influence of style on information reception has to do with the manner in which we present ourselves to others. The way we "come across" to those with whom we interact can have a substantial impact on the way they react to us, and this will influence both the quality and quantity of information they make available. People who are overly talkative, for instance, often have less verbal information available to them than they otherwise might, because the people with whom they converse are limited in their interest and in the time available to speak. Our greetings, tone, word choice, level of openness, dress, and appearance also have an impact upon the messages other persons make available to us, and this, in turn, has a direct bearing on our selection, interpretation, and retention.

EXPERIENCE AND HABIT

We develop a number of information reception tendencies as a result of our experiences. These habits are no doubt the major guiding influence in how we select, interpret, or retain messages at any moment in time. Whether one thinks of reading a daily newspaper, viewing a particular television show, exchanging pleasantries with an acquaintance on the way to work, or arguing with a friend or family member, our previous experiences, and the communication patterns we have developed as a result of these experiences, influence our message reception in very fundamental ways. See Figure 5–7.

Message Influences

In addition to the *receiver,* the nature of the *message* also has a major impact on selection, interpretation, and retention. Five particularly important characteristics are origin, mode, physical character, organization, and novelty.

ORIGIN

Some of the messages we attend to have their origins in our physical environment. When we select an item on which to sit, identify a landmark to measure our movement, pick out an apartment in which to live, decide whether the temperature in our living room is too high, or develop a theory of why apples fall from trees, we do so using information based on the objects, events, relationships, or substances in the physical environment.

We also make frequent use of messages we create ourselves through a process called *interpersonal* communication. When we listen to and think about what we have said to someone else, try to recall our knowledge about a particular topic, talk to ourselves, or look at ourselves in a mirror before leaving for an important engagement, we are dealing with messages of which we ourselves are the source. We also use messages we ourselves create to assess our own internal feelings. Our sense of

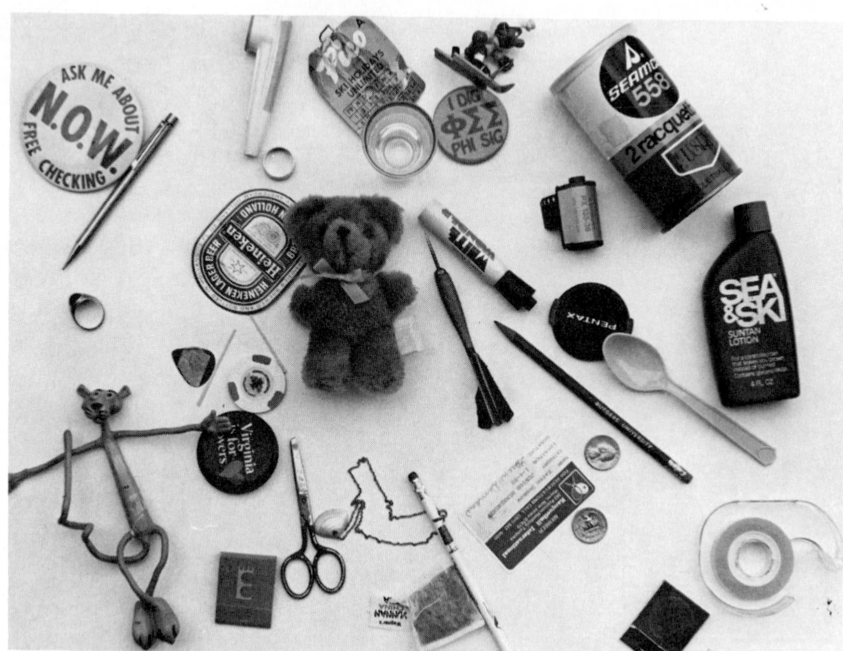

FIGURE 5–7 Glance at the items in the illustration above for 5 to 10 seconds, close the book, and list the items that you can remember on a sheet of paper. When one compares the resulting list with the picture, it is obvious that many items were forgotten and others were perhaps never noticed in the first place. Further study of those things noticed and remembered, and those not, can underscore aspects of the information reception process, the impact of memory on selection and retention of new information, and the complexity of information processing. Generally speaking in any situation what one notices and remembers is greatly influenced by one's accumulated past experience. Sometimes an item is taken note of precisely because one cannot relate to and identify it. In any case, those things noticed and remembered and those forgotten in any situation generally say as much or more about the individual involved—his or her past experiences, priorities, hobbies, and so on—as they do about the actual messages and message sources present in the environment.

illness, fear, happiness, frustration, confusion, excitement, pain, and anxiety result from messages that originate in our own physiological functioning.

Certainly the great majority of information of significance to us in our environment arises either directly or indirectly from the activities of other persons—through *interpersonal communication.* Often the messages that have importance to us originate out of face-to-face interaction with others. Other interpersonal messages are the product of the

TABLE 5–1 Factors Affecting Message Reception

1. THE RECEIVER —Needs —Attitudes, Beliefs, Values —Goals —Capabilities —Uses —Communication Style —Experience and Habit 2. THE MESSAGE —Origin —Mode —Physical Character —Organization —Novelty	3. THE SOURCE —Proximity —Attractiveness —Similarity —Credibility and Authoritativeness —Motivation and Intent —Delivery —Status, Power, and Authority 4. THE MEDIA AND THE ENVIRON MENT —Context and Setting —Repetition —Consistency —Competition

activities of persons separated from us in either time or space or both, transported to us by means of various communication media. A favorite television program, the evening news, a letter from a friend far away, a best-selling novel, the morning paper, a cherished painting, or the latest CD by a favorite recording group can satisfy some of the same needs as face-to-face encounters, though the originator and receiver of the information are separated from one another physically.

In many circumstances we are limited as to which of these message sources we can use. If, for example, we wish to find out the temperature in Tokyo last night, we have little choice but to rely on messages provided by other people through media. If we want to know how we feel about some situation facing us tomorrow, we rely on information we create ourselves. If we need to determine the exact temperature of our swimming pool, that information can be best derived by placing a thermometer in water.

There are many other instances in which we can choose among these sources. We can seek an answer to the question, "Is it hot in here?" using any of these sources: We can make a determination based on our personal "feelings"; we can ask the opinion of one or several other people; or we can use a nearby thermometer. A similar situation occurs when we undertake a project such as figuring out how to use a new piece of stereo equipment. We may choose to tackle the chore ourselves making use of the manufacturer's instructions. We could seek the assistance of a neighbor, or, we may "dig right in" without consulting the instructions, relying on our own resources and prior experience with similar projects. Alternatively, as many of us do in such situations, we can use a combination of these message sources.

The availability or lack of availability of various message sources has an obvious and direct impact upon the way in which we attend to, interpret, and retain information. Individuals may vary in terms of their preferences for particular types of sources; however, when there is a choice many of us rely on "self-created" messages first. That is, if we think we already have the information necessary in a particular circumstance, we may go no further. When we feel we lack the internal resources to make sense of or handle a particular situation on our own, we turn to other sources. For instance, when we get a stomach ache, we are likely to dismiss its significance initially. If it persists, we seek the advice of a doctor, consult a medical book, or undergo various diagnostic procedures. Similarly, when we enter a grocery store to shop for particular items, we will probably go directly to the shelves where we expect to find them. If, however, the store is an unfamiliar one, or the items are not where we expected, we are likely to glance at the signs hanging above the aisles or to ask a clerk for assistance.

MODE

Information reception varies depending upon whether visual, tactile, auditory, gustatory, or olfactory modes are involved. In any number of situations, a touch or reassuring embrace will be taken note of and interpreted in quite a different way than spoken words of encouragement. In such an instance, actions may speak louder than words. Likewise the smell of decaying garbage may be a much more poignant message than a newspaper story about the consequences of a garbage strike or a description of the odor from a friend who witnessed the accumulating trash. In other circumstances, however, words may be more salient than actions, such as in a brainstorming session, a term paper, a letter to a friend, a legal brief, or a debate.

PHYSICAL CHARACTER

Physical characteristics such as size, color, brightness, and intensity can also be important to message processing. In general, symbols, actions, objects, or events that are large or prominent will attract more attention than those which are not. A bright light is more salient than a dim light; large type more noticeable than small type.

Actions and circumstances that have major consequences for large numbers of people—a fire, natural disaster, or international conflict for instance—are more likely to be taken note of than less important events of less widespread impact. These events appear on the front page of the newspaper or on the evening news. The extent of their impact is a major factor in the information-reception processes of reporters and editors, who recognize that readers and viewers are also likely to attend to and be interested in these events.

Other things being equal, messages that have vivid color, brightness, or intensity are more apt to be noticed and taken account of than those lacking these characteristics. A four-color advertisement, a brightly colored sport coat, a high intensity light are likely to be attended to before objects lacking these attributes. The intensity of potential visual or verbal messages can also be an important consideration in message reception. Visual nudity, explicit sexuality, and graphic violence, for example, may well be responded to quite differently than images without these characteristics.

ORGANIZATION

A good deal of research in the area of persuasion has been directed toward determining the way in which the ordering of ideas or opinions affects reception. More recent research on information processing has added to our knowledge in this area. This work suggests that when we are presented with a series of items, we devote greatest attention to the items listed first. As a result, this information has the greatest likelihood of becoming a part of our long-term memory.[26] When asked to recall items from a list after it has been completed, individuals do best with those things presented near the beginning and those near the end. The items at the end are thought to be recalled because they are still a part of one's short-term memory, while those at the beginning are remembered because the information can be retrieved from long-term memory.[27]

The significance of organization of information is evident in a variety of settings. Within a picture or a report the arrangement of elements can have a substantial impact on the overall impression created. The ordering of material within a database is also an important factor in whether and how that material will be used. Even the arrangement of foods at a grocery store often has an impact on our message processing. How many times do we pick up grocery items we hadn't intended to because we noticed them while on our way to the place in the store where bread or milk were shelved?

NOVELTY

Often messages that are novel, unfamiliar, or unusual stand out, "grabbing our attention" if only for the moment. While we may generally devote very little attention to the color of automobiles, a pink or purple car is likely to "catch the eye" of even the most preoccupied motorist.

The same principle applies in other areas such as dress, language, appearance, or greetings, to which most of us devote little conscious attention unless messages dramatically violate what we have come to expect. An unfamiliar foreign language, unusual dress, or a normally tidy room in disarray often become very salient to us. Other examples are provided in Figures 5–8 and 5–9. Though we are typically only somewhat aware when we engage in a ritualistic handshake greeting, we certainly do take note when the other person squeezes our hand too firmly, too loosely, or continues to shake for seven or eight pumps.

Source Influences

Some of the most interesting and complex information-reception decisions we make involve interpersonal sources. Why do we listen to and believe some people more than others? Our decisions depend on a number of factors including: *proximity, attractiveness, similarity, credibility, authoritativeness, motivation, intent, delivery, status, power,* and *authority.*

PROXIMITY

Our distance from a source can have a major influence on the likelihood of our attending to particular messages. We are more likely to be exposed to sources that are close at hand than to those that are further away.[28] The closer we are, the less time, effort, and money that must be expended to expose ourselves of the message.

For example, if we are setting out to assemble a new bicycle, we are much more likely to ask for the assistance of a neighbor if we reside in a housing development than if our home is two miles from the next residence. If we walk into a library to find a reference and must pass by the librarian, we may decide to ask his or her advice simply because of proximity. For this same reason, we are far more likely to attend to the ac-

FIGURE 5–8 Persons, objects, events, or patterns that are unique or novel often grab our attention far more than the usual, commonplace, or predictable. Barbara Cartland reports, for example, that during the two years after the Mona Lisa was stolen from the Louvre in Paris in 1911, more people came to stare at the place in the museum where the famous painting had hung than had come to see the actual painting during the 12 previous years.

Niagara Falls provides another interesting case in point. One of the first things that strikes most visitors to the falls is the pervasive sound created by the pounding of the falls to the river below. To residents of the area, however, the noise goes generally unnoticed. Ironically, it was the sudden absence of the thundering falls during a hard freeze in the winter of 1936 and previously in 1909 that reportedly awoke the residents.

Source: Barbara Cartland, *Barbara Cartland's Book of Useless Information.*

tions and reactions of a next-door neighbor or colleague at work than to those of persons who live a block away or work in the next building.

The significance of distance as a factor in message reception is illustrated by considering the function of communication media. By means of television, radio, newspapers, magazines, books, and newer electronic technologies, information from thousands of miles away becomes available without leaving the comfort of one's home. It is, in fact,

FIGURE 5–9 Unusual objects, events, individuals, or actions often command attention and interest.

the ease of access to television and other media which has helped to make these media and the messages they transport such a central part of our lives.

PHYSICAL AND SOCIAL ATTRACTION, AND SIMILARITY

The way in which we process interpersonal messages often has a great deal to do with how attractive we believe a particular message source to be. Particularly when we are first meeting an individual, we react largely to his or her general appearance. If, based on any of these messages, we are attracted to the person, it is likely that we will pay increased attention to, remember, and attach special significance to his or her words. In this way, attraction plays a significant, though often subtle, role in influencing the nature of selection, interpretation, and retention.

Though we tend to think of attractiveness primarily in physical terms, we often find persons appealing for other reasons as well. An individual who appears to be friendly, warm, empathetic, and concerned, and who expresses interest in or respect for us, may be quite attractive to us as a social companion. Like physical attractiveness, *social attractiveness* also can be an important influence in information reception.

Similarity is another factor of significance to message reception. The more like a source we are, or believe ourselves to be, the more likely we are to pay special attention to that person and what he or she says.[29] Sometimes similarities that interest us in others are basic characteristics such as gender, level of education, age, religion, background, race, hobbies, or language capacity. In other instances, we are drawn to people because they share our needs, attitudes, goals, or values.

The influence of similarity on reception is vividly illustrated by the great impact of our peer group, beginning in our early school years. Our cohorts have a role in shaping our reactions to clothing, movies, school, books, various occupations, and also to our parents, friends, and acquaintances. Preferences for persons with similar cultural, religious, racial, occupational, and educational backgrounds continue to influence message selection, interpretation, and retention through the course of our lifetime.

CREDIBILITY AND AUTHORITATIVENESS

We are likely to attend to and retain messages from sources we believe to be experienced and/or knowledgeable.[30] Certain people—or categories of people—may be viewed as credible and authoritative, regardless of the topic. Information provided by medical doctors, clergymen, professors, or lawyers, for example, is often regarded as more noteworthy than messages from people with other vocations, even on topics that are outside the professional's areas of expertise. Similarly, many of us afford actors, television personalities, politicians, and other persons who are in the public eye particular attention and significance. Thus, the actor speaking on politics or the medical doctor lecturing on religion may be given more than the usual level of attention by receivers because of the credibility attached to the person by virtue of education or notoriety.

In some instances, the credibility accorded a particular person depends upon the topic in question. Other things being equal, we are more likely to attend to and retain information on international affairs presented by a network news commentator than to messages on the same topic offered by our next-door neighbor. When the topic is insurance, however, we may well attach more credibility to our neighbor who has twenty-five years experience working in that field than to reports provided by the newscaster.

MOTIVATION AND INTENT

The manner in which we react to a particular interpersonal message source also depends upon the way we explain his or her actions to ourselves.[31] Depending upon what motives we attribute to an individual, our response may vary substantially. If we assume a person intends to inform us, we are likely to react to and interpret the messages in a different way than if we believe the intention is to persuade or deceive us. If we believe someone "has our best interests at heart," we are likely to be more receptive than if we believe that person is just looking out for himself or herself.

DELIVERY

The manner in which a source delivers a message can be an important influence in information reception and processing. Among the factors that come into play in delivery of spoken messages are volume, rate of speaking, pitch, pronunciation, and the use of pauses. Other visual factors, such as gestures, facial expressions, and eye contact may be influential.

STATUS, POWER, AND AUTHORITY

The presence or lack of *status*—position or rank—can also be important in determining how likely it is that a source or particular message will be selected and acted upon. The *power* or *authority* of a source—the extent to which the source is capable of dispensing rewards or punishment for selecting, remembering and interpreting messages in a particular way—is also influential in information processing.

Generally speaking, parents, teachers, employers, supervisors, or others who have status, power, or authority relative to us have a better than average chance of obtaining our attention to their messages. The significance we attach to their role directs our attention to their words and actions in an effort to be aware of their opinions or to seek their favor. To the extent that we can be rewarded or punished through grades, money, favors, or praise for interpreting their messages in particular ways, we may be especially attentive.

Media and Environmental Influences

Beyond the *receiver,* the *message,* and the *source,* the *medium* and *environment* also have a substantial impact on selection, interpretation, and retention.

THE MEDIUM

The media, or channel, through which messages reach us can be a significant factor in information reception. Differences, such as whether messages are presented via print or illustration, gesture or dress, film or microfiche, radio broadcast or the spoken words of a friend, can have have a direct, and in some cases obvious, influence. Simply in terms of availability, some media provide a greater likelihood of exposure to information than others. More people watch television than read academic journals, and the size of both of these is much larger than the group that uses electronic consumer databases.

Beyond obvious assets and liabilities of particular mass media, there are less apparent distinctions in terms of information reception. Recent studies have shown, for instance, that among many people, newspapers have been declining as primary sources of national and international news. However, it appears that newspapers are a major information source for local news.[32] It has also been noted that in many circumstances, information provided by several media is more influential than when available on a single medium alone.[33]

The manner in which messages are presented *within* a medium can also have a bearing on information processing. In newspapers, for instance, factors such as sentence length, the number of different words used, punctuation, and language level can have an influence on comprehension, credibility, and interest associated with a publication.[34]

Of the various mass media, television has no doubt received the most attention among scholars in the past several decades. This interest is not surprising given the central role of television in the lives of most Americans. Even as early as the 1950s, families viewed television on the average of four and one-half hours a day. That number jumped to over five hours in the 1960s, over six hours in the 1970s, and nearly seven hours in the 1980s.[35] In terms of exposure to messages alone, television is clearly a major force in our lives.

As noted in the recent summary of a National Institute of Mental Health report, *Television and Behavior,* "Television can no longer be considered as a casual part of daily life, as an electronic toy."[36]

> The simplest representations (on television) are literal visual and auditory pictures of something in the real world, for example, a car moving along a highway. To process this information, children probably depend on the same perceptual and cognitive skills they use in processing information in the real world. . . . At the next level are the forms and conventions that do not have real-world counterparts. Some of them are analogs of real-world experiences. . . . For example, a "zoom in," in which the object in front of the camera seems to get larger and more focused, is similar to moving closer to something in real life. But some effects, for example, slow motion, do not appear in the real world, and children—and others who are unfamiliar with television—must learn what they mean.
>
> Once they are learned, these media conventions can be used by people in their own thinking. For example, children may learn to analyze a complex stimulus into its smaller parts by watching the camera zoom in and out. The forms can take on meaning, sometimes as a result of associations seen on television.[37]

The report also indicates that the rapid movement and visual and audio contrasts presented by television are particularly salient to very young viewers, who often become "passive consumers of audio-visual thrills."[38]

THE ENVIRONMENT

Context. The manner in which a particular person or event is reacted to depends on whether we are at home or on vacation, at work or engaged in a leisure activity. It will depend also on whether the messages are received in an office, a church, a bedroom, or an auditorium. It is not difficult to think of examples of how the same message would be interpreted very differently depending upon the context in which it was encountered. See Figure 5–10.

The presence of others often has a very direct bearing on how we select as well as interpret and retain information. How we want to be seen, how we think other people see us, what we believe others expect from us, and what we think they think about the situation we are in are among the considerations that shape the way we react in social situations.

If we are in the company of colleagues or friends, we may pay particular attention to the people, events, and circumstances they attend to. In our effort to decide how well we liked a particular movie, lecture, painting, or person, the reactions of other persons are often of major significance to our own judgments. Sometimes, we conform our own infor-

FIGURE 5–10 The context or setting in which potential information sources are encountered can be an important factor influencing whether and how messages are selected, interpreted, and remembered.

mation processing to that of others for appearances only; in many other instances the influence is more subtle and far-reaching.

Repetition. We are likely to take into account and remember messages that are repeated often. Advertising slogans and jingles, the lyrics of popular songs, the multiplication table, an often-called phone number, and the birth dates of family members stand out in our minds, in part because they have been repeated so often. Repetition also contributes to our learning of our native language, our parents' and friends' opinions, the slang and jargon of our associates, and the accent of our geographic region.

Consistency and Competition. Where a person has been exposed over a long period of time to one religious orientation, one political philosophy, or one set of values, there is a likelihood that the individual will come to select and accept messages consistent with that position. *Brainwashing* is the extreme example of this sort of communication phenomenon. In such circumstances, the individual is bombarded with messages that advocate a particular position, and information supporting alternative points of view is systematically eliminated from the environment. When coupled with the promise of reward (or absence of punishment) and consistency, the lack of competitive messages becomes a powerful shaping force influencing the probability of message selection and the manner of interpretation and retention.

In considerably less extreme forms, the educational process makes use of these same principles. Math, language, reading, and spelling are taught not only through repetition but also through consistency. Through the arrangement of classroom furniture and the use of examinations, lectures, books, and homework assignments substantial effort is directed toward minimizing the influence of competing messages.

An Active and Complex Process

Selection, interpretation, and reception are basic to message reception. These activities are influenced by any number of the factors discussed in this chapter, making information processing one of the most active and complex facets of human communication. Morton Hunt makes this point eloquently in discussing the opening sentence of Gibbon's *Decline and Fall of the Roman Empire:*

> "In the second century of the Christian era, the Empire of Rome comprehended the fairest part of the earth, and the most civilized portion of mankind."
>
> A reader who finds this sentence perfectly intelligible does so not because Gibbon was a lucid stylist but because he or she knows when the Christian era began, understands the concept of "empire," is familiar enough with history to recognize the huge sociocultural phenomenon known as "Rome," has enough information about world geography so that the phrase "the fairest part of the earth" produces a number of images in the mind, and, finally, can muster a whole congeries of ideas about the kinds of civilization that then existed. What skill, to elicit that profusion of associations with those few well-chosen cues—but what a performance by the reader! One hardly knows which to admire more. . . .[39]

Without doing any injustice to Hunt's intent, we could extend the point to apply equally to the impressive accomplishments of a listener in a personal, group, or public setting, or to the observer of visual images in an art gallery, a baseball game, or a television program.

Implications and Applications: Listening, Observing, Interpreting, and Remembering

- Message reception is a fundamental aspect of our communication behavior—an aspect to which we often pay little attention.
- Listening and observing are our primary means for gathering information about the people, events, problems, and opportunities in our environment.
- Listening and observing involve selection. While we attend to and attach importance to some people, circumstances, and objects, we inevitably ignore others.
- Our selections, interpretations, and memories of messages are subjective and are influenced by what we, personally, bring to the situation, as well as by available messages, sources, media, and environmental influences.
- Our personal characteristics and previous experiences have a major influence on what we see, hear, understand, believe, and remember.
- Competence in listening and observing requires conscious effort,

an awareness of factors influencing the process, and an understanding of ourselves and our own capabilities, needs, attitudes, values, and goals.

Summary

In this chapter, our focus has been upon the nature of information reception, and the processes involved in sensing and making sense of the people, objects, and circumstances in our environment. Individuals play an active role in this process though they may have little awareness that it is taking place.

Selection, interpretation, and retention are primary facets of information reception. The first involves the selective attention to particular environmental messages from all those to which an individual is exposed. The second consists of the transformation of those messages into a form that has value and utility for the individual. The third involves retention and short- and long-term, episodic and semantic, memory. In actual operation, selection, interpretation, and retention are very much interrelated activities.

A number of factors influence selection, interpretation, and retention. Many of them have to do with the receiver and his or her needs, attitudes, beliefs, values, goals, capabilities, uses, style, experience, and habits.

Other factors that influence information reception have to do with messages—their origin, mode, physical character, novelty, and organization. Sources also have an impact on message reception, through their proximity, attractiveness, credibility, motivation, intention, delivery, status, power, and authority. Message reception may also be affected by factors related to the medium and environment.

Notes

1. See Stuart M. Albert, Lee Alan Becker, and Timothy C. Brock, "Familiarity, Utility, and Supportiveness as Determinants of Information Receptivity," *Journal of Personality and Social Psychology*, Vol. 14, 1970, pp. 292–301. D. E. Broadbent, "A Mechanical Model for Human Attention and Immediate Memory," *Psychological Review*, Vol. 64, 1957, pp. 205–215. Robert T. Craig, "Infor-

mation Systems Theory and Research: An Overview of Individual Information Processing," in *Communication Yearbook 3.* Ed. by Dan Nimmo (New Brunswick, NJ: Transaction, International Communication Association, 1979), pp. 99–120. D. Deutsch and J. A. Deutsch, "Attention: Some Theoretical Considerations," *Psychological Review,* Vol. 70, 1963, pp. 80–90. Lewis Donohew and Philip Palmgreen, "An Investigation of 'Mechanisms' of Information Selection," *Journalism Quarterly,* Vol. 48, 1971, pp. 624–639. Lewis Donohew and Philip Palmgreen, "Reappraisal of Dissonance and the Selective Exposure Hypothesis," *Journalism Quarterly,* Vol. 48, 1971, pp. 412–420. Anne M. Treisman, "Strategies and Models of Selective Attention," *Psychological Review,* Vol. 76, No. 3, 1969, pp. 282–299.

2. Samuel L. Becker, "Visual Stimuli and the Construction of Meaning," in *Visual Learning, Thinking and Communication.* Ed. by Bikkar S. Randhawa (New York: Academic Press, 1978), pp. 39–60.

3. Broadbent, 1957.

4. Craig, 1979, p. 102.

5. See Norman F. Dixon, *Preconscious Processing* (London: Wiley, 1981).

6. The issue of *what* is recalled under hypnosis and drugs is relatively controversial. While it was long believed that the information remembered was in its "original, unaltered" form, recent studies have suggested that often it is a transformed, elaborated, and often distorted version, changed by time and circumstance. For a discussion of these issues, see Elizabeth Loftus, *Memory* (Reading, MA: Addison-Wesley, 1980), pp. 54–62.

7. Craig, 1979, p. 103.

8. Morton Hunt, *The Universe Within* (New York: Simon & Schuster, 1982), p. 85.

9. Hunt, 1982, p. 86.

10. Hunt, 1982, p. 86.

11. For a more detailed description of information-processing stages and dynamics see Geoffrey R. Loftus and Elizabeth F. Loftus, *Human Memory: The Processing of Information* (Hillsdale, NJ: Lawrence Erlbaum), 1976; and Peter H. Lindsay and Donald A. Norman, *Human Information Processing* (New York: Academic, 1977).

12. Hunt, 1982, p. 104.

13. G. Loftus and E. Loftus, 1976, p. 8. The authors provide a useful overview and model of information processing and memory in their "Introduction." See also Hunt, 1982, especially Ch. 3, and Elizabeth Loftus, 1980, especially Ch. 2.

14. G. Loftus and E. Loftus, 1976, p. 8.

15. George Mandler, *Cognitive Psychology: An Essay in Cognitive Science* (Hillsdale, NJ: Lawrence Erlbaum, 1985), pp. 92–94. Lists of distinguishing characteristics are presented here in shortened form.

16. E. Tulving, *Elements of Episodic Memory.* (Oxford, England: Oxford University Press, 1983). See discussion in Mandler, 1985, pp. 106–107; and Gillian Cohen, *Memory in the Real World* (Hillsdale, NJ: Lawrence Erlbaum, 1989), pp. 114–115.

17. Cohen, 1989, pp. 114–115.

18. Cohen, 1989, pp. 114–115.

19. Based on a listing and discussion by Cohen, 1989, pp. 217–221.

20. One of the most widely cited classifications in recent years was provided in the writings of Abraham Maslow, "A Theory of Human Motivation," *Psychological Review,* Vol. 50, 1943, pp. 370–396. The framework differentiates between basic biological needs and "higher order" psychological and social needs.

21. Maslow, 1950.

22. Maslow, 1950.

23. See Elihu Katz, Jay G. Blumler, and Michael Gurevitch, "Utilization of Mass Communication by the Individual," in *The Uses of Mass Communications,* Jay G. Blumler and Elihu Katz, eds. (Beverly Hills, CA: Sage, 1974) pp. 22–23.

24. Lawrence R. Wheeless, "The Effects of Attitude, Credibility, and Homophily on Selective Exposure to Information," *Speech Monographs,* Vol 41, April 1974, pp. 329–338.

25. Cf. Philip Zimbardo, *Shyness* (Reading, MA: Addison-Wesley); James C. McCroskey, "Oral Communication Apprehension: A Summary of Recent Theory and Research," *Human Communication Research,* Vol. 4, 1977, pp. 78–96; Gerald M. Phillips and Nancy J. Metzger, "The Reticent Syndrome: Some Theoretical Considerations about Etiology and Treatment," *Speech Monographs,* Vol. 40, 1973.

26. Loftus, 1980, pp. 24–25.

27. Ibid.

28. See Nan Lin, *The Study of Human Communication* (New York: Bobbs-Merrill, 1973), pp. 44–46.

29. Wheeless, 1974.

30. Carl I. Hovland and W. Weiss, "The Influence of Source Credibility on Communication Effectiveness," *Public Opinion Quarterly,* Vol. 15, 1951, pp. 635–650; for a discussion of the role of credibility in communication see James C. McCroskey, *An Introduction to Rhetorical Communication* (Englewood Cliffs, NJ: Prentice Hall, 1978), especially Ch. 4.

31. The way we explain behavior to ourselves is the focus of work in an area called *attribution theory.* See, for instance, Edward E. Jones, David E. Kanouse, Harold H. Kelley, Richard E. Nisbett, Stuart Valins, and Bernard Weiner, eds., *Attribution: Perceiving the Causes of Behavior,* (Morristown, NJ: General Learning Press, 1971) for an overview of the area.

32. R. C. Adams, "Newspapers and Television as News Information Media," *Journalism Quarterly,* Vol. 58, No. 4, Winter 1981, pp. 627–629.

33. Steve K. Toggerson, Media Coverage and Information-Seeking Behavior," *Journalism Quarterly,* Vol. 58, No. 1, Spring 1981, pp. 89–92.

34. See Judee K. Burgoon, Michael Burgoon, and Miriam Wilkinson, "Writing Style as Predictor of Newspaper Readership, Satisfaction, and Image," *Journalism Quarterly,* Vol. 58, No. 2, Summer 1981, pp. 225–231.

35. "What Is TV Doing to America?" *U.S. News and World Report,* August 2, 1982, p. 29.

36. *Television and Behavior: Ten Years of Scientific Progress and Implica-*

tions for the Eighties, Volume 1: Summary Report (Rockville, MD: National Institute of Mental Health, 1982), p. 87.

37. *Television and Behavior,* 1982, p. 24.

38. *Television and Behavior,* 1982, p. 26.

39. Hunt, 1982, pp. 119–121.

References and Suggested Readings

ADAMS, R. C. "Newspapers and Television as News Information Media." *Journalism Quarterly.* Vol. 58, No. 4, Winter 1981, 627–629.

ALBERT, STUART M., LEE ALAN BECKER, and TIMOTHY C. BROCK. "Familiarity, Utility, and Supportiveness as Determinants of Information Receptivity." *Journal of Personal and Social Psychology.* Vol. 14, No. 4, 1970, 292–301.

ASHCRAFT, MARK H. *Human Memory and Cognition.* Glenview, IL: Scott, Foresman, 1989.

BADDELEY, ALAN. *Your Memory: A User's Guide.* New York: Macmillan, 1982.

BAKER, STEPHEN. *Visual Persuasion.* New York:McGraw-Hill, 1961.

BECKER, SAMUEL L. "Visual Stimuli and the Construction of Meaning." In *Visual Learning, Thinking and Communication.* Ed. by Bikkar S. Randhawa. New York: Academic Press, 1978, pp. 39–60.

BEGLEY, SHARON. *"Memory." Newsweek.* September 29, 1986, pp. 48–54.

BETTINGHAUS, ERWIN P. *Persuasive Communication.* New York: Holt, 1968.

BOLLES, EDMUND BLAIR. *Remembering and Forgetting: An Inquiry into the Nature of Memory.* New York: Walker, 1988.

BROADBENT, D. E. "A Mechanical Model for Human Attention and Immediate Memory." *Psychological Review.* Vol. 64, No. 3, 1957, 205–215.

BUDD, RICHARD W., and BRENT D. RUBEN. *Beyond Media: New Approaches to Mass Communication,* Second Ed. New Brunswick, NJ: Transaction, 1987.

BURGOON, JUDEE K., MICHAEL BURGOON, and MIRIAM WILKINSON. "Writing Style as Predictor of Newspaper Readership, Satisfaction, and Image." *Journalism Quarterly,* Vol. 58, No. 2, Summer 1981, 225–231.

BURGOON, MICHAEL K., and GERALD R. MILLER. *New Techniques of Persuasion.* New York: Harper, 1973.

COHEN, GILLIAN. *Memory in the Real World.* Hillsdale, NJ: Lawrence Erlbaum, 1989.

CRAIG, ROBERT T. "Information Systems Theory and Research: An Overview of Individual Information Processing." In *Communication Yearbook 3,* Ed. by Dan Nimmo. New Brunswick, NJ: Transaction, International Communication Association, 1979, 99–120.

CRAIK, FERGUS I. M. "A Process View of Short-Term Retention." In *Cognitive Theory, Volume 1.* Ed. by Richard M. Shiffrin, N. John Castellan, Harold R. Lindman, and David B. Pisoni. Hillsdale, NJ: Lawrence Erlbaum, 1975, 173–192.

DANCE, FRANK E. X. "The Functions of Human Communications." In *Informa-*

tion and Behavior: Volume 1. Ed. by Brent D. Ruben. New Brunswick, NJ: Transaction, 1985, 62–75.

DEUTSCH, D., and J. A. DEUTSCH. "Attention: Some Theoretical Considerations." *Psychological Review,* Vol. 70, No. 1, 1963, 80–90.

DIXON, N. F. *Preconscious Processing.* London: Wiley, 1981.

DONOHEW, LEWIS, and PHILIP PALMGREEN. "An Investigation of 'Mechanisms' of Information Selection." *Journalism Quarterly* Vol. 48, 1971, 624–639.

———. "Reappraisal of Dissonance and the Selective Exposure Hypothesis." *Journalism Quarterly* Vol. 48, 1971, 412–420.

FARNHAM-DIGGORY, SYLVIA. *Information Processing in Children.* New York: Academic Press, 1972.

FREEDMAN, JONATHAN L., and DAVID O. SEARS. "Selective Exposure to Information: A Critical Review." *Public Opinion Quarterly,* Vol. 31, 1967.

GORDON, WILLIAM C. *Learning and Memory.* Pacific Grove, CA: Brooks/Cole, 1988.

GREGG, VERGON H. *Introduction to Human Memory.* London: Routledge and Kegan Paul, 1986.

GUMPERT, GARY, and ROBERT CATHCART, eds. *Intermedia Third Ed.* New York: Oxford University Press, 1986.

HOVLAND, CARL I., and W. WEISS. "The Influence of Source Credibility on Communication Effectiveness." *Public Opinion Quarterly.* Vol. 15, 1951, 635–650.

HUNT, MORTON. *The Universe Within.* New York: Simon and Schuster, 1982.

KATZ, ELIHU, JAY G. BLUMLER, and MICHAEL GUREVITCH. "Utilization of Mass Communication by the Individual." In *The Uses of Mass Communications.* Ed. by Jay G. Blumler and Elihu Katz. Beverly Hills, CA: Sage, 1974, 19–32.

LEVINSON, DANIEL J. (with CHARLOTTE N. DARROW, EDWARD B. KLEIN, MARIA H. LEVINSON, and BRAXTON MCKEE). *The Seasons of a Man's Life.* New York: Ballantine, 1978.

LIN, NAN. *The Study of Human Communication.* New York: Bobbs-Merrill, 1973.

LOFTUS, ELIZABETH. *Memory.* Reading, MA: Addison-Wesley, 1980.

LOFTUS, GEOFFREY R., and ELIZABETH F. LOFTUS. *Human Memory: The Processing of Information.* Hillsdale, NJ: Lawrence Erlbaum, 1976.

LOFTUS, ELIZABETH, and JONATHAN W. SCHOOLER. "Information-Processing Conceptualizations of Human Cognition: Past, Present, and Future," in *Information and Behavior: Volume 1.* Ed. by Brent D. Ruben. New Brunswick, NJ: Transaction, 1985, 225–250.

MANDLER, GEORGE. *Cognitive Psychology: An Essay in Cognitive Science.* Hillsdale, NJ: Lawrence Erlbaum, 1985.

MCCROSKEY, JAMES C. "Oral Communication Apprehension: A Summary of Recent Theory and Research." *Human Communication Research.* Vol. 4, 1957, 78–96.

MCCROSKEY, JAMES. "Oral Communication Apprehension: A Reconceptualization. " In *Communication Yearbook 6.* Ed. by Robert N. Bostrom. Beverly Hills: Sage, 1982, 136–170.

MCGUIRE, WILLIAM, J. "The Nature of Attitudes and Attitude Change." In *The Handbook of Social Psychology, Volume 3.* Ed. by Gardner Lindzey and Elliot Aronson. Reading, MA: Addison-Wesley, 1969, 136–314.

——. "Psychological Motives and Communication Gratification." In *The Uses of Mass Communications.* Ed. by Jay G. Blumler and Elihu Katz. Beverly Hills, CA: Sage, 1974, 167–195.

McLeod, Jack M., Carl R. Bybee, and Jean A. Durall. "Evaluating Media Performance by Gratifications Sought and Received." *Journalism Quarterly.* Vol. 59, No. 1 Spring 1982, 3–12, 59.

Maslow, Abraham. "A Theory of Human Motivation," *Psychological Review.* Vol. 50, 1943, 370–396.

Maslow, Abraham H. *Motivation and Personality.* Second Ed., New York: Harper, 1954.

Paivio, Allan. "On Exploring Visual Knowledge." In *Visual Learning, Thinking, and Communication.* Ed. by Bikkar A. Randhawa. New York: Academic Press, 1978, 113–131.

Palmgreen, Phillip. "Uses and Gratifications: A Theoretical Perspective." In *Communication Yearbook 8.* Ed. by Robert N. Bostrom. Beverly Hills: Sage, 1984, 20–55.

Paris, Scott G. "Integration and Inference in Children's Comprehension and Memory." In *Cognitive Theory, Volume 1.* Ed. by Richard M. Shiffrin, N. John Castelan, Harold R. Lindman, and David B. Pisoni. Hillsdale, NJ: Lawrence Erlbaum, 1975, 223–246.

Phillips, Gerald M., and Nancy J. Metzger. "The Reticent Syndrome: Some Theoretical Considerations About Etiology and Treatment." *Speech Monographs.* Vol. 4, 1973.

Randhawa, Bikkar S., ed. *Visual Learning: Thinking and Communication.* New York: Academic Press, 1978.

Sigel, Irving E. "The Development of Pictorial Comprehension." In *Visual Learning, Thinking and Communication.* Ed. by Bikkar S. Randhawa. New York: Academic Press, 1978, 93–111.

Television and Behavior: Ten Years of Scientific Progress and Implications for the Eighties. Volume 1: Summary Report. Rockville, MD: National Institute of Mental Health, 1982, 87.

Toggerson, Steve K. "Media Coverage and Information-Seeking Behavior." *Journalism Quarterly.* Vol. 58, No. 1, Spring 1981, 89–92.

Treisman, Anne M. "Strategies and Models of Selective Attention." *Psychological Review.* Vol. 76, No. 3, 1969, 282–299.

Tulving, E., *Elements of Episodic Memory.* Oxford, England: Oxford University Press, 1983.

Warnock, Mary. *Memory.* London: Faber and Faber, 1987.

Wheeless, Lawrence R. "The Effects of Attitude, Credibility, and Homophily on Selective Exposure to Information." (April 1973). *Speech Monographs.* Vol. 41, 1974, 329–338.

Wheeless, Lawrence R., and John A. Cook. "Information Exposure, Attention, and Reception." In *Information and Behavior: Volume 1.* Ed. by Brent D. Ruben. New Brunswick, NJ: Transaction, 1985, 251–286.

Zillman, Dolf, and Jennings Bryant. *Selective Exposure to Communication.* Hillsdale, NJ: Lawrence Erlbaum, 1985.

Zimbardo, Phillip. *Shyness.* Reading, MA: Addison-Wesley, 1979.

In order for elections to serve the pe
controlling political policy four condition
peting candidates should offer clear policy
voters; (2) Voters should be knowledgeable
(3) Assuming the issues are clear, the majo
also be identified; and (4) After the elect
didate should be bound by his election mand
However, in the American political sys
are not fulfilled and the people do not
policy. In actuality, parties
ternatives simply b
Candidates
In order for elections to serve th
public policy four
candidates or parties
Voters sh

6

Verbal Codes

Introduction: Message Production

Producing messages is as fundamental to our lives as receiving them. Virtually every aspect of our behavior—our language, tone of voice, appearance, eyes, actions, even our use of space and time—is a potential source of information that may be selected for attention, interpreted, remembered, and acted upon by others.

AN ILLUSTRATION

As a way of introducing the topic of message production, consider the following scenario involving a job interview:

> It's time to get serious about finding a job. A friend calls your attention to an advertisement in the newspaper for a position that sounds interesting at a firm whose name you recognize. You prepare a resume and send it off with a cover letter.
>
> Several days later you get a call and an interview is scheduled.
>
> You decide that it's wise to spend time preparing. You gather some information on the organization and plan what you'll say if they ask why you want the position and why you are not working now. You also make up a list of questions you would like to ask them and give some thought to the kind of impression you would like to create.
>
> When the day of the interview arrives, you make it a point to dress well and arrive a few minutes early. You feel well-prepared and have yourself "psyched-up" to make a good impression. When the interviewer arrives, you greet her with a hearty, "Hello, there! How are you, today?" shake her hand, and take a seat next to the desk. You take a deep breath, hoping that will help you relax.
>
> As the questions begin to come, you try to respond in a way that will lead the interviewer to see you as comfortable yet not overly informal, interested but not overly aggressive, composed yet spontaneous, self-assured but not arrogant, interested in the job but not desperate.
>
> After what seems like about an hour, she says she has no more questions, and asks if you do. You inquire about starting salary, opportunities for advancement, and benefits—questions you selected because they would yield information you needed, while creating the impression of competence and alertness.
>
> After brief responses, she thanks you for coming, and indicates that she

will be in touch with you as soon as all the applicants for the position have been considered. You respond, "OK," get up, and leave.

Now let's examine the situation from the organization's point of view: The task of finding a qualified person was initiated long before the interview, with the collection of information and the preparation of the job description and advertisement. In a more general sense, the recruitment process actually began with the firm's advertising and public relations efforts over the years.

After screening many applications, the list of people to be interviewed was finalized. The goal of the interview itself was to create a positive, yet realistic, impression of the organization and the job and to evaluate candidates' suitability for the position.

Questions were asked from a standardized interview guide. They were designed to help probe candidates' technical qualifications, while giving the interviewer a sense of how much "homework" applicants had done to prepare for the interview, how composed and confident they were, how they approached problems, how they dealt with people, and how they felt about themselves:

- How did you learn about the position?
- How much do you know about the company?
- Where did you go to school?
- What was your major? Why did you select that field?
- What experience have you had that is relevant to this job?
- Why are you thinking of leaving your present position?
- What are your greatest strengths and weaknesses?
- What are you looking for in this position?
- What questions do you have about the job?
- What are your long-term career objectives?

Encoding and Decoding

In a situation such as the one described, each party is putting forth a good deal of effort to provide information and to create particular kinds of impressions. The individuals involved have specific goals in mind and create messages designed to achieve them. This process—converting an idea into a message—is termed *encoding*. Some of the messages that become significant for others are intentionally encoded. Our hope is that the individuals for whom our messages are prepared will *decode* them—translate the message into an idea—more or less as we intend. Message production is generally considered to be effective when encoding and decoding occur in such a way that an idea is interpreted by the receiver in more or less the same way the source had in mind—when message received corresponds to message sent.

Even in circumstances like the job interview discussed previously—where interactants have a clear idea of the meaning they want to convey through their messages—they are also likely to create messages which are unintended. This happens no matter how well we plan or rehearse. An inappropriate greeting, evasiveness in answering a question, a shaky voice, an abrupt change of topic, a misspelled or misused word, a poorly pronounced phrase, the lack of eye contact, or a sweaty brow can easily have as much—or more—impact as the messages we encode intentionally.

The messages we produce fall into two broad categories: verbal and nonverbal. In this chapter, we will examine verbal codes in some detail. Nonverbal codes are the focus of the next chapter.

The Nature of Language

Verbal codes make use of alphanumeric language, one of humankind's most impressive accomplishments. About 10,000 distinct languages and dialects are in use today, and each is unique in some respects.[1] There are also a number of commonalities among languages. All spoken languages, for instance, make use of a distinction between vowels and consonants, and in nearly all languages the subject precedes the object in declarative sentences.[2] Every language has an identifiable pattern and set of rules relative to:

- Phonology—the way sounds are combined to form words;
- Syntax—the way words are combined into sentences;
- Semantics—the meanings of words on the basis of their relationship to one another and to elements in the environment; and
- Pragmatics—the way in which language is used in practice.

PHYSIOLOGICAL FACTORS

Some general similarities among languages may be the result of a common ancestry. Major similarities, however, appear to be more the result of human physical and mental capacities. Although a number of animal species can produce auditory messages, even primates with their ability for vocalization lack the basic physiological capacity of humans.

As shown in Figure 6.1, the human larynx located at the upper end of the trachea or windpipe is strengthened by cartilage that supports the vocal cords. When air from the lungs passes over the vocal cords with a greater force than occurs during normal breathing, the cords vibrate. The vibrations that result are called *voicing*. As the vocal cords are tightened, the pitch of the voice rises; as they are loosened, the pitch lowers. The position of the tongue provides additional variation in sound production. As the air is projected with voice-producing force, it is affected by the vocal cords and the tongue, as well as by the lips, mouth, teeth, and jaw.

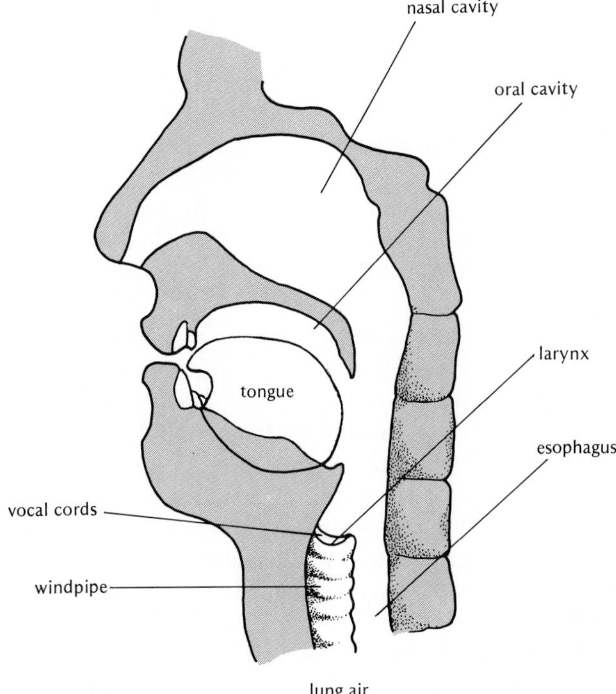

FIGURE 6–1 *Human Sound Production.* The larynx is located at the upper end of the trachea or windpipe. Air passing through the vocal cords causes vibrations that produce human voice patterns. Tightening of the vocal cords produces high-pitched sounds; loosening the cords results in a lower pitch.

The position of the tongue, lips, and jaw are the primary factors involved in the creation of the vowel sounds. When the out-flowing breath creates friction against the teeth, lower lip, or the upper parts of the mouth or tongue, sounds such as the English pronunciation of f, v, s, z, th, sh, and zh are produced. If the breath is stopped momentarily by movement of the lower lip or some part of the tongue, another sort of friction results, creating such sounds as the English pronunciation of p, b, t, d, k, and g. When the breath is rapidly and intermittently stopped, trills or flips result, which are associated with the pronunciation of rr in Spanish, and tt in words such as butter or letter in English. If the breath stream is stopped in the mouth such that it is forced through the nasal passages, the result is a nasal sound common to French and to the English pronunciation of b, m, d, n, and g.[3] Sounds of letters are combined to form words, and words to form phrases and sentences.

COGNITIVE FACTORS

As with other animals, human physiology only partially explains the workings of the communication process. Controlling these mechanisms are the brain and nervous system, which enable us to sense, make sense of, and relate to our environment and one another. Here, the differences between humans and other animals are even more apparent.

One example will help to illustrate the point. Studies of chimps and gorillas who have been taught American sign language indicate clearly that primates can be taught to use language. However, the total vocabulary of the most successful of these students was four hundred words. In contrast, the average human has a vocabulary nearly two hundred times that large.[4]

Findings from neurophysiological research have pointed to the importance of particular areas of the brain for linguistic functioning. Especially important in this regard are what are termed *Broca's Area* and *Wernicke's Area,* both of which are located in the left half or hemisphere of the brain.[5] Research suggests that ideas or feelings that an individual wishes to vocalize are translated into an appropriate auditory pattern in Wernicke's Area and then transmitted to Broca's Area, which activates the electrical impulses needed to mobilize the voice-producing mechanisms and to create the intended vocalization.[6] See Figure 6–2. This conclusion is supported by studies which have shown that damage to Broca's Area of the brain disturbs the production of speech but has much less impact on comprehension, whereas damage to Wernicke's area disrupts all aspects of language use.[7]

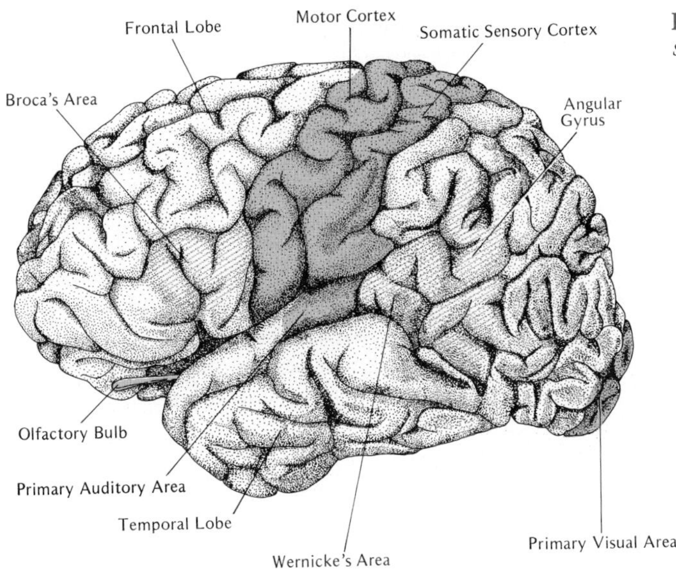

FIGURE 6–2 *Left Hemisphere of the Human Brain.*

Language Acquisition

A good deal of attention has been devoted to determining precisely how and when we first develop competency in the use of language. Some linguists contend that the basic structure of language is innate in humans and that the child needs to learn only the surface details of the language spoken in his or her environment. Others seen language acquisition as a part of the general development of the individual.[8] Both groups agree that interaction between the individual and the environment is essential to linguistic competence. Studies have demonstrated that without the capacity and opportunity to talk with others, no language capability develops.[9]

We can distinguish two broad perspectives on language development—the psycholinguistic approach and the sociolinguistic approach:[10]

1. The Psycholinguistic Approach: Early utterances—*protowords* (the forerunners of words) and words themselves—are based on the

child's personalized understanding of the world. Language is a means for the expression of meanings he or she has learned.

2. The Sociolinguistic Approach: Language development occurs when the child experiences a need to communicate. Language is learned through social interaction and is a means for accommodating the demands of social life.

Studies of the first few months of life suggest that language acquisition begins with random "coos" and "giggles" in the presence of family members and other familiar persons, as illustrated in Figure 6–3. At age six to nine months, the "coos" and "giggles" are replaced by babbling sounds; and by eighteen months, most children can form a few simple words—dada, papa, mama, or nana.[11]

The speech patterns of others in the environment are important during this stage and throughout language acquisition. Generally, the speech of those who care for the child differs from standard language use. The vocabulary is simplified; intonation patterns are exaggerated; sentences are simple; frequent questions are asked by mothers; and frequent assertions are made by fathers.[12]

During the earliest stages of language development, single words are utilized to label, assert, or question.[13] In addition to describing an important person, for example, "mama" may be used as an assertion. "Mama!" may mean, "I want you!" or "I need you, now!" Posed as a question, "Mama?" is a way of saying, "Where are you?" or "Will you come help me?" or "Is that you?" By the time most children reach the age of two, they are able to use language to express any number of meanings:[14]

- Nomination—naming
- Recurrence—acknowledging recurrence or reappearance
- Denial—rejecting an idea
- Nonexistence—acknowledging the absence or disappearance of something or someone
- Rejection—preventing an activity or appearance of something or someone
- Location—specifying the relationship between two objects
- Possession—associating an object with someone or something
- Attribution—relating objects to one another
- Experience + Experiencer—a living thing affected by an event

CHILD'S AGE	COORDINATION	LANGUAGE
4 months	 Holds head up.	Coos and chuckles when people play with him/her.
6 to 9 months	 Can sit alone and pull himself/herself up into a standing position.	Babbles continually, sounding like this: "gagagag; yayayaya: dadadada."
12 to 18 months	 First stands alone, then walks along furniture, and, finally, walks alone.	Uses a few words, follows simple commands, and knows what "no" means.
18 to 21 months	 Walking looks stiff and jerky, sits in a chair, can crawl down stairs, and throw a ball (clumsily).	Understands simple questions and begins to put two or three words together in sentences.
24 to 27 months	 Runs well, but falls when making a quick turn. Can also walk up and down stairs.	Uses short sentences composed of words from a 300 - 400 word vocabulary.
30 to 33 months	 Has good hand and finger coordination and can manipulate objects well.	Vocabulary increases in size, and three and four word sentences are prevalent; language begins to sound adultlike.
36 to 39 months	 Runs smoothly and negotiates sharp turns; walks stairs by alternating feet; can ride a tricycle, stand on one foot (briefly), and jump twelve inches in the air.	Talks in well-formed sentences, following rather complex grammatical rules; others can generally understand what he/she is talking about.

FIGURE 6–3 *The Development of Language Skills.*

Source: Reprinted from *The Genesis of Language* by Smith and Miller. By permission of The MIT Press, Cambridge, Massachusetts.

- Action + Actor—a living thing receives the force of an action
- Action + Object—an object affected by an action or activity

As illustrated in Figure 6–3, when the child reaches the age of two and beyond, he or she begins to form two-word sentences: "The two-word stage is a time for experimenting with many binary semantic-syntactic relations such as possessor-possessed ("Mommy sock"), actor-action ("Cat sleeping"), and action-object ("Drink soup").[15]

Although the child's vocabulary is growing, words are being used primarily to define specific, concrete actions and objects. A "car" may be understood as "a way to go to the store," and a "jack-in-the-box" is "what plays music and pops up." From this point on, the child's vocabulary and ability to form sentences progresses rapidly. Before youngsters are three, most are able to use their three-hundred to four-hundred word vocabularies to create well-formed sentences of three, four, and more words.[16]

As the child grows older, his or her phonetic, syntactic, semantic, and pragmatic skills increase. Words are used in increasingly more abstract ways. Whereas "dog" to the toddler meant "my dog Spot," to the youngster it may refer to "my dog Spot and John's dog Rusty." And in later stages of development, "dog" becomes "a kind of pet" and later "a specific kind of four-legged animal."

What began as the use of words and sentences to refer to the immediate and the tangible gradually evolves to a capability for referring to the abstract and the distant. Thus, as a child develops increasing skill in the use of language, the linkage between his or her words and the particular events of the immediate surroundings becomes progressively more remote. For an adult, any word's meaning is an abstraction based on a lifetime of experiences. With the development of skill in using spoken language comes competency in the use of written forms.

> In 1945, the average number of words in the written vocabulary of an American child age 6 to 14 was 25,000. In 1990, that number has dropped to 10,000.

FIGURE 6–4

Source: Harper's Index, October, 1990, p. 17. Based on a national sample of writing by children in grades 1 to 8 as reported by Gary Ingersoll, University of Indiana (Indianapolis), 1990; and H. D. Rinsland, *A Basic Vocabulary of Elementary School Children* (New York: Macmillan, 1945).

Language in Everyday Use

Language is an incredibly powerful tool. We use language not only in vocal but also in written form, not only in single messages but in lengthy documents and databases, not only face-to-face but also in situations involving communication media. We can classify the major everyday uses of language into three categories: (1) Representation; (2) Conversation; and (3) Social and Public Communication.

Representation

LANGUAGE AND REALITY

At the most basic level, language enables us as individuals to name and symbolically represent elements of our world. It therefore provides a means for understanding and organizing ourselves with the environment and one another. Some of the labels refer to the tangible and concrete—friends, teachers, books, courses, reading, and writing. Language also provides the means through which we represent abstract concepts—friendship, learning, love, knowledge, freedom. Through language, we are able to manipulate symbols in our thinking. We can create, test, and refine our theories or understandings of the world.

The relationship between language and the reality it represents is a very complex and intimate one. One example of the relationship between the world of language and the world of physical realities is suggested in the opening passage of the Old Testament in which the spoken word is described as being used by God to create the world—God said, "Let there be light, and there was light." Another vivid illustration comes from the Middle East, where the word *abracadabra* was thought to have the power to cure a fever, as explained in Figure 6–5. The word was written on a triangular piece of flax and worn around the patient's neck. After nine days the flax was thrown backwards over the shoulder into a stream. It was believed that when the word disappeared, the illness would be cured. The sense of relationship between language and the reality it represents is also apparent in an ancient Jewish spell designed to protect against a demon named "Shabriri." To get rid of the demon, one would say, "Shabriri, Briri, Rir, Iri, Ri," whittling him away

ABRACADABRA
ABRACADABR
ABRACADAB
ABRACADA
ABRACAD
ABRACA
ABRAC
ABRA
ABR
AB
A

FIGURE 6–5 The nature of the relationship between language and the elements in the physical environment to which they refer has long been an issue of importance in human life. In the Middle Ages, for example, the word *Abracadabra* was believed to be capable of curing fever. Apparently, the first prescription for its use came from a poem on medicine by Quintus Serenus Sammonicus, a doctor who accompanied the Roman Emperor Severus on an expedition to Britain in 208 AD. The word was to be written on a triangular piece of paper. The sheet of paper was to be worn on a piece of flax around the patient's neck for nine days and then thrown backwards over the shoulder into a stream that ran eastward. Presumably, when the word disappeared, so would the ills of the patient.

Source: Man, Myth, and Magic, Volume 1, New York: Marshall Cavendish, 1970.

to nothing. It was believed that when the word was "gone," so too was the demon.[17]

The words and concepts we have available to represent experience guide us toward particular ways of understanding reality. In English, a common arrangement of nouns and verbs is:

subject→verb→object

Two examples are: "Bill hit Mary," or "You make me mad." The pattern is "one person or thing causing another person or thing." Implicit in the form is a sense of one-way causality—the subject (noun) causes (verb) the outcome in the object (noun). Patterns of representational language use are more than just ways of talking. They imply and encourage ways of thinking—in this instance, they encourage us to see things in terms of "this" causing "that."

By the same token, the realities which confront us have a great impact on our language and the language usage patterns we come to develop and use. In a society whose livelihood depends upon fishing, for instance, the language will be replete with words and phrases that capture subtleties of weather, the sea, boats, and fishing. These subtleties are absent in the common language of more technologically-oriented societies in which computer and electronics terminology abound. Similarly, the language available to an engineer to describe the structures of his world fall on deaf ears when spoken to a friend who is a lawyer or a psychologist.

The use of language is such a basic and subtle aspect of human life, that its representational and "artificial" nature are often overlooked. This is especially so when particular language use patterns are widely shared. If I am the only one around who thinks a particular word is obscene, for instance, I might well question whether my meaning for the term is correct. However, so long as others seem to share my meaning, I am comforted in my view that representation and "reality" are one in the same. Unfortunately, there are many instances where we *assume* our words are being understood and their meanings shared when they may not be. Researchers have shown that even terms like "always," "often," and "rarely," when used by health professionals in the context of laboratory reports, are subject to a wide range of interpretation. A study of physicians and health care administrators in several settings showed that estimates as to the meaning of "always" varied from 60 percent to 100 percent. For "sometimes," estimates ranged from 0 to 90 percent; and for "rarely," meanings varied from 0 to 95 percent.[18]

Generally, then, language seems to work "as if it were real." Most often, when we ask someone to pass the salt, their arm extends, grasps a salt container, and, without much difficulty at all, places the salt container in front of us. But there are also a number of circumstances in life which remind the reflective person that an uncritical belief in the "reality of language" can lead to difficulties. Getting a message through to someone who should quit smoking, lose weight, change lifestyles, or "turn over a new leaf" is a much more difficult proposition.

Similarly, a man saying that he is "in love" may not tell us much about the way he feels, how he will behave, or what he really thinks about the concept and person to whom his words refer. We use the words "I do," for example, to seal the bonds of marriage. Although these two words have great symbolic value to the parties involved at that moment, the stability of the marriage will depend not upon the words but upon the behaviors and ideologies to which they refer.

Beyond the problems that arise from confusing words with the people, behaviors, actions, or ideas to which they refer, additional complexity in language results because in actual use words seldom represent the same things to two different people. As noted earlier, the precise meanings each of us attaches to words and phrases depend upon our experiences. As a consequence, the meanings of words are subjective and, to some extent, unique to each individual. The following exchange illustrates the point:

LYNN: "Marty, I need that breakdown on the Johnson deal that you've been working on for this afternoon's meeting."

MARTY: "Okay, Lynn, you'll have it."

MARTY: "Sally, that memo for sales has got to go out this morning."
SALLY: "I'll get it right out."
LYNN: (4:30 that afternoon) "Ray, where's that information you promised to get me this afternoon?"
MARY: "You should have had it this morning. I asked Sally to get it right over to you."
LYNN: "Well, it's not here and you know this isn't the first time something like this has happened . . . "

As a result of the day's events, Marty has accumulated more evidence that Sally is incompetent. Lynn has decided once and for all that she simply can't count on Marty, and Sally is convinced that Marty is always looking for a reason to criticize her. Although all of these conclusions may be justified, it is also quite possible that at least a partial explanation of what occurred is to be found in the words and phrases each person used and how they were interpreted. Initially, Lynn indicated to Marty that she needed the information for the afternoon meeting. Marty told Sally that it had "to go out this morning." But what did "go out this morning" mean? To Sally, who sent it out at 11:00 through the interoffice postal system—it meant *go out* this morning. To Lynn and Marty it meant *be delivered* this morning.

The same kind of difficulties arise in many other settings. For instance, hour after hour is spent in labor negotiations, for instance, arguing over the precise terminology to be used in a contract. Seemingly innocent words like "should," "will," "are," or "may" can become very problematic in these circumstances. See Figure 6–6.

LIMITATIONS OF LANGUAGE FOR REPRESENTATION

As intimate as is the relationship between language and reality, general semanticists caution that several characteristics of language limit its usefulness.[19]

The Principle of Nonidentity (A is not A). The principle of nonidentity reminds us that words are not the same order of "stuff" as the "realities" to which they refer. The world is perpetually in the process of changing, while our language available for making sense of it may not be. The reverse may also occur when language changes but the reality doesn't, as illustrated in Box 6–1.

A dramatic illustration of the representational limitations of language—and the manner in which these limitations can be overcome—is provided by the New Revised Standard Version of the Bible. The 1990

FIGURE 6–6 Minor differences in word choice—such as "should" versus "are" in the signs shown—may have a substantial impact on the significance a message will have.

Verbalize—Speak
Visualize—See
Within the framework of—Within
At this point in time—Now
Counterintuitive—Surprising
Is of the opinion—Believes
Oversight—Mistake

BOX 6–1 *Contemporary Words and Phrases and Their Translations.*
Source: Paul Dickson, *Slang! The Topic-by-Topic Dictionary of Contemporary American Lingoes*, New York: Pocket Books.

version is an update of the 1952 version, both of which are descendents of the 1611 *King James Bible.* Changes in the latest edition aim to make language more accurate, clearer, more contemporary, and more gender- and racially-sensitive, as shown in Box 6–2.[20]

As another example: who would have imagined fifty years ago that advances in electronics would mean that terms like floppy disk, joy stick, VCR, or compact disk would become household terms for so many of us?

The Principle of Non-allness (A is not all A). The principle of non-allness asserts that "the map is not the territory"—our language can

Mathew 4:4
  1952 Version: "Man does not live by bread alone."
  1990 Version: "One does not live by bread alone."
II Corinthians 11:25
  1952 Version: "Once I was stoned."
  1990 Version: "Once I received a stoning."
Song of Solomon 1:5
  1952 Version: "I am very dark, but comely."
  1990 Version: "I am black and beautiful."
Exodus 20:17
  1952 Version: "You shall not covet your neighbor's wife, or his manservant, or his maid-servant. . . .
  1990 Version: "You shall not covet your neighbor's wife, or male or female slave. . . . "

BOX 6–2 *Changing Language in the Bible.*
Source: Ari L. Goldman, "New Bible: 'He' Goes the Way of All Flesh," *The New York Times*, Sept. 28, 1990, p. A10.

never represent all of the object, event, or person to which we are referring. As Anatol Rapoport explains:

> . . . no matter how good a map you make, you cannot represent all of the territory in it. Translated into terms of language, it means that no matter how much you say about some "thing," "event," "quality," or whatnot, you cannot say all about it.[21]

The Principle of Self-reflexiveness. The principle of self-reflexiveness calls attention to the problems that can arise when we use language to talk about our use of language. When we use concepts to talk about concepts, we become increasingly abstract and move progressively into the world of words and away from the world of the tangible.

For example, our self-reflexive capability allows us to label ourselves "successes" or "failures" as if these were actual characteristics that have an existence apart from our representations of them. We may easily forget that one cannot *be* a success or failure but can only be *seen* or *interpreted* as such by someone.

Conversation

NEGOTIATION OF MEANINGS

We can also look at language from a social and interactional perspective. Through language we are able to coordinate our own activities with those of others, to undertake joint projects, to discuss and solve problems, and to share in the pursuit of personal and social needs.

From an interactional perspective, language is a tool for the negotiation of meanings between and among individuals. When we create a spoken or written message, our language serves as the medium to convey our representations. It is our means of projecting ourselves and our ideas into the environment.

As we have discussed previously, the messages we encode are based on meanings influenced by our own experiences, needs, and goals; and, to some extent at least, we are each unique in these terms. When others decode our messages, they do so in terms of the meanings our words have for them—based on their experiences, needs, goals, and capabilities. When I talk to you about my feelings about "dogs," I, of course, am using the word dog to refer to the "dogs-of-my-experience." When you decode my message, you do so in terms of the "dogs-of-your-experience." See Figure 6–7.

Thus, in any conversation (or written exchange), language serves as a medium through which individuals: (1) code or externalize meanings, and (2) decode and internalize meanings. As the interaction continues, language serves as the channel through which interactants may: (3) discover discrepancies and/or similarities in their meanings, and (4) consciously—and more often unconsciously—negotiate a mutuality of meaning appropriate to the purposes at hand. In some circumstances, we may be able to get along fine in a discussion about dogs if you are thinking of a poodle and I am thinking about a German shepherd. In other situations, a greater level of mutual understanding would be essential.

RULES AND RITUALS

We take our ability to converse with others very much for granted, so much so that it may seem like quite a simple activity. Clearly, this is not the case. As communication researcher Margaret McLaughlin indi-

"I can't think of a better companion than a dog. They are faithful, kind, affectionate. . . Sunshine is like a member of the family."

"I'd never think of going out at night without my dog by my side"

"DOG"

"I've never cared much for dogs as pets."

"I agree, dogs make great pets."

FIGURE 6–7 In everyday usage, we speak and listen based on the meanings words have for us, rather than in terms of dictionary definitions.

cates, our ability to engage in social intercourse presupposes that we have and can use an incredible amount of knowledge:

> . . . not only what we might call *world knowledge* (that groceries cost money, that parents love their children, that dogs bite, etc.), but also more specific knowledge bases, such as the rules of grammar, syntax, etiquette, and so on, as well as specifically *conversational rules* such as "When someone has replied to your summons, disclose the reason for the summons," and "Before saying good-bye to a telephone caller, reach agreement that all topical talk is completed." What is fascinating about conversation is that the ordinary person rarely reflects upon the vastness of the knowledge store that is required to carry it on.[22]

A *rule* is a prescription, regulation, or requirement. Some rules are obvious and explicit—like the rules of tennis, traffic regulations, or the requirements for membership in a formal group or organization. Other rules are implicit and subtle, like tennis etiquette, or the informal norms and practices expected of members of a group or organization. *Conversational rules* are those largely implicit and subtle regulations that guide our behavior in verbal interaction. They describe how one must, should, or should not behave in interactions with others.[23] Conversational rules facilitate cooperative effort, help to structure and regularize interaction, provide a basis for predicting patterns of communication, and guide us in interpreting the actions of others.

Speech scholars have identified a number of rules that guide our behavior in conversations. We can group these rules into the following categories:[24]

- Cooperativeness: Be sincere and make your contributions reasonable, given the agreed upon purpose of the conversation.
- Informativeness: Make your contributions as informative as possible or necessary.
- Responsiveness: Take account of and be responsive to the informational needs of others.
- Interactiveness: Share responsibility with other interactants for guiding and managing the conversation.
- Conformance: Know and follow accepted conversational practices. Inform others when you violate a rule.

Cooperativeness. Without some degree of cooperativeness and willingness to commit to interaction, conversation is impossible. H. Paul Grice, an important contributor to our understanding of conversational rules, called this general rule the *cooperative principle,* out of which flows other maxims of cooperation:[25] Don't state the obvious, or restate what others already know; don't be superfluous—don't say too much, and make your comments relevant to the topic at hand.

Informativeness. Conversation also normally involves a commitment to be informative: Don't knowingly mislead or say something you believe is false; don't exaggerate or say more than you know; and don't withhold or say less than you know.

Responsiveness. The obligation to be aware of and accommodating to the needs of other interactants involves inferring and responding to other's knowledge and beliefs, responding to questions and requests for information, using a manner and tone that takes account of the needs of other interactants, being clear, being courteous, and avoiding excessive boasting and self-promotion.

Interactiveness. Interactiveness also refers to rules governing the management of the conversation. These commitments have to do with conversational sequences and rituals, including:

1. Initiating interaction—initiating conversations and/or responding to the initiation efforts of others. If, for example, I say: "How are you?" the expectation is that you will participate in the initiation ritual by responding and will do so along the lines of: "Fine, and you?"
2. Establishing a conversational agenda—participating in the process of setting the agenda for discussion. If, for example, I say: "I guess our main topic of discussion today is how to handle the labor problem," the expectation is that you will either agree with the agenda as defined and allow it to guide the conversation or disagree and take the lead in suggesting another agenda.
3. Turn taking as the conversation progresses—sometimes termed *interaction management.* This is the expectation that interactants will "take turns" in speaking as a conversation progresses, avoiding monopolizing on the one hand and nonparticipation on the other.
4. Topic shifting—changing topics and/or responding to the topic changes of others. The expectation is that topic changes are suggested and agreed to or explicitly negotiated, rather than unilaterally imposed. If you are in the middle of an enthusiastic description of a recent trip to Europe, it is expected that I will not interrupt in the middle of your sentence or paragraph and begin talking about a

course I am thinking of taking. Rules call for me to wait until a natural break in the conversation occurs or to introduce a transition that is responsive to you. Thus, I might say: "Your talking about the trip reminds me of a new course I learned about while you were away. I really want to tell you about it. It sounds interesting."

5. Closing—terminating conversations and responding to termination initiatives by others—sometimes termed *leaving-taking.* The expectation is that leave-taking occurs by mutual agreement. That is, it is expected that I will not get up and walk away while you're in the middle of telling me about your trip. As with openings, there are a number of conversational rituals and conventions associated with conversational closings. Thus, a closing like, "OK, then, take care," and a response, such as, "You, too!" serve to signal the desire of the initiator to terminate conversation and provide a standardized way of dealing with what would otherwise be an ambiguous and potentially awkward circumstance.

Conformance. Conformance refers to the obligation to adhere to conversation rules or to provide an explanation when a violation occurs. The expectation is that we will follow rules in our conversations. When violations occur, the consequences are frequently negative. They may include confusion, frustration, misunderstanding, a loss of trust or liking among interactants, or a reinterpretation of the value and goals of the conversation by one or more of the parties involved.

There are any number of circumstances in which we violate rules. We may shift a topic abruptly, get up to leave in the middle of a conversation, exaggerate or understate, or say things we don't mean. There may be good reasons for these actions. When rule violations occur, we are expected to indicate this by explaining the reason for the violation. For instance, when you must interrupt or exit a conversation abruptly, an explanation that you just realized you're late for an important meeting, together with an apology, will help to excuse the rule violation.

One of the most blatant examples of rule violation happens when one interactant knowingly engages in deception. In such a circumstance, the informativeness rule and, hence, the sharing of information, have been undermined. When all other rules are followed, efforts to deceive may be quite successful. For instance, we may find ourselves persuaded by a cooperative, responsive, and interactive salesperson, even when some of the information provided about a product is incorrect. One of the reasons this occurs, of course, is that we are often better able to make accurate judgements about whether other rules are being followed than whether we are being told the truth. If the deception is detected, it is likely to have a substantial impact on the conversation and the meanings which result. The consequences of an attempt at deception will depend on the topic, the nature of the relationship between interactants, and the situation.

In some situations, interactants may say things that are untrue, but without the goal of deception. For example, we may say, "That's a lovely dress she bought," but when we are being sarcastic and don't intend our message to be taken literally, we can indicate this through tone of voice or facial expressions.

Rules and the significance of rule violations depend a good deal on the situation or context. Our expectations may differ depending upon whether we are interacting with an intimate friend or a stranger, a child or an adult, a member of the same or opposite sex, a salesperson or a member of the clergy, one other person or several others. Thus, contextual, gender, ethnic, racial, and cultural differences may all have an impact on conversational protocol.

LANGUAGE AND SEX DIFFERENCES

Researchers have identified differences between men and women in their use of language in conversation. The areas in which differences have been noted include: initiation, verbosity (the amount of talking), interruptions, conversational maintenance and question asking, and lexical and phonological characteristics.[26]

Initiation. Women generally spend more time initiating conversations than men. However, topics introduced by men are more likely to be taken note of and carried on by other interactants. The following exchange at a restaurant illustrates an all-too-familiar pattern:[27]

> MAUREEN: "What are you going to order?"
> TOM: "The bacon and cheddar burger."
> MAUREEN: "That sounds good. I think I'll have the chicken salad."
>
> After the order is taken, and a moment of silence. . . .
>
> MAUREEN: "I went to the mall yesterday to look for a dress for my sister's wedding."
> TOM: "Yeah?"
> MAUREEN: "But I couldn't find anything I liked. I guess I'll have to keep looking around."
> TOM: No response.

As Lea Stewart and colleagues explain: "This example illustrates one way men speaking with women inhibit conversations by giving minimal responses such as 'yeah' or 'oh' to topics introduced by women . . . and thereby violate turn-taking rules for conversation."[28]

Verbosity. Contrary to the stereotype, studies suggest that men generally talk more than women. In some studies, men talked four times as much as women. Men also use more words per utterance than women, especially if they are responding to negative criticism.

Interruptions. Men are more apt to interrupt than women, particularly in conversations between men and women. Some studies of recorded conversations indicate that as much as 75 percent of all interruptions were done by males.[29] Research on college-age students suggests that this difference may be decreasing as gender roles evolve. However, it appears that men use interruptions primarily as a means of controlling content, while women are more likely to use it for expressing support or meeting expectations for turn taking.

Conversational Maintenance and Question Asking. Women generally spend more time and effort facilitating the continuation of conversation, as is well illustrated in the restaurant dialogue discussed previously. Researchers have also found that when they analyzed tapes of actual conversations, 70 percent of the questions asked by interactants were posed by women.[30]

Lexical and Phonological Characteristics. Not surprisingly, studies show that women use a larger vocabulary to discuss topics about which they have greater interest and experience. And, conversely, in areas where men have greater expertise, their vocabularies are broader. There are also differences in the adjectives used by the two sexes. Words like *adorable, charming, sweet* and *lovely* are more likely to be used by women, while men are more apt to use terms such as *nice, good,* or *pretty.* Studies suggest that women use intensifying adverbs more than men—for example, I *really* enjoyed the book, or I'm *so* disappointed.

CONTENT AND RELATIONSHIP

Whether we use our words in a planned, intentional way or in a less systematic, unintentional fashion, verbal messages provide potential information of two types: (1) information about *content*—the topic under discussion, and (2) information about *relationships*—about the source and how the source regards the intended recipient(s).[31] A written or spoken presentation designed to convince us to vote for a particular candidate, for instance, includes *content* about the candidate, his or her qualifications, campaign promises, and potentials. Also, the presentation provides messages as to the level of preparation, interest, education, intelligence, attitudes, beliefs, mood, and motives of the speaker. And the speech may provide clues as to how the speaker regards the intended audience. Does the speaker "look down" on the audience? Does he or she consider them to be powerful, authoritative, educated? Does he or she fear or resent them?

To further clarify the distinction, consider the following statement:

MARGE: "Carol is an incompetent and uncaring person!"

From a content point of view, Marge is indicating that there are some things about Carol that bother her. Beyond that, Marge may also be providing some clues about herself. She seems to feel quite strongly about Carol. Perhaps she is a fairly outspoken individual. She may be quite an emotional person. Perhaps she is judgmental and intolerant of individual differences. Perhaps she is jealous or envious of Carol.

In her messages about Carol and herself, Marge may also be providing clues as to how she regards the person to whom she is speaking. It is likely that Marge sees herself as being, or wanting to be seen as being, closer to the person she's talking to than she is to Carol. It is also probable that Marge assumes the listener is closer to her than to Carol. One could also infer that she trusts the listener, that she simply doesn't care who knows how she feels about Carol, or that she is pursuing a specific personal motive. At the least, we can safely assume that Marge has some reason for wanting to share her reaction with the listener. In any case, her message has both a content and relationship component.

Consider two more complex examples:

1. Daddy: (Following the sound of breaking glass) "Marc."
   Marc: "Daddy, I didn't do it."
2. Ed: "Mary, I want to talk to you."
   Mary: "Ed, I know what you're going to say. I'm sorry, I never intended for you to get hurt . . . It just happened."

In all respects except the content, these two exchanges are quite similar. In each instance the first speaker is really saying very little from a topical point of view. In fact, in both cases, the speakers provide no information that identifies a topic for discussion. The second speakers, however, provide the basis for a number of inferences. Both Marc and Mary seem to assume they are being asked about a particular act, even though this is not necessarily the case. They respond *defensively*—as though they have been attacked. Their responses, perhaps motivated by guilt, fear, or both, are messages from which one could infer something about their feelings and attitudes. Their messages also provide the basis for inferences as to how they feel about the persons with whom they are interacting. Both Marc and Mary are concerned about their relationships, by necessity or choice. For whatever reasons, both seem to see themselves in a "one-down" or inferior position, in which they must justify, explain, and/or seek forgiveness or approval from Daddy or Ed.

Let's examine a slightly more complicated situation:

BILL: "My wife and I are really excited. We've got a chance to go to Las Vegas this weekend on a special half-price package. It wasn't really the time we had picked to go, but we just can't pass it up . . . Doubt we'll ever have a chance to go so cheaply again."

TODD: "I considered going, but with the economy the way it is, I decided it's not smart to spend money on travel this year."

In the brief exchange, Bill is providing information about the prospect of an upcoming trip. He's also explaining that it will cost only one-half the normal amount. The fact that Bill is talking about the trip at all may suggest that he's the type of person who enjoys sharing his excitement. Or he may be boasting; perhaps he is seeking attention or recognition.

By explaining that he got a special price, Bill may provide a clue that he wishes to be seen as clever, shrewd, or economical. Or, alternatively, his message may suggest that he is the kind of person who feels the need to justify or apologize for his good fortune. The decision to share his plans with Todd suggests that Bill cares about or values Todd, or that he wants to impress Todd, or to solicit support or encouragement.

Todd says that he does not think it is a smart time to spend money on a trip. Beyond this, his response may provide a clue that he is unwilling to share in Bill's excitement. He may be jealous. Or he may fail to detect Bill's excitement. Todd's response also may suggest that he wishes to be seen as more rational than Bill—at least in this instance. From a relationship perspective, it seems that he feels no obligation to acknowledge or contribute to Bill's excitement and has no particular interest in providing an audience for further discussion of Bill's trip.

METACOMMUNICATION

Sometimes we engage in conversations about our conversation; or to put it differently, we communicate about communication. This is termed *metacommunication.*[32]

1. Brenda: "Matt, let's go to a movie tonight."
2. Matt: "Oh, I don't know, Brenda. Can we talk about it later?"
3. Brenda: "That's becoming a pattern around here Matt. You never want to carry a discussion through to a conclusion."
4. Matt: "The pattern I see is the one where you refuse to end a conversation until you've gotten the decision you want."
5. Brenda: "Same old story. You can't handle any negative feedback. One small criticism, and you get real defensive"

In the first exchange above—(1) and (2)—Matt and Brenda are discussing the possibility of going to a movie. With Brenda's response (3), there is a shift from talking about the movie to talking about the way Matt responded. In his next response (4), Matt comments on Brenda's communication. Brenda continues the process of metacommunication as she replies (5), carrying forth a fairly common pattern of communication.

Social and Public Communication

PRODUCTION AND DISTRIBUTION OF SOCIAL REALITIES

Language is the primary means used for social and public expression. We are bombarded by public speeches on all topics, as well as by news, entertainment, advertisements, and public relations messages. These messages are a pervasive part of the environment in which we live. Messages and meanings which are widely distributed and popularized through public communication become accepted realities. As communication scholar Lee Thayer explains:

> What is uniquely characteristic of human communication . . . is the fact that (human) . . . sophistication . . . has made possible the emergence and evolution of a purely communicational environment or reality . . . i.e., an environment or reality comprised of anything that can be and is talked about. Whatever can be talked about comprises a reality in the sense that

> it must be adapted to and dealt with in much the same way as that reality which is subject to sensory validation (the physical environment).[33]

Thus, it is largely through social and public communication that the shared realities of language and meanings are created, perpetuated, reaffirmed, or altered. The story of the "Emperor's New Clothes" (Box 6-3) gives us insight into the powerful and pervasive nature of the basic process by which this happens. Messages are produced, distributed, believed, used, socially accepted, and eventually take on an objective reality that is seldom questioned.

Implications and Applications: Representation, Talk, Conversation, and Writing

- Language is our primary means for recording information for ourselves, and for producing and transmitting messages for others.

- Our use of language provides messages from which inferences are drawn about our interest in a particular topic, our preparation, attitudes, education, mood, motives, age, personality, concepts of ourselves, and our regard for our listeners, readers, or viewers.

- Verbal messages may be either oral or written. Written messages are well-suited to situations in which we desire a high degree of control and predictability over the message that is produced and transmitted, or in which a document or record of communication is required. However, compared to oral communication, written message sending and feedback require more time; and it is sometimes more difficult to change one's position once it has been committed to writing. Oral messages create a sense of spontaneity and provide for instantaneous feedback and adjustment of one's position or approach. They leave no document behind, which can be an asset in some circumstances and a liability in others.

- Our words and concepts are our tools for labeling the people, objects, and events around us.

- The relationship between language and reality is an intimate one. In everyday use, language often seems to work "as if it were real."

- There are many circumstances in life which remind us of the dangers of reacting to words as if they were the objects, people, or events to which they refer.

- Our representations are seldom, if ever, neutral or value free. They

The Emperor's New Clothes

In the great city in which he lived many strangers came every day. One day two rogues came. They said they were weavers, and declared they could weave the finest stuff anyone could imagine. Their colors and patterns were unusually beautiful, they said, and explained that the clothes made of the stuff possessed the wonderful quality that they became invisible to anyone who was unfit for the office he held or was not very bright or perceptive.

"Those would be most unusual clothes!" thought the Emperor. "If I wore those, I should be able to find out what men in my empire are not fit for the places they have; I could tell the clever ones from the idiots." He asked the men to begin weaving immediately.

They put up two looms, and pretended to be working. They at once demanded the finest silk and the costliest gold; this they put into their own pockets, and worked at the empty looms till late into the night.

After a few weeks passed, the Emperor said to himself, "I should like to know how far they have got on with the stuff." But he felt quite uncomfortable when he thought that those who were not fit for their offices could not see it. He believed, of course, that he had nothing to fear for himself, but he preferred first to send someone else to see how matters stood.

"I will send my honest old Minister to the weavers," thought the Emperor. "He can judge best how the stuff looks, for he has sense, and no one understands his office better than he." So the good old Minister went out into the hall where the two rogues sat working at the empty looms.

"Mercy!" thought the old Minister, and he opened his eyes wide. "I cannot see anything at all! Can I indeed be so stupid? Am I not fit for my office? It will never do for me to tell that I could not see the stuff."

"Haven't you anything to say about it?" asked one of the rogues, as he went on weaving. "It is charming—quite enchanting!" answered the old Minister, as he peered through his spectacles. "What a fine pattern, and what colors! Yes, I shall tell the Emperor that I am very much pleased with it."

The Emperor soon sent another honest officer of the court to see how the weaving was going on, and if the stuff would soon be ready. He fared just like the first: he looked and looked. "Isn't that a pretty piece of stuff?" asked the two rogues; and they displayed and explained the handsome pattern which was not there at all.

"I am not stupid!" thought the man. "Yet it must be that I am not fit for my office. If that is the case, I must not let it be noticed." And so he praised the stuff which he did not see, and expressed his pleasure at the beautiful colors and charming pattern. "Yes, it is enchanting," he told the Emperor.

All the people in the town were talking of the gorgeous stuff. The Emperor wished to see it himself while it was still upon the loom. With a whole crowd of chosen men, among whom were also the two honest statesmen who had already been there, he went to the two cunning rogues.

"Isn't that splendid?" said the two statesmen, who had already been there once. "Doesn't your Majesty approve of the pattern and the colors?" And they pointed to the loom, assuming that the others could see the stuff.

"What's this?" thought the Emperor. "I can see nothing at all! That is terrible. Am I stupid? Am I not fit to be Emperor?" He said aloud, "Oh, it is very beautiful! It is our highest approval." He nodded in a contented way, and gazed at the loom. . . .

BOX 6–3 The fable of "The Emperor's New Clothes," provides an excellent, though exaggerated illustration of the process by which our realities are created through language.

are influenced by our ways of thinking, and, in turn, they guide our thinking. Sometimes the influence is liberating; sometimes it constrains us. For instance, when we use sentences in which the structure is noun→verb→noun, we are more likely to think about the world, and communication, in cause-and-effect terms.

• The labels we use for ourselves—such as intelligent, attractive, poor, or unhappy—direct our thinking about ourselves down particular paths and not others. Likewise, the labels we use for other people—Moslem, wealthy, white, Jewish, or aggressive, for instance—also guide our ways of thinking about these people in particular ways, while discouraging other ways of viewing them.

• Language is also the means through which we converse and share points of view with others.

• In our conversations we expect others to follow a number of rules and rituals—regarding social initiation, turn taking, agenda setting, topic shifts, and leave-taking, for instance.

• We tend to think little about conversational rules until they are violated. When rules are broken, they often have a great impact on the conversation, on our impression of the rule breaker, and on our concept of the relationship.

• In some instances, women and men use language differently, as a consequence of different patterns of experience. Women are more forthcoming as conversation initiators, question askers, and conversation maintainers. Men may interrupt more often and may work harder to maintain control of conversations.

• Our verbal messages to others, and theirs to us, do two things simultaneously: (1) they relate specific content; and (2) they establish, comment on, reinforce, or alter relationships.

• As we engage in social or public communication, we take part in creating, distributing, reinforcing, or altering the meaning of language and the rules for its use.

Summary

Through our words, sentences, tone, appearance, actions, and other behaviors, we produce messages that are potentially significant sources of information for others. Some of the messages we encode intentionally, others more by accident. Decoding occurs when our messages are attended to and interpreted.

Most of our purposefully-created messages involve the use of language. Languages are similar to one another in several respects. All have rules relative to phonology, syntax, semantics, and pragmatics. Still more basic similarities result from the physiological and cognitive capacities of humans. The physiology of human speech is more advanced than that necessary for vocalizations in other species, and the differences between human mental abilities and those of other animals are even more pronounced. Particular areas of the brain—*Broca's Area* and *Wernicke's Area*—both of which are located in the left hemisphere, are thought to be critical to language use.

Our capacity for language develops from the time we are infants through a progressive series of stages. As adults, we use language not only to refer to the immediate environment as does the child, but also to record, describe, assert, express emotion, question, identify ourselves, entertain, humor, defend, and for a number of other purposes.

Language plays a central role in human interaction in terms of representation, conversation, and social and public communication. At the most basic level it is our means for representing and labelling elements of our environment and one another.

It is also by means of language that we negotiate understandings through conversation. Understanding the nature of conversation requires an awareness of the influence of rules and rituals, language and sex differences, content and relationship messages, and metacommunication. Additionally, language provides the medium through which social and public communication take place and the means through which shared communication realities are created.

Notes

1. William S-Y Wang, "Language and Derivative Systems," in *Human Communication: Language and Its Psychobiological Basis.* Ed. by William S-Y Wang (San Francisco: Freeman, 1982) p. 36.

2. Wang, 1982, p. 36.

3. Harold Whitehall, "The English Language," in *Webster's New World Dictionary of the American Language* (Cleveland: World, 1964), pp. xv–xxix.

4. Morton Hunt, *The Universe Within* (New York: Simon and Schuster, 1982), pp. 36–37.

5. What is named Broca's Area is based on the pioneering research by Paul Broca during the late 1800s. Wernicke's Area is named for German neurologist Karl Wernicke, who is acknowledged as the first to discover that damage to that section of the left hemisphere would lead to difficulties in speech comprehension. For a detailed discussion of the history and significance of this work to neurophysiology and speech, see *Left Brain, Right Brain,* by Sally P. Springer and George Deutsch (San Francisco: Freeman, 1981); "Specializations of the Human Brain," by Norman Geschwind in *Scientific American* (September 1979); Ross Buck, "Spontaneous and Symbolic Nonverbal Behavior and the Ontogeny of Communication," in *Development of Nonverbal Behavior in Children.* Ed. by R. S. Feldman (New York: Springer-Verlag, 1982) pp. 29–62; and an overview provided by Hunt, 1982.

6. Norman Geschwind, "Specializations of the Human Brain," in Wang, 1982, pp. 113–115.

7. Geschwind, 1982, p. 112. Also see discussion in Hunt, 1982, pp. 33–36.

8. Breyne Arlene Moskowitz, "The Acquisition of Language," in Wang, 1982, p. 122.

9. Moskowitz, 1982, p. 123.

10. Judith Coupe and Juliet Goldbart, *Communication before Speech.* London: Croon Helm, 1988, pp. 20–21.

11. The summary of stages in language acquisition is based upon an in-depth discussion provided in Barbara S. Wood, *Children and Communication* (Englewood Cliffs, NJ: Prentice Hall, 1976), pp. 24–27, adapted from Eric Lennedberg, "The Natural History of Language," in *The Genesis of Language.* Ed. by Frank Smith and George A. Miller (Cambridge, MA: M.I.T. Press, 1968), p. 222. See also, Moskowitz, 1982.

12. Moskowitz, 1982, p. 123.

13. Wood, 1976, pp. 112–113.

14. Adapted from Coupe and Goldbart, 1988, p. 25. Based originally on L. Leonard, "Semantic Considerations in Early Language Training," in *Developmental Language Intervention.* Ed by K. Ruder and M. Smith (Baltimore: University Park Press, 1984).

15. Moskowitz, 1982, p. 125.

16. Wood, 1976, pp. 25–26.

17. *Man, Myth, and Magic, Volume 1* (New York: Marshall Cavendish, 1970).

18. William O. Robertson, "Quantifying the Meanings of Words," *Journal of the American Medical Association,* Vol. 249, No. 19, 1983, pp. 2631–2632.

19. See discussion by Richard Budd in "General Semantics," in *Interdisciplinary Approaches to Human Communication.* Ed. by Richard W. Budd and Brent D. Ruben (Rochelle Park, NJ: Hayden, 1979). Reprinted by Transaction Books, New Brunswick, NJ.

20. Ari L. Goldman, "New Bible: 'He' Goes the Way of All Flesh," *The New York Times,* Sept. 28, 1990, p. A10.

21. Anatol Rapoport, "What Is Semantics," in *The Use and Misuse of Language.* Ed. by S. I. Hayakawa (New York: Fawcett, Premier Books, 1962), pp. 19–20.

22. Margaret McLaughlin, *Conversation: How Talk Is Organized* (Newbury Park, CA: Sage, 1984), pp. 13–14.

23. Adapted from Susan Shiminoff, *Communicative Rules: Theory and Research* (Beverly Hills, CA: Sage, 1980); See discussion in McLaughlin, 1984, p. 16.

24. Adapted from Mark Ashcraft, *Human Memory and Cognition* (Glenview, IL: Scott, Foresman, 1989), pp. 447–467, especially framework presented on p. 459. Based on the framework developed by H. Paul Grice, "Logic and Conversation," in *Syntax and Semantics, Vol. 3: Speech Actions.* Ed. by P. Cole and J. L. Morgan (New York: Seminar Press, 1975), pp. 41–58. And D. A. Norman and D. E. Rumelhart, *Explorations in Cognition* (San Francisco, Freeman, 1975); Ronald Wardhaugh, *How Conversation Works,* Oxford, England: Blackwell, 1985; and McLaughlin, 1984.

25. Grice, 1975; See discussion in Stephen W. Littlejohn, *Theories of Human Communication,* 3rd ed. (Belmont, CA: Wadsworth, 1989), pp. 165–166.

26. The framework and research summary presented in this section is based on Lea P. Stewart, Alan D. Stewart, Sheryl A. Friedley, and Pamela J. Cooper, *Communication between Sexes: Sex Differences and Sex-role Stereotypes,* 2nd ed. (Scottsdale, AZ: Gorsuch Scarisbrick, 1990), pp. 48–59. See also discussion in John Pfeiffer, "Girl Talk-Boy Talk," *Science,* Vol. 6, No. 1, Feb. 1985, pp. 58–63.

27. Based on dialogue provided Stewart and Associates, 1990, p. 52.

28. Stewart and Associates, 1990, p. 52.

29. Candice West and D. H. Zimmerman, "Small Insults: A Study of Interruptions in Cross-Sex Conversations between Unacquainted Persons," in *Language, Gender and Society.* Ed. by B. Thorne, C. Kramarae, and N. Henley (Rowley, MA: Newbury House, 1983), pp. 102–117, discussed in Pfeiffer, 1985.

30. P. M. Fishman, "Interaction: The Work Women Do," *Social Problems,* Vol. 25, pp. 397–406, 1978, discussed in Pfeiffer, 1985.

31. Paul Watzlawick, Janet H. Beavin, and Don D. Jackson, *Pragmatics of Human Communication* (New York: Norton, 1967), pp. 51–52.

32. Watzlawick and Associates, 1967, pp. 53–54.

33. Lee Thayer, "Communication—Sine Qua Non of the Behavioral Sciences," in Budd and Ruben, 1979. Reprinted by Transaction Books, New Brunswick, NJ.

References and Suggested Reading

ASHCRAFT, MARK. *Human Memory and Cognition.* Glenview, IL: Scott, Foresman, 1989.

BLOOMFIELD, LEONARD. *Language.* New York: Holt, 1933.

BROWN, ROGER. *Words and Things.* New York: Free Press, 1958.

BUDD, RICHARD W. "General Semantics." In *Interdisciplinary Approaches to Human Communication.* Ed. by Richard W. Budd and Brent D. Ruben. Rochelle Park, NJ: Hayden, 1979, 71–94.

BURLING, ROBBINS. *Man's Many Voices.* New York: Holt, 1970.

CHOMSKY, NOAM. *Aspects of the Theory of Syntax.* Cambridge, MA: M.I.T. Press, 1965.

COUPE, JUDITH, and JULIET GOLDBART. *Communication before Speech.* London: Croon Helm, 1988.

DE SAUSSAURE, F. *Course in General Linguistics.* Translated by W. Baskin, New York: Philosophical Library, 1959.

DEVITO, JOSEPH. *The Psychology of Speech and Language.* New York: Random House, 1970.

FISHMAN, P. M., "Interaction: The Work Women Do." *Social Problems,* Vol. 25, 1978, pp. 397–406.

FODOR, A., and J. J. KATZ. *The Structure of Language.* Englewood Cliffs, NJ: Prentice Hall, 1964.

GESCHWIND, NORMAN. "Specializations of the Human Brain." *Scientific American.* September 1979, 180–182.

GRICE, H. PAUL. "Logic and Conversation." In *Syntax and Semantics—Vol. 3: Speech Actions.* Ed. by P. Cole and J. L. Morgan. New York: Seminar Press, 1975.

HAYAKAWA, S. I. *Language in Thought and Action.* New York: Fawcett, 1962.

HUNT, MORTON. *The Universe Within.* New York: Simon and Schuster, 1982.

JOHNSON, WENDELL. *People in Quandaries.* New York: Harper, 1946.

KORZYBSKI, ALFRED. *Science and Sanity.* Lakeville, CT: The International Non-Aristotelian Library, 1948.

LAKEOFF, ROBIN. *Language and Woman's Place.* New York: Harper & Row, 1975.

LEE, IRVING. J. *Language Habits in Human Affairs.* New York: Harper, 1941.

LITTLEJOHN, STEPHEN W. *Theories of Human Communication. Third Ed.* Belmont, CA: Wadsworth, 1989.

NORMAN, D. A., and D. E. RUMELHART. *Explorations in Cognition.* San Francisco, Freeman, 1975.

MCLAUGHLIN, MARGARET. *Conversation: How Talk Is Organized.* Newbury Park, CA: Sage, 1984.

MILLER, GEORGE A., and F. SMITH, Eds. *The Genesis of Language.* Cambridge, MA: M.I.T. Press, 1966.

MOSKOWITZ, BREYNE ARLENE. "The Acquisition of Language." *Scientific American.* November 1978, 92–94.

PFEIFFER, JOHN. "Girl Talk-Boy Talk." *Science.* Vol. 6, No. 1, February 1985, 58–63.

RAPOPORT, ANATOL. "What Is Semantics." In *The Use and Misuse of Language.* Ed. by S. I. Hayakawa. New York: Fawcett, Premier Books, 1962.

SAPIR, EDWARD. *Language.* New York: Harcourt, 1921.

SEARLE, JOHN. *Speech Acts: An Essay in the Philosophy of Language.* Cambridge, England: Cambridge University Press, 1969.

SHIMINOFF, SUSAN. *Communicative Rules: Theory and Research.* Beverly Hills, CA: Sage, 1980.

SPRINGER, SALLY, and GEORGE DEUTSCH. *Left Brain, Right Brain.* San Francisco: Freeman, 1981.

STEWART, LEA P., ALAN D. STEWART, SHERYL A. FRIEDLEY, and PAMELA J. COOPER. *Communication Between Sexes: Sex Differences and Sex-role Stereotypes. Second Ed.* Scottsdale, AZ: Gorsuch Scarisbrick, 1990.

THAYER, LEE. "Communication—Sine Qua Non of the Behavioral Sciences." In *Interdisciplinary Approaches to Human Communication.* Ed. by Richard W. Budd and Brent D. Ruben. Rochelle Park, NJ: Hayden, 1979. Reprinted by Transaction Books, New Brunswick, NJ.

WARDHAUGH, RONALD. *How Conversation Works.* Oxford, England: Blackwell, 1985.

WANG, WILLIAM S-Y. "The Chinese Language." *Scientific American.* February 1973, 50–60.

———. "Language and Derivative." In *Human Communication: Language and Its Psychobiological Basis.* Ed. by William S-Y Wang. San Francisco: Freeman, 1982, 36–38.

WATZLAWICK, PAUL, JANET H. BEAVIN, and DON D. JACKSON. *Pragmatics of Human Communication.* New York: Norton, 1967, 51–52.

WEST, CANDICE, and D. H. ZIMMERMAN. "Small Insults: A Study of Interruptions in Cross-Sex Conversations between Unacquainted Persons." In *Language, Gender and Society.* Ed. by B. Thorne, C. Kramarae, and N. Henley. Rowley, MA: Newbury House, 1983, 102–117.

WHORF, BENJAMIN L. *Language, Thought, and Reality*. Ed. by J. B. Carroll. New York: Wiley, 1956.

WILLIAMS, FREDERICK, ROBERT HOPPER, and DIANA S. NATALICIO. *The Sounds of Children*. Englewood Cliffs, NJ: Prentice Hall, 1977.

WOOD, BARBARA S. *Children and Communication*. Englewood Cliffs, NJ: Prentice Hall, 1976.

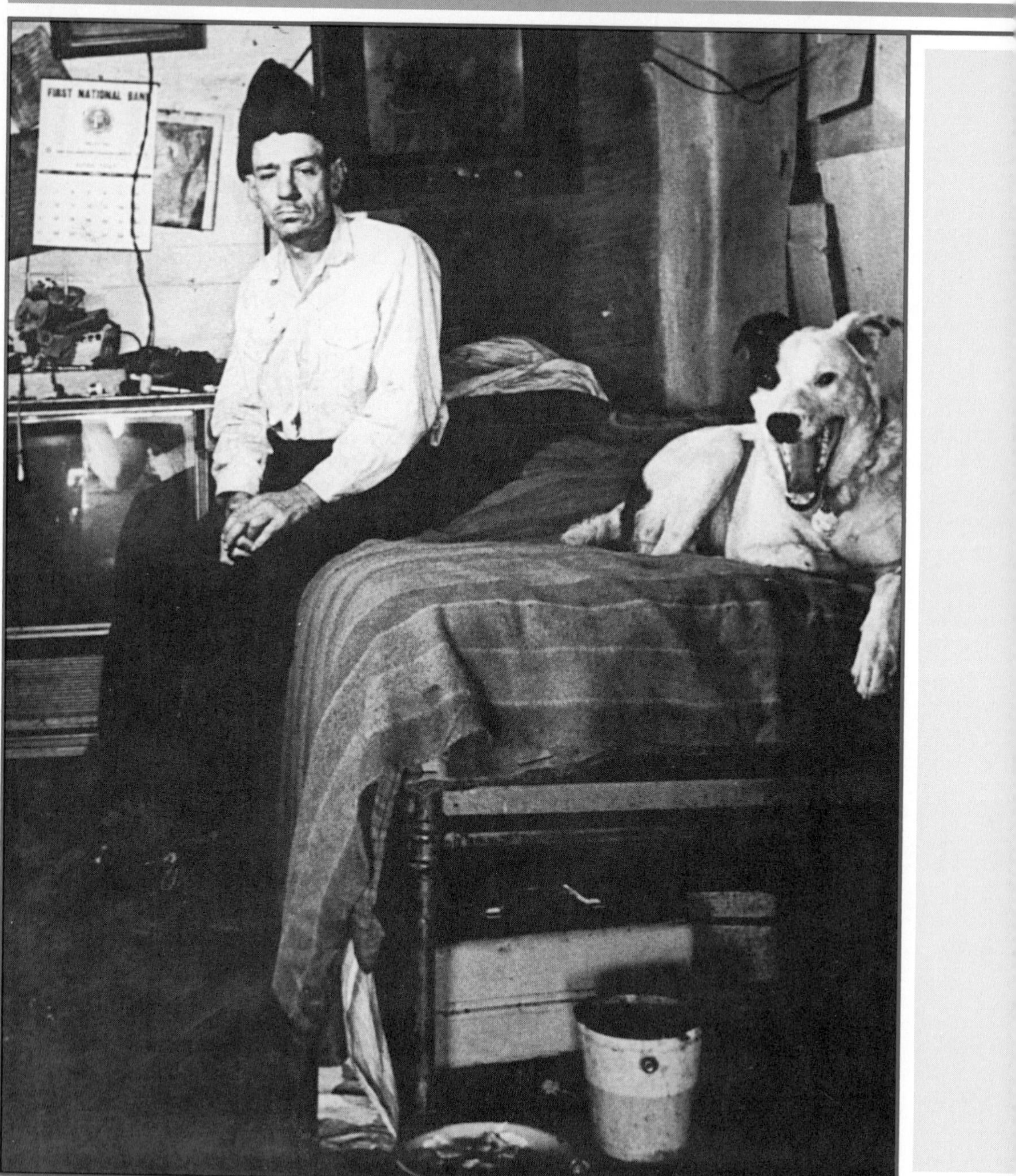
FIRST NATIONAL

7

Nonverbal Codes

> Kim walks over to a row of unoccupied chairs, places the briefcase and purse she is carrying on the seat to her right, and situates a Saks Fifth Avenue bag near her on the floor. She begins to leaf through the pages of *The Wall Street Journal,* glancing periodically at her watch and the TV monitor listing incoming flights.
>
> After about five minutes have passed, a middle-aged man dressed in a three-piece suit with a "carry-on" over his shoulder walks over and takes a seat directly across from her. As Kim glances up, her eyes catch his. He smiles, and she looks away. Kim concentrates her attention on the newspaper in front of her, but senses that the man is still staring. Finally, she notices him get up and walk away.
>
> Several minutes later he reappears, walks over to the seat next to her and sits down without saying a word. Seconds later, Kim picks up her briefcase, the newspaper, and shopping bag and walks rapidly toward the concourse. Shortly thereafter, the man gets up and heads off in the same direction.

Though no words are spoken in this scenario, the individuals' appearance, facial expressions, dress, actions, use of space and time provide important cues that are interpreted and acted upon. Based on the man's smile, eye contact, and physical movement, Kim concludes that the onlooker is taking more than a casual interest in her and removes herself from the situation.

You have probably also formed initial impressions of the two individuals based on nothing more than the sparse description of their nonverbal behavior. For instance, you may have concluded that Kim is

- carrying items she purchased at Saks Fifth Avenue;
- very conscious of the time;
- waiting for a plane; and
- employed in a professional position, probably finance.

The man in the three-piece suit, you may assume to be

- traveling;
- interested in initiating contact with Kim; and
- employed in business or a profession.

The formation of your reactions to the characters—and theirs to one another—based on nonverbal cues is not unique to this situation. Particularly in circumstances where we are forming first impressions, or where there are conflicts between words and actions, nonverbal codes are often far more influential than verbal codes. In fact, researcher Albert Mehrabian suggests that where we are confused about how we feel about another person, verbal messages account for only 7 percent of our overall impression, the remainder being accounted for by nonverbal factors:[1]

$$\text{Total Feeling} = 7\%\ \text{Verbal Impact} + 38\%\ \text{Vocal Impact} + 55\%\ \text{Facial Impact}$$

A great many nonverbal factors contribute to the global impressions people form. Sometimes impressions are accurate; often they are incorrect, exaggerated, or incomplete. In the situation just described, our first impressions may be correct. However, a number of other interpretations are possible. The Saks Fifth Avenue bag may have been given to Kim to carry several reports from her office. The frequent glances at her watch could have simply been a nervous gesture, and she may have been leafing through *The Wall Street Journal* for no better reason than she found it on the chair next to her. She might have been passing time before going to work at one of the shops in the airport. Or perhaps she was a plainclothes airport security guard.

The man in the suit may have been interested in establishing a personal relationship or simply a friendly person with no intentions that involved Kim. His actions may have been a response to hers, or any apparent connection could have been coincidental. Or, *he* may have been a member of the security staff with questions about the contents of the Saks bag and growing suspicions about Kim's very nervous behavior.

Even from this simple example, three important characteristics of nonverbal communication are apparent:

1. A number of factors influence nonverbal communication;
2. Nonverbal messages have a variety of meanings; and
3. The interpretation of nonverbal codes depends on the nonverbal messages themselves and also on the circumstance and the observer.

Similarities between Verbal and Nonverbal Codes

RULE-GOVERNED

Rules can be identified in nonverbal, as well as in verbal, codes. Some of these patterns pertain to the production of nonverbal messages and to the ways in which emotions are displayed. Still others are necessary to comprehend the significance of messages.

Rules associated with the creation of many nonverbal behaviors—a handshake, for instance—are similar to phonetics. Rules prescribing the appropriate sequence of nonverbal cues relative to one another—in meeting someone for the first time, for example—are a type of syntax. There are also general semantic patterns for many nonverbal behaviors that can be identified, and there are conventions as to when and how particular cues are to be used—a kind of pragmatics of nonverbal codes.

As with verbal codes, some patterns are common to the behavior of all individuals, regardless of personal or cultural differences. In facial expressions, for instance, studies suggest that there is a predictable relationship among emotions such as happiness, sadness, anger, or fear, and distinctive movements of facial muscles regardless of a person's personal and cultural background.[2] Gestures, such as the head nodding, which we associate with "yes" and "no," also seem to be universal, though their precise meanings may not be. Beyond the universal characteristics of nonverbal and verbal code systems are a great many more patterns that are unique to particular individuals, groups, regions, occupations, or cultures.

INTENTIONALITY

Most often, language is consciously used by people for the purpose of sending messages. This is the case in spoken, and especially written, communication. This is also often the case with nonverbal codes. We may consciously use particular facial expressions, gestures, and dress on a first date, job interview, or a group meeting, with the intention of creating a desired effect.

Both verbal and nonverbal messages may also be produced and transmitted unintentionally. Unintentional cues, like frowning out of nervousness when being introduced to someone for the first time, can have as much information value as poor grammar or run-on sentences.

COMMON MESSAGE FUNCTIONS

Verbal or nonverbal behavior may bear any one of several relationships to one another.[3] (1) Messages may be *redundant* and duplicate one another, as when a person says, "I am going to sit down," and then walks over to a chair and sits. (2) They can also *substitute* for one another, as when a handshake substitutes for "Hello, it's nice to meet you." (3) Verbal and nonverbal messages may be *complementary*, as when an individual smiles and says, "Come in, I'm glad to see you." (4) A verbal or nonverbal code may also be used to add *emphasis* to the other, such as making a fist to underscore a point being made verbally. (5) Verbal and nonverbal codes can also be sources of *contradiction*, as would be the case if we were told how interested another person was in hearing our thoughts, while the "listener" stared across the room at a member of the opposite sex. (6) Both types of codes can be used for *regulation*—controlling the communication process, determining who will speak, for how long, and even when changes in topic will occur.

Differences between Verbal and Nonverbal Codes

AWARENESS AND ATTENTION

There has been general lack of awareness of the nonverbal codes in comparison with language. Only during the last several decades has nonverbal communication emerged as an area of extensive scholarly study and a topic of popular articles and books.

This contrast is most apparent when one considers the manner in which training in the two areas is handled in our schools. Proficiency in the use of verbal codes is, in fact, considered to be so important that it is regarded as one of "the basic skills;" and great effort is expended to ensure that we are taught rules of pronunciation, syntax, semantics, and pragmatics as a part of our formal education. Theory and practice in the written and oral use of language are provided at virtually all educational levels.

By comparison, nonverbal skills receive little attention in most schools. Music, art, and physical education *are* generally included as part of the curriculum. However, no proficiency training comparable to composition, literature, or public speaking is provided for the nonverbal competencies that are so vital to human communication.

OVERT AND COVERT RULES

One of the explanations for the relatively greater emphasis placed on verbal codes is that there are *overt rules* and structure for language and language use. As a consequence, this information is provided in various sources. Nothing comparable exists for nonverbal codes. There are no nonverbal dictionaries or style manuals. And, other than books on etiquette, fashion, and body language, there are no guides to nonverbal code usage.

We learn the *covert rules* of nonverbal communication more indirectly, through observation, and subtle—and sometimes not so subtle—patterns of reward and punishment.[4] Thus, we "know the rules" for greeting and expressing affection to others nonverbally—when to shake hands, for how long, how hard to squeeze the other person's hand, and when hugs and kissing are appropriate—but these rules are covert. Few of us are conscious of their role in governing our behavior or are able to articulate the rules involved.

CONTROL

While we devote considerable attention to managing our nonverbal communication in some situations, we are often more successful in controlling our verbal messages. If the goal is to convey our competence or grasp of a situation, for example, most of us are better able to control the impression we create verbally than nonverbally. Through planning and rehearsal, we will probably be able to gain predictability regarding the messages we will send verbally. However, despite our best efforts to manage our nonverbal behavior, nervousness or embarrassment may be quite apparent through *nonverbal leakage*—a trembling voice or sweaty palm, for instance.

PUBLIC VS. PRIVATE STATUS

Language usage patterns have long been regarded as a topic that is appropriate for public discussion and scrutiny. Teachers, parents, or friends are generally quite willing to ask us questions when they don't understand what is being said or to comment when they disagree. However, matters relating to one's appearance, gestures, mannerisms, and body positions are generally considered private, personal, and even taboo topics, and are therefore far less likely topics of open discussion, analysis, or critique.

HEMISPHERIC SPECIALIZATION

Another major difference and a topic of scholarly interest is the location in the brain in which nonverbal activities are centered. As we noted, the left hemisphere of the brain is thought to play a predominant role in language processes.[5] Other activities which require the sequential processing of information, such as mathematics, seem also to rely heavily on the left hemisphere. The right hemisphere is of special significance in the recognition of faces and body images, art, music and other endeavors where integration, creativity, or imagination are involved.[6]

Studies show that some individuals with damage in the right hemisphere have difficulty with location and spatial relationships, recognition of familiar faces, or recognition of scenes or objects. Other research, which argues convincingly in favor of right-hemisphere specialization, has shown that even where damage to the language centers in the left hemisphere is so severe that the patients may have difficulty speaking, the ability to sing is often unaffected.[7]

There is substantial evidence that the contributions of the two hemispheres of the brain are in some sense distinctive. Recent research by Ross Buck indicates, however, that *symbolic* (intentional) activity is processed in the right hemisphere while *spontaneous* (unintentional) behavior occurs primarily in the left brain.[8] This means that some verbal processing takes place in the right brain, and some nonverbal activity occurs in the left brain. What remains to be determined is whether differences in the *locations* of verbal and nonverbal information processing are indicative of more fundamental differences in the *manner* in which these codes are handled by the brain.

Types of Nonverbal Codes

In the remainder of this chapter, we will examine six categories of nonverbal cues:

- Paralanguage
- Appearance
- Gestures
- Touch

- Space
- Time

Paralanguage

What we say—using words, phrases, and sentences—is obviously important to communication. However, the way we use language can be even more important than our words as sources of information. *Paralanguage* refers to any message that accompanies and supplements language. Technically speaking, any supplemental nonverbal message can be viewed as an instance of paralanguage.

VOCALIC FORMS

One focus of our discussion of paralanguage will be on *vocalics*—auditory messages, other than words, created in the process of speaking.[9] Vocalics, which includes pitch, rate of speech, rhythm, coughs, and giggles, nasality, pauses, even silence, are very significant sources of impressions in face-to-face communication.[10] Recall that Mehrabian found that when an individual is confused in his or her feelings about another person, vocal messages accounted for 38 percent of the impression that is formed.[11]

Long before children develop skill in language use, they have a familiarity with the tonal pattern of the language in their surroundings. Some recent studies suggest that from the tonal contours of the babbling, it is possible to identify the language environment in which a child lives, even as early as the second year of life.[12] The paralinguistic patterns acquired by children reflect not only the language patterns of the region in which they are being raised but also the unique patterns of family and friends.

With spoken language, paralinguistic cues such as loudness, rate of speaking, tone, interjections, pitch variation, and use of pauses can have a major influence on whether and how one reacts to the individual and his or her verbalizations. On the basis of pitch, for example, we are able to determine whether a particular utterance is a statement or a question, a serious comment, or a sarcastic barb. Whether "really" spoken orally is interpreted as "Really?" or "Really!" is determined through paralanguage rather than through the word itself. In the same way, we decide whether, "That's beautiful," is to be taken literally or to mean quite the opposite.

Pitch is also the difference between whether "Can I help you?" creates a positive or negative impression. Spoken with a raised pitch at the end of the sentence, the sense is one of politeness and genuine interest. The same words, spoken in a monotone are likely to be taken as rudeness and disinterest.

In some languages, paralanguage is even more essential to communication than it is in English. In Chinese, tones determine the meaning of words, as illustrated in Figure 7–1. Standard Chinese has only four tones: falling (as in *MA*), rising *(MA)*, level *(MA)* and dipping, or falling and then rising *(MA)*.[13] The drawings on the right show the voice pattern as the words are spoken. Changing the tone has the same kind of effect on the meaning of a word as changing a vowel or a consonant would in English.

Interjections *(nonfluencies)*—such as "like," "a," "huh," "so," or "you know"—and stuttering may also have an impact upon the way an utterance is interpreted. Consider the potential difference in the impressions and likely impact created by each of the following:

> Sam: "Like do you want to like go now or like later?"
> Shawn: "Do you want to go now or later?"

Although the words used are essentially the same, the meanings we would attach to these two messages, and the inferences we would draw about their sources, are likely to be very different. Based on first impressions, would you rather hire Sam or Shawn to represent your company to the public? With whom would you prefer to go out on a date?

As suggested by previous examples, paralanguage provides a basis for inferences about a speaker, as well as having a potential influence on the impact of the content of the message. Rate of speed and accent, for example, can provide the basis for inferences as to nationality, the region of the country in which the person was raised, and other characteristics associated with stereotypes about the geographic locale. The linguistic patterns of the "fast-talking New Yorker" or "the slow-speaking Southerner," are often associated with behavioral, as well as geographic, characteristics. Paralanguage can also provide the basis for assumptions about the speaker's educational level, interest in the topic, and mood. Moreover, tone, pitch, rate of speech, and volume provide clues as to an individual's emotional state.

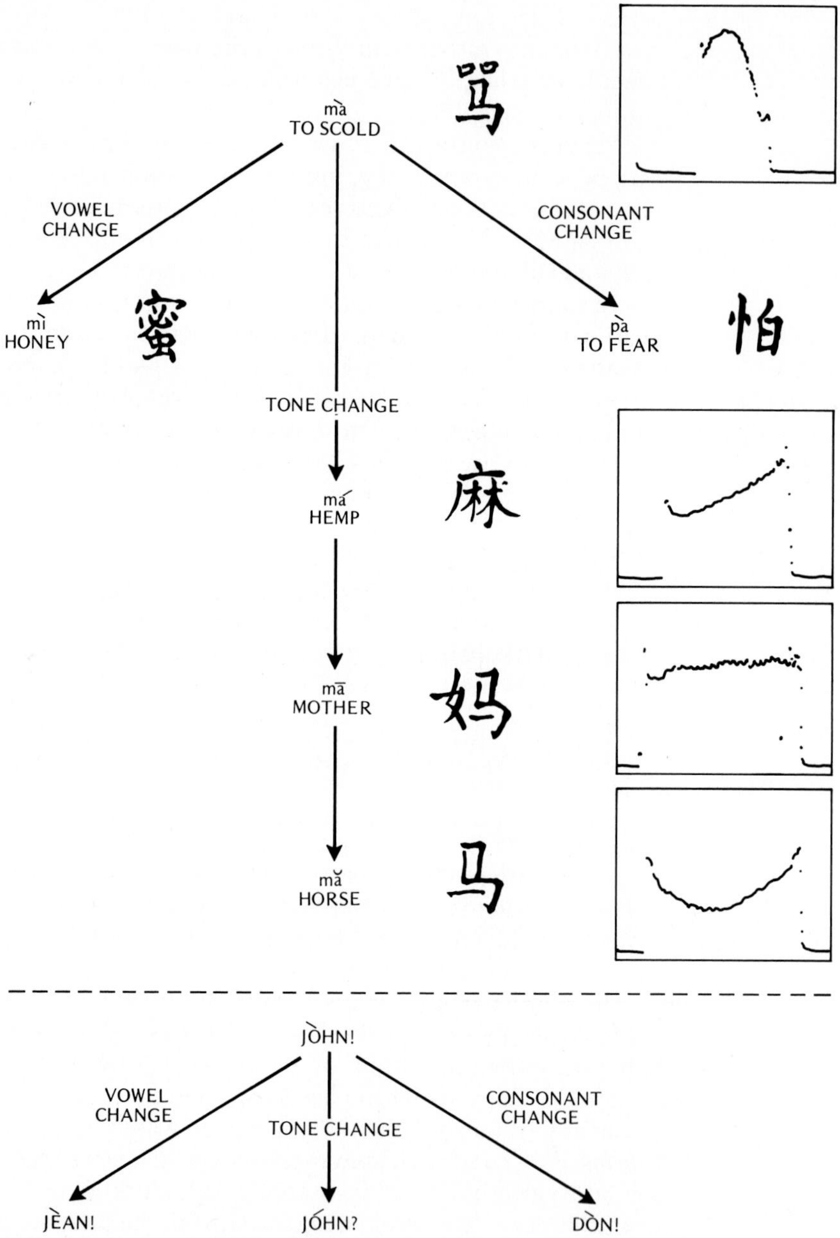

mà
TO SCOLD 骂

VOWEL CHANGE

CONSONANT CHANGE

mì
HONEY 蜜

pà
TO FEAR 怕

TONE CHANGE

má
HEMP 麻

mā
MOTHER 妈

mǎ
HORSE 马

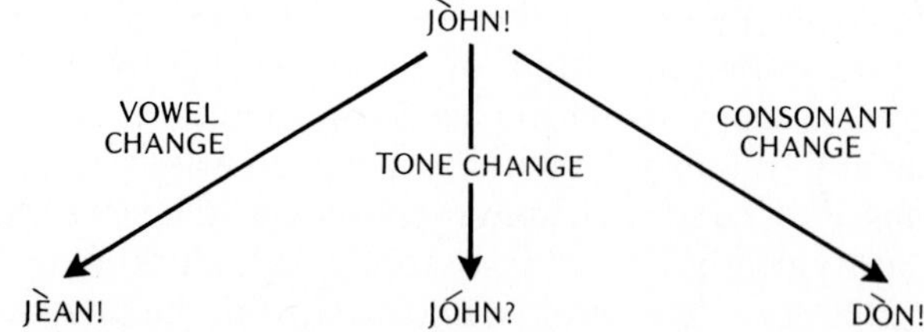

FIGURE 7–1 *Paralanguage Is Essential to Language Use in Chinese.*

Source: William S—Y Wang, "The Chinese Language," in *Human Communication: Language and Its Psychobiological Bases.* Copyright © 1973 by Scientific American, Inc. All rights reserved.

WRITTEN FORMS

Up to this point we have been discussing paralanguage as it relates to *spoken* language. The form of a word or statement is also important to interpretation in *written* language use. The visual appearance of written materials, in terms of punctuation, spelling, neatness, the use of space for margins and between words, whether the document is typed or handwritten, and even the color of ink are likely to influence the reader's reaction to the words and its source.

In written language, paralinguistic cues serve as a basis for generalized inferences as to how educated, careful, respectful, or serious a person is, and may provide clues as to his or her mood or emotions at the time of writing. See Figure 7–2. These in turn, may affect the way others think about and relate to the author.

Appearance

It is said that "Beauty is only skin-deep," and "You can't judge a book by its cover." However, there is little doubt that, particularly when other

FIGURE 7–2

sources of information are lacking, "surface-level" messages play a critical role in human communication.

Particularly in the formation of initial impressions, appearance is probably the single most important information source. Perhaps the most dramatic evidence as to the importance of appearance comes from studies of dating preferences, from which it has been determined that attractiveness was more important than such factors as religion, race, self-esteem, academic achievement, aptitude, personality, or popularity, in determining how well partners would like one another.[14] Evidence from other studies suggests that physical attractiveness is not only important to dating preferences but also is often a predictor of how successful, popular, sociable, sexually attractive, credible, and even how happy people are.[15]

A number of factors contribute to appearance, among them one's *face, hair, eyes, physique, dress, adornment,* and *artifacts.*

THE FACE

Generally speaking, we react to a person's face holistically. That is, when we look at someone's face, we get an overall impression and seldom think the face in terms of its distinctive features. Yet as nonverbal communication researcher Mark Knapp explains:

> The human face comes in many sizes and shapes. There are triangular, square, and round faces; foreheads may be high and wide, high and narrow, low and wide, low and narrow, protruding or sunken; the complexion of a face may be light, dark, coarse, smooth, wrinkled, or blemished; eyes may be balanced, close, far apart, recessed or bulging; noses can be short, long, flat, crooked, "hump-backed," a "bag," or a "ski slope"; mouths may be large and small with thin or thick lips; ears, too, may be large or small, short or long, and can bulge or appear sunken.[16]

Beyond their significance in contributing to one's overall appearance, facial expressions serve as message sources in their own right, providing probably the best source of information as to an individual's emotional state—happiness, fear, surprise, sadness, anger, disgust, contempt, and interest.[17] Our feelings are often, as the adage suggests, "written all over our faces." It has been estimated that our faces are capable of creating 250,000 expressions.

Researchers believe that the role of the face in relation to emotion is common to all humans. Describing what has been termed a "neurocultural theory of facial expression," Paul Ekman explains: "What is universal in facial expressions of emotion is the particular set of facial muscular movements when a given emotion is elicited."[18] The specific events and circumstances that *trigger* emotions vary from one individual and culture to another.[19] The emotions evoked by ceremonies accompanying death, for instance, may vary greatly from one person to another depending upon the individual's personality and the way the event is viewed in the given culture.

The customs and rules guiding the *display* of particular emotions also may vary from person to person, and culture to culture. For any emotion, exaggeration, understatement, and masking (deception) may occur.[20] An employee might exaggerate or mask an emotion, for example, when learning that a promised "healthy raise" only amounts to two percent.

TABLE 7–1 **Nonverbal Information Sources**

***Paralanguage* (Vocalics)**
- Vocalic Forms
- Written Forms

Appearance
- Face
- Hair
- Eye Gaze
- Pupil Dilation
- Physique
- Dress
- Adornment
- Artifacts

***Gestures* (Kinesics)**
- Baton Signals
- Guide Signs
- Yes-no Signals
- Greetings and Salutation Displays
- Tie Signs
- Isolation Gestures
- Preening Gestures

***Touch* (Haptics)**

***Space* (Proxemics)**
- Personal Space
- The Physical Environment

***Time* (Chronemics)**
- Timing
- Timeliness

TABLE 7–2 Specific Nonverbal Behaviors That Contribute to Attractiveness Beyond Dress and General Appearance

Warm Behaviors	Cool Behaviors
Looks into eyes	Gives cold stare
Touches hand	Sneers
Moves toward individual	Gives a fake yawn
Smiles frequently	Frowns
Works eyes from head to toes	Moves away
Has a happy face	Looks at the ceiling
Smiles with mouth open	Picks teeth
Grins	Shakes head negatively
Sits directly facing individual	Cleans fingernails
Nods head affirmatively	Looks away
Puckers lips	Pouts
Licks lips	Chain-smokes
Raises eyebrows	Cracks fingers
Has eyes wide open	Looks around the room
Uses expressive hand gestures while speaking	Picks hands
Gives fast glances	Plays with hair
Stretches	Smells hair

Source: G. L. Clore, N. H. Wiggins, and S. Itkin, "Judging Attraction from Nonverbal Behavior: The Gain Phenomenon," *Journal of Consulting and Clinical Psychology* 43 (1975), pp. 491–497. Copyright © 1975 by the American Psychological Association. Adapted by permission of the author.

HAIR

Hair and beard length, color, and style also are important nonverbal message sources. These factors contribute to overall attractiveness and may also serve as the basis of inferences as to one's personality, age, occupation, attitudes, beliefs, and values.

EYE GAZE

Probably the most impactful features of the face in terms of communication are the eyes.

As Ellsworth notes:

> Unlike many nonverbal behaviors having a potential cue-value that is rarely realized, such as foot movements, [or] subtle facial or postural changes, a direct gaze has a high probability of being noticed. For a behav-

TABLE 7–3 Stages in Emotional Development and Nonverbal Expression

Stage	Age	Characteristics	Sample Emotions
1	to 3 mos.	Wild, irregular, jerky movements of the entire body.	excitement, distress
2	3-5 mos.	Regular, rhythmic movements of the entire body.	anger, delight
3	5-14 mos.	Making faces, turning the head and poking: specific movements.	affection, fear, elation
4	14-24 mos.	Contact movements (pokes, hits, caresses) to others.	affection for child, affection for adult, jealousy, joy

Source: Barbara S. Wood. *Children and Communication* (Englewood Cliffs, N.J.: Prentice Hall, 1976), p. 197, adapted from "Emotional Development in Early Infancy," *Child Development,* 1932, 3.

ior that involves no noise and little movement, it has a remarkable capacity to draw attention to itself even at a distance.[21]

As significant as eye behavior is to human communication, most of us are relatively unsophisticated in our awareness of eye behaviors and our ability to characterize them with any precision. Among those who study this facet of our nonverbal behavior, a number of terms have been advanced that assist in description:[22]

- Face contact—looking at a person's face.
- Eye contact (or eye gaze)—looking at a person's eyes.
- Mutual gaze—mutual gazing by two individuals at one another's face.
- One-sided gaze—one person looking at another's face, but the behavior is not reciprocated.
- Gaze avoidance—one person actively avoiding another's eye gaze.
- Gaze omission—one individual failing to look at another, but without the intention of doing so.

As children, we have heard many times that "it's not polite to stare;" and, as adults, there are frequent reminders of the "rule." If one stops at a traffic light, and the person in the next car looks interesting, one may "steal a glance;" but one is careful not to appear to stare. Similarly, while waiting in line at a grocery store, or sitting in a restaurant or other public place, we may casually glance at the people around, but generally

FIGURE 7–3

must at the same time try to appear as though we are not noticing the other person or persons at all.

Actually, the rule that we apply as adults is, "It's not polite to stare at people whom you don't know very well, unless you can do so with-out having them notice you." When and if we are noticed, we pretend not to have been looking, unless the intent is to violate the other's expectations.

The rules for eye contact with friends and acquaintances are quite different from those for strangers. When conversing verbally with even a casual acquaintance, some degree of mutual eye gaze is customary. "Looking" may help in grasping the ideas being discussed and is an indication of attention and interest. Among close friends, extended eye con-

FIGURE 7–4 In addition to contributing to overall appearance, one's face and hair provide the basis for inferences as to one's emotional state, age, mood, interest level, personality, and reaction to events and people.

tact is not only acceptable, but is expected. In the case of intimate friends and lovers, prolonged glances may be exchanged periodically even when no accompanying words are spoken.

There are a number of other situations where eye glances are "optional." For instance, when a speaker asks a question of a large audience, each member of the group may choose to engage or avoid the glance of the speaker. Generally, the likelihood of being called on to answer the question is considerably greater if one looks at the speaker than if one looks away.

At what and whom we look, for how long, under what circumstances, whether the gaze is one-sided or mutual, and whether we are engaged in gaze omission or gaze avoidance, provide the basis for inferences as to our focus of attention, interests, intentions, and even attitudes. Looking may be a matter of observing, orienting, inspecting, concealing, avoiding, or searching for pacification.[23]

Researchers have demonstrated that a primary function of eye gaze, or the lack thereof, is to regulate interaction. Eye contact serves as a signal of readiness to interact, and the absence of such contact, whether intended or accidental, tends to reduce the likelihood of such interaction.[24] Other studies suggest that eye gaze also plays an important role in personal attraction. Generally speaking, positive feelings toward an individual and high degree of eye contact go together. Perhaps for this reason, we often assume that people who look our way are attracted to us. Studies indicate, further, that individuals who engage in high levels of eye gaze are typically seen as more influential and effective in their dealings than others.

A number of factors have been shown in research to be related to the extent of eye gaze, including distance, physical characteristics, personality, topic, situation, and cultural background.[25] Based on this research, one can predict that, generally, more eye contact will occur when one is physically distant from others, when the topic being discussed is impersonal, and when there is a high degree of interest in the other person's reactions. Greater eye contact also occurs when one is trying to dominate or influence others, comes from a culture that emphasizes eye contact during conversation, is generally outgoing, striving to be included, listening rather than talking, or when one is dependent on the other person.[26]

One would expect less gazing between persons who are physically close, when intimate topics are being discussed, when there are other relevant objects or people nearby, or when they are not particularly interested in another's reactions or are embarrassed. Similarly, if an individual is submissive, shy, sad, ashamed, attempting to hide something, or of higher status than the person with whom he or she is talking, less eye contact is likely.[27] Obviously, these are generalities which may not apply in a given circumstance.

PUPIL DILATION

The pupils of the eye can be an indication of one's interest or attraction. As one looks at people or objects that are seen as appealing, the pupils tend to enlarge; and, in at least some experimental settings, there is evidence that pupil size can be a factor in judgments of a person's attractiveness. In these studies, pictures of females with enlarged pupils were consistently rated as more attractive by males than were those of women with small pupils.[28] It is also interesting to note, in this regard, that the drug Belladonna (meaning literally, "beautiful woman") has a tradition of use by women as a cosmetic to increase the size of their pupils with the thought that in so doing they would enhance their attractiveness.

The extent to which pupil size is actually a useful source of information is still a question. Particularly in a culture such as ours, in which we stand so far apart during most conversations, it is difficult to discern the size of another person's pupils, even when making an effort to do so. In Middle Eastern cultures, however, where the standard distance separating people during conversations is much smaller, information based on pupil size is more usable. Some authors have noted in this connection that sunglasses are often worn by persons in these cultures as a means of concealing pupil size.[29]

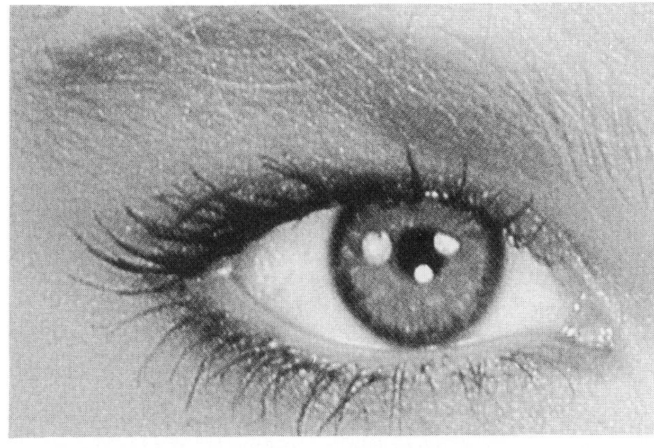

FIGURE 7–5 Research suggests that when one looks at an individual or object that is of interest or seen as attractive, the viewer's pupils dilate. Baby pictures shown to single women, married but childless women, and mothers resulted in pupil dilation. The same pictures shown to single men and married but childless men resulted in pupil constriction. Fathers viewing the pictures experienced pupil dilation.

Source: H. Hess, *The Tell-Tale Eye* (New York: Van Nostrand Reinhold, 1975) and Desmond Morris, *Manwatching* (New York: Abrams, 1977).

PHYSIQUE

An additional factor that contributes to appearance is physique. Studies have suggested, for example, that inferences are often drawn about personality based on *somatype*—body shape and size. People who appear to be "soft," "round," and overweight may be assumed to be affable, affectionate, calm, cheerful, complacent, extroverted, forgiving, kind, softhearted, and warm. People who appear to be muscular, bony, and athletic-looking are often stereotyped as being active, argumentative, assertive, competitive, confident, dominant, hot-tempered, optimistic, reckless, and nonconforming; and people who are tall and thin in appearance are often assumed to be aloof, anxious, awkward, cautious, cool, introspective, meticulous, sensitive, shy, and conforming. Although most studies find a match between particular physical traits and people's *perceptions*, there is little correlation between somatypes and actual behavioral characteristics.

One's height alone may also provide the basis for stereotyping. For males in our culture, greater height is often associated with positive qualities, while, beyond a certain point, the opposite is the case for females. Where these biases operate, they may be a consequence of primitive, subconscious reactions. Canadian psychologist John Gillis in his book *Too Tall, Too Small* provides the following interesting findings:[30]

- All U.S. presidents except for James Madison (5-foot-4) and Benjamin Harrison (5-foot-6) have been taller than the average height of men of their time.
- In the past twenty-one presidential elections, the taller man won seventeen times.
- Richard Nixon was perceived by his supporters to be taller than John F. Kennedy; Kennedy's supporters believed he was taller. Both men were actually six feet tall.
- Michael Dukakis was the shortest nominee of a major party since Thomas E. Dewey (5-foot-8) in 1944, and Harry S Truman (5-foot-9) in 1948.

DRESS AND ADORNMENT

Dress fulfills a number of functions for us as humans, including decoration, physical and psychological protection, sexual attraction, self-assertion, self-denial, concealment, group identification, and display of status of role.[31] Cosmetics, jewelry, eyeglasses, tatoos, hair pieces, false eyelashes, and permanents serve many of these same ends.

Nonverbal communication scholar Dale Leathers writes: "Our social identity and image is defined, sustained and positively or negatively modified by communication through appearance."[32] Dress is the major facet of appearance through which we can exercise control over communication. We generally assume that people make conscious choices about what they wear and therefore take their dress to be an important source of messages about them.[33]

Dress and adornment are noteworthy and often utilized as the basis for judgments as to gender, age, approachability, financial well-being, class, tastes, values, and cultural background.

Dress also provides the messages from which inferences are drawn relative to more basic facets of our personalities. It has been suggested by some researchers, for instance, that individuals who show particular interest in their dress tend to be conventional, compliant, persistent, suspicious, and insecure.[34] Persons who were particularly concerned with economy in dress were found to be responsible, efficient, precise, and intelligent. Others who dressed in close conformity with current styles were generally sociable, traditional, and submissive.

Badges of various kinds also provide information about the identity,

FIGURE 7–6 In addition to providing a source of basic information as to sex, age, occupation, and group affiliation, dress also often plays a critical role in first impressions.

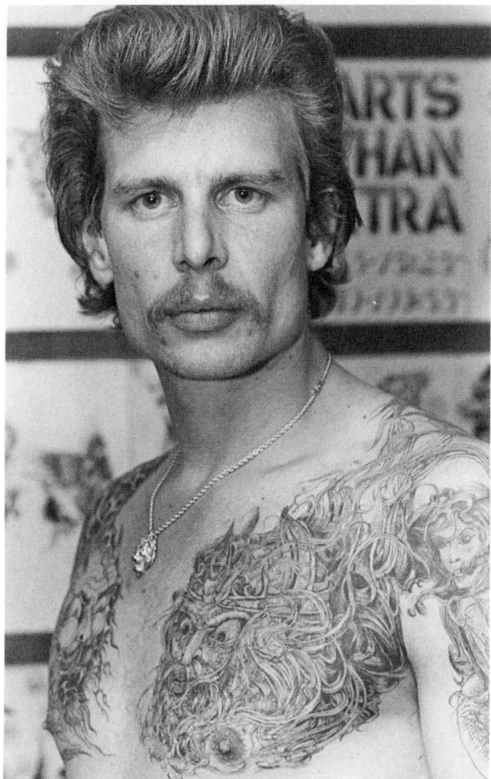

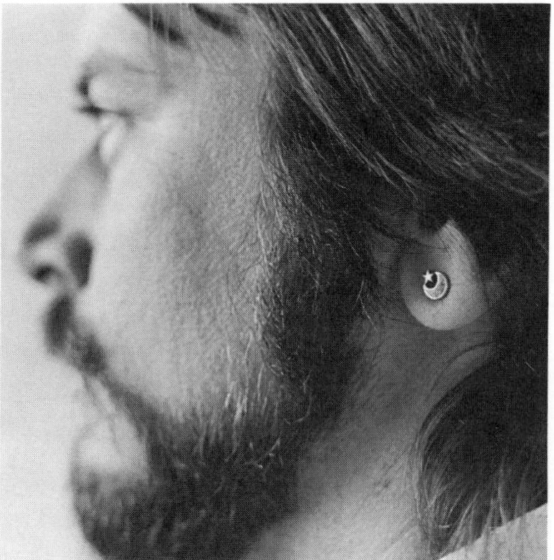

FIGURE 7–7 Jewelry, hair, beards, make-up, and other bodily adornments are also potential information sources.

status, or affiliations of an individual. Often one's dress serves as an occupational badge, as is generally the case with police officers, nurses, prostitutes, doctors, priests, military personnel, and members of particular athletic teams. In such instances, the "costume" each wears is designed, standardized, and used with the goal of making one's occupation easy to determine. The "uniforms" of college students, businessmen, factory workers, or housewives may serve much the same function, though they are not necessarily intended to do so.

Other badges are hats, shirts, sweatshirts, or jackets that bear the name of an individual, school, employer, manufacturer, favorite auto, or musical performer. Specialized jewelry such as a fraternity or sorority pin, a wedding or engagement ring, or a necklace with a name or religious symbol, may also serve to provide information as to one's identity, status, group, or organizational affiliation.

ARTIFACTS

One's car and home are artifacts—objects—that provide additional messages from which others may draw inferences as to financial resources, aesthetic preferences, personality, status, or occupation. A particular credit card, briefcase, or a business card may serve as artifactual cues to which people react as they form impressions based on one's appearance.

Gestures—Kinesics

Movements of body, head, arms, legs, or feet—technically termed *kinesics*—also play an important role in human communication. Studies suggest that we progress in the development of our capacity for gesturing through four basic stages.[35] In the first stage, from birth to three months, irregular, jerky movements of the entire body indicate excitement and distress. In the next stage, three to five months, the infant is able to move the entire body more rhythmically, in patterns associated with anger and delight. In the third stage, five to fourteen months, children develop specialized gestures such as making faces, turning the head, and poking. Between the ages of fourteen and twenty-four months, the child is able to express affection for particular people, as well as joy and jealousy, through contact movements such as poking, hitting, and caressing.

Gestures, as well as other cues, may either be *purposeful*—messages which are intended to achieve a particular purpose—or *incidental* and *unintended.* Some gestures may be used as complements for language, such as if we shake our head back and forth while saying "no," when asked a question. In other instances we use gestures in place of words. A shrug of the shoulders, for instance, is used to indicate confusion or uncertainty, a frown and slow horizontal back-and-forth motion of the head to indicate frustration or annoyance, or the circle sign made by the thumb and forefinger to mean "OK."

INHERITED, DISCOVERED, IMITATED, AND TRAINED ACTIONS

Desmond Morris, an anthropologist who has intensely studied this area, suggests that gestures are acquired through *inheritance, discovery, imitation,* and *training.*[36] Examples of actions that are inborn include the sucking response of the baby, the use of body contact gestures as a part of courtship, and the pattern of greeting between individuals when coming together or parting company.

Some gestures we discover as we identify the limitations and capabilities of our bodies. The way people cross their arms is an example. There is little variation from one culture to another, but there are differences between individuals within any one culture, and each individual tends to be fairly consistent over time. Some of us fold left hand over right, and others right over left. Regardless of which we have become accustomed to, it is difficult to reverse the pattern without considerable effort, as shown in Figure 7–8.[37]

A good many of our gestures we acquire unknowingly from the people around us as we grow up. The typical handshake, for instance, is acquired through imitation, as are many other greeting forms and cultural and subcultural mannerisms.

Actions such as winking, playing tennis, jumping on one foot, whistling, or walking on one's hands, require active training in order to master. The wink, for example, taken so much for granted by the adult, is a formidable challenge for a child. Like other trained actions, substantial observation and systematic effort is required for mastery.

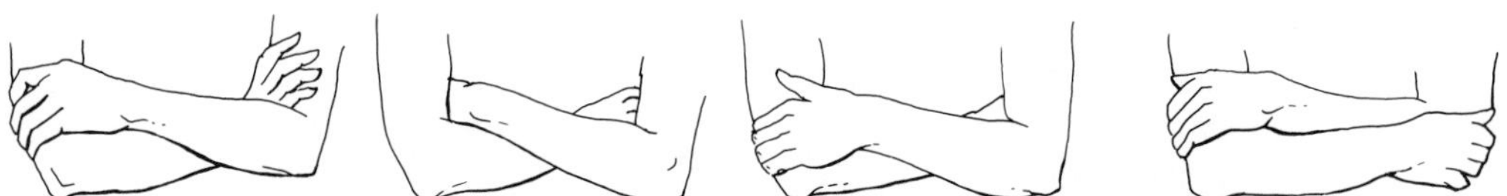

FIGURE 7–8 Folding one's arms can be considered a *discovered action.* There are no significant differences from one culture to another as to how individuals cross their arms, but there are differences between persons. These differences occur because we "discover" the action rather than learn it from others. Once one has arrived at a way of crossing his or her arms, it becomes very natural, and it is only with some difficulty and conscious attention that it can be done in another way.

Source: Desmond Morris, *Manwatching* (New York: Abrams, 1977).

ORIGINS OF GESTURES

It is interesting to speculate as to the origins of human gestures. Some gestures displayed by adults seem to be carried over from our activities as children. Smoking, pencil chewing, nail biting, candy and gum chewing, and "nervous eating" may well have their roots in our early feeding experiences when oral satisfaction was associated with safety and security.

Other gestures may have cultural origins. Kissing and erotic gestures of the tongue associated with lovemaking may have their roots in the feeding habits of our ancestors. At early points in human history, mothers apparently fed their young by chewing food in their mouths first and then passing the food to their child's mouth in a gesture which very much resembles the tongue-kissing of adult lovers today.[38]

Another gesture, the horizontal head shaking which we use to say "no," may well have its origins in the infant's side-to-side head shaking gesture indicating he or she wants no more milk from the mother's breast, a bottle, or a spoon.[39]

TYPES OF GESTURES

There are many ways of classifying gestures. Morris, who provides what is perhaps the most exhaustive listing, includes the following.[40]

Baton Signals and Guide Signs. One type of gesture, the baton signal, is used to underscore or emphasize a particular point being made verbally. Examples of baton signals include a downward clipping motion of the hand, a forward jabbing movement of the fingers and hand, and the raised forefinger. Another similar kind of gesture is the *guide sign,* by means of which we indicate directions to others, as when we point, direct, or beckon another person nonverbally.

Yes-No Signals. *Yes-no Signals* are another category of gesture. Movements of the head are the primary means for creating these signals. While many gestures are unique to one or several cultures, the vertical, "yes" head nod appears to be fairly universal. Even though we might assume that the meaning of the "yes" nod is fairly specific, further thought reminds us that there are a number of variations:

The Acknowledging Nod: "Yes, I am still listening."

The Encouraging Nod: "Yes, how fascinating."

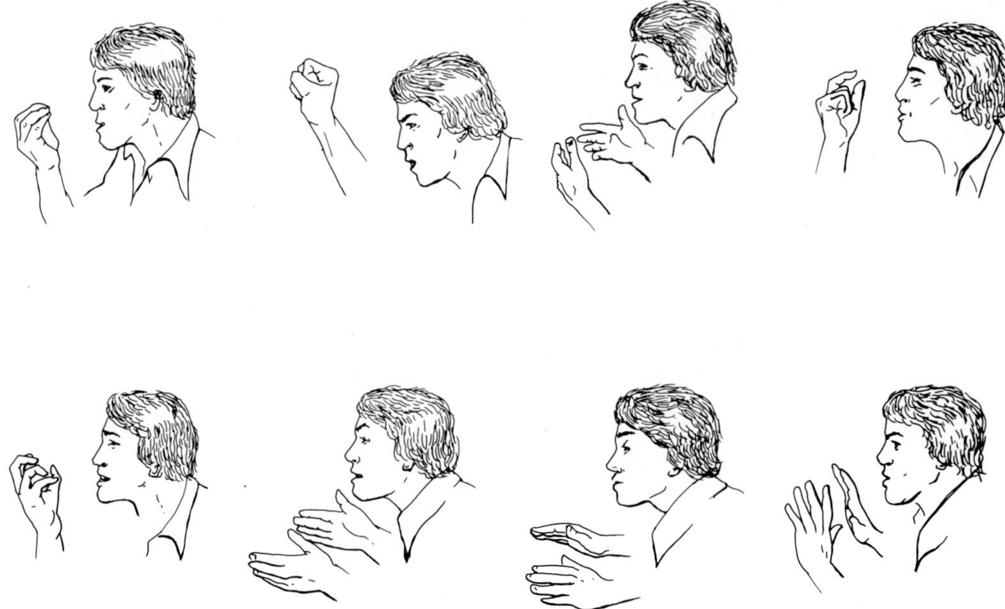

FIGURE 7–9 *Baton Gestures.*
Source: Desmond Morris, *Manwatching* (New York: Abrams, 1977).

The Understanding Nod: "Yes, I see what you mean."

The Agreeing Nod: "Yes, I will."

The Factual Nod: "Yes, that is correct."[41]

The "no" gesture, of course, consists of a horizontal movement of the head. In many parts of the world a side-to-side swaying of the head is also used to say "maybe yes, maybe no." In addition to the head, the hand and fingers can also be used to express yes-no signals. For instance, in our North American culture a shaking of the forefinger from side to side is a way of saying "no." See Figure 7–10.

Greetings and Salutation Displays. The most familiar greeting forms are the handshake, embrace, and kiss by which we signal our pleasure at someone's arrival or the significance of their departure.

One can differentiate several stages in the greeting or salutation process. The first phase is the *inconvenience display:*

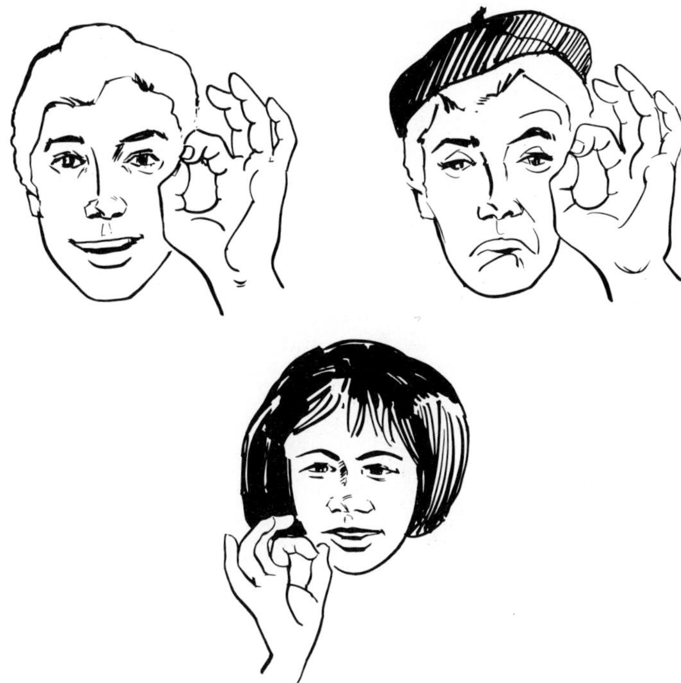

FIGURE 7–10 A circle sign made with the thumb and forefinger illustrates how the significance of a single gesture can vary substantially from one culture to another. In England and North America, the sign means, "okay." For the French, it signifies "okay" when the gesture is made while smiling. If it is accompanied by a frown, it is taken to mean "worthless" or "zero." In Japan, the same sign is often used as a sign for "money."
Source: Desmond Morris, *Manwatching* (New York: Abrams, 1977).

To show the strength of our friendliness, we "put ourselves out" to varying degrees. We demonstrate that we are taking the trouble. For both host and guest, this may mean "dressing up." For the guest it may mean a long journey. For the host it entails a bodily shift from the center of his home territory. The stronger the greeting, the greater the inconvenience. The Head of State drives to the airport to meet the important arrival. The brother drives to the airport to greet his sister returning from abroad. This is the maximum form of bodily displacement that a host can offer. From this extreme there is a declining scale of inconvenience, as the distance travelled by the host decreases. He may only go as far as the local station or bus depot. Or he may move no farther than his front drive, emerging from his front door after watching through the window for the moment of arrival. Or, he may allow a child or servant to answer the door and remain in the room, the very center of his territory, awaiting the guest who is then ushered into his presence. The minimal inconvenience display he can offer is to stand up when the guest enters the room, displacing himself vertically but not horizontally.[42]

The second stage is the *distant display.* From the moment the guest and host see each other, they indicate the other's presence by several other gestures including a smile, eyebrow flash, head tilt, wave, and sometimes an outstretching of arms indicating an upcoming embrace. As the two individuals approach one another, they signify pleasure at the other's presence by hugging, squeezing, patting, kissing, or pressing their checks together, coupled often by extended eye contact, laughing, smiling, sometimes even crying. The particular greeting used depends upon a number of factors including the nature of the relationship, the situation in which they are meeting one another, the length of time that has passed since they have seen one another, and the extent of change in either person's status since last they were together.

Tie Signs. The *bonding,* or *tie sign* is a category of gesture through which individuals indicate that they are in a relationship. In much the same way that wedding rings, fraternity pins, or matching clothing suggest the existence of a relationship between two or more people, certain gestures serve the same purpose. Handholding, linked arms, a single drink shared by two people, close physical proximity when sitting or walking, and the simultaneous sharing of objects of all kinds provide cues about the individuals and the nature of their relationship.

Isolation Gestures. Other common gestures are the body positionings such as crossing arms or legs, through which we conceal or block portions of the body from view. In some instances, *isolating gestures* may serve as intentional messages, though more often they are less purposeful. These and other gestures, including hugging oneself, supporting the chin or cheek with an arm, or touching one's mouth, may signal discomfort or anxiety, even though one may be unaware of these feelings.[43]

Other Gestures. Gestures also play a major role in courtship, mating, and sexual affairs. In addition to hand holding, kissing, petting, and forms of sexual contact, *preening behavior*—for instance, stroking one's hair, adjusting makeup or clothing in the mirror, or stroking one's own arms or legs—can also play a role in sexual attraction.[44]

In religion, gestures have significant functions. Kneeling, standing at appropriate times, bowing, and folding one's hands in prayer are symbolic means through which one participates in the central rituals of any faith.

FIGURE 7–11 Even when no words are spoken, nonverbal codes often provide clues as to who "goes with" whom in any given situation.

Touch—Haptics

When a gesture is extended to the point where physical contact is involved, tactile messages are created. For humans the significance of tactile messages, also termed *haptics,* begins well before birth in the prenatal contact between mother and infant. From the first moments of life, touch is the primary means by which child and parents relate to one another. Through this tactile mode, feeding takes place and affection is expressed.

During the early years, touch continues to be the central means for expressions of warmth and caring among family members and close friends. Beginning with the preschool and elementary years, physical contact also takes on a role in play and sports and, particularly among boys in our culture, fighting. We also learn the significance of tactile messages in greeting rituals such as the handshake, hug, and kiss during this period.

In the teenage and preadult years, touching takes on increasing significance in expressions of warmth, love, and intimacy. Tactile messages are important in athletic endeavors, in the actual activity of the sport, and in the pats and slaps of assurance and encouragement among players and coaches. For some, the role of touch in aggression continues during this period. Among adults, most physical contact is associated with (1) informal greetings and gestures of departure between friends and colleagues, (2) expressions of intimacy and sexual activities, and (3) expressions of hostility and aggression.

Two of the interestings facets of tactile messages are their power and their inherent ambiguity. In health care settings, one of the sources of discomfort for many patients is the fact that examinations and treatment involve being touched by relative strangers in a manner that we normally associated with intimate relations. Another type of difficulty occurs when a person intends a particular touching gesture to convey warmth and affiliation, but it is interpreted as aggressiveness. This has become a problem with sexual harassment cases and child abuse, especially in preschools. People may read sexuality where it is not intended, or others may have that intent, but deny it.[45]

Levels of contact and comfort with touching vary to some extent from one culture to another. In some Asian or African cultures, for example, male friends may walk down the street hand-in-hand as they talk. In Middle Eastern cultures, casual acquaintances stand so close together when talking that North Americans assume they are intimates.

FIGURE 7–12

By comparison, ours is a low-contact culture. In general, North Americans go to great lengths to avoid touching whenever possible. In an elevator or crowded shopping mall, for instance, we generally touch strangers only when absolutely necessary and then often with discomfort.

Depending upon the circumstance, persons involved, and the culture, touch may lead us to react with considerably more intensity than we would to verbal or other nonverbal cues. Touching another person without his or her consent is regarded in most societies as far more disturbing than verbal abuse and obscene gestures.

Space—Proxemics

The use of space, *proxemics,* plays an important role in human communication. To some extent the intensity of tactile messages occurs because we have well-defined expectations as to how much personal space we will have around us. When our *personal space,* the *portable territory* we carry with us from place to place, is invaded, we respond. Being bumped unnecessarily in an elevator, having a beach towel walked across or practically shared by a stranger, or being unnecessarily crowded while shopping generally cause us discomfort for this reason. Our response is to readjust our own position to regain the amount of space we think we need. Research suggests that in some instances the extreme violation of personal space over a time, such as occurs in hysterical crowds and very high density neighborhoods, can lead to extreme reaction, frustration, and even aggression.

Edward Hall has done much to broaden our understanding of the way space is used during face-to-face conversations.[46] Hall found that the distance between interactants varied predictably depending upon the setting and the content of conversation:

- Public conversations—12 feet to the limits of visibility
- Informal and business conversations—4 to 12 feet
- Casual conversations—$1\frac{1}{2}$ to 4 feet
- Intimate conversations—0 and 18 inches

Fluctuations with each category depend upon a number of factors: the culture in which the conversation takes place, the ages of the individuals, topic being discussed, setting, nature of the relationship, attitudes and feelings of the individuals, and so on.[47]

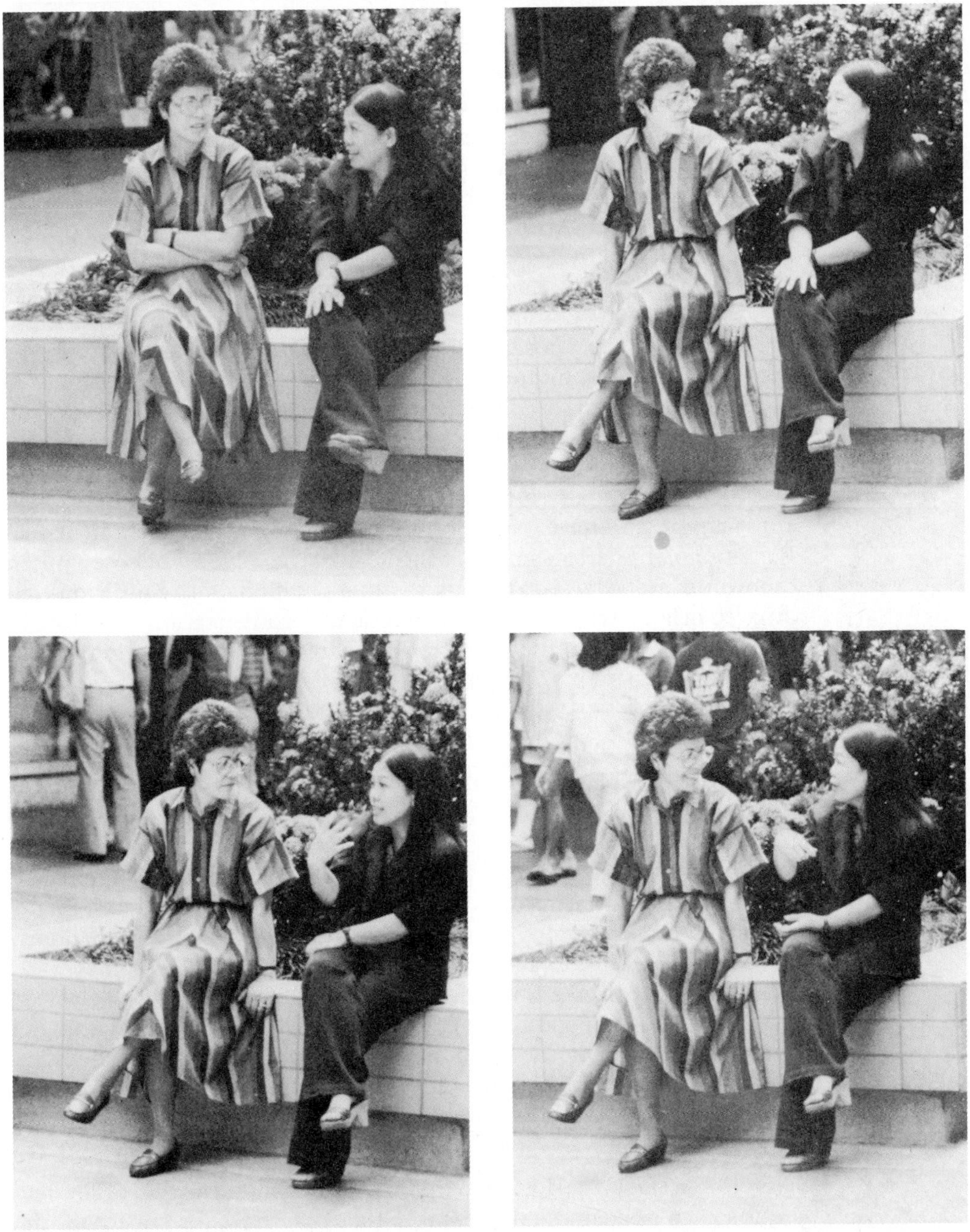

FIGURE 7–13 Body positioning and the way space is used play an important role in human interaction.

The use of space and position is also important in seating. In a group situation, for instance, certain positions are more often associated with high levels of activity and leadership than others. Being in front of a group, separated more from the group as a whole than are any of the individual members from one another, affords the isolated individual a position of distance and authority. Examples are a teacher in front of a class, a judge in front of the court, a religious leader at the front of the church, and so on.

A person's position within a large room—a classroom, for example—can also have an influence on verbal behavior. In typical classes, over fifty per cent of the comments are initiated by class members located in the front and center positions within the room. For many individuals, position is the most influential factor explaining their participation.[48] In smaller groups, particularly where furniture is involved, the head of the table is traditionally a position of leadership, honor, respect, and power. See Figures 7–14, 7–15, and 7–16. In a conference room, a similar association often attends to the individual sitting at the head of a table. Some researchers have found, for instance, that in experimental jury deliberations, the person sitting at the head of the table was chosen much more often as leader than persons in other positions.[49] Our positions relative to others, whether in silence or active conversation, standing or sitting, can be a significant factor in shaping communication and in contributing to others' impressions of us and ours of them.

THE PHYSICAL ENVIRONMENT

Our buildings, furniture, decor, lighting, and color schemes are the result of human decision making. In addition to providing shelter and housing, and facilitating our various activities, the man-made elements of our physical environment also serve a number of informational functions—some intentionally, many by accident.

Whether one thinks of the arrangement of furniture and the selection of wall hangings in one's own apartment, the design and furnishing of an elegant restaurant, the layout of an outdoor mall or park, or the architecture of a massive airport complex, all have much in common in terms of communication.

Directing Behavior. Each environment with its furniture, decor, and color serves as a source of messages that may have an impact on the people present. Some of the information is "designed-in" by the archi-

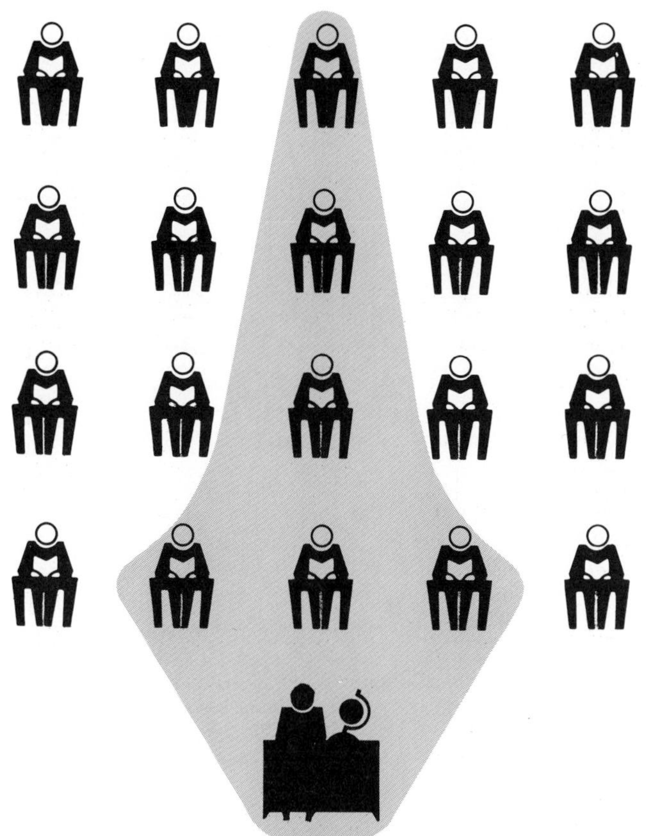

FIGURE 7–14 Studies suggest that classroom participation is highest in the front and center sections of a room. Researchers studying interaction in grades one, six, and eleven found that sixty-three percent of the contributions came from students located in only three positions, one behind another, down the center of the classroom.

Source: Mark L. Knapp, *Essentials of Nonverbal Communication,* and R. S. Adams and B. Biddle, *Realities of Teaching: Explorations with Video Tape* (New York: Holt, Rinehart, Winston, 1970). Copyright © 1980, Holt, Rinehart, Winston. By permission.

tect or designer to shape the way the environment or its parts are used. Sidewalks in a park, for example, direct our movement as we walk about. Similarly, chairs used in some fast-food restaurants are designed to be comfortable for only a short period of time and may well influence our decisions about how long to remain in the environment.

Provide Symbolic Value. Structures and their contents, by virtue of their size, shape, use of space, and decor, may also have symbolic significance for us. Religious buildings and their contents, for example, are often symbolic by their very nature. Large rooms with high ceilings, stained glass windows, dimly-lit interiors, deep colors, and sacred books and objects, each have information value to those who use the environment.

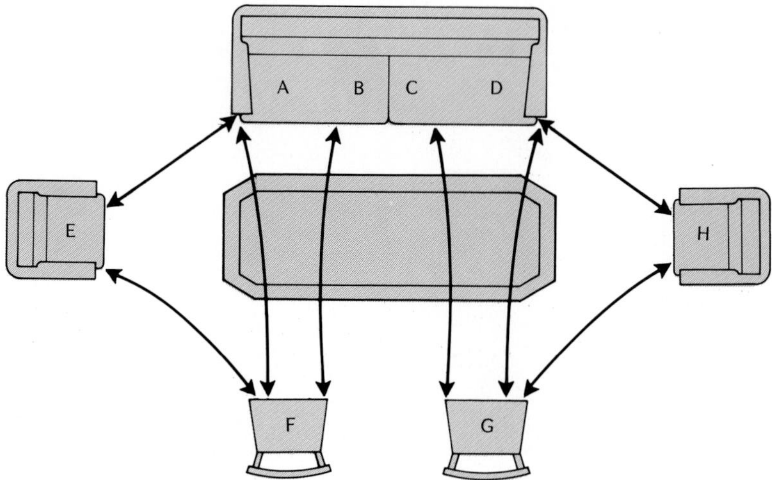

FIGURE 7–15 The arrangement of furniture and seating patterns play an important role in the level and direction of conversation. All other things being equal, the pairs marked by arrows would engage in the most frequent conversation. Those persons seated on the couch would be least likely to engage in interaction.

Source: Albert Mehrabian, *Public Places and Private Spaces: The Psychology of Work, Play, and Living Environments.* Copyright © 1976 by Basic Books, Inc. By permission.

The symbolic properties of houses of worship have their parallels in shopping malls, parks, restaurants, as well as in the structure and decor of homes and apartments. The differences, for instance, between dining in a candlelit room with elegantly upholstered armchairs and soft dinner music compared to the experience of having dinner at the counter of a truck stop are quite substantial.

Regulating Interaction. Environments may also provide the basis for information that regulates—encourages or discourages—interaction. The study carrels of the library, for example, serve to separate and isolate their users, discouraging interaction, while a business office with no private offices or partitions encourages interchange. In a similar sense, a classroom with permanently attached chairs contributes to "one-way" message flow. Robert Sommer provides the following lucid description of the typical classroom and its impact.

> The American classroom is dominated by what has been called the rule of two-thirds—two-thirds of the time someone is talking and two-thirds of

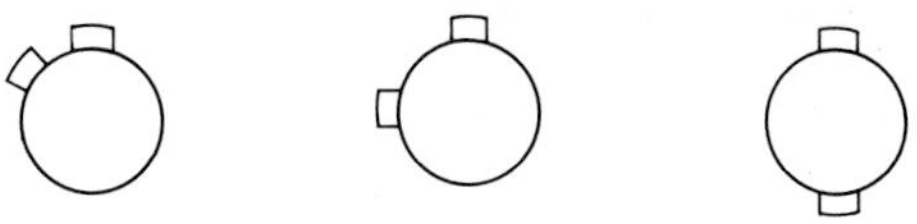

	Round (corner)	Round (side by side)	Round (opposite)
Conversation	63%	17%	20%
Cooperation	83	7	10
Co-action	13	36	51
Competition	12	25	63

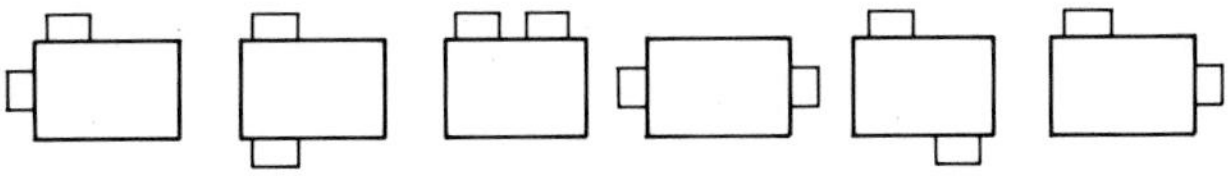

Conversation	42%	46%	11%	0%	1%	0%
Cooperation	19	25	51	0	5	0
Co-action	3	32	7	13	43	3
Competition	7	41	8	18	20	5

FIGURE 7–16 In studies of relationships and seating preference, Robert Sommer asked students to indicate how they would prefer to situate themselves for each of the following situations:
(1) *Conversation:* Casual discussions for a few moments before class.
(2) *Cooperation:* Sitting and studying together for a common exam.
(3) *Co-action:* Sitting and studying for different exams.
(4) *Competition:* Competing to see which person would be first to solve a se ries of puzzles.
Students were asked to indicate their preferences for round and rectangular tables, each with six possible seating positions. The results of the studies are shown under the diagrams.

Source: Robert Sommer, "Further Studies of Small Group Ecology," *Sociometry*, 28, 1965, pp. 337–348, and Mark Knapp, *Essentials of Nonverbal Communication* (New York: Holt, Rinehart, Winston, 1980), pp. 85–90.

the time it is the teacher, and two-thirds of the time that the teacher is talking, she is lecturing, giving directions or criticizing behavior. Movement in and out of classrooms and the school building itself is rigidly controlled. Everywhere one looks there are "lines"—generally straight lines that bend around corners before entering the auditorium, the cafeteria, or the shop. . . . The straight rows tell the student to look ahead and ignore everyone except the teacher, the students are jammed so tightly together that psychological escape, much less physical separation, is impossible. The teachers have 50 times more free space than the students with the mobility to move about. He writes important messages on the blackboard with his back to his students. The august figure can rise and walk among the lowly who lack the authority even to stand without explicit permission. Teacher and children may share the same classroom but they see it

FIGURE 7–17 The objects of our physical environment also serve as nonverbal information sources, providing clues as to how they are to be understood, related to, and whether and how they are to be used.

differently. From a student's eye level, the world is cluttered, disorganized, full of people's shoulders, heads, and body movements. His world at ground level is colder than the teacher's world. She looms over the scene like a helicopter swooping down to ridicule or punish any wrongdoer.[50]

The Use of Time—Chronemics

The use of time and timing—*chronemics,* as it is technically termed—is another critical, and often overlooked, factor in communication. In fact, the reactions to our words and deeds often depend far more on *when* we speak or act, than upon the content of the action.

TIMING

Timing plays a role in interaction at two levels of analysis: (1) micro and (2) macro. Micro-conversational time-use characteristics include the speed at which we talk, the number and extent of pauses and interruptions, our "talk-to-silence" ratio, and our patterns of conversational "turn taking." These factors can play an important role in terms of message transmission, reception, and interpretation; and each also serves as a basis for the formation of impressions about the individuals involved. Too little talking, for instance, can be read as disinterest, shyness or boredom, whereas too much can be construed as aggressiveness, self-assuredness, presumptuousness, overconfidence, or rudeness.

At the macrolevel are our more general decisions as to whether to even engage in conversation at a particular point in time. It comes as no surprise to anyone who has ever asked for a raise or to borrow the family car that there are certain "times" that are better than others for presenting ideas or suggestions. The decisions people make about when to speak and when to be silent, when they have said too much and when too little, when to "speak their piece" and when to "keep it to themselves" are among the most critical decisions they make relative to communication.

TIMELINESS

Sayings like "Time is money," "Never put off until tomorrow what you can do today," "A stitch in time saves nine," and "The sooner the better" reflect the common North American view that time is a precious commodity. The faster we can get something done, the less time we "waste."

Our "time-is-money" philosophy shows up in a great many of our activities. We find ourselves rushing to meet deadlines, keep appointments, avoid waste, and increase productivity. We drive as fast as we legally can, so we'll get where we're going quicker. When we have an appointment with someone, we like to get business transacted in as little time as possible so we can get on the next task. We want to leave work "on time" whenever possible to hurry home. En route every red light, wait at a pedestrian crossing, or slow-moving car is an annoyance as we rush home. We want to get home quickly to relax and enjoy our "leisure time."

Given the significance of *time* in our daily lives, it is not surprising that our use of it can have an important impact on behavior. Being "early" or "late" is a message. The meaning provided by such messages varies depending on a number of factors, including the amount of time one is early or late, the purpose of an appointment, the length of the relationship between the persons involved, the relative status of the parties involved, and the orientation toward time of each of the individuals.

Being fifteen minutes late for a visit with a heart specialist may lead to the cancellation of the appointment, while being fifteen minutes late for a cocktail party may result in being embarrassingly "early." Being late for a business meeting carries different consequences than being late for a social engagement. Arriving two hours late—even with a good reason—for a first date will probably be reacted to differently than being as late for a meeting with one's spouse. In such circumstances, timeliness and the use of time—being on time, late, or early—may be as significant a source of information to other persons as whatever one does or says after arriving.

There are very significant intercultural differences in the use of this code. In Latin America and the Middle East, one can arrive at a time that an American or Canadian would consider "late," and still be considered "on time" or even "early."

Messages and Meanings—MS $\neq$ MR

We have seen how verbal and nonverbal behaviors play a pervasive role in human communication. Through the use of verbal and nonverbal codes, individuals create cues that can and often do become significant to others. Sometimes the behaviors are intentional, as with a planned speech or the wave of a hand. Often they are accidental, as with a blush or an avoidance of eye contact in embarrassment.

The process of verbal, and especially nonverbal, message making is automatic. Both occur as a natural and basic part of human activity. The nonverbal and verbal behaviors of any one individual can be seen as contributing to the vast pool of messages comprising the symbolic environment that surrounds us at any point in time.

It is important to keep in mind that the presence of particular verbal or nonverbal messages in the environment provides little or no assurance that they will be attended to or interpreted in a particular way. Bill tells Mary "I love you." Mary says, "I love you, too." Each has attended to the verbal message provided by the other, and the message each is sending is the same. Can we assume the message has the same meaning for both Bill and Mary? Not necessarily. Whether we think in terms of ourselves as "senders" or "receivers" of messages in a relationship, group, organization, society or mass audience, messages sent (intentionally or not), do not necessarily equal messages received. Common messages do not necessarily result in shared interpretation. Maybe Bill and Mary have the same meanings in mind. Or, perhaps, Bill means he wants to get married, while Mary means she wants to go out only with Bill.

The same distinction between message and meaning, is important in the realm of nonverbal codes: Eye engagement intended as a sign of interest by one person may be read as aggressiveness by another; a gesture interpreted as an isolation gesture by one person may be regarded as a way of keeping warm in a cold room to others. Verbal and nonverbal behaviors are *sources* of meaning, but they are not, in and of themselves, meaningful.

The meanings verbal and nonverbal messages have depend not only on the messages that are available but also on our individual ways of processing information and on our social interactions with others. Whether we regard a particular person as attractive or intelligent will depend minimally on: (1) the nonverbal and verbal behaviors of the person in question; (2) the way we personally attend to and interpret those behaviors; and (3) the social interactions with our peers and other members of our society that have helped to define and shape our notion of what constitutes attractiveness or intelligence.

To determine the meanings of particular messages, we have to look beyond the verbal and nonverbal messages to the processes involved in information reception. We must look also to the relationships, groups, organizations, cultures and societies, which provide the contexts in which verbal and nonverbal messages are created, shared and interpreted.

Implications and Applications: Paralanguage, Appearance, Gestures, Touch, Space, and Time

- Paralanguage, appearance, gestures, touch, space, and time are important sources of messages in a wide range of situations.
- Nonverbal codes are the primary means through which we create impressions of ourselves, and form impressions of others.
- Our nonverbal behaviors are governed by rules we have learned through experience over the course of our lifetime.
- We are largely unaware of the rules that guide our nonverbal behaviors and our reactions to them.
- When others violate nonverbal rules, we generally have global, overgeneralized, sometimes emotional reactions. For instance, a person may be perceived to be a wimp if he or she doesn't squeeze firmly enough while shaking hands, or we may feel angry when someone is continually late for appointments.
- We are generally aware of only a small percentage of the nonverbal messages we create and convey in any situation.
- Some facets of nonverbal codes, such as dress, greetings, and time, we can easily manage if we choose to do so. Others, like paralanguage, eye contact, gestures, and the use of space can be managed with effort and practice. Still others—a blush of embarrassment or a nervous gesture—we may be unable to control.
- Nonverbal competence requires awareness and attention to the codes of communication, and conscious effort to be sensitive to the impact of our nonverbal behavior on others.

Summary

Nonverbal codes play an important role in human communication. There are a number of similarities between verbal and nonverbal codes. They: (1) are rule-governed; (2) make possible the production of unintended, as well as purposeful messages; and (3) share in common a variety of message functions.

There are also key differences: (1) Compared to language, there has been a lack of awareness and attention to nonverbal cues and their impact on behavior; (2) nonverbal codes involve rules which are primary covert rather than overt; and (3) verbal codes are thought to occur primarily in the left hemisphere of the brain, while the right hemisphere is essential for processing information related to nonverbal activity.

Paralanguage, appearance, gestures, touch, space, and time are six primary sources of nonverbal messages. Appearance plays an important role in interpersonal relations, particularly in initial impressions. Dress, adornment and physique are facets of appearance that serve as potential information sources. The face is a central aspect of one's appearance, providing the primary source of information as to one's emotional state. Hair is also a message source.

The eyes are perhaps the most important component of the facial system in terms of communication. Based upon direction and duration of eye gaze, or the absence thereof, cues are provided that serve as the basis of inferences as to interest, readiness to interact, and attraction. Pupil size may also be important.

Gestures are potential sources of information. Among the most common types of gestures are: baton signals and guide signs, yes-no signals, greetings and salutation displays, tie signs, and isolation gestures.

Touch is another source of messages that play a central role in greetings, the expression of intimacy, and acts of aggression. The intensity of reactions to tactile cues is suggestive of the importance of space in communication. When our personal space is invaded in other than intimate relationships, discomfort—and often "fight" or "flight"—results.

The significance of spatial cues is also apparent in seating patterns. Certain seating positions are often associated with high levels of participation and leadership. The nature and placement of elements in the physical environment—furniture, decor, lighting, and color schemes—also generate messages that are potentially significant to behavior. They often provide cues that influence their use, symbolic value, and interaction patterns.

Time, timing, and timeliness can also be significant in the communication process. The way time is shared in conversations, for instance, can be a source of information that is even more influential than the content of those discussions. Timeliness—being "late" or "early"—can itself be a potential information source. Substantial cultural variations exist.

Our verbal and nonverbal behaviors—some intentionally enacted—create a pool of messages that is part of the environment that surrounds us. The presence of verbal and nonverbal messages provides no assurance that they will be attended to or be of particular significance to individuals within that environment. Messages sent (intentionally or not) do not equal messages received.

Notes

1. Albert Mehrabian, *Silent Messages* (Belmont, CA: Wadsworth, 1971), pp. 42–47; and *Nonverbal Communication* (Chicago: Aldine-Atherton, 1972), pp. 181–184.

2. See Paul Ekman, Wallace Friesen, and P. Ellsworth, *Emotion in the Human Face: Guidelines for Research and an Integration of the Findings* (New York: Pergamon Press, 1972); Paul Ekman, "Universal and Cultural Differences in Facial Expressions of Emotions," in *Nebraska Symposium on Motivation*, Ed. by J. K. Cole (Lincoln: University of Nebraska Press, 1972), pp. 207–283; and discussion of these and other related works in Robert G. Harper, Arthur N. Wiens, and Joseph D. Matarazzo, eds., *Nonverbal Communication: The State of the Art* (New York: Wiley, 1978), p. 212.

3. For a detailed discussion on functions of nonverbal cues, on which this summary is based, see Judee K. Burgoon and Thomas Saine, *The Unspoken Dialogue: An Introduction to Nonverbal Communication* (Boston: Houghton Mifflin, 1978), pp. 10–14.

4. I am indebted to Valerie Manusov for suggesting the distinction between covert and overt rules in discussing nonverbal and verbal codes.

5. Robert E. Ornstein, *The Psychology of Consciousness* (San Francisco: Freeman, 1977), pp. 20–21. See more detailed discussion in Sally P. Springer and George Deutsch, *Left Brain, Right Brain* (San Francisco: Freeman, 1981), and Norman Geschwind, "Specializations of the Human Brain," *Scientific American*, September, 1979, pp. 180–182.

6. Springer and Deutsch, 1981.

7. Springer and Deutsch, 1981, p. 15.

8. Ross Buck, "Spontaneous and Symbolic Nonverbal Behavior and the Ontogeny of Communication," in *Development of Nonverbal Behavior in Children*. Ed. by R. S. Feldman (New York: Springer-Verlag, 1982) pp. 29–62.

9. Burgoon and Saine, p. 80.

10. See discussion in Burgoon and Saine, 1978, pp. 80–84.

11. Mehrabian, 1972, pp. 181–184.

12. William S-Y Wang, "The Chinese Language," in *Human Communication: Language and Its Psychobiological Bases* (San Francisco: Freeman, 1982), p. 58.

13. Wang, 1982, p. 58.

14. Mark L. Knapp, *Essentials of Nonverbal Communication* (New York: Holt, 1980), p. 100.
15. Knapp, 1980, pp. 98–99.
16. Knapp, 1980, pp. 161–162.
17. Ekman, Friesen, and Ellsworth, 1972, p. 50.
18. Ekman, 1972, p. 216.
19. See discussion in Harper, et al., 1978 pp. 98–105; and Ekman, 1972.
20. See Harper, 1978, p. 101.
21. P. C. Ellsworth, "Direct Gaze as a Social Stimulus: The Example of Aggression," in *Non-verbal Communication of Aggression* Ed. by P. Pliner, L. Krames, and T. Alloway, (New York: Plenum, 1975), pp. 5–6.
22. Harper, 1978, p. 173.
23. G. Nielsen, *Studies of Self-Confrontation* (Copenhagen, Denmark: Munksgaard, 1962).
24. An excellent summary of research findings on the functions and perceived impact of eye gaze is provided in Harper 1978, pp. 181–215.
25. See discussion in Knapp, 1980, pp. 190–194.
26. Knapp, 1980, pp. 198–199.
27. Knapp, 1980, p. 199.
28. A discussion of research on pupil dilation by E. H. Hess, *The Tell-Tale Eye* (New York, Van Nostrand Reinhold, 1975); and E. H. Hess, A. L. Seltzer, and J. M. Shlien, "Pupil Responses of Hetero-and Homosexual Males to Pictures of Men and Women: A Pilot Study," *Journal of Abnormal Psychology,* Vol. 70, 1965, pp. 587–590. A useful summary is provided in Knapp, 1980, pp. 169–172 and Desmond Morris, *Manwatching* (New York: Abrams, 1977), pp. 169–172.
29. Edward T. Hall, "Learning the Arabs' Silent Language," *Psychology Today,* August 1979, pp. 47–48.
30. Gillis, John S., *Too Tall, Too Small* (Champaign, IL: Institute for Personality and Ability Testing, 1982); and Painter, Kim, "How Bush, Dukakis Measure Up in '88," *USA Today,* Vol. D4, Sept. 22, 1988.
31. Knapp, 1980, p. 116.
32. Dale G. Leathers, *Nonverbal Communication Systems* (Boston: Allyn and Bacon, 1976), p. 96.
33. Valerie Manusov, Unpublished notes on nonverbal communication, January 1991.
34. See discussion by L. Aiken, "Relationship of Dress to Selected Measures of Personality in Undergraduate Women," *Journal of Social Psychology,* Vol. 59, 1963, pp. 119–128; in Knapp, 1980, p. 118.
35. A discussion of research and writings on the development of nonverbal capabilities in children is provided in Barbara S. Wood, *Children and Communication* (Englewood Cliffs, NJ: Prentice Hall, 1976), pp. 194–200.
36. Morris, 1977, pp. 17–23. The term *imitated actions* is used to refer to what Morris has labeled *absorbed actions.*
37. Morris, 1977, pp. 16–17.
38. Morris, 1977, p. 52.
39. Morris, 1977, pp. 68–69.

40. The discussion of baton signals, yes-no signs, guide signs, salutations displays, tie signs, and isolation gestures is based upon the work of Morris, 1977, pp. 56–100.

41. Morris, 1977, p. 68.

42. Morris, 1977, p. 79.

43. See Morris discussion of "barrier signals," 1977, pp. 133–135, and "auto contact behaviour" pp. 102–105.

44. Knapp, 1980, pp. 136–137.

45. Valerie Manusov, Unpublished notes on nonverbal communication, January, 1991.

46. See discussion of personal space provided in *The Silent Language*, Edward T. Hall (New York: Doubleday, 1959), especially Chapter 10.

47. A useful discussion of the work of Edward Hall and others in the area of personal space is provided in Knapp, 1980, pp. 81–87, and Burgoon and Saine, 1978, pp. 92–97.

48. A summary of research on position and participation is provided in Knapp, 1980, pp. 67–68 and 87–90.

49. F. Strodtbeck and L. Hook, "The Social Dimensions of a Twelve Man Jury Table," *Sociometry*, Vol. 24, 1961 pp. 297–415. See, also, discussion of additional research on this topic in Knapp, 1980, p. 87.

50. Robert Sommer, *Personal Space* (Englewood Cliffs, NJ: Prentice Hall, 1969), p. 99.

References and Suggested Readings

ADAMS, R. S., and B. BIDDLE. *Realities of Teaching*. New York: Holt, 1970.

AIKEN, L. "Relationships of Dress to Selected Measures of Personality in Undergraduate Women." *Journal of Social Psychology*. Vol. 59, 1963, 119–228.

ANGELOGLOU, MAGGIE. *A History of Make-up*. New York: Macmillan, 1970.

BASS, BERNARD M., and S. KLUBECK. "Effects of Seating Arrangement on Leaderless Group Discussions." *Journal of Abnormal and Social Psychology*. Vol. 47, 1952, 724–726.

BERSCHEID, E., and E. H. WALSTER. *Impersonal Attraction*. Reading, MA: Addison-Wesley, 1969.

———. "Physical Attractiveness." In *Advances in Experimental Social Psychology*. Ed. by L. Berkowitz. Vol. 7. New York: Academic, 1974, 158–215.

BICKMAN, L. "The Social Power of a Uniform." *Journal of Applied Social Psychology*. Vol. 4, 1974, 47–61.

BUCK, ROSS, "Spontaneous and Symbolic Nonverbal Behavior and the Ontogeny of Communication," in *Development of Nonverbal Behavior in Children*. Ed. by R. S. Feldman. New York: Springer-Verlag, 1982.

BURGOON, JUDEE K., and THOMAS SAINE. *The Unspoken Dialogue.* Boston: Houghton Mifflin, 1978.

BYRNE, D., O. LONDON, and K. REEVES. "The Effects of Physical Attractiveness, Sex, and Attitude Similarity on Interpersonal Attraction." *Journal of Personality.* Vol. 36, 1968, 250–272.

COOMBS, R. H., and W. F. KENKEL. "Sex Differences in Dating Aspirations and Satisfactions with Computer-Selected Partners." *Journal of Marriage and the Family.* Vol. 28, 1968, 62–66.

CORTES, J. B., and F. M. GATTI. "Physique and Propensity." *Psychology Today.* Vol. 4, 1970, 32–34, 42–44.

———. *Telling Lies.* New York: Norton, 1985.

EKMAN, PAUL, "Universal and Cultural Differences in Facial Expressions of Emotions." In *Nebraska Symposium on Motivation, 1971.* Ed. by J. K. Cole. Lincoln: University of Nebraska Press, 1972, 207–283.

EKMAN, PAUL, and WALLACE V. FRIESEN. "The Repertoire of Nonverbal Behavior: Categories, Origins, Usage, and Coding." *Semiotica.* Vol. 1, 1969, 49–98.

———, and WALLACE V. FRIESEN, "Constants Across Cultures in the Face and Emotion." *Journal of Personality and Social Psychology.* Vol. 17, 1971, 124–129.

———, and WALLACE V. FRIESEN. *Unmasking the Face.* Englewood Cliffs, NJ: Prentice Hall, 1975.

EKMAN, PAUL, WALLACE FRIESEN, and P. ELLSWORTH. *Emotion in the Human Face: Guidelines for Research and an Integration of the Findings.* New York: Pergamon, 1972.

ELLSWORTH, P. C. "Direct Gaze as a Social Stimulus: The Example of Aggression." In *Nonverbal Communication of Aggression.* Ed. by P. Pliner, L. Krames, and T. Alloway. New York: Plenum, 1975, 53–76.

GESCHWIND, NORMAN. "Specializations of the Human Brain." *Scientific American,* September, 1979, 180–182.

GIBBINS, K. "Communication Aspects of Women's Clothes and Their Relation to Fashionability." *British Journal of Social and Clinical Psychology.* Vol. 8, 1969, 301–312.

GUREL, L. M., J. C. WILBUR, and L. GUREL. "Personality Correlates of Adolescent Clothing Styles." *Journal of Home Economics.* Vol. 64, 1972, 42–47.

HALL, EDWARD T. *The Silent Language.* Garden City, NY: Doubleday, 1959.

———. *The Hidden Dimension.* Garden City, NY: Doubleday, 1969.

———. "Learning the Arabs' Silent Language." *Psychology Today.* August, 1979.

HARE, A., and R. BALES. "Seating Position and Small Group Interaction." *Sociometry.* Vol. 26, 1963, 480–486.

HARPER, ROBERT G., ARTHUR N. WIENS, and JOSEPH D. MATARAZZO, eds. *Nonverbal Communication: The State of the Art.* New York: Wiley, 1978.

HARRISON, RANDALL P. *Beyond Words.* Englewood Cliffs, NJ: Prentice Hall, 1974.

HENLEY, NANCY M. *Body Politics.* Englewood Cliffs, NJ: Prentice Hall, 1977.

HESS, E. H. "The Role of Pupil Size in Communication." *Scientific American.* Vol. 233, November 1975, 110–112, 116–119.

———. *The Tell-Tale Eye.* New York: Van Nostrand Reinhold, 1975.

HESS, E. H., and J. M. POLT. "Pupil Size as Related to Interest Value of Visual Stimuli." *Science.* Vol. 132, 1960, 349–350.

HEWES, GORDON W. "The Anthropology of Posture." *Scientific American,* 1957.

HOWELLS L. T., and S. W. BECKER. "Seating Arrangement and Leadership Emergence." *Journal of Abnormal and Social Psychology,* Vol. 64, 148–150.

ILIFFE, A. M. "A Study of Preference in Feminine Beauty." *British Journal of Social and Clinical Psychology.* Vol. 51, 1960, 267–273.

ITTELSON, WILLIAM H., ed. *Environment and Cognition.* New York: Seminar Press, 1973.

JOSEPH, NATHAN. Uniforms and Nonuniforms: Communication Through Clothing. New York: Greenwood, 1986.

JOURARD, S. M. "An Exploratory Study of Body-Accessibility." *British Journal of Social and Clinical Psychology.* Vol. 5, 1966, 221–231.

KENDON, A. "Some Functions of Gaze-Direction in Social Interaction." *Acta Psychologica.* Vol. 26, 1967, 22–63.

KNAPP, MARK L. *Essentials of Nonverbal Communication.* New York: Holt, 1980.

KROUT, MAURICE H. "Symbolism." In *The Rhetoric of Nonverbal Communication.* Ed. by Haig A. Bosmajian. Glevniew, IL: Scott, Foresman, 1971.

LEATHERS, DALE G. *Nonverbal Communication Systems.* Boston: Allyn & Bacon, 1976.

LYNCH, KEVIN. *The Image of the City.* Cambridge, MA: M.I.T. Press, 1960.

MEHRABIAN, ALBERT. *Public Places and Private Spaces.* New York: Basic Books, 1976.

———. *Silent Messages.* Belmont, CA: Wadsworth, 1971.

———. *Nonverbal Communication.* Chicago: Aldine-Atherton, 1972.

MOLLOY, JOHN T. *Dress for Success.* New York: Warner, 1975.

MORRIS, DESMOND. *Intimate Behavior.* New York: Random House, 1971.

———. *Manwatching.* New York: Abrams, 1977.

NIELSEN, G. *Studies in Self-Confrontation.* Copenhagen, Denmark: Munksgaard, 1962.

NORBERG-SCHULZ, CHRISTIAN. *Existence, Space and Architecture.* New York: Praeger, 1971.

ORNSTEIN, ROBERT E. *The Psychology of Consciousness.* San Francisco: Freeman, 1977.

PARRY, ALBERT. *Tattoo.* New York: Simon & Schuster, 1933.

RICHMOND, VIRGINIA P., JAMES C. MCCROSKEY, and STEVEN K. PAYNE. *Nonverbal Behavior in Interpersonal Relations.* Englewood Cliffs, NJ: Prentice Hall, 1987.

ROSENFELD, L. B., S. KARTUS, and C. RAY. "Body Accessibility Revisited." *Journal of Communication.* Vol. 26, 1976, 27–30.

RUBEN, BRENT D., and PAOLO SOLERI. "Architecture: Medium and Message." In *Beyond Media.* Second Ed. Ed. by Richard W. Budd and Brent D. Ruben. New Brunswick, NJ: Transaction, 1987, 214–233.

SCHEFLEN, ALBERT L. "Quasi-Courtship Behavior in Psychotherapy," *Psychology.* Vol. 28, 1965, 245–257.

SHELDON, W. H., *Atlas of Man.* New York: Harper, 1954.

SOMMER, ROBERT. *Personal Space.* Englewood Cliffs, NJ: Prentice Hall, 1969.

SPIEGEL, JOHN, and PAVEL MACHOTKA. *Message of the Body.* New York: Free Press, 1974.

SPRINGER, SALLY P., and GEORGE DEUTSCH. *Left Brain, Right Brain.* San Francisco: Freeman, 1981.

STRASS, J. W., and F. N. WILLIS, JR. "Eye Contact, Pupil Dilation, and Personal Preference." *Psychonomic Science.* Vol. 7, 1967, 375–376.

STRONGMAN, K. T., and C. J. HART. "Stereotyped Reactions to Body Build." *Psychological Reports.* Vol. 23, 1968, 1175–1178.

STRODTBECK F., and L. HOOK. "The Social Dimensions of a Twelve Man Jury Table," *Sociometry.* Vol. 24, 1961, 297–415.

WALSTER, E., V. ARONSON, D. ABRAHAMS, and L. ROHMANN. "Importance of Physical Attractiveness in Dating Behavior." *Journal of Personality and Social Psychology.* Vol. 4, 1966, 508–516.

WANG, WILLIAM S-Y, "The Chinese Language." In *Human Communication: Language and Its Psychobiological Bases.* San Francisco, CA: Freeman, 1982.

———. "Explication and Test of Communication Competence," *Human Communication Research.* Vol. 3, 1977, 195–213.

WOOD, BARBARA S. *Children and Communication.* Englewood Cliffs, NJ: Prentice Hall, 1976.

phone
phone

LOTTO

24 Hour
Green Thumb Teller
FDIC

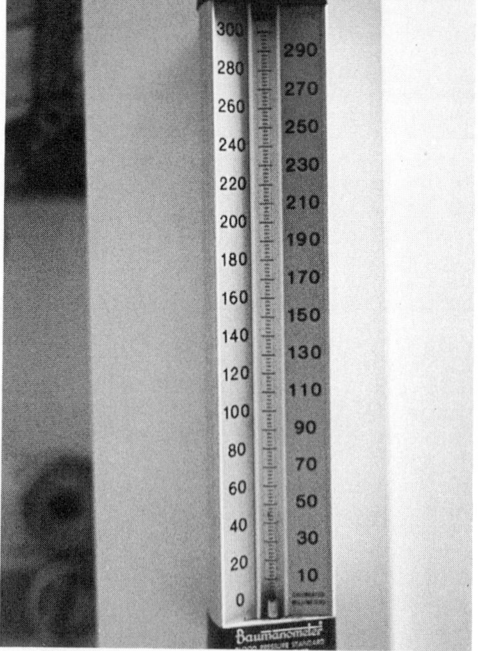
300
280
260
240
220
200
180
160
140
120
100
80
60
40
20
0
290
270
250
230
210
190
170
150
130
110
90
70
50
30
10
Baumanometer

8

Mediated Communication

6:15 A.M. Clock radio clicks on. "Hostilities continue in the Middle East . . . Dow-Jones closed up 30 in light trading . . . lows in the mid 50s, possibility of showers early this evening. . . . " Up and at 'em. Get into jogging gear, grab the "Walkman" and a tape, and out the door.

7:00 A.M. Back from running. Pick up the newspaper. Glance at the headlines, turn on the TV, and grab a quick bite to eat.

7:20 A.M. Set the car radio to the station with the "Eye-in-the-Sky" traffic reporters: "Overturned truck causing delays on I-380; otherwise, traffic conditions normal . . . " Off with the radio, in with the audiocassette. Almost forgot! Swing by the video rental store to return videotapes. Take out the bank card and pull in next door to the automated bank teller.

7:30 A.M. On the way again. Meant to call Rick before leaving home. Better call him now on the car phone.

7:45 A.M. Arrive at work. Check the answering machine and electronic mailbox for messages.

8:00 A.M. Contracts arrive from client via FAX. Sign and FAX copy back.

8:30 A.M. Turn on desktop computer. Should work on the report!! Must be done by tomorrow morning.

5:00 P.M. Report still not completed. Take home portable computer to work on it.

6:00 P.M. Home again. Check the phone answering machine and read mail. Leaf through magazines, junk mail, and a catalogue of products for the busy executive.

6:45 P.M. Watch the news, then listen to CDs while eating dinner.

9:00 P.M. Watch the HBO movie, while writing memos on the computer.

11:00 P.M. Back to work on the report!

The Tool-Making Animal

Beyond our capacity for creating and using messages for communication, one of our other basic human skills is the capacity to create tools.

This capability has aided us greatly in our efforts to adapt to our human environment. It has given us great advantages over other animals in terms of our capability to grow food, build shelters, and carry out the many other activities necessary for our basic survival.

Our tool-making facility has given us another unique advantage over other animals—the ability to create communication *media*—technological devices that extend our natural ability to create, transmit, receive, and process visual, auditory, olfactory, gustatory, or tactile messages. In this chapter, our focus is on media and *mediated communication*—communication which occurs when media intervene, *or mediate,* between message sources and receivers.

Media and Their Functions

At first consideration, tools like telephones, pencils, typewriters, and computers may not seem to have much in common. However, on further reflection, it becomes apparent that in one way or another each of these extends our ability to engage in human communication.

Without basic communication media, such as writing instruments and surfaces on which to write—or electronic substitutes—there would be no way to preserve messages, nor to move them from one place to another. And, if there were no printing presses, telegraph or telecommunication, it would be impossible to rapidly distribute a single message to a number of distant points on the globe. Without tools like computers, copying machines, microfilm, tape recorders, and VCRs, we would be severely limited when it comes to copying, organizing, storing, and retrieving information for future use. Media extend human communication by enhancing (1) message production and distribution, and (2) information reception, storage, and retrieval.

PRODUCTION AND DISTRIBUTION

When we examine the communication media that we take so much for granted, we find that one of the most basic functions they perform is to extend our ability to produce and distribute information at great distance in space or time from the point of origin. *Production* involves the creation of messages using communication media. *Distribution* has three components:

1. Transmission: moving messages.
2. Reproduction and Amplification: duplicating, amplifying, or multiplying messages.
3. Display: making messages physically available once they arrive at their destination.

Often messages are auditory in form, consisting of spoken language or music produced by human performers or musical instruments, and conveyed by media such as telephones, letters, radio, or recordings.

Visual information in the form of words, illustrations and other symbols may be created, transmitted and displayed by means of hand and arm signals, signs, printing, and photographic equipment. Television, film, and satellites have extended our auditory and visual capacities simultaneously. Other tools serve these same functions, though we are less accustomed to thinking of them in this way. Pencils, pens, typewriters, and paints and brushes serve as media in creating visual messages. They also further our human capacity for transmitting and displaying these messages, as do computers, video games, and even hand-held calculators. Communication media that duplicate or amplify include carbon paper, printing presses, and copying equipment.

Without too much stretch of the imagination, even such devices as heating pads, saunas, and hot tubs would qualify as communication technologies in that they extend our tactile capacities. See Table 8–1.

RECEPTION, STORAGE, AND RETRIEVAL

Media that aid in production, distribution, reproduction and/or amplification also play an important role in reception in that they serve to make messages accessible. As noted in Table 8–2, tools such as radio and TV receivers, magnifying glasses, radar, and telescopes, assist with the reception of visual information, while earphones and hearing aids expand capabilities for receiving auditory messages.

Though we are unaccustomed to thinking of written documents as communication media, they also serve very basic functions in extending our information storage and retrieval efforts. Certainly the most noteworthy information-recording tools to be developed in recent years are computers, with their enormous capacity to code, store, manipulate, and retrieve messages.

TABLE 8–1 Message Production and Distribution Media

Auditory Media	
Spoken Languages	Telephones
Musical Instruments	Telegraphs
Amplifers	"Beepers" (Paging devices)
"Walkie-talkies"	CB radios
Phonograph Recording	CDs
Audio and Video Duplication	Audiocassettes
AM, FM, Other Band Radios	
Visual Media	
Alphabet	Bumper Stickers
Smoke Signals	Skywriting
Cave Drawings	Print Media
Hand and Arm Signals	Billboards
Pens and Pencils	Typewriters
Carbon Paper	Reprography/Copying Equipment
Lanterns	Ribbons and Badges
Artists and Graphics Materials Signs	Blackboards
Photography and Photographic Equipment	Signs
Flags	T-shirts/Sweatshirts
Pins	
Auditory-Visual Media	
Cinematography and Films	Cable Systems
Broadcast Television	Video Disks
Projection Systems	Video Cassettes
Microwaves	Electronic Games
Teleconferencing	Fiber Optics
Tactile Media	
Braille	Medical Palpation
Heating Pads	Ice Packs

Evolution of Communication Media: From Smoke Signals to Cellular Phones

It was about 20,000 B.C. when early humans first carved symbols on the walls of caves and used drums and smoke to signal one another. While smoke signals and cave drawings served their intended purposes well, they lacked the capacity for making messages permanent and portable.

TABLE 8–2 Information Reception, Storage and Retrieval Media

Auditory Reception Media	
Hearing aids	Radio Receivers
Earphones	Stethoscopes
Visual Reception Media	
Eyeglasses	Sonograms
Mirrors	CRT (Cathode Ray Tube)
Contact Lenses	Digital Scanners
X-ray Systems	Medical Imaging Devices
Microscopes	NMR
Magnifying Glass	CAT SCAN
Binoculars	Telescopes
Radar	Periscopes
Storage and Retrieval Media	
Written Documents	Books
Computers	CDs
Diaries	Microfiches and Microfilms
Wills	Magnetic Disks
Appointment Calendars	CD Roms
Flight Recorders	Scrolls
Phonograph Records	Audio and Video Tapes/Recorders
Files	
Audio and Audio/Video Laser Disks	Computers and Software

By about 1000 B.C., early hieroglyphic and pictographic drawings had given way to systems of writing that made use of an alphabet.[1] Paper was invented around A.D. 100, and the oldest-known printed work is a Sutra printed in Korea in A.D. 750. Writing extended the natural human capacity for memory by providing a means for creating a lasting record of our messages.

The ancient Greeks built a series of high walls stretching across the countryside from which messages were relayed using fire and smoke. The Persians and Romans had postal systems; official correspondence was carried by horseback between stations on a more or less regular basis.

By 1500 Johannes Gutenberg had completed the printing of a Bible using movable type. Although printing as it is known today began in Germany during the mid-fifteenth century, Chinese, Japanese, and Koreans actually had developed the process much earlier. Printing made it

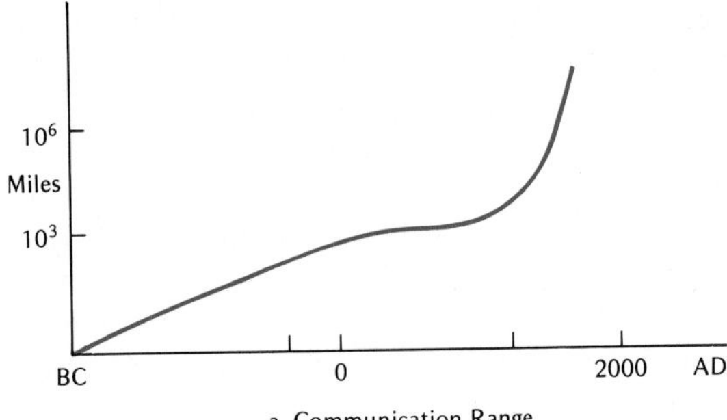

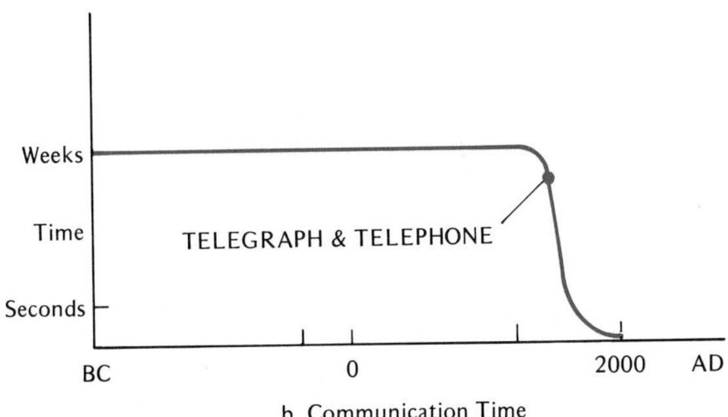

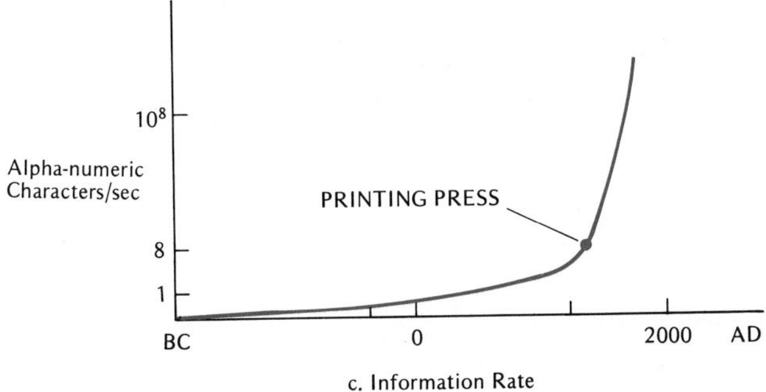

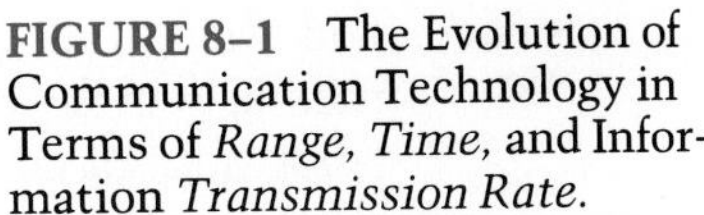

FIGURE 8–1 The Evolution of Communication Technology in Terms of *Range, Time,* and Information *Transmission Rate.*

Source: Understanding Communications Systems, Don L. Cannon and Gerald Luecke. Copyright © 1980, Texas Instruments Learning Center, Dallas, Texas. By permission.

possible to rapidly duplicate and transmit messages, as shown in Figure 8–1. Together, writing and printing had a revolutionary impact on communication and on virtually all facets of life—education, government, commerce, and religion.[2]

Newspapers appeared in their present-day form in the 1600s. It was during this period that regular mail service was established to link major cities in Europe, and by the 1700s postal services were operating in many countries. The mid-1800s brought the advent of the telegraph and the Morse code, and with them the introduction of electronic media, which greatly increased both *range* (distance) and *immediacy* (shortness of delay between message transmission and message reception). See Figure 8–1.

Prior to Marconi's development in 1895 of the wireless telegraph—radio, as it is commonly termed today—the source and the destination had to be physically connected by wire. With a means for sending coded signals and later voice through the air, many new alternatives became available. As shown in Figure 8–1, these advances paved the way for the introduction of television in the 1930s.

There were a number of other notable advances in the 1800s. In 1866, cable was laid across the seabed of the Atlantic, further extending the capability for rapid message transmission. The telephone—a medium that has come to play an incredibly pervasive role in human communication—was patented during the same period.

The 1950s saw the widespread adoption of television. In 1950, only 10 percent of U.S. households had television sets; ten years later that figure had jumped to a remarkable 89 percent. Communication satellites were developed in the 1960s. See Figure 8–2.

In the decade that followed, a number of new communication media became widely available, including miniaturized transistor radios, stereophonic audio equipment, home movie systems, photocopiers, and eight-track and cassette audio recorders. Developments in the more recent past include new and hybrid media such as video games, cable television, home computer systems, computerized databases, cellular phones, FAX, electronic mail systems, telephone answering machines, VCRs, CDs and CD players.

Impact of Media on Everyday Life

Communication media and mediated communication have affected a great many aspects of our personal and professional lives, our groups and organizations, our own society and the world community. Evidence of the impact of new media is all around us. For the most part, we take our media environment very much for granted. We wake up to a radio and think nothing of it. And imagine not being able to use a telephone for a day!

It is also interesting to consider the proportion of the space in department stores and shopping malls allocated to media—television, video cassettes, videodiscs, video games, stereo systems, photographic equip-

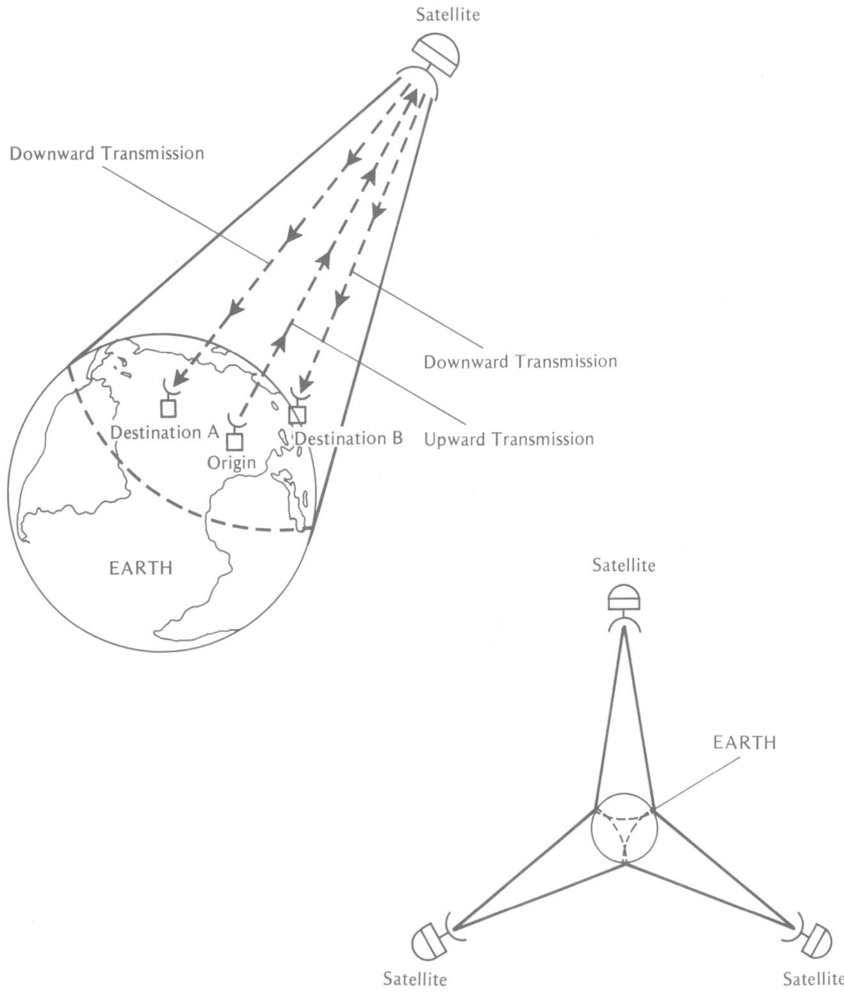

FIGURE 8–2 By means of telecommunication technology, messages originated at one point on the earth's surface can be relayed via satellite to any number of remote destinations and back again.

ment, telephones, electronic watches, calculators, computers, and a variety of other technologies. This is the *hardware*—the physical tools—of the Information Age. Additional space is devoted to *software* such as records, tapes, computer programs, video game cartridges, and a multitude of new magazines and books about these media.

The impact of media on everyday life has also been apparent in economic terms. Since 1980, the annual amount of money individuals spend on electronic media has grown by 45 percent, from 1.1 to 1.6 percent for a national total of $54.6 billion. By way of comparison, during this same time period, spending on furniture did not change, accounting for roughly 5 percent of annual personal consumption.[3] Even in the years between 1985 and 1990, growth of communication media consumption has been dramatic, as shown in Table 8–3.

Communication media have also had an impact on our language and thought. Terms such as "VCR," "CD," "word processing," "joystick," "byte," "software," and "Mario" have become familiar parts of our vocabulary. Moreover, personal and portable tape and CD players, the latest video game, and cellular phones have become symbols of status in our homes and on our streets.

Cable television, telecommunications, videogames, and recording and playback devices have greatly broadened the number of leisure outlets available to us; and portable video and audio devices provide greater flexibility as to *when, where,* and *how* we are entertained. At work, word-processing systems, sophisticated photocopy equipment, phone conferences, FAX machines, cellular mobile phones and other media are the accepted standard even for small businesses. Within larger organizations, management information systems (MIS), corporate video, and electronic mail provide access to vital information at the touch of a keyboard. See Box 8–1 and Figure 8–3.

Few occupations are unaffected by media. In the news media and the publishing industry, the new technologies have changed the way information is collected, processed, and distributed. Writers and editors have access to a variety of databases to supplement information gathered through interviews and other means. Articles are written, revised, edited, and arranged on-screen. The finished product— a newspaper, magazine, or book—may be printed in a traditional manner or transmitted

TABLE 8–3 New Communication Media Ownership: 1985 and 1990

Home Computers	*Answering Machine*	*Videocassette Recorder*
1985: 13%	1985: 5%	1985: 17%
1990: 23%	1990: 31%	1990: 68%
Cordless Telephones	*Compact Disk Player*	
1985: 10%	1985: 1%	
1990: 25%	1990: 19%	

(*Source:* Trish Hall, "Electronics: It's Not Home Without It," *New York Times,* Mar. 29, 1990, pp. C1, C6, based on Electronic Industries Association figures on the percentage of the estimated 91.4 million U.S. households that owned the indicated products during January, 1985 and January, 1985 and January, 1990, respectively)

- Sending unit scans document detecting light and dark areas
- Scanner creates corresponding audible tones
- Tones are sent over telephone lines
- Receiving unit converts the tones into signals
- Signals trigger print to recreate a copy of the original document

BOX 8–1 *How FAX Works.*

via satellite or cable to remote printing sites, as is the case with newspapers like *USA Today* and *The Wall Street Journal.* See Figure 8–4.

Broadcast journalism has also been greatly affected by communication technology. In earlier times, television news and entertainment broadcasts could be originated only in studios and then broadcast from fixed transmitting stations. Today's telecommunication media make it possible for journalists to originate and broadcast events to and from

TO: Dr. Ruben SCILS/Rutgers 0021-201-932-6916

From: Mei-Mei Wu, Taipei, ROC

Date: December 19, 1990

Re: Season Greetings!

****

Dear Dr. Ruben and Friends at the Ph.D. Program:

Especially thinking of you at the time of the year.

Wishing you a very wonderful holiday!

MERRY CHRISTMAS & HAPPY NEW YEAR!

Season Greetings

FIGURE 8–3 *A FAX Christmas Card.*

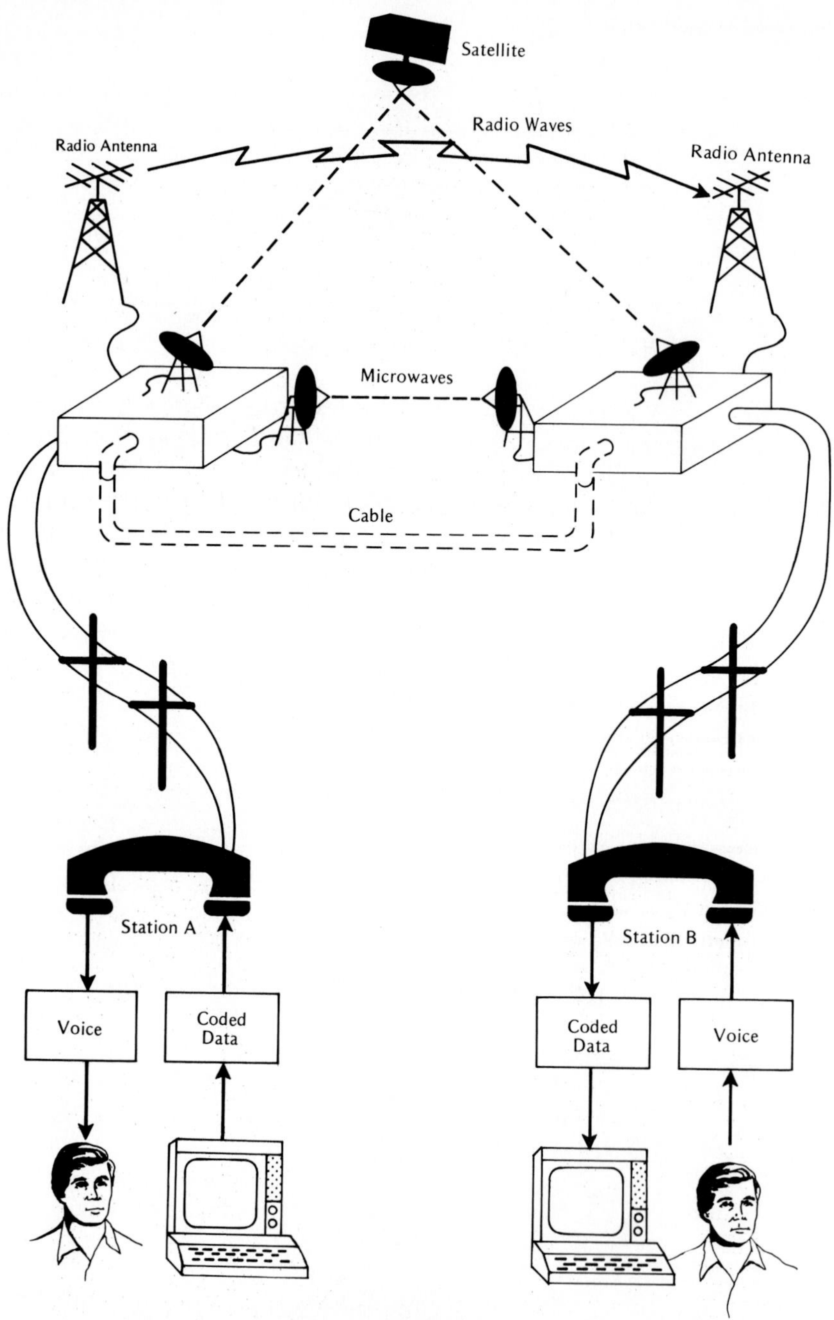

FIGURE 8–4 Voice and coded auditory or visual data can be transmitted between home, office, or production studios via satellite, radio wave, microwave, or cable.

Source: Understanding Communications Systems. Don L. Cannon and Gerald Leucke. Dallas: Texas Instruments Learning Center, 1980. By permission.

remote sites around the world by means of transmitting "dishes" and communication satellites.

With developments such as *videotex,* which uses television or computer monitors to display text and graphic content, information can be transmitted directly to the consumer via cable or phone lines or to an intermediary computer. But, unlike the more familiar uses of television, videotex systems allow audience members to play a role in selecting the information they receive. In this way, consumers can "personalize" what has traditionally been standardized *mass* media programming.

In medicine, media play a critical role in diagnosis, communication between caregivers, and treatment. Libraries are also being transformed by media. The concept of the library as a building where people come to read and check out books and articles is giving way to a view of a service institution that aims to serve the broad-based information needs of its clients using a variety of media.

In the field of law, computers and telecommunications systems are used in the storage and retrieval of information regarding legal decisions, regulations, and statutes. Word processing also facilitates the "personalized" preparation of standardized documents, such as wills and contracts, in a fraction of the time that was required when each legal document had to be created from scratch. For scientists, scholars, inventors, and engineers, improved communication media leads to broader access, with greater ease and in less time, to better organized information.

Additionally, advances in media have created a growing number of entirely new jobs in information management, information services, and communication and information policy. See Box 8–2.

As we look to the future, new work and leisure communication options will be provided by media such as cellular phones that slip into a shirt pocket, minipagers the size of wrist watches, plane-to-plane calling, home computers and FAX machines, personalized brochures and mailings, and nationwide access to any number of telephone calling and answering options, including voice messaging, caller-identification, and caller-blocking.

INCREASING NUMBER OF MESSAGES AND MEDIA

Each new technological advance, particularly those with the capability of multiplication, amplification, or duplication, brings an increase in the volume of messages and the number of media available to us. By some estimates, the total number of words available from all media in the U.S. has more than quadrupled in the last quarter century.[4] Unfortu-

Information brokers, offering a wide range of services that are often otherwise unavailable to small companies and individuals, are playing an increasingly important role in our information-intense economy. Though the field is believed to have developed in the 1940s, the dramatic growth of information brokering is directly attributable to the explosion of computerized information services. Now, with no more than a computer and a modem, familiarity with computerized databases, and an enterprising approach, one or several individuals can begin their own information service.

Potential customers for information brokers exist throughout our economy. Large corporations generally maintain their own information centers and archives. Smaller organizations and companies cannot justify this expense, yet they have dramatic information needs. And, even the most highly educated among them usually have no idea how to get the information that their tasks require. The information broker who is willing to work with individuals or small businesses can find an enormous untapped market in this country. As a service business within our service economy, information brokering is likely to gain importance in the years ahead.

BOX 8–2 *Information Brokering.*
Source: Excerpted and adapted from: "Information Brokering" by Karen Smalletz in *Bulletin of the American Society for Information Science,* April/May 1988, p. 28.

nately, our own ability to select, interpret, and retain this information has not increased at a similar rate. With access to more media and messages, the problem of *information overload*—the availability of more messages than can be effectively utilized—becomes more critical. As this occurs, the real challenge facing humans will shift from "how to get it" to "what to do with it." How many telephone messages do we want to answer? Is there a limit to how much information we can use on any one topic? How many CDs and audiotapes can we listen to, and how many videotapes can we watch? How many newspapers, magazines, and books are we able to read?

Because the number of messages and media grows larger while our abilities to use them remain more or less constant, we are actually less fully informed about what is available in our environment now than we were ten or twenty years ago. Table 8–4 compares the number of words

TABLE 8–4 Percent of Words Consumed Compared to Words Produced in the U.S.—1960 and 1980.

Radio	*Broadcast TV*	*Newspapers*	*Books*
1960 .3%	1960 2.5%	1960 3.8%	1960 45.6%
1980 .1%	1980 .9%	1980 2.0%	1980 34.8%

(*Source:* Ithiel De Sola Pool, Hiroshi Inose, Nozomu Takaski and Roger Hurwitz, *Communication Flows: A Census in the United States and Japan* (New York: North-Holland Press, 1984), p. 21.)

consumed to estimates of words produced by radio, broadcast TV, newspapers, and books in 1960 and 1980. In each of these cases, the percentage of total words that we are able to consume has dropped substantially during the twenty year period, and it seems certain that this gap will continue to increase.

New human competencies are needed to deal more effectively with an increasing number of media and messages. These skills include[5]

- identifying available media and assessing their attributes.
- diagnosing information needs.
- accessing and retrieving information.
- organizing, classifying and managing information.
- using computers and other communication technologies.
- assessing the value and importance of information.
- selecting, ignoring, and resisting messages when appropriate.

INCREASING CAPACITY FOR INFORMATION STORAGE AND RETRIEVAL

Some new communication technologies—particularly computers and other electronic devices—have the capability of assisting us to select, organize, and retrieve information more efficiently. The advent of electronic technologies has brought dramatic increases in the capacity for information storage and retrieval. With videodisks, for example, it is possible to store 108,000 separate color television images together with sound on each disk. At this rate, it will be possible to store and easily retrieve the text of about 3,200 separate books on one two-sided disk. As the quality of television monitors improves, it will be feasible to display desired portions of the text from any of these books on the screen in a matter of seconds. Currently, 3.5 inch double-sided disks used by many personal computers have a capacity of approximately 800 kilobytes (800K), or about 160 pages of text. Internal hard disks of these same computers often have the capacity to store from twenty-five to fifty times as much as can be recorded on the 3.5 inch disks. One twenty megabyte disk has the capacity to store approximately 4000 pages of text for easy access and retrieval. We are moving progressively toward a time when we will have electronic access to virtually all current news and entertainment, as well as documents of all kinds.

SUBSTITUTING COMMUNICATION FOR TRANSPORTATION

There has always been an interesting relationship between the functions of transportation technology and those of the tools of communication. Even with the earliest media this relationship was apparent. Instead of delivering a message in person, one could send it on horseback or by ship via courier. It was not necessary to deliver a message personally, if the information could be transported. See Figure 8–5.

Moving messages across time and space can be an effective, efficient, and economical alternative to moving things or people. Business conferences may be held between individuals across the continent using telephones and video hook-ups. Using telephone lines, doctors at a hospital monitor the vital signs of a patient miles away; and with similar technology, medical personnel also have access to current research findings in their efforts to diagnose and treat illness. Automated teller machines allow us to withdraw and deposit funds from our account without traveling to a bank. Lawyers can search through the equivalent of whole libraries to find key cases or legal opinions, when connected to a nationwide network and computerized database, without leaving their offices.

FIGURE 8–5 In terms of their functions, transportation technology and communication have much in common.

Advances in the years ahead promise to extend further the capability for substituting communication for travel.

EVOLVING CONCEPTS OF OFFICE AND HOME

With the capabilities of today's communication media, concepts of home and office have become far less distinct than they once were. For most of us, *work* has traditionally been a place away from home. However, because of new media, work is increasingly becoming less "a place" and more "an activity." The idea of an office filled with individuals conversing face-to-face about social and business matters is being joined by an understanding of *office* that includes an individual at home in leisure attire, conducting business via phone, computer or FAX machine. As one home-worker comments: "You can work in your pajamas if you want to. There's no dress code to worry about. And there are perks that come from being in your own house, such as easy access to your favorite coffee and being able to position your desk so that you have a view."[6]

CHANGING USES OF MEDIA

Traditionally, there has been a reasonably clear distinction between various communication media and their uses. Newspapers, for example, historically provided their audience with the summary of events of the day. Television, radio, and film were primarily entertainment media. Telephones have been used socially and in business contexts, generally as a substitute for short, face-to-face conversation.

Many of these traditional distinctions are rapidly becoming obsolete. Those who have cable television may now select channels for shopping, music, religious programming, weather, comedy shows, and adult movies. Cable users also have a channel that functions as a local bulletin board, much like what one is accustomed to finding in the newspaper or on the wall of a local supermarket. Other cable channels are available on a subscription fee basis, bringing films to television via satellite. Other cable channels display stock market quotations, wire service copy, and the local weather.

With some fairly inexpensive equipment and a flip of the switch, television can become a video arcade game. Connected to a microcomputer, television becomes a book—a self-instructional guide to French, finance, the stock market, or computer programming. With some additional hardware and software programming, the telephone also changes its function to become a device for the transmission of alphanumeric messages to or from a computer.

Together, the computer, telephone, and television can become a newspaper, magazine, game, reference tool, catalog, index, and a variety of other things. When a printer is added, these same tools become a typewriter and paper, a card catalog and the stacks of books at a reference library in medicine or law. When connected to a videodisk or videocassette, the television set becomes a movie screen. When the tapes were recorded on a portable videotape unit, television becomes a home movie—a family album.

Commenting on this trend today, Everett Dennis, Executive Director of the Gannett Center for Media Studies at Columbia University, remarked: "If there is a single concept that marked the last decade, it is surely the convergence—the coming together of communication devices and forms into . . . electronically-based, computer-driven . . . systems that retrieve, process and store text, data, sound and image."[7] Over twenty years ago, Edwin Parker observed the beginnings of this trend, which he correctly predicted would lead to:

1. Increased amounts of information available to the public, and increased efficiency . . . since everything need not be distributed to everyone in the audience.
2. Greater variety in the ways information packages can be constructed.
3. Individual receiver selection of information (both in content and timing) as opposed to source control of information selection, packaging and transmission.
4. Improved "feedback" capability (since the individual subscriber can "talk" to the system). . . .
5. Greater convenience to the user . . . [8]

INCREASING VALUE OF INFORMATION AS A COMMODITY

The economics of communication and information refers to the *value* associated with communication technology, products, and services. The evidence of value is the willingness of individuals, groups, organizations and societies to pay for these media and information products or services. Researchers point to an increasing number of individuals within the U.S. whose occupational roles involve information production or use; and the production of communication media and messages are central to a great many of the largest and most significant corporations.[9] As communication scholars Jorge Schement and Leah Lievrouw explain:

> Information has been exchanged in the marketplace since ancient times. But before the twentieth century it was rarely sold as a commodity in its own right, and, when it was, it was always treated as an exceptional good. Now it is exchanged as routinely as "ordinary" commodities . . .[10]

Information products, unlike many other products, can often be easily duplicated and are generally not consumed when they are used. Several pages of an article or songs on a cassette can be copied without detracting from the value of the original product. Moreover, a book or CD can be passed along from one person to another, with each person deriving equivalent value. This is not the case with products like foods or fuels which cannot be easily copied and lose their value as they are consumed.

As scholar Alfred G. Smith noted: "Today our primary resource is information. Today knowledge is the primary wealth of nations and the prime base of their power. Today the way we trade messages and allocate information is our information economy."[11] In the case of media, use requires the purchase, lease, or rental of hardware. Typically, when first introduced, technologies are not widely affordable. As sales and production increase, costs generally drop, and an increasing number of consumers can afford the media. This has been the clear pattern with radios, television, computers, CD players and VCRs. Video recorders, for instance, when first introduced in 1979, sold for an average of $771. In 1990, the average price was $265, and basic models could be purchased for slightly over one hundred dollars. CD players were introduced in 1983 at an average price of $1,000; today they sell for an average of $350.[12]

However, even with economies resulting from production, contemporary communication technologies carry a substantial price tag, and many people cannot afford them. Beyond the cost of media hardware, are the costs associated with maintenance, software (such as computer programs, CDs, or video games), or use (such as cable subscription costs) by both producers and consumers. Often the one-time cost of buying equipment is small compared to costs of continued use and "upgrading" as the technology is refined.

For individuals, organizations, and societies alike, the potential of the Information Age is available primarily for those who can afford the necessary hardware and software. To the extent that these resources are unevenly distributed—and this is certainly the case today—advantage goes to those who can afford to acquire these products and services. Thus, it may be argued that rather than narrowing the gap between the information rich and poor, as so many had hoped would happen, advanced media of the Information Age may further increase that gap.

INCREASING AVAILABILITY OF SYNTHETIC EXPERIENCE

Communication media often present messages that may be unlike any we experience first hand. As Ray Funkhouser and Eugene Shaw note:

> Until the nineteenth century, for most people actual experience was limited to events occurring within the 'natural sensory envelope'—the limits of the human nervous system to detect physical stimuli, governed by natural, physical processes.[13]

Today, communication media increasingly enable us to experience what may be termed a "synthetic reality." Funkhouser and Shaw list the following as examples:

- Altered speeds of movement, either slow or fast motion
- Reenactments of the same action (instant replay)
- Instantaneous cutting from one scene to another
- Excerpting fragments of events
- Juxtaposing events widely separated in time or space
- Shifting points of view, via moving cameras, zoom lenses, or multiple cameras
- Combined sight from one source and sound from another (e.g., background music, sound effects, dubbed dialogue)
- Merging, altering, or distorting visual images, particularly through computer graphics techniques and multiple-exposure processing
- Manufacturing "events" through animations or computer graphics[14]

Thus, communication media not only extend our capability to experience the realities available to our senses but actually add a number of "artificial" experiences as well.

Media Characteristics

ASYNCHRONOUS—SYNCHRONOUS

In some communication situations, there is a substantial time lag between the message production and consumption; with others there is little or no gap. In face-to-face communication, for instance, there is little or no time or space gap. Our verbal and nonverbal behaviors create messages which may be instantaneously attended to by other interactants. In such a situation, communication is *synchronous*. In other situations, the creation and transmission of messages is not synchronized in time with message reception and use. There may be a delay of seconds, minutes, hours, days or even years—as, for example, between the printing of a book and its being read in different regions or countries. In such a circumstance, communication is *asynchronous*.

We can think of a continuum of situations, ranging from virtually synchronous to extremely asynchronous, in which communication media are involved. At one extreme are communication situations involving media such as books, films, and CDs; at the other are face-to-face interaction, concerts, and events involving "live" media like television, radio, and telephones. Nearer the center of the continuum are personal correspondence, voice messaging, and telephone answering machines.

Generally speaking, new media provide greater flexibility in bridging time and space than many of the earlier media. For example, FAX machines were used as an international news medium by Chinese students living in various countries in 1989 to flood their homeland with reports of the massacre in Tiananmen Square. In 1990, the same technology was used to facilitate voting by GIs stationed in Saudi Arabia. Normally, when done by mail, the process takes at least a month. By FAX, voting was completed within twenty-four hours.[15] Depending upon the specific application and the needs of interactants, media like FAX, teleconferencing, computers and answering machines can be used in ways that either minimize or expand the gap in time between production and consumption.

LOW INTERACTIVITY—HIGH INTERACTIVITY

Communication media vary in the extent to which message content and timing are controlled by the source rather than by the user. Mass media such as books, television, newspapers, and magazines are essentially source-controlled in terms of content and timing of production and distribution. Audience members engage in active decision making about whether to give attention to particular mass media offerings and, in many instances, can actively and consciously choose *how* to use the information received. Consumer decisions—as well as letters to the editor and other forms of feedback—have an impact on content, but the influence is delayed and often indirect. In the short-term individuals have no way to interact with or control message content or timing. Such media have limited potential for *interactivity*.

Other media, such as telephones, FAX, VCRs, tapes, home video, and many computer applications, are more interactive. They permit audience members to exert greater control over the content, timing, and locale. To take one example, there are thousands of audiocassette tapes available for use at whatever time of day or night we choose to listen to them. And we may choose to play these tapes at home, at work, in the car, or while walking or jogging. We can "fast-forward" through selections we don't care for, "pause" for interruptions, and "freeze" or "rewind" to repeat messages or message segments that we particularly like. Similarly, voice mail, E-mail, and inexpensive home answering machines provide a high level of user control. See Box 8–3.

Increasingly, the capabilities of more interactive media like telephones and computers, are being combined with traditionally less interactive media like television or radio to produce interesting hybrids. For example, reality-based crime shows, like Fox Networks' "America's Most Wanted" and NBC's "Unsolved Mysteries," encourage viewers to call in tips on a toll-free 800 number. In the case of "America's Most Wanted,"

Technological advances promise to make broadcast television a far more interactive, user-controlled medium. For about the price of a movie channel, cable system subscribers in Montreal are able to play a direct and active role in creating sports and news coverage. With the new system, viewers may select from among four different views of the event on four different channels. In the case of sporting events, one channel provides the traditional "wide angle" coverage. Other channels offer close-ups of players, while yet another provides continuous instant replays. For news programs, the system allows viewers to break away from the standard newscast at various points to receive more in-depth information on a news story of particular interest and later to return to the "standard" broadcast. Other applications are being developed and market tested.

BOX 8–3 *Television Viewers Become Producers.*

153 of the 231 criminals profiled to date are now in custody, 101 as a direct result of viewer tips to (800) CRIME-90.[16]

Communication researcher Carrie Heeter provides the following list of dimensions of interactivity that may be used to classify media.[17]

- Complexity of choices available—how much choice users have regarding content and timing of utilization.
- Effort users must exert—how the activity required by the user compares to the activity level of the medium.
- Responsiveness to users—how actively a medium responds to users; the degree to which media are "conversational"—that is, operate like human conversations.
- Monitoring information use—how able a particular medium is to monitor behaviors of users and adjust its operation based on this feedback.
- Ease of adding information—how easily users are able to create and distribute messages for other user audiences. Based on this criterion, broadcast television has very low interactivity, call-in radio has moderate, and computerized bulletin boards have very high levels of interactivity.
- Facilitation of interpersonal communication—how difficult interaction is between specific and known interactants.

LOW SOCIAL PRESENCE—HIGH SOCIAL PRESENCE

In some circumstances, we may have a sense that a communication event is quite personal, sociable, and warm. In other situations, the process seems impersonal, unsociable, and cold.[18] When the former occurs, the event is described as high in *social presence;* the latter is considered to be low. Not surprisingly, face-to-face communication is generally regarded as higher in social presence than mediated communication. There are also differences between media in terms of social presence, as shown in Table 8–5.

A primary difference between face-to-face and mediated communication that affects social presence is nonverbal communication. In all mediated situations some communication modes are restricted in this regard. In the case of written media, cues related to oral paralanguage, appearance, eye gaze, kinesics, proxemics, and haptics are absent. In the case of audio mediation, visual and tactile cues are missing, and so on.

TABLE 8–5 Social Presence Rating of Five Media

Communication Mode	Social Presence Rating*
Face-to-face	0.81
Television	0.24
Multispeaker Audio	−0.18
Telephone Audio	−0.52
Business Letter	−0.85

(*Source:* J. Short, E. Williams, and B. Christie, *The Social Psychology of Telecommunications* (New York: Wiley, 1976), p. 71.

*Social presence scores range from +0.9 to −0.9.

Moreover, many of the conversational cues that are so important in face-to-face interaction may be missing in mediated situations. Researchers point out however, that, depending on the goals, the situation, and the relationship between interactants, the limitations on social presence may be unimportant. And, with care and attention, the social presence of any medium can be enhanced.

PUBLIC—PRIVATE

There was a time when viewing a movie was, of necessity, a public and mass communication event. To see a particular film, one went to a public theatre and watched the film with a large audience at one of the preset times. Today, with cable television and videocassette recorders and video rental centers, movie viewing can take place in a private—individual or group—context, at any time one chooses. Personal preferences guide film selections; and there are a variety of individualized viewing options like replay, slow motion, "freeze," and fast-forward.

Much the same can be said of banking. Electronic tellers permit a shift from the public setting of the bank during regular working hours established for the public at large to an individualized context and time that is more private and personally convenient.

Not all traditional media require public consumption. Television viewing and radio listening have always potentially been private experiences. Newspaper, magazine, and book reading also may be private and do not require that all audience members engage in the experience simultaneously.

Personal and Organizational Media

Communication media may extend any form of communication, including face-to-face. We use media in this way when we call a friend on the phone, write a letter to a relative, leave a message on an answering machine, or interact with a colleague via computer.

Communication media that assist in exchanges between two or among several people in this way are *interpersonal media*. They are being used to enhance interpersonal communication. By means of interpersonal media, time and space may be overcome in our interactions with others. These and other media are also used to expand our capabilities for communication within and between groups, organizations, and societies.

Media can be thought of as *intrapersonal communication media*, when they expand our ability to produce, store or retrieve messages of which we ourselves are the source.

We can therefore classify media as follows:

- Intrapersonal Media: tools used to extend intrapersonal communication capabilities. *Examples:* tape recorder, home video, diary, mirror.
- Interpersonal Media: tools used to extend interpersonal communication capabilities. *Examples:* letters, greeting cards, telephones.
- Group and Organizational Media: tools used to extend group and organizational communication capabilities. *Examples:* telephones, intercoms, paging systems, computers.

Mass Media and Mass Communication

DEFINITIONS

Mass communication is the most familiar form of mediated communication. It is a process through which information products are created and distributed by a mass communication organization for consumption by an audience.[19] See Figure 8–6. Most often mass communication involves *mass media* such as newspapers, magazines, books, radio, and television. Mass media technologies multiply, duplicate, or amplify messages for distribution to a large audience.

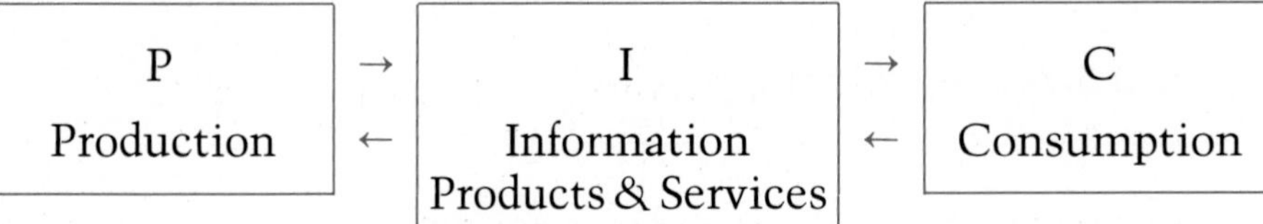

Production	Information Products & Services	Consumption
Description: Mass communication organizations create and distribute information products and/or services	**Description:** Information products and/or services are distributed to an audience	**Description:** Information products and services compete for attention, acceptance, and use among audiences.

ORGANIZATIONS:
- Television Network
- Newspaper Publishers
- Movie Producers
- Magazine Publishers
- Book Publishers
- Record Companies
- Advertising Agencies
- Public Relations Firms
- Libraries
- Museums
- Information Services
- Etc.

PRODUCTS/SERVICES:
- Television Programs
- Newspapers
- Movies
- Magazines
- Books
- Records/Tapes
- Ads
- Public Relations Campaigns
- Documents
- Exhibits
- Research Reports/Databases
- Etc.

AUDIENCES:
- Individuals
- Couples, Families, Co-Workers, Etc.
- Groups
- Organizations
- Societies

USES/IMPACT:
- Information
- Entertainment
- Persuasion
- Education
- Diversion
- Motivation
- Deception
- Socialization
- Etc.

FIGURE 8–6 *P↔I↔C Model of Mass Communication.*

Production, Distribution, and Consumption. The industrial revolution brought an age in which the mass production, distribution, and consumption of *industrial* goods was central to the economic and social fabric of our society. In a similar way, the communication revolution has brought us to an age in which the basic commodity is *information. Mass communication organizations* mass produce, distribute, and market information products and services.

- *Production* refers to the creation, gathering, packaging, or repackaging of messages.
- *Distribution* relates to the movement of mass communication products from the point of production to the point of consumption. The movement may occur immediately, as with a live television broadcast, or it may involve substantial time delays, as with magazines, books, films, or taped programs.

- *Consumption* refers to the uses, impacts, and effects that mass communication can have for a single individual, a relationship, group, organization, or society. Examples include: being informed, entertained, persuaded, educated, humored, motivated, or deceived. For a society, the influences of mass communication may be social, political, cultural, economic, or technological.

The economic relationship between the consumers and producers may be direct, indirect, or a blend of the two. In the case of movies, consumers directly underwrite production costs through their ticket purchases. Television and radio producers and distributors are supported by advertisers who want to gain access to consumers of those mass communication products. In such instances, consumers provide indirect financial support of production and distribution each time they purchase advertisers' products. With newspapers and magazines, the economic link between consumers and producers is partially direct—through payment of subscription charges. It is also partially indirect—through the purchase of advertisers' products. In the case of software products—computer programs, video games, CDs, videocassettes—audience members pay directly.

Information Products and Services. *Information products* are collections of messages organized in a particular way for a particular purpose or use by a particular audience. The term "information product" includes not only news but also entertainment, public relations and advertising, computerized databases, even museum exhibits or theatrical performances.

Information services are activities associated with the preparation, distribution, organization, storage, or retrieval of information. Information services include: news or editorial research, public relations consulting, and electronic information delivery.

The Audience. The term *audience* refers to the group of individuals who have the potential for being exposed to and using an information product or service. In the terminology of the Information Age, the audience is the *user group.*

Traditionally, when talking about mass communication, "audience" evokes an image of a very large, diverse group of viewers or readers all being exposed to the same information at more or less the same time and all unknown to the information producers. However, the advent of some of the new technologies like VCRs, CDs, portable cassette tape players, and personal computers suggests the value of a broadened concept of audience. New media make it easier to direct messages to specific segments of a mass audience. This view of "audience" does not presume that the user group must be of a specific size, nor be particularly diverse, nor that all of its members be exposed to the same information at a similar point in time, nor that members of the group be unknown to the information producers. More basic is the requirement that the information product involved must have been purposefully produced and distributed by a mass communication organization for a particular constituency. A network television program fits this definition, as does a videotape produced for a corporation, a church newsletter, or a museum exhibit.

This approach to mass communication takes account of:

- traditional mass media and newer technologies.
- convergence among once-distinct mass communication media, products, and services.
- interactive capabilities of many mass communication media.
- active decision-making roles played by mass communication producers *and* consumers.
- complex individual, social, economic, and cultural dynamics that contribute to the interplay between mass communication producer and consumer groups.
- general and specialized mass communication producers, products, services, and consumer groups.

FOUR BASIC FUNCTIONS OF MASS COMMUNICATION

Mass media and mass-mediated communication serve a number of functions. Sociologist and mass communication scholar, Charles Wright describes four: surveillance, correlation, socialization, and entertainment.[20]

Surveillance. Media provide a constant stream of news-related messages that enables audience members to be aware of developments in the environment that may affect them. *Surveillance* may consist of a *warning function,* alerting members of the audience to danger—a hurricane or pollution of the water or air, for example.

Mass-mediated communication also serves a *status conferral function;* individuals, organizations, and issues that are reported on by mass media tend to be seen as significant by members of the audience. Additionally, mass-mediated communication serves an *agenda-setting func-*

tion in that it helps to set the public agenda as to issues, individuals, and topics of concern to mass media audience members.

Correlation. Mass media serve to interrelate and interpret messages about the events of the day. The *correlation function* serves to help audience members determine the relevance that surveillance information has for them.

Socialization. Partly as an extension of the surveillance and correlation function, mass-mediated communication socializes individuals for participation in society. Mass media provide common experiences, foster shared expectations as to appropriate and inappropriate behaviors, and contribute to the creation of a common culture and cultural consensus. Mass-mediated communication also plays a central role in the transmission of cultural heritage from generation to generation.

Entertainment. Mass media are a pervasive source of mass entertainment and provide the basis for diversion and release for audience members.

By extending these concepts, we can see that mass media play a role in the production and distribution of social realities discussed in earlier chapters. In our society, and in most others, the mass media are the major providers of standardized messages regarding persons, products, situations, and events—messages that often have a major influence on the images members of the audience develop relative to them.

OTHER FUNCTIONS OF MASS COMMUNICATION

Social Contact and Sense of Community. Mass communication consumption can serve as a substitute for human contact, helping individuals avoid isolation and loneliness. As noted by mass communication researchers Robert Kubey and Mihaly Csikszentmihalyi:

> Those who lack structured interactions with other people due to unemployment, divorce, widowhood, personality factors, or declining health are more likely than others to turn to television for companionship, information, and escape. Older people who are widowed and/or retired, for example, are among the heaviest television viewers.[21]

Especially new interactive media—listener call-in radio, 900 phone numbers, and computer bulletin boards—may be seen as serving mass communication and interpersonal communication functions at the same time. See Figure 8–7.

Mass communication also gives people a sense of community and connection to others. It can also provide a stimulant to interaction to the extent that we share the same interests as other information consumers. Reading the morning newspaper, attending a particular concert, or viewing the weekend football or basketball game may facilitate interaction by providing topics for conversation.

Reassurance and Confirmation. Mass media give their audience members a "recipe" for living; the media reassure members of the audience that their sense of the way they live is reasonable, moral, and acceptable. Mass media also help audience members deal with fundamental questions about life, purpose, illness, and death.

Encountering others who share the same experiences also reaffirms the appropriateness of our own actions. As communication scholar Lee Thayer notes:

FIGURE 8–7 Recently married, Louise Broussard and Mark Tracy, pictured here, are the third couple in three years to meet through CompuServe's "CB Simulator," a network which permits users to send and receive messages through their computers. Through the system, Mark, a deaf sheet metal mechanic in Texas, was able to interact with Louise, a systems analyst in California, without having his disability present a barrier to communication. Mark and Louise interacted electronically for six months before meeting face-to-face. Their wedding was held on June 21, 1986, at a CompuServe-sponsored party in Columbus, Ohio. At the ceremony, the couple exchanged vows by typing them into a computer, as hundreds of friends looked on electronically. Reportedly, some of their friends sent presents ordered from CompuServe's "Electronic Mall" home-shopping service. Louise and Mark sent the digitized photo, above, through the CompuServe network.

> To the extent that we believe "everyone else" takes a daily newspaper, and to the extent that being like "everyone else" is vital to our own sense of being "in" the world, we will go through the ritual of "taking" a daily newspaper. If large numbers of people believed that "everyone else" attended a museum once a week, more people than now do so would go through the ritual of attending a museum. Suffering the nth repetition of a "top ten" tune being played that day, young people are no longer hearing it; they are performing a ritual—one that keeps each one tacitly in touch with all the "others."[22]

Mediated Communication: A Mixed Blessing

Mediated communication extends the basic capacities of human communication. We generally think of this expansion in very positive terms, pointing to the capability of media to traverse time and space in a manner and at a pace that would otherwise be impossible. However, mediated communication is a mixed blessing, on the one hand enhancing and enlarging the potentialities of message sending and receiving, while on the other hand limiting and constraining communication or human experience.

LIMITED COMMUNICATION MODES

One potential limitation imposed by mass communication is the reduction of the range of potential modes of communication available. In face-to-face encounters, an individual has the potential for processing visual, auditory, tactile, olfactory, and gustatory modes. Communication media limit the number of these modalities and, hence, the *richness* of the information they provide.[23] In the case of telephone, radio, or print, one mode is involved. Television or film utilize two.

In one sense, of course, any restriction on the number of available modes can be seen as limiting the richness of human communication. For some purposes, however, one or two communication modes may be quite adequate. A newspaper or magazine account of an event in the Middle East certainly may provide consumers with an overview of noteworthy events that have transpired during the period in question. However, even with the most sophisticated communication media, many of the sights, sounds, and smells that were present for the reporter are unavailable to audience members.

At times, this limitation is not a liability but is, in fact, a positive and desirable characteristic. A case in point is a work of fiction. In reading a novel, it is often the absence of fully-functioning face-to-face communication modes which both requires and allows readers to play a very active role in creating the visual images themselves. In such an instance, it can be argued that the media constraint actually enhances the richness of the communication experience.

DECREASED CONTROL

In contrast with the typical face-to-face communication situation, the receiver or audience member in mediated communication often has much less influence on the content and directions of interaction. As suggested previously, this is particularly the case in mass-mediated situations in which the only option available to an audience member who wishes to alter the content of communication is to "turn off" the message—an option that at times we might wish were available in interpersonal situations! On a longer-term basis, mass communication consumers may exercise control by writing letters or making phone calls to the station—or in the case of print media, by cancelling subscriptions. However, in these instances, the controlling feedback from the consumer is delayed, and it is unlikely that any one audience member can exercise great control over the producers or products.

New technologies, like answering machines and VCRs, have lessened the significance of this limitation of traditional media. This attribute helps to explain the popularity of many of these newer communication technologies.

It is important to note that from a source's perspective, mediated-communication situations often afford *more,* rather than *less* control. A videotaped speech, prerecorded television program, or written correspondence may be revised many times before being released. In contrast, all face-to-face communication is "live," meaning that messages are produced and transmitted in the same act. There are no opportunities for rewriting, editing, reshooting, retouching, or lip-synching.

ANONYMITY AND DEPERSONALIZATION

In mediated communication situations, interactants often have no direct knowledge of one another. In many mass communication situations, for instance, audience members may know the producer, reporter, or author by name but may have little broader knowledge of the individuals involved. Despite this relatively limited information, it is interesting that consumers may think of themselves as having personal relationships with media celebrities. Meg Ryan, co-star of the film "When Harry Met Sally," reports that she has been approached on the street by people who want to share their own dating experiences with "Sally." Even those of us who may not go to such an extreme may be momentarily surprised that a media personality we encounter in a face-to-face situation doesn't seem to recognize us as readily as we do them!

The problem of anonymity and depersonalization is particularly apparent from the perspective of mass media sources. If mass communication producers know their audience members at all, it is generally in terms of their aggregate market characteristics such as age, sex, occupation, political orientation, or brand preferences.

While this limitation may seem to be a liability, there are a number of instances in which mediated communication serves as well as it does for the very reason that interactants do not know one another personally. The success of listener call-in radio programs can be partly attributed to the anonymity afforded by the medium. One need not identify himself or herself in order to share an opinion about a controversial topic or seek advice on a personal problem. In such instances, mass communication provides a vehicle for mediated therapeutic communication.[24] The attraction of 900 number "dial-a porn" for some consumers can, similarly, be traced to the anonymity afforded by media.

It is important to remember that, in a sense, face-to-face interaction is also often mediated—by makeup, perfume, clothing, furniture arrangement, eyeglasses, scarves, and so on. Human encounters may also be mediated by shyness and apprehension, and these barriers are often less limiting in situations where technology is mediating than in face-to-face situations. It can certainly be argued that an encounter with a van Gogh portrait is more "personal" and less "anonymous" than one with a state trooper in mirrored sunglasses.

DECREASED RESPONSIBILITY AND ACCOUNTABILITY

The decreased control, anonymity, and depersonalization that sometimes occur in mediated communication situations can foster a sense of detachment, increased passivity, and a decreased sense of responsibility for directing the communication process and its outcomes. To a greater extent than in face-to-face encounters, the sense that we are actively engaged in a human communication act can be lost.[25] Because interactants are removed in time and space from one another, the dynamic nature of the process is obscured. These consequences can "spill over" to nonmediated situations, encouraging passivity and a lack of responsibility for one's role in the communication process generally.

Media and the Quality of Life

MEDIA FORMS

Over the course of human history, the forms of communication media have changed in dramatic complex ways. Our first messages using communication tools were fashioned from sticks, rocks, smoke, and fire. We have progressed today to the point where we are surrounded by a wide variety of machines and electronic devices that extend our information-processing modalities incredibly. The advent of television made it possible to view as well as listen to local and national programming for the first time. We now have cable television, projection television, and even television sets that double as telephones. While we once made our program selections from among a handful of stations, we are now able to choose among any number of offerings in most locales in the country. And, with videocassettes, we are not limited in our selections to programs being broadcast to us. In effect, we are able to create our own programming with such luxuries as rewind, slow motion, stop-action, fast-forward, and stereo sound.

Further advances in computers, cable, and telecommunication networks provide still other options. Using relatively inexpensive microcomputers and software, one can send and receive acoustically-coded alphanumeric data through telephone lines. With this media, the user has access to a number of large data bases that contain current newspapers, airline schedules, and a variety of games. Using this same equipment, it is possible to bank, shop, make restaurant reservations from home, order "hard" printed copies of desired materials, and "converse" with other computers.

As impressive as these home technologies are, there is little doubt that they will seem elementary compared to the home communication centers to which we will become accustomed in the years ahead. In all likelihood, these installations will combine the information storage and retrieval capacity of the computer and videodisks, with video display, stereophonic audio reproduction, and print capability. With these systems we will have at our disposal a wide variety of programming from which to choose—films, network shows, video concerts, news programs, documentaries, games, national and international wire services, stock market quotation services, airline schedules, weather and travel data, a range of newspapers and magazines, and even off-track betting. Through these home centers, we will be able to access and electronically display back issues of newspapers and magazines, or single out articles on particular topics of our choosing. With a press of a key, we will receive a printed, permanent copy of any of these documents.

Through the system, we will scan the pages of store catalogs and lists of sale items at supermarkets. With a touch of the keyboard, the order will be placed, the bank notified to forward payment, and our balance updated and displayed on the screen in front of us. If we need to know the telephone number of a friend, or whether a particular book is available in the local library, that information, too, will be available. A few additional keystrokes may well dial the necessary call or display the pages of the selected book on the screen.

Interconnected burglar and fire alarm systems will be linked to the center; and in the event that sensors detect a fire or break-in, information will be automatically conveyed to the fire or police department for immediate action. Our health records, favorite books, sets of encyclopedias, even family pictures, can all be stored on disks for immediate access and display, with "hard" copies available whenever desired. Writing a book, composing a song, creating visual art forms, and "personal publishing" of all sorts will be options for anyone who has access to the center.

MEDIA FUNCTIONS

For all the obvious changes in the *forms* of our communication media over the years, it is important to question the extent to which their *functions* have also changed. There can be little doubt that communication media today are quicker and more flexible than ever before. To what degree, however, have these changes led to an improvement in the quality of human communication or the quality of life? In any given day, how much more do we know as a result of all the technology we have available? Are people more satisfied in their jobs? How much better entertained are we by all the new media? Are we better organized, or happier? Do we have better relationships? Do people understand each other better? Is the promise of improved cross-cultural relations becoming a reality?

Questions such as these remind us that communication media are only extensions of our own communication abilities and liabilities. They can do little more than display, transport, store, duplicate, amplify, or display the messages *we* create. The nature and significance of messages and the uses to which they are put will depend, in the final analysis, upon us and not upon our media.

Implications and Applications: Media and Mediation

• Media play a pervasive role in our personal, social, and occupational activities.

• Through mediated communication we are able to overcome natural limitations of space and time.

• Mediated communication also provides a means for supplementing human memory by expanding our capacity for storing, arranging, and retrieving information.

• The ever-increasing array of messages and media in our environment makes it increasingly difficult to be "on top of" all the information resources available to us.

• Increasingly, we need the capacity to analyze media and messages to determine their quality, value, and appropriateness for particular purposes. We need to know when and how to select particular media and messages and when and how to *deselect*—disregard, distrust, or ignore—media and messages. This implies that we must also develop skills for assessing our own and others' communication needs and goals.

• There are many circumstances in which mediated communication can be substituted for—and may be more effective than—face-to-face communication. In such situations, we must be able to determine the trade-offs between these two types of communication—as sources and receivers.

• As our forms of personal, organizational, and mass media become increasingly sophisticated, it is easy to conclude that the qualities of human communication and of human life are advancing at a similar pace. Changes in media forms, however, do not necessarily result in corresponding changes in function. More news sources, channels, watts, remote controls, CDs, video games, and videotapes do not necessarily result in our being better informed, better entertained, happier, or more successful. A critical question is: As individuals in relationships, groups, organizations, and societies, are we *using* mediated or face-to-face communication in a way that can fulfill the desired functions?

Summary

Our tool-making facility has given us the ability to create communication media—technological devices that extend our natural ability to create, transmit, receive, and process visual, auditory, olfactory, gustatory, or tactile messages. The basic functions media serve involve: message production and distribution, and reception, storage, and retrieval.

Communication media have had major impacts on contemporary life. These include an increase in the number of messages and media, an increase in the capacity for information storage and retrieval, a substitution of communication media for transportation technology, the initiation of new concepts of office and home, the changed uses of media, an increase in the value of information as a commodity, and the increasing availability of synthetic experience. Characteristics of media include their degree of synchronicity, interactivity, social presence, and public versus private nature.

Media may extend any form of communication, including face-to-face. Mass communication, the most familiar form of mediated communication, is a process through which information products are created and distributed by a mass communication organization for consumption by an audience. Mass media and mass-mediated communication serve a number of functions, including: surveillance, correlation, socialization, entertainment, social contact, sense of community, reassurance, and confirmation. Mediated communication is a mixed blessing, in that it provides limited communication modes, decreased control, anonymity and depersonalization, decreased responsibility, and accountability.

Over the course of human history, the forms of communication media have changed in dramatic ways. For all the changes in the *forms,* it is important to question the extent to which their *functions* have also changed. Have these changes led to an improvement in the quality of human communication or in the quality of life? Questions such as these remind us that the nature and significance of messages and the uses to which they are put will depend, in the final analysis, upon us and not upon our media.

Notes

1. For detailed discussions of the history of communication media see George N. Gordon, "Communication," in *World Book Encyclopedia* (Chicago: World Book, 1981), Vol. 4, pp. 711–723; and Colin Cherry, *World Communication: Threat or Promise? A Socio-Technical Approach* (New York: Wiley, 1971). See also Jorge Reina Schement and Daniel A. Stout, Jr., "A Time-Line of Information Technology," in *Information and Behavior: Volume 3. Mediation, Information, and Communication.* Ed. by Brent D. Ruben and Leah Lievrouw (New Brunswick, NJ: Transaction, 1989), pp. 395–424.

2. Anthony Smith, *Goodbye Gutenberg: The Newspaper Revolution of the 1980s* (Oxford: Oxford University Press, 1980), p. 3.

3. Trish Hall, "Electronics: It's Not Home without It," *New York Times,* Mar. 29, 1990, p. C1, C6.

4. Ithiel De Sola Pool, Hiroshi Inose, Nozomu Takaski and Roger Hurwitz, *Communication Flows: A Census in the United States and Japan* (New York: North-Holland Press, 1984), p. 44. Based on data covering 1960 to 1980 for radio, television, cable television, records, tapes, movies, classroom education, newspapers, books, direct mail, first class mail, telephone calls, telex, telegrams, mail grams, FAX and data communication.

5. Further discussion of these issues is provided in Todd Hunt and Brent D. Ruben, *Mass Communication: Producers and Consumers* (New York: Harper-Collins, 1992).

6. "Running Your Business from Home," *Aide Magazine,* Feb. 9, 1991 p. 10.

7. Everette E. Dennis, "Director's Commentary," *Communique,* Vol. 4, No. 5, January, 1990, p. 2.

8. Edwin Parker, "Information Utilities and Mass Communication," in *The Information Utility and Social Choice.* Ed. by H. Sackman and Norman Nie (Montvale, NJ: AFIPS Press, 1970). p. 53.

9. Further discussion of these issues is provided in Hunt and Ruben, 1992, Chapter 20; and Jorge Reina Schement and Leah Lievrouw, *Complex Visions, Complex Realities: Social Aspects of the Information Society* (Norwood, NJ: Ablex, 1987).

10. Schement and Lievrouw, 1987, p. 3.

11. Alfred G. Smith, "The Cost of Communication," Presidential Address, International Communication Association, 1974. Abstracted as "The Primary Resource," *Journal of Communication,* Vol. 25, 1975, pp. 15–20.

12. The *New York Times,* Dec. 1, 1990, p. F6, based on figures from the Electronic Industries Association, Communication Research, Inc., and *Consumer Reports Magazine.*

13. Ray Funkhouser and Eugene F. Shaw, "How Synthetic Experience Shapes Social Reality," *Journal of Communication,* Vol. 40, No. 2., 1990, p. 78.

14. Funkhouser and Shaw, 1990, p. 79.

15. The *New York Times,* November 2, 1990, p. A 34.

16. Dylan Jones, "Show Brings 101st Fugitive to Justice," *USA Today*, Mar 13, 1990 p. 5.

17. See listing, discussion, and review of additional writings on this topic by Carrie Heeter, "Implications of New Interactive Technologies for Conceptualizing Communication," in *Media Use in the Information Age: Emerging Patterns of Adoption and Consumer Use*. Ed. by J. L. Salvaggio and J. Bryant (Hillsdale, NJ: Lawrence Erlbaum) pp. 217–235; Ronald E. Rice, "New Media Technology: Growth and Integration," in *The New Media*. Ed. by R. Rice and Associates (Beverly Hills: Sage, 1984), pp. 33–54; and William Paisley, "Computerizing Information: Lessons from a Videotex Trial," *Journal of Communication*, Vol. 33, No. 1, 1983, pp. 153–161.

18. See Ronald E. Rice, "Computer-Mediated Communication System Network Data: Theoretical Concerns and Empirical Examples," *International Journal of Man-Machine Studies*, Vol. 32, 1990, pp. 627–647; Ronald E. Rice and Gail Love, "Electronic Emotion: Socioemotional Content in a Computer-Mediated Communication Network," *Communication Research*, Vol. 14, No. 1, 1987, pp. 85–108; and Rice, 1984, pp. 57–62, for a detailed discussion.

19. See Hunt and Ruben, 1992, especially Chapter 1, for a detailed presentation of this approach to mass communication.

20. Charles R. Wright, *Mass Communication: A Sociological Perspective*. 3rd ed. (New York: Random House, 1986).

21. Robert Kubey and Mihaly Csikszentmihalyi, *Television and the Quality of Life: How Viewing Shapes Everyday Experience* (Hillsdale, NJ: Lawrence Erlbaum, 1990), p. 168.

22. Lee Thayer, "On the Mass Media and Mass Communication: Notes Toward A Theory," in *Beyond Media: New Approaches to Mass Communication*. Ed. by Richard W. Budd and Brent D. Ruben (New Brunswick, NJ: Transaction, 1988), p. 65.

23. See discussion and review of literature on information richness in Ronald E. Rice and Associates, "Task Analyzability, Use of New Media, and Effectiveness: A Multi-Site Exploration of Media Richness," *Organization Science*, 1991, in press.

24. Gary Gumpert and Sandra L. Fish, eds., *Talking to Strangers: Mediated Therapeutic Communication* (Norwood, NJ: Ablex, 1990) provide an excellent collection of articles examining therapeutic uses of communication technologies.

25. See Kubey and Csikszentmihalyi, 1990, for a discussion of the impact of television viewing on passivity.

References and Suggested Readings

BELL, DANIEL. *The Coming of Post-industrial Society*. New York: Basic Books, 1973.

BENIGER, JAMES. *The Control Revolution.* Cambridge, MA: Harvard University Press, 1986.

BUDD, RICHARD D., and BRENT D. RUBEN. *Beyond Media: New Approaches to Mass Communication. Second Ed.* New Brunswick, NJ: Transaction, 1988.

CHERRY, COLIN. *World Communication.* New York: Wiley, 1971.

DIDSBURY, H. F., JR. *Communication and the Future: Prospects, Promises, and Problems.* Bethesda, MD: World Future Society, 1982.

DIZARD, WILSON P., JR. *The Coming Information Age: An Overview of Technology, Economics, and Politics.* New York: Longman, 1989.

EDELSTEIN, ALEX S., J. E. BOWES, and SHELDON M. HARSEL. *Information Societies: Comparing the Japanese and American Experiences.* Seattle, WA: University of Washington Press, 1978.

FUNKHOUSE, RAY, and EUGENE F. SHAW. "How Synthetic Experience Shapes Social Reality." *Journal of Communication,* Vol. 40, No. 2, 1990, 75–87.

GUMPERT, GARY, and ROBERT CATHCART. *Inter/Media: Interpersonal Communication in a Media World.* New York: Oxford University Press, 1986.

GUMPERT, GARY, and SANDRA L. FISH, eds. *Talking to Strangers: Mediated Therapeutic Communication.* Norwood, NJ: Ablex. 1990.

HAMMER, D. P. *The Information Age: Its Development and Impact.* Metuchen, NJ: Scarecrow Press, 1976.

HEETER, CARRIE. "Implications of New Interactive Technologies for Conceptualizing Communication." In *Media Use in the Information Age: Emerging Patterns of Adoption and Consumer Use.* Ed. by J. L. Salvaggio and J. Bryant. Hillsdale, NJ: Lawrence Erlbaum, 217–235.

HUNT, TODD, and BRENT D. RUBEN. *Mass Communication: Producers and Consumers.* New York: HarperCollins, 1992.

KRAUT, ROBERT E. "Telework as a Work-Style Innovation." In *Information and Behavior: Volume 2.* Ed. by Brent D. Ruben. New Brunswick, NJ: Transaction, 1988, 116–146.

KUBEY, ROBERT, and MIHALY CSIKSZENTMIHALYI. *Television and the Quality of Life: How Viewing Shapes Everyday Experience.* Hillsdale, NJ: Lawrence Erlbaum, 1990.

MACHLUP, FRITZ. *The Production and Distribution of Knowledge in the United States.* Princeton, NJ: Princeton University Press, 1962.

MASUDA, YONEJI. *The Information Society as Post-industrial Society.* Washington, DC: World Future Society, 1980.

MIRABITO, MICHALE M., and BARBARA L. MORGENSTERN. *The New Communications Technologies.* Boston: Focal, 1990.

MOWLANA, HAMID. *Global Information and World Communication: New Frontiers in International Relations.* New York: Longman, 1986.

OETTINGER, ANTHONY G. "Information Resources: Knowledge and Power in the 21st Century. *Science,* Vol. 209, No. 4, 1980.

POOL, ITHIEL DE SOLA. *Technologies of Freedom.* Cambridge, MA: Belknap, 1983.

POOL, ITHIEL DE SOLA, HIROSHI INOSE, NOZOMU TAKASKA, and ROGER HURWITZ.

Communications Flows: A Census in the United States and Japan. New York: North-Holland, 1984.

PORAT, MARC. *Information Economy: Definition and Measurement.* Washington, DC: U.S. Department of Commerce, Office of Telecommunications, May, 1977.

RICE, RONALD E. *The New Media: Communication, Research, and Technology.* Beverly Hills, CA: Sage, 1984.

RICE, RONALD E., and GAIL LOVE. "Electronic Emotion: Socioemotional Content in a Computer-Mediated Communication Network." *Communication Research,* Vol. 14, No. 1, 1987, 85–108.

RICE, RONALD E., and ASSOCIATES. "Task Analyzability, Use of New Media, and Effectiveness: A Multi-Site Exploration of Media Richness." *Organization Science,* 1991.

ROGERS, EVERETT. *Communication Technology.* New York: Free Press, 1986.

RUBIN, M. R., and M. T. HUBER. *The Knowledge Industry in the United States: 1960-1980.* Princeton, NJ: Princeton University Press, 1986.

SALVAGGIO, JERRY L. *Telecommunications: Issues and Choices for Society.* New York: Oxford University Press, 1983.

SCHEMENT, JORGE R., and LEAH LIEVROUW, eds. *Competing Visions, Complex Realities: Social Aspects of the Information Society.* Norwood, NJ: Ablex, 1987.

SCHEMENT, JORGE, REINA SCHEMENT, and DANIEL STOUT. "A Time-line of Information Technology." In *Information and Behavior, Vol 3: Information, Mediation, and Communication.* Edited by Brent D. Ruben and Leah Lievrouw. New Brunswick, NJ: Transaction, 1989.

SMITH, ANTHONY. *Goodbye Gutenberg.* New York: Oxford University Press, 1980.

THAYER, LEE. "On the Mass Media and Mass Communication: Notes Toward A Theory." In *Beyond Media: New Approaches to Mass Communication.* Ed. by Richard W. Budd and Brent D. Ruben. New Brunswick, NJ: Transaction, 1988.

———. *Communication and Communication Systems.* Homewood, IL: Richard D. Irwin, 1968.

WILLIAMS, FREDERICK. *The Communications Revolution.* Beverly Hills: Sage, 1982.

WRIGHT, CHARLES R. *Mass Communication: A Sociological Perspective. Third Ed.* New York: Random House, 1986.

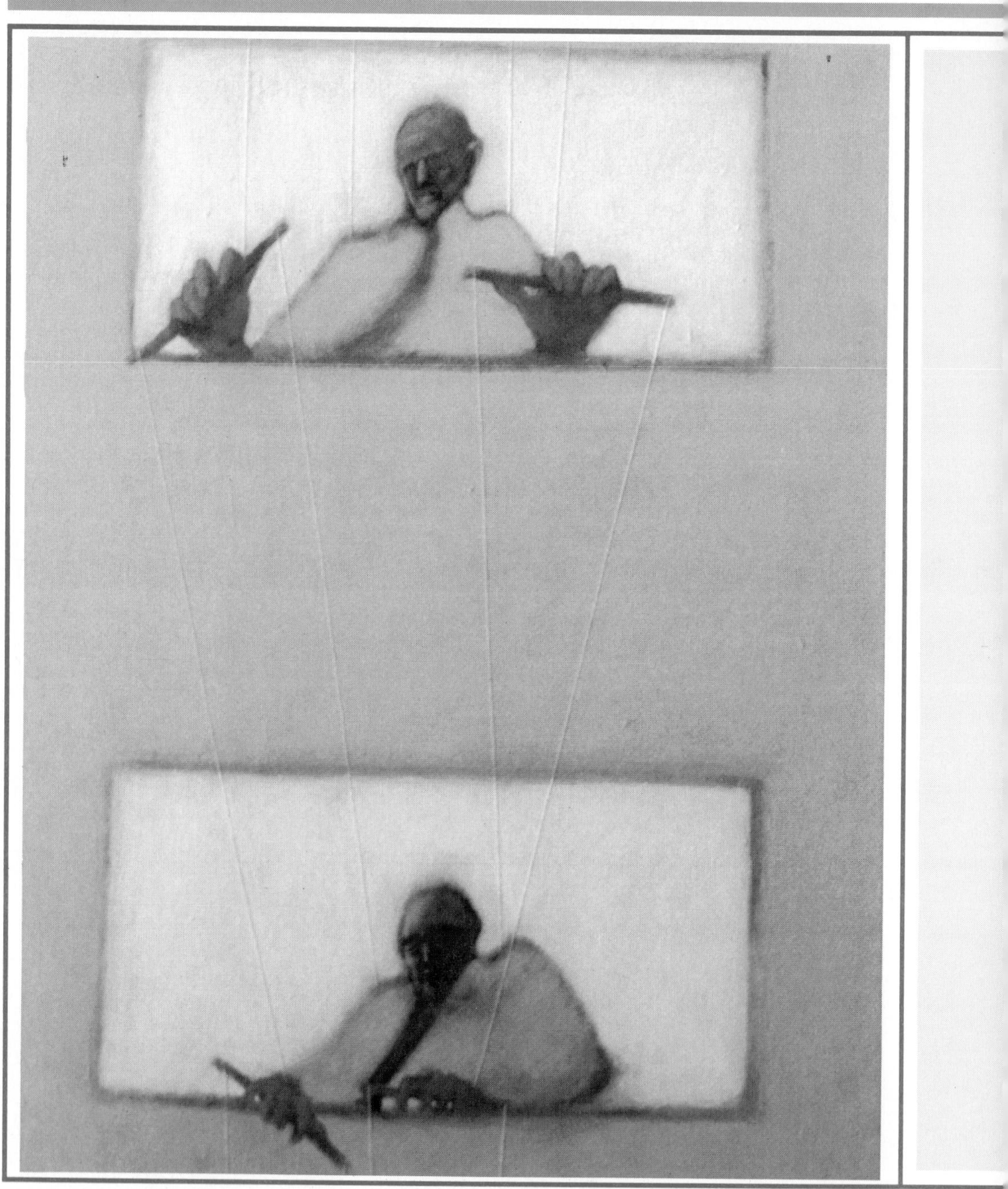

9

The Individual

Reaction, Action, and Interaction

In Part 2 of the book we discussed message reception, verbal and nonverbal codes, and the nature and role of communication mediation in some detail. When we examine these separately, we "freeze" and dissect the communication process in order to gain a better understanding of its components. The chapters in this section extend this framework to consider broadly the role of communication in the ongoing activities of individuals, relationships, groups, organizations, cultures, and societies. We begin with a focus on the individual and the role communication processes play in our everyday lives and in our long-term development.

Through message receiving and sending we *sense, make sense of,* and *act toward* the people, circumstances, and objects in our environment. As we process visual, auditory, tactile, olfactory, or gustatory messages, we are *reacting* to our environment. When we initiate verbal and nonverbal communication, we are *acting.* We are *interacting* when we are involved in message-sending, message-receiving exchanges with other interactants.

Reacting, acting, and interacting are the most basic activities of human communication. They are essential to basic functions like navigation, parent-child relations, and courtship, and are equally vital to decision making, cognitive development, self-development, self-expression, and self-reflexiveness.

Decision Making

In the ongoing dynamics of human life, we must not only select, interpret, and remember messages, but we must also use the resulting information as the basis for the decisions that guide our behavior. Our decision making occurs in what may be termed an *information-use environment.* We can distinguish four general types of information-use environments.[1]

- Geographical—defined by physical or geographical limits. Examples: a room, building, neighborhood, city, state, region, or country.
- Interpersonal—defined by the presence of other individuals in face-to-

face situations. Examples: ritual greeting situations, riding with others on an elevator, an interview, a conversation, or a date.

- Group or Organizational—defined by presence of individuals in a group or organizational unit formed for a specific purpose. Examples: a club, a fraternity or sorority, a religious organization, a corporation, a public institution.
- Cultural or Societal–defined by the presence of individuals who may be personally unknown to each other, but who are linked by a common cultural, ethnic, or national affiliation. Examples: Chicano, Black, Canadian.

We carry out decision-making activities in any of these circumstances by employing an *information-use sequence* through which messages are used as the basis for description, classification, evaluation, and action. See Figure 9–1.

In nearly every circumstance, a primary use of a message is to *describe:* to determine the nature, characteristics, or appearance of an object, situation, or person. Description is necessary for the most basic communication functions like navigation, food finding, and courtship, as well as in relationships, groups, organizations, or societies.

Based on our descriptions, *classification* is possible. When we classify, we compare our new observations with information stored from previous experience to see where a person, object, or event "fits."

Through *evaluation* we identify the range of possible relationships between ourselves and the objects, situations, or persons in our environment, and determine what, if any, actions or reactions are appropriate and/or necessary.

A fourth step in the message-processing sequence is carrying out particular verbal or nonverbal actions, based on our descriptions, classifications, and evaluations. Then, after *acting,* we often gather information as "feedback" to monitor and assess the impact of those actions. In so doing, we are once again involved in the description, classification, and (re)evaluation and action sequence. See Figure 9–2 on page 289.

We can illustrate this sequence by considering a very simple activity. Imagine for a moment that you have just opened the door of your hotel room and stepped out into the corridor looking for a place to relax and spend ten minutes before your dinner reservation. As you begin to move through the hallway, you notice a chair ahead of you. Actually, of course, you don't notice a chair. Instead, you see a physical object from a particular point of view. Based upon the visible characteristics of that object, you infer the existence of portions of it that you cannot see. You may only be able to make out two legs, for instance, connected by what

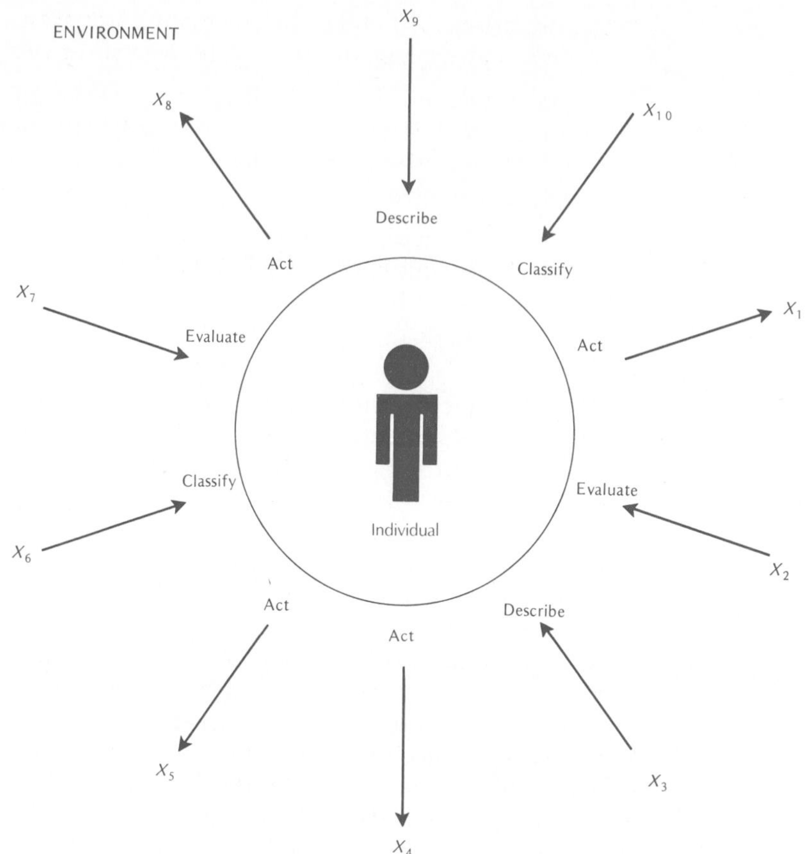

FIGURE 9–1 We use messages to which we react to describe, classify, and evaluate the objects, people, and circumstances in our environment. When we *act* based upon our reactions, we *create* messages, completing the information processing sequence.

appears to be a one-inch horizontal plane. Given your observation that the object is standing evenly on the floor, however, it seems safe to conclude that there are probably two additional legs which are not visible because of your position relative to the object. See Figure 9–3.

As you continue to process information, you eventually classify the object as a chair, by which you mean "something to sit on." In the split second that this information-processing sequence requires, you observe it, walk over, and sit down, in full confidence that the object will support your weight.

With but a slight change in circumstance, the outcomes of informa-

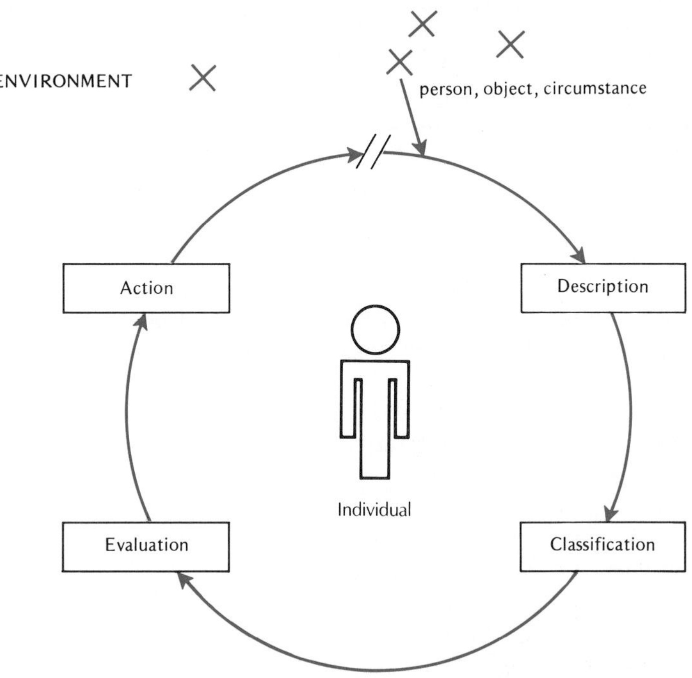

FIGURE 9–2 Information Use Sequence

tion processing might be quite different. If, for example, the hallway were crowded with people and you were in a hurry, your attention might well be focused on *avoiding* rather than *using* the chair. In such a situation, the objective would be to maneuver past the object, perhaps without ever giving a thought to it as "something to sit on." The chair would be a "stationary object to be avoided," and you would act to move rapidly past it.

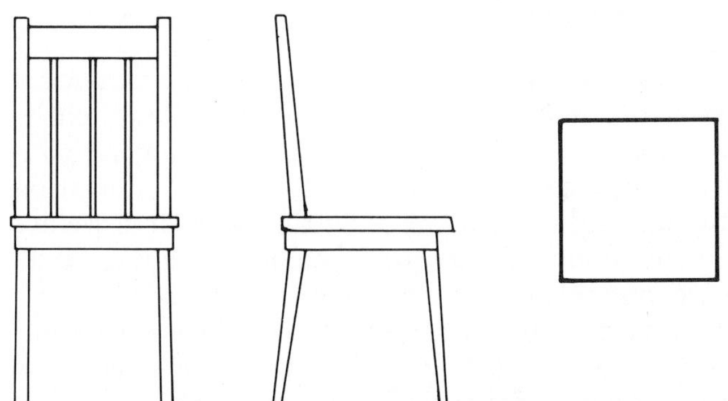

FIGURE 9–3 In observing an object such as a chair we infer—based on past experience—elements, properties, and characteristics that we often cannot actually see.

From the perspective of decision making, the way we process information about people, circumstances, and objects is similar. If you noticed someone walking toward you in the hotel hallway, his or her appearance, expressions, eye movements, actions, use of time and space would serve as message sources in the same way as did the properties of the chair. His or her nonverbal (and perhaps, verbal) behavior would serve as the basis for information as to age, sex, race, attractiveness, and perhaps even willingness to converse.

If, from your description, classification, and evaluation the person seemed friendly, interesting, and receptive, you might exchange glances, smile, or speak. If, however, you were in a hurry to check out and catch a plane, it is likely that you would relate to the individual in the hallway precisely as you would to the chair in the previous example. He or she would be classified essentially as "an object to be avoided," with the major difference between a person and a chair being that the former is "mobile" and the latter "stationary." Thus, whether the message sources that matter to us in a particular situation are people, objects, or circumstances, we go through a similar process of describing, classifying, evaluating, and then acting. Because of differing goals, needs, habits, and other factors, however, the outcomes of this sequence may vary greatly from one situation to another.

When decision making involves other people, the process of reacting to and acting toward often gives rise to a process of *interacting.* In such a circumstance the decision-making activities of each person are contingent on behavior of the other. As we shall see in the next chapter, it is by means of interpersonal communication and reciprocal decision making that relationships are developed.

Cognitive Development

As psychologist O. J. Harvey noted so succinctly, "That the individual will come to structure or make sense of the personally relevant situation is one of psychology's most pervasive tenets."[2] During each instant, we are involved in reacting to, acting toward, and interacting with our environment and the people in it. At the same time we are engaged in a far more subtle activity with major long-term consequences for us. As we routinely process information, we are also developing internalized representations of our world that allow us to think and comprehend what we experience around us. These personal theories or representations—which are variously termed *images, mental models, cognitive maps,* and *semantic networks*—provide the means for relating to the environment and one another.[3]

LEARNING

Our images develop over time in a very complex manner. The process begins early in life.

> The newborn baby is not capable of speech, symbolic understanding, or directing skillful mobility. It has no ideas, words, or concepts, no tools for communication, no significant sensory experience, no culture. The newborn baby never smiles. He (or she) is unable to comprehend the loving phrases of his (or her) mother or to be aware of the environment.[4]

Facilitated and limited by the physiological potentialities we inherit—our "cognitive hardware"—we begin to learn about our environment and our relation to it and to develop our personalized theories—our "cognitive software."

> For some time . . . (the baby) see(s) just a mass of shifting shapes and colors, a single, ever-changing picture in front of (him or her). . . . The picture . . . is not made up, as it is for us, of many separate elements, each of which we can imagine and name, by itself, and all of which we can combine in our minds in other ways.
>
> When we see a chair in a room, we can easily imagine that chair in another part of the room, or in another room, or by itself. But for the baby the chair is an integral part of the room he (or she) sees. . . . This may be the reason, or one of the reasons, why when we hide something from a very young baby, it ceases to exist for him (or her). And this in turn may be one of the reasons why peek-a-boo games are such fun for small babies to play, and may contribute much to their growing understanding of the world.[5]

The infant's awareness of mother, father, food, and objects as potential sources of satisfaction represents perhaps the first elements of the child's lifelong map-making enterprise. Gradually, the infant's world view expands to take account of the rapidly broadening environment of his or her experience. The fascination and attention to fingers, hands, and mouth broadens to toys in and around the crib and to the physical environment itself. The map continues to expand to define more and more detail of the child's room, other rooms in the dwelling, the neighborhood, the community, and eventually, the country and world. At the same time, the child is developing the verbal and nonverbal communi-

FIGURE 9–4 As we respond to the many circumstances, objects, and persons in our environment, we are developing our internalized theories of the world.

cation rules necessary for making sense of and relating to his or her social environment—first family, then friends, relatives, acquaintances, teachers, peers, colleagues at work, and so on.

As children grow, they select, interpret, and retain information, and they begin to learn about the physical and social environment and their relationship to it. The physical and social world provides an extensive menu of message sources, as the developing human individual embarks upon a life-long quest to make sense of and cope with the situations he or she encounters.

As suggested in earlier discussions, much remains to be learned about the ways in which selected environmental cues are transformed into interpretable information and stored in a way that makes it quickly and easily accessible to us. It is thought by scholars working in this area that much of the information is processed and stored in long-term memory in what cognitive psychologists term a *semantic network,* whereby incoming messages are linked systematically to previously stored information based on common characteristics.

A *canary,* for instance, might become significant to an individual through a process of comparing its properties to those of previously observed and classified objects. That it "has wings," "flies," and is "quite small" suggests it is similar to other animals one has learned to call *birds*—about which information has been previously processed and retained. That this *bird* "sings" and is "in a cage in a friend's house," suggests that while this canary has much in common with other birds, it also is different in some respects. A *canary* is a special kind of bird—a *pet bird.* See Figure 9–5.

As Morton Hunt explains:

> New material is added to this network by being plunked down in a hole in the middle of an appropriate region, and then gradually . . . tied in, by a host of meaningful connections, to the appropriate nodes in the surrounding network.

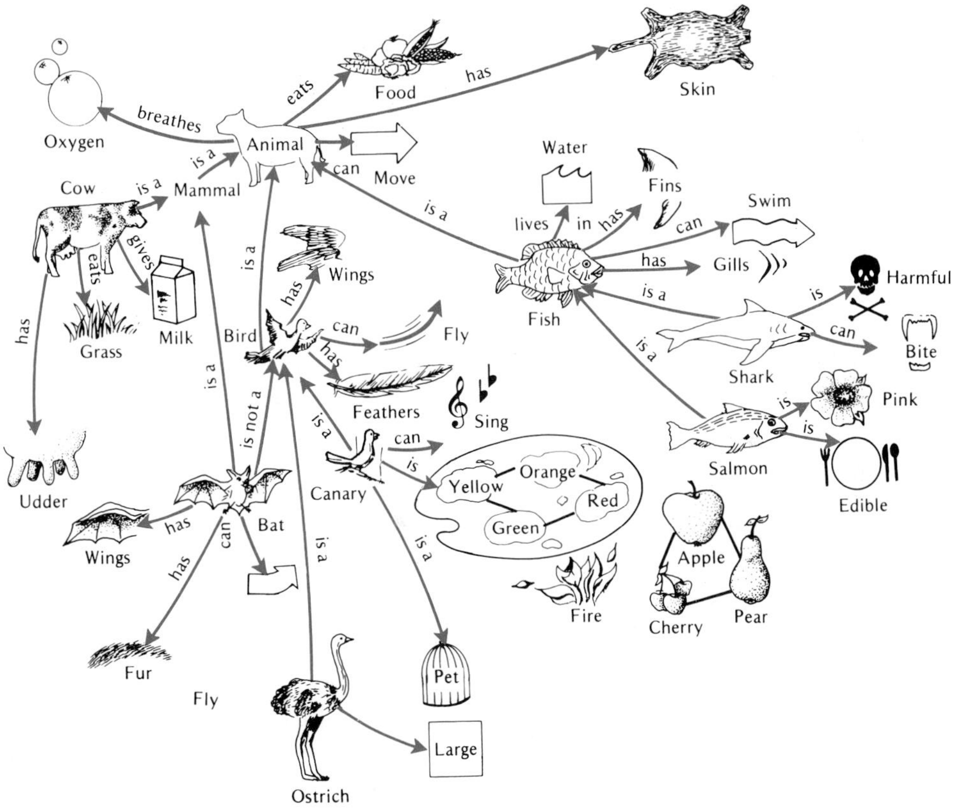

FIGURE 9–5 Humans interpret, store, and retrieve information according to the associations and meanings the objects, phenomena, and events of their experience have for them.

Source: Adapted from *Cognitive Psychology and Information Processing,* R. Lachman, J. L. Lachman, and E. C. Butterfield. Coypright © 1979 by Lawrence Erlbaum Associates. By permission.

> Thus, although remembered information is arranged by categories of subject matter, the arrangement is far less orderly and regular than in reference works or libraries. But also far more redundant: we have many ways of getting to something filed in long-term memory, many cues and routes to the item we are seeking. When no cue or route takes us directly to it, we can guide ourselves to the general area and then mentally run through the items in that area until we come across the one we're looking for.[6]

Our personal theories and representations are the long-term informational consequence of our efforts to adapt to the messages with which we are confronted over the course of our lifetimes.[7] They are not simply the result of an accumulation of messages to which we have been exposed, though these messages certainly play an important role.[8]

MEDIATED COMMUNICATION AND DEVELOPMENT

Mediated communication plays a critical role in the developmental process. In our culture, television is the first medium to which children are exposed, and it rapidly becomes a noteworthy part of their lives.[9] Studies indicate that by four years of age, many children have become regular viewers.[10] Researchers have found that television use begins even earlier for some children, based on observations that babies six to twelve months old respond visually and verbally to TV for one to two hours daily.[11]

Books, and later newspapers and magazines, begin to take on significance during the grade school years. Studies find that one-third of six to eight year olds have read a newspaper. The percentage increases to 61 percent for nine to eleven year olds, 75 percent for twelve to fourteen year olds, and more than 80 percent for fifteen to seventeen year olds.[12]

A similar pattern occurs for radio and recordings. One-third of six to eight year olds listen to radio or recordings on a daily basis; the figure increases to 60 percent of fifteen to seventeen year olds.[13] Particularly in the past decade, the availability of video games, VCRs, walkman units, computers, and other media has further extended the role of mass communication in the daily routines of children.

CHARACTERISTICS OF PERSONAL REPRESENTATIONS

Through a subtle self-programming process, as a consequence of communication, we acquire the personal theories and mental models and associations that direct our behavior in any given situation. Whether we are aware of it or not, our models and our rules tell us what to say, when to say it, how to act in this and that circumstance, how to tell one kind of circumstance from another, what to pay attention to and what to ignore, what to value and what to despise, what type of people to seek out and which to avoid, what and whom to believe, and so on.

These representations are our means for navigating about in our symbolic and physical environment and the basis for our functioning as human beings. They enable us to act and react and to carry our knowledge of our environment forward in time. Without them, each experience would be totally new and bewildering.

The significance of these theories is clearest when one considers an illustration such as the simple act of putting a key in a lock or opening a door. Our image of doors and our rules for door opening tell us how to locate and use the handle and whether to pull or push the door in order to open it. Without this stored knowledge, each door opening would be a wholly novel experience. Were it not for our representations, even the identification of a door would be a trial-and-error matter, because we would have no way other than by means of our maps to identify doors in the first place.

Models are also invaluable in dealing with interpersonal facets of our environment. Standardized greetings such as a handshake and "Hi, how are you?" and "Fine, thanks, and you?" are easily accomplished. This is the case because we have categorized a particular situation as being like certain other situations in the past, for which we have learned a particular conversational pattern. Our models also guide us in deciding when "Hi! How are you?" is simply a request for a "routine" acknowledgement, and when the person wants more detailed information on our physical or mental health.

In emphasizing the obvious assets and values of our internal theory building capability, it is quite possible to overlook some of the shortcomings and dysfunctions of this capacity. Primary among these liabilities is the fact that once our internal representations become fairly well defined, they take on an objective quality. Often, they seem so real to us that we lose sight of their representational nature, and forget that they are in many senses our own personal creations. We seldom give a second thought, for instance, to whether a paper dollar has buying power, or to the meaning of symbols like "dog" or "mother," "Protestant" or "Catholic," "Democrat" or "Republican," "son," or "father." We have so thoroughly internalized our images of "dollars," "mother," "father," "Catholics," and "dogs," that we may behave as if our representations were, in fact, identical to the persons, objects, situations, or ideas to which they refer.

This kind of problem comes about for several reasons:[14]

1. The environment is constantly changing while our representations are relatively fixed.
2. Any representation is necessarily incomplete.
3. Representations are personal and subjective.
4. Representations are social products.
5. Representations are resistant to change.

Change. Like a paper map and the territory it characterizes, there can never be a point-for-point correspondence between our cognitive map and our environment. General semanticists, to whom we must be grateful for the map-and-territory analogy, point out several reasons why this match between our internal maps and external physical and symbolic reality is never complete. The first has to do with the process-like nature of the environment. The environment is ever-changing, and one "can never step in the same river twice."[15] Our symbols and symbolic images are not always changing in the same way or at the same rate as the environment. For instance, long after we have moved a clock or wastebasket to a new location, we persist in looking for it where it used to be because of our well-learned maps.

The point to be mindful of is that the usefulness of our representations is often time-dependent. Images and models appropriate at one point in time may be useless, even harmful at other times. The world and the behavior of its inhabitants may change substantially from one time to another, and there is unfortunately no guarantee that our maps will be sensitive to these changes. If for no other reason, we should perhaps be grateful that our memories are imperfect, since forgetting contributes to the potential for change in our maps.[16]

Incomplete. A second reason for mismatches between our maps and the environment is that our representations are always less complete and comprehensive than what they symbolize. Details are invariably left out. Much as a highway map highlights some features of the landscape and ignores others, our personal images are also selective. They are generalizations that categorize or stereotype selected aspects of the environment for our convenience. See Figure 9–6.

The symbol "dog," to which we have previously referred, illustrates this point. Each person has a different image of the animal to which the word refers. When we think of dog, our images are based on our own personal experience, which bears an arbitrary relationship to the four-

The United States: The Country

The United States: The States

FIGURE 9–6 Our maps, like physical maps of geographic territories, are necessarily selective. Maps highlight some characteristics of a territory and obscure others.

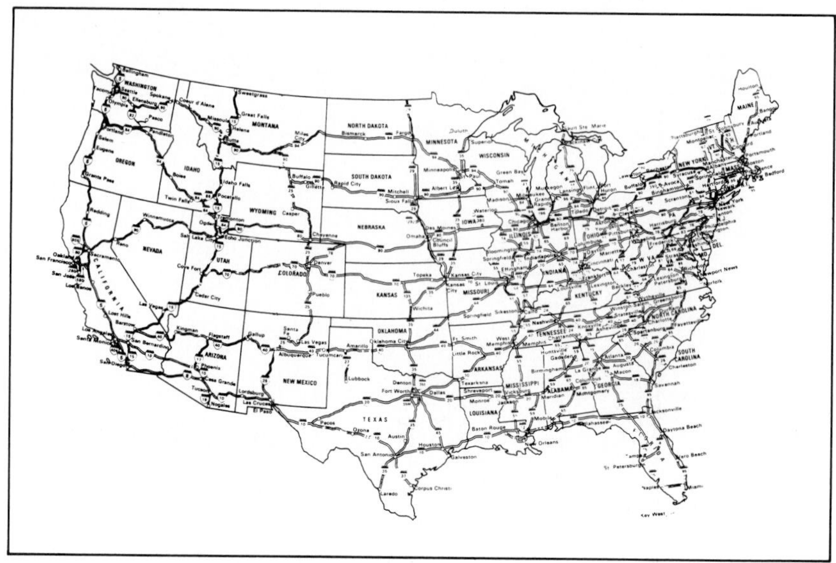

The United States: Interstate Routes and Major Cities

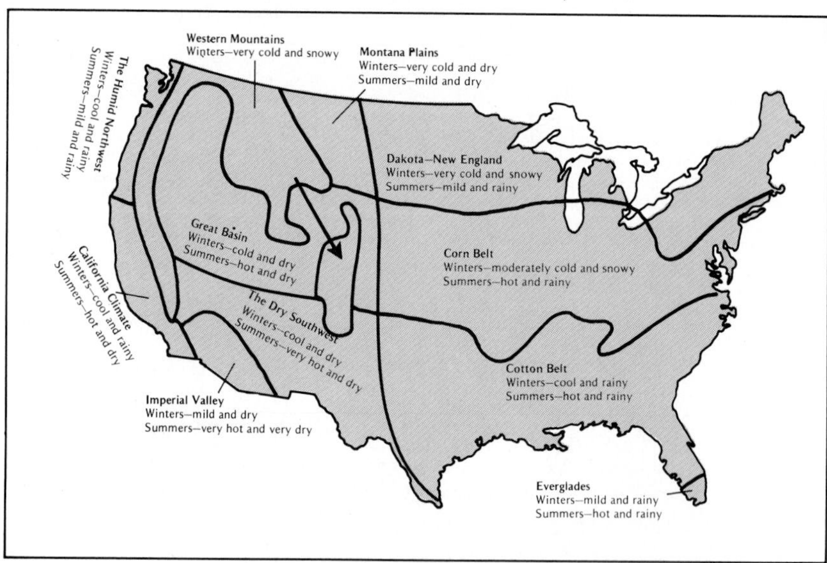

The United States: Climates

FIGURE 9–6 *(continued).*

legged animal we refer to as "dog." Further, one's personal meaning of "dog" is very likely to be far less comprehensive than the collective standardized definitions of the word.

Personal and Subjective. As we know, our images develop in our effort to adapt to the situations that confront us in our lives. We are not all confronted with the same situations, and the images and rules we develop as a result of our experiences vary greatly from person to person.

An exchange between two characters in the film *Eye of the Beholder* makes this point. The scene takes place on a sidewalk in an urban area. A landlord (Copplemeyer) and his artist tenant (Michael Garrard) gaze across the street at a passing woman:

GARRARD: "Do you see that woman over there? She isn't real."
COPPLEMEYER: "That woman over there isn't real, huh? I made her up from my imagination?"
GARRARD: "Yes, exactly. One man looks and sees nothing, another looks and falls in love. Today I will put on a canvas what I see in a woman. To me the painting will be as real as that woman. To you it will be only a painting."
COPPLEMEYER: "The painting will be as real as that woman?"
GARRARD: "Yes, Copplemeyer, yes! Do you understand?"
COPPLEMEYER: "I understand you are a lunatic!"
GARRARD: (laughing) "You see, Copplemeyer, you prove my point. The man you see in me does not exist."[17]

In a sense suggested so clearly by the dialogue, we each create our images.

Social Product. Whether one considers a child striving to make sense of a toy jack-in-the-box, a physicist trying to integrate a new observation into his or her theory, or a salesperson trying to make a sale, the influence of other persons is unmistakable. From our earliest days, parents, family, and previous generations play a role in determining the messages and experiences to which we will be exposed. Even the language we use is a product of our having developed the necessary knowledge and skills through social learning.

We are influenced not only by these informal, developmental experiences but also by our formal education and training. These social processes direct our attention in a highly selective fashion, highlighting certain phenomena and situations while minimizing others, shaping our representations in a host of subtle and not-so-subtle ways through the course of our lifetime.

Stable and Rigid. After our images are fairly well established, new messages generally produce very little fundamental change. After we have developed a preference for one political party, for instance, it is unlikely that a single or even several advertisements or news articles will lead us to change our affiliation. Similarly, once we have decided we don't care for a particular job, television program, or individual, it is seldom that any single exposure to potentially contradictory information will change our minds.

Our maps and force of habit tend to guide us toward messages and message sources that are generally consistent with the representations we have developed. In most instances, our tendency is to ignore or distort information that contradicts or disconfirms our image.

Like the scholar who has great difficulty discarding a particular theory or scientific paradigm even in the face of seemingly disconfirming information, we part reluctantly with elements of our personal paradigms—our representations of reality. Nonetheless, in some instances, changes in our models do occur. Sometimes the weight of accumulating evidence, the influence of persons who are important to us, and perhaps even accidents of history lead us to change our ways of acting, reacting, and interacting. Even a single incident can have a rather dramatic impact. Sometimes, for instance, a car accident, illness, disappointment, or a particular achievement can be a trigger for significant change.

Self-Development

Becoming is a term coined by Gordon Allport to capture the dynamic process by which we as humans develop, modify, and refine our personal identity—our "self" and our concept of our "self."[18] The role of communication in this "becoming process" can be viewed as beginning with the very act of conception, at which instant the information necessary to the blueprint of growth for the offspring begins its work. The potentials we inherit are nurtured and shaped by our life experiences in our physical and communicational environment. Collectively, these experiences exert a subtle yet pervasive influence upon us.

We know that our self-development is very much shaped by our earliest interactions with those who care for us as infants and children. For the most part, our care givers create and control the environment to which we are exposed and with which we must cope. As we grow, our care givers are our models for how we are to act and how we are to think and feel about ourselves:

> If a child lives with criticism
> He learns to condemn
> If a child lives with hostility
> He learns to fight
> If a child lives with ridicule
> He learns to be shy
> If a child lives with shame
> He learns to be guilty
> If a child lives with tolerance
> He learns to be patient
> If a child lives with encouragement
> He learns confidence
> If a child lives with praise
> He learns to appreciate
> If a child lives with fairness
> He learns justice
> If a child lives with security
> He learns to have faith
> If a child lives with approval
> He learns to like himself
> If a child lives with acceptance and friendship
> He learns to find love in the world.[19]

While the process is obviously somewhat more complex and unpredictable than this passage may imply, the role of our care givers is very fundamental.

As we grow and become mobile, the number and diversity of shaping influences increase. As shown in Figure 9–7, encounters with family members are supplemented by face-to-face dealings with peers, and by broadening experiences in relationships, groups, organizations, and society. The impact of these interactions is sometimes quite dramatic. We come to use the same "buzz words" and slang phrases as friends and family members, and we often share their values, opinions, occupational preferences, outlooks, and political preferences. We may adopt similar styles of dress and even develop the same gestures. Some of these shaping influences have a fundamental and lasting impact on our development, others much less so.

Mass communication and communication technologies also play a role in our self-development in that they provide us with a wealth of information relative to such facets of life as masculinity and femininity, age, race, occupation, consumption, violence, criminality, eating and nutrition, and family and interpersonal relations.

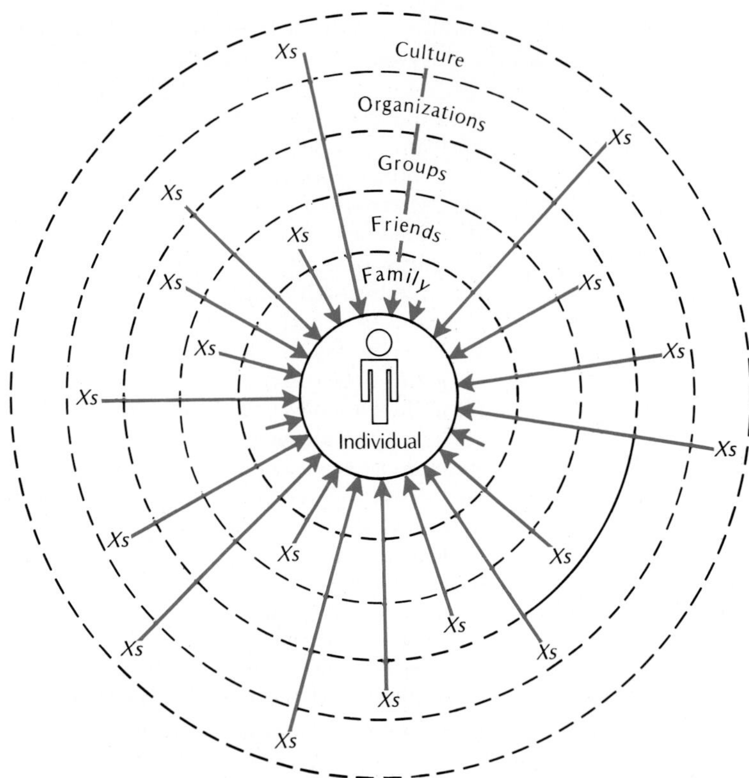

FIGURE 9–7 To a large extent our individual identities and self-concepts are a consequence of having adapted to the messages (*Xs*) created for us by our family and the relationships, groups, organizations, and culture of which we have been a part.

STRESS AND GROWTH

Self-development is an ongoing process of adjusting and readjusting oneself to the many influences, challenges, and opportunities we encounter. As such, it is necessarily a stressful process.

From a biological point of view, the *stress-adjustment cycle* we go through directly parallels that of other living things, whose day-to-day existences are also fraught with continual threats and challenges to their growth and development.[20] However, in terms of the origins of the stress, and the means available for dealing with it, we are quite unlike other animals. Most animals detect and react to threats and challenges in their environment in a direct, reflex-like manner. For instance, upon hearing a loud noise, a gazelle instinctively begins to run away from the source of the noise. It detects a challenge to its well-being, comfort, or safety, and it flees. This instinctive reaction to stressful situations is known as the *fight-or-flight response.*

Human stress is usually the consequence of a second-order information-processing event, involving symbolic meaning. Many of the situations that are stressful for us threaten our psychological, rather than physical, well-being. The threat of rejection by a loved one, a heated argument with a colleague, the prospect of a failure on an important exam, or the pressure of an approaching deadline for an incomplete project are frequently potent stressors for us. Other common stresses are listed in Box 9–1. These symbolic threats are capable of triggering the same hormonal, muscular, and neural reactions that for other animals are associated only with the physical threats to their safety and well-being.

Unlike other animals, we do not generally cope with challenge by physical fleeing or fighting; we have learned that physical combat and running away are not regarded as "civilized" ways for us to deal with problems. Because of this learning, we hold our bodies "in check" and usually react by "fight" or "flight" only in a symbolic sense.

Though stress and adjustment are normal aspects of human life, evidence suggests that chronic and accumulated stress can have serious physical, as well as emotional, consequences, as suggested in Box 9–1. Research indicates that stress lowers our resistance to illness and can play a contributory role in diseases of the kidney, heart, and blood vessels, as well as contributing to high blood pressure, migraine and tension headaches, and gastrointestinal problems such as ulcers, asthma, allergies, respiratory diseases, arthritis, and even cancer.[21]

Though there are a number of negative consequences of stress, it is an inevitable part of the process of life and of becoming. It is also a very positive force in the sense that stress presents opportunities for personal and social growth and change.[22] Ultimately, the consequences of stress for us depend on the way in which we take advantage—or fail to take advantage—of the opportunities environmental challenges can provide.

This duality is expressed clearly by physician M. Scott Peck in *The Road Less Traveled:*[23]

> What makes life difficult is that the process of confronting and solving problems is a painful one. Problems, depending upon their nature, evoke in us frustration . . . grief . . . sadness . . . loneliness . . . guilt . . . regret . . . anger . . . fear or anxiety. These are uncomfortable feelings . . . often as painful as any kind of physical pain. . . .
>
> Yet it is in this whole process of meeting and solving problems that life has its meaning. . . . It is only because of problems that we grow mentally and spiritually.

Rank	Life Event	Mean Value
1	Death of a Spouse	100
2	Divorce	73
3	Marital separation	65
4	Jail term	63
5	Death of a close family member	63
6	Personal injury or illness	53
7	Marriage	50
8	Fired at work	47
9	Marital reconciliation	45
10	Retirement	45
11	Change in health of family member	44
12	Pregnancy	40
13	Sex difficulties	39
14	Gain of new family member	39
15	Business readjustment	39
16	Change in financial state	38
17	Death of a close friend	37
18	Change to different line of work	36
19	Change in number of arguments with spouse	35
20	Mortgage over $10,000	31
21	Foreclosure of mortgage or loan	30
22	Change in responsibilities at work	29
23	Son or daughter leaving home	29
24	Trouble with in-laws	29
25	Outstanding personal achievement	28
26	Wife begins or stops work	26
27	Begin or end school	26
28	Change in living conditions	25
29	Revision of personal habits	24
30	Trouble with boss	23
31	Change in work hours or conditions	20
32	Change in residence	20
33	Change in schools	20
34	Change in recreation	19
35	Change in church activities	19
36	Change in social activities	18
37	Mortgage or loan less than $10,000	17
38	Change in sleeping habits	16
39	Change in number of family get-togethers	15
40	Change in eating habits	15
41	Vacation	13
42	Christmas	12
43	Minor violations of the law	11

Becoming is not a passive process. In reacting to, acting upon, and interacting with these influences, we provide the fuel for the becoming process. Each encounter builds upon the last, as we negotiate our way through the demands and opportunities around us and as we fashion our identities. In a very real sense, we become what we live. Whatever we are, have been, and will be—whether dominant or submissive, withdrawn or outgoing, self-confident or insecure, rigid or flexible, passive or aggressive—is very much influenced by the communication experiences we have had up to that point and the ways we have adapted to them.

Self Expression

Self-expression is a fundamental facet of human activity. Whether it involves speaking, writing, painting, singing, or engaging in other forms of performance, the process is one of communication.

In a wide range of communication situations, a great deal of our energy is expended not only "making statements," but also "making a statement." "Making statements" serves *instrumental* communication functions. In the case of instrumental communication, we have information we want to convey or receive, and our efforts are directed toward ensuring the clarity of message and accuracy of meanings. In contrast, "making a statement" has to do with *expressive* functions of communication. Here, our concerns may be more with impression, tone, and mood.

In his classic book, *The Presentation of Self in Everyday Life,* sociol-

---

BOX 9–1 The relationship between stress and illness has been dramatically demonstrated by Thomas Holmes and Richard Rahe, who have developed a scale (Social Readjustment Rating Scale) for classifying the severity of various stressful changes in life and relating these changes to the probability of becoming ill. Results of their research suggest that as stress increases, so does the likelihood of illness.

To complete the scale, check those events that have occurred within the past year and sum the point values. Holmes and Rahe found that with a score of 150 the chance of undergoing a major health change or contracting an illness was roughly 50%. With a score over 300 points within a single year the likelihood of illness or health change jumped to nearly 90 per cent.

Source: Reprinted with permission from Thomas H. Holmes and Richard H. Rahe, "The Social Readjustment Rating Scale," *Journal of Psychosomatic Research,* 11 (2) (1967) Pergamon Press, Ltd.

ogist Erving Goffman makes a similar distinction. He notes that there are two kinds of communication: expressions *given* and expressions *given off*.[24] Goffman describes self-expression using a theatrical metaphor, in which individuals are actors on a stage, presenting themselves to an audience. In this perspective, people encounter one another in face-to-face engagements and take turns presenting dramas or telling stories to one another. In distinguishing between instrumental and expressive forms of communication, Goffman says:

> . . . often what talkers undertake to do is not to provide information to a recipient but to present dramas to an audience. Indeed, it seems that we spend most of our time not engaged in giving information but in giving shows. And observe, this theatricality is not based on mere displays of feelings of faked exhibitions. . . . The parallel between stage and conversation is much, much deeper than that. The point is that ordinarily when an individual says something, he is not saying it as a bold statement of fact on his own behalf. He is recounting. He is running through a strip of already determined events for the engagement of his listeners.[25]

Thus, if the goal of instrumental communication is information transfer, *impression management* is the goal of expressive communication. But it is important to note that expressive communication is not

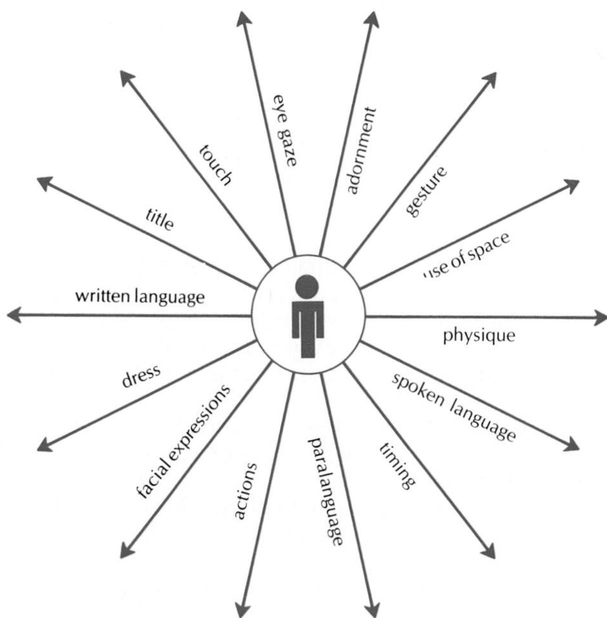

FIGURE 9–8 Every facet of our behavior is a potential source of instrumental and expressive communication.

necessarily an intentional process as suggested by Figure 9–8. Through verbal and nonverbal behaviors, we create the basis for impressions—and form impressions of others—whether we intend for this to occur or not. See Figure 9–9.

LANGUAGE: LABELS AND NAMES

One of the simplest, yet nonetheless important, forms of self-expression is the way we refer to ourselves. The importance of names as a means of self-expression is underscored by the use of names on everything from coffee mugs to license places. See Figures 9–10 and 9–11.

We have options as to how to label ourselves. Consider the possibilities available to Professor Robert C. Johnson when identifying himself: He can present himself as "Professor Robert C. Johnson," "Professor Johnson," "Mr. Johnson," "Robert C. Johnson," "Robert," "Rob," "Bob," "Robbie," or "Bobby."

Research suggests that names can be a meaningful form of expression. There is evidence, for example, that first names can be important in impression formation. Studies also suggest that certain first names are more often seen as being associated with qualities such as intelligence, attractiveness, strength, or femininity than others, as shown in Box 9–2. For instance, "John" and "Robert" are regarded far more positively than "Frederick," and "Joan" is regarded more favorably than "Donna" or "Cynthia."

PERSONALS

Single-White-Male—very successful genuine professional, interesting mid 50's, handsome, silver haired, distinguished, affectionate and understanding seeks mature attractive, well groomed sophisticated, intelligent, liberated, sexy, devoted, fun type S/W/F (under 35 yrs, 5′ 6″, 36″ 24″ 35″, approx 120 lbs.) with no dependents, for romantic, meaningful, permanent loving relationship. Private dinners, informal parties, social affairs, political functions, theatre, movies, recreational activities, sporting events, picnics, lost weekends, continental and foreign vacations and traveling. Kindly respond by sincere and descriptive letter enclosing recent color photo. Reply to Box #04211.

FIGURE 9–9 *"All the world's a stage . . ."*

FIGURE 9–10

NONVERBAL CODES: EMBLEMS AND ARTIFACTS

Not all expressive communication involves the use of verbal codes. Clothing, jewelry, hair styles, and makeup are vehicles for self-expression. See Figure 9–12 on page 311. Styles and brand names—of clothing, cars, luggage, stereo systems—are also ways of making a personal statement. Gestures, posture, and the use of space and time may also play a role.

FIGURE 9–11

Women's Names	Men's Ranking	Women's Ranking
Anne	9	5
Barbara	10	12
Carol	6	15
Cheryl	7	14
Cynthia	20	18
Diane	11	19
Donna	16	17
Janet	8	4
Jean	12	3
Joan	4	2
Judith	15	11
Karen	1	7
Kathleen	5	16
Linda	19	10
Margaret	17	8
Mary	3	6
Nancy	2	13
Patricia	18	9
Sharon	14	20
Susan	13	1

BOX 9–2 What's in a name? Names are not necessarily the neutral, value-free labels that many people might assume or desire them to be. Often, for example, surnames serve as messages from which nationality and/or religion can be inferred. And based upon these inferences, first impressions may be formed.

There is also evidence to suggest that even first names by themselves provide the basis for impressions. In several studies individuals were asked to indicate how much they associate qualities such as goodness, strength, and potency with various men's and women's names. The results indicate that people do associate certain qualities with particular names, and that, in general, people are more positively disposed toward some names than others. The list shows the ranking of preferences for men's and women's names that resulted.

Source: "Men's First Names, Nicknames, and Short Names: A Semantic Differential Analysis," *Names,* 21:1 (March, 1973), pp. 22-27. By permission. E. D. Lawson, "Women's First Names: A Semantic Differential Analysis," *Names* (June, 1974), pp. 542-58.

Self-Awareness

SELF-REFLEXIVENESS AND SELF-MONITORING

As we mentioned previously, the capacity for self-reflexiveness is one of the fundamental characteristics of human communication. Our self-

	Men's Names	Men's Ranking	Women's Ranking
First Names			
	Daniel	10	13
	David	7	9
	Edward	18	10
	Frederick	25	25
	James	13	17
	John	11	1
	Joseph	9	2
	Robert	1	12
	Thomas	19	24
	Ronald	16	8
Short Names			
	Dan	24	15
	Dave	2	3
	Ed	13	16
	Fred	16	27
	Jim	3	5
	Jack	6	6
	Joe	4	19
	Bob	8	4
	Tom	5	11
	Ron	22	7
Nicknames			
	Danny	23	26
	Davey	28	28
	Eddy	27	30
	Freddy	29	23
	Jimmy	20	21
	Johnny	26	14
	Joey	30	29
	Bobby	11	18
	Tommy	14	20
	Ronnie	21	22

BOX 9–2 (*continued*).

reflexive capability allows us to look upon and analyze ourselves, our thoughts, and our actions. It also permits us to turn our attention inward upon ourselves in order to examine our own communication behavior. Through self-reflexiveness, we can replay and think about our actions, reactions, and interactions. Similarly, we can examine our own self-development and the ways we express ourselves. We also can reflect upon our decision making, cognitive development, and self-development.

When we engage in any of these forms of self-reflexiveness, we do so by means of *intrapersonal communication*—the processing of messages

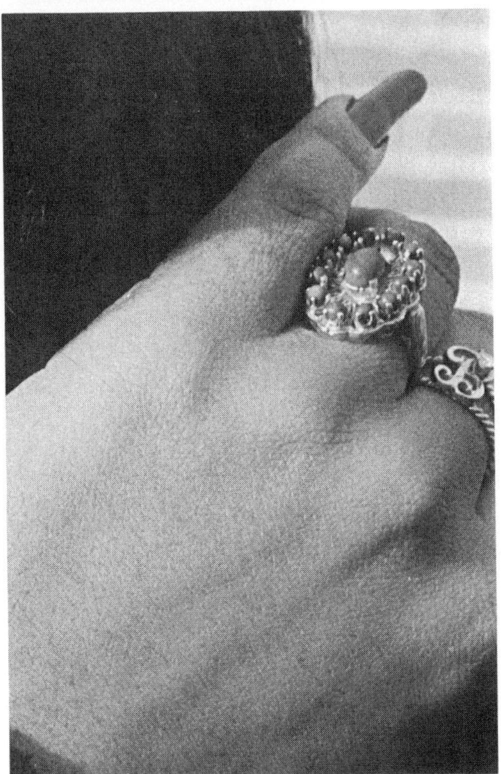

FIGURE 9–12 As individuals we express our identities through a variety of means, nonverbally as well as verbally.

of which we, ourselves, are the source. By means of intrapersonal communication and self-reflexiveness, we are able to engage in what can be termed *self-monitoring*—the analysis and adjustment of our actions in order to achieve a particular communication goal (or goals). We are engaged in self-monitoring when we analyze our communication behavior in a public speaking situation, in a job interview, on a date, or in exchanges with colleagues. In each of these cases and so many others, we have one or more communication goals we want to achieve. If we are aware of our goals and understand the nature of human communication, we can monitor and adjust our communication behavior, our goals or both.

The *Johari Window* provides a useful way to think about the dynamics of self-awareness of behavior, feelings, and motives. Shown in Figure 9–13, the *Johari Awareness Model,* as it is also termed, includes four quadrants:

- Quadrant 1, the open quadrant, refers to behavior, feelings, and motivation known to self and others.
- Quadrant 2, the blind quadrant, refers to behavior, feelings, and motivation known to others but not to self.
- Quadrant 3, the hidden quadrant, refers to behavior, feelings, and motivation known to self but not to others.
- Quadrant 4, the unknown quadrant, refers to behavior, feelings, and motivation known neither to self nor others.[26]

In discussing the model, Luft contends that we should strive to in-

	Known to self	Not known to self
Known to others	1 OPEN	2 BLIND
Not known to others	HIDDEN 3	UNKNOWN 4

FIGURE 9–13 *The Johari Model.*
Source: Joseph Luft, *Of Human Interaction.* Belmont, CA: Mayfield, 1969; and *Group Process: An Introduction to Group Dynamics., 3rd Ed.* Palo Alto, CA: National Press Books, 1984. By Permission.

crease self-awareness by reducing the size of Quadrant 2—our blind area. Quadrant 2 is an area of vulnerability in that it includes what others know about our behavior, feelings, and motivation that we are unaware of, or choose to ignore or deny. Decreasing our blind area also has the effect of increasing Quadrant 1—the open area—and this in turn holds promise for improving interpersonal relationships as well as self-awareness. Luft offers a number of suggestions for how one can enhance self-awareness:

- Threat tends to decrease awareness; mutual trust tends to increase awareness.
- Forced awareness (exposure) is undesirable and usually ineffective.
- Interpersonal learning means a change has taken place so that Quadrant 1 is larger, and one or more of the other quadrants has grown smaller.
- Sensitivity means appreciating the covert aspects of behavior, in Quadrants 2, 3, and 4 and respecting the desire of others to keep them so[27].

Self-reflexiveness and self-monitoring provide us with a means of assessing our actions, reactions, and interactions, being "in touch with" ourselves, benefiting from experiences, enhancing our interpersonal effectiveness, learning from our failures as well as our successes, and growing as human beings. They can be incredibly powerful tools, providing some of our most important opportunities for applying our understanding of human communication and human behavior to the betterment of our own lives.

SELF-TALK

One of the ways to increase self awareness is to focus our attention periodically on how we talk to ourselves. Many of us spend time analyzing how we talk to others and how they talk to us, but how often do we think about how we talk to ourselves? How do we talk to ourselves when we have failed at something? When we have succeeded? Are we as supportive and forgiving of ourselves as we would be of others?

Self-talk provides clues as to the kind of relationship we have with ourselves.[28] As much as our relationships with others can typically benefit from care and attention, so too can our relationships with ourselves.

Implications and Applications: Looking Within

• A basic communication need is to make sense of the situations we encounter.

• As individuals we engage in decision making in any number of differing information-use environments. Our decisions involve the use of incoming messages for the purposes of describing, classifying, evaluating, and acting.

• We use messages to make decisions about the physical environment, and we also use them to make decisions about the human and social environment.

• Over time, the consequences of our individual decisions form patterns. These patterns form the basis for the personal theories, or representations, that guide our ways of sensing, making sense of, and acting toward the people, objects, and circumstances we encounter.

• Personal representations are mixed blessings. On the one hand, they are invaluable as guides to orient ourselves in what would otherwise seem like a forever new and unpatterned world. On the other hand, our personal representations may also allow us to mislead ourselves because they may not correspond well to the changing world in which we live, and because they are necessarily incomplete, personal, subjective, socially-based, and resistant to change.

• Throughout our lives, we are developing as individuals through communication encounters in a variety of relationships, groups, organizations, and culture. We are very much influenced by these communication experiences; in a sense, we are created by them.

• The popular phrase, "no pain, no gain," is one way to express the relationship between stress and growth—both of which are inevitable aspects of human communication. When we experience the pain of failure, fear, or loss, it is extremely difficult to see the experience as positive. However, the raw material for intellectual and emotional growth is present in such circumstances.

• Impression management is one of the major communication activities in which we engage as individuals. We want to be seen and thought about in particular ways; and most of us devote substantial quantities of time, money, and energy in an effort to achieve this communication goal.

• Self-reflexiveness can be very beneficial in enhancing our ability to understand and use our communication knowledge. It is this capacity that allows us to make plans and set goals for ourselves. And it is self-awareness and self-monitoring that later allow us to assess our own performance, evaluate it against our goals, and identify ways to improve our performance the next time around. Self-talk can be one of the most important forms of human communication.

Summary

We have examined a number of uses and consequences of communication from the individual perspective. By sending and receiving messages, we react to and act toward the people, objects, and events in our environment. It is also through communication that we interact and negotiate meanings with others.

Decision making is a fundamental process in which communication plays an important role. In making decisions, we engage in an information-use sequence, whereby we use messages to describe, classify, evaluate, and act in information-use environments.

Communication is also basic to cognitive development. Through message processing we learn and develop the personalized theories and representations of the world that guide our behavior. These representations have limitations because they may fail to keep pace with changes in the environment. Additionally, they are incomplete, subjective, socially-influenced and sometimes overly rigid.

"Becoming" is a term coined to refer to the process of self-development. The role of communication in development begins with the act of conception and continues throughout our lives, as we adjust to a variety of individuals, influences, and circumstances.

In the developmental process, we undergo stress in our efforts to adapt to the challenges and opportunities that present themselves. Many of the stressors to which we react are symbolic and themselves the product of communication. Through communication, we identify these stressors; and message processing is a primary means by which we react to and cope with such circumstances.

Self-expression is a fundamental part of human activity. Whether it involves speaking, writing, painting, singing, or engaging in other forms of performance, the process is one of communication. Communication serves instrumental and expressive functions. Instrumental communication involves conveying information; expressive communication involves impressions. Our names and other labels serve expressive functions, as do nonverbal emblems and artifacts.

Self-awareness involves reflecting upon and monitoring our own behavior. Awareness involves intrapersonal communication—the processing of messages of which we ourselves are the source. By means of selfreflexiveness and self-monitoring, it is possible to adjust our communication behaviors to achieve particular goals. Analysis of "self-talk" provides insights into the kind of relationship we have with ourselves. Self-awareness gives us an important opportunity to apply our understanding of human communication on our own behalf.

Notes

1. Adapted from Robert S. Taylor, *Value-Added Processes in Information Systems* (Norwood, NJ: Ablex, 1986), p. 35.
2. O. J. Harvey, *Motivation and Social Interaction* (New York: Ronald, 1963), p. 3.
3. The term "map" is drawn from the writings of general semantics. See Richard W. Budd, "General Semantics," in *Interdisciplinary Approaches to Human Communication,* 2nd. ed. Ed. by Richard W. Budd and Brent D. Ruben (New Brunswick, NJ: Transaction, 1988) for a discussion of the history of the term. "Image" was first used in the present context by Kenneth Boulding in *The Image* (Ann Arbor, MI: University of Michigan Press, 1956). The phrase "semantic network" comes from cognitive psychology. See Morton Hunt, *The Universe Within* (New York: Simon & Schuster, 1982) for a general discussion of the origin and uses of the term.
4. Jose M. R. Delgado, *Physical Control of the Mind* (New York: Harper, 1969), p. 45. See also "Neurophysiology" in Budd and Ruben 1988, p. 126. Parenthetical material added.
5. John Holt, *How Children Learn* (New York: Pitman, 1969), p. 61. Parenthetical material added.
6. Morton Hunt, *The Universe Within* (Simon & Schuster, 1982), pp. 107–108.
7. See George Kelley, *A Theory of Personality* (New York: Norton, 1963), for a discussion of a similar notion that he refers to as personal constructs. See also the discussion of schemata in Edward E. Jones, David E. Kanouse, Harold H. Kelley, Richard E. Nisbett, Stuart Valins, and Bernard Weiner, *Attribution: Perceiving the Causes of Behavior* (Moorestown, NJ: General Learning Press, 1971).
8. See Kenneth Boulding, "General Systems Theory—The Skeleton of Science," *General Systems,* Vol. 1, 1956, p. 15.
9. An excellent overview of this topic is presented by Ellen Wartella and Byron Reeves, in "Communication and Children." In *Handbook of Communi-*

cation Science, Ed. by Charles R. Berger and Steven H. Chaffee (Newbury Park, CA: Sage, 1987), pp. 619–650.

10. Roberts D., and C. Bachen, "Mass Communication Effects." In *Mass Communication Review Yearbook*. Ed. by D. Charles Whitney and Ellen Wartella (Newbury Park, CA: Sage, 1982), pp. 29–78.

11. J. Hollenbeck, and R. G. Slaby, "Infant Visual Responses to Television," *Child Development*, Vol. 50, 1979, pp. 41–45.

12. Newspaper Advertising Bureau, 1980.

13. Newspaper Advertising Bureau, 1980.

14. See Budd, 1979. See also Wendell Johnson, *People in Quandaries* (New York: Harper, 1946).

15. Johnson, 1946.

16. See discussion of adaptive function of forgetting in Hunt, 1982, p. 111, and Elizabeth Loftus, *Memory* (Reading, MA: Addison, 1980), p. 19.

17. Dialogue based on *The Eye of the Beholder*, Stuart Reynolds Productions.

18. Gordon Allport, *Becoming* (New Haven CT: Yale University Press, 1955).

19. Dorothy Law Nolte, "Children Learn What They Live," in *Looking Out/Looking In*. Ed. by Ron Adler and Neil Towne (San Francisco: Holt, 1975), p. 43.

20. See Hans Seyle, *The Stress of Life*, rev. ed. (New York: McGraw-Hill, 1976).

21. A review of research and a discussion of the relationship between stress and illness is provided by Kenneth R. Pelletier, in *Mind as Healer, Mind as Slayer* (New York: Delacorte, 1977), pp. 117–188.

22. See Brent D. Ruben, "Communication and Conflict: A System Theoretic Perspective," *Quarterly Journal of Speech*, Vol. 64, No. 2, 1978, pp. 202–210.

23. M. Scott Peck, *The Road Less Traveled* (New York: Simon & Schuster, 1979), p. 17.

24. Erving Goffman, *The Presentation of Self in Everyday Life* (Garden City, NY: Doubleday, 1959), p. 4.

25. Erving Goffman, *Frame Analysis: An Essay on the Organization of Experience* (Cambridge: Harvard University Press, 1974), p. 508. See overview in Stephen W. Littlejohn, *Theories of Human Communication* (Belmont, CA: Wadsworth, 1988), pp. 106–108.

26. Joseph Luft, *Of Human Interaction* (Palo Alto, CA: Mayfield, 1969).

27. Luft, 1969.

28. Linda C. Lederman, "Intrapersonal Relationships: New Agenda for Relational Research," Unpublished paper, Rutgers University, 1989.

References and Suggested Readings

ALLPORT, GORDON W. *Becoming*. New Haven: Yale University Press, 1955.

BATESON, GREGORY, and JURGEN RUESCH. *Communication: The Social Matrix of Society*. New York: Norton, 1951.

BLUMER, HERBERT. "Symbolic Interaction." In *Interdisciplinary Approaches to*

Human Communication. Ed. by Richard W. Budd and Brent D. Ruben. New Brunswick, NJ: Transaction, 1979, 135–151.

BOULDING, KENNETH. *The Image.* Ann Arbor, MI: University of Michigan Press, 1956.

BUDD, RICHARD. W. "General Semantics." In *Interdisciplinary Approaches to Human Communication.* Ed. by Richard W. Budd and Brent D. Ruben. New Brunswick, NJ: Transaction,1979, 71–93.

BUDD, RICHARD W., and BRENT D. RUBEN, eds. *Beyond Media: New Approaches to Mass Communication. Second Ed.* New Brunswick, NJ: Transaction, 1988.

DELGADO, JOSE M.R. "Neurophysiology." In *Interdisciplinary Approaches to Human Communication.* Ed. by Richard W. Budd and Brent D. Ruben. New Brunswick, NJ: Transaction, 1979, 119–134.

GOFFMAN, ERVING. *The Presentation of Self in Everyday Life.* Garden City, NY: Doubleday, 1959.

———. *Frame Analysis: An Essay on the Organization of Experience.* Cambridge: Harvard University Press, 1974.

GUMPERT, GARY, and ROBERT CATHCART. *Intermedia. Ed.* New York: Oxford University Press, 1986.

GUMPERT, GARY, and SANDRA L. FISH, eds. *Talking to Strangers: Mediated Therapeutic Communication.* Norwood, NJ: Ablex, 1990.

HUNT, MORTON. *The Universe Within.* New York: Simon & Schuster, 1982.

JOHNSON, WENDELL. *People in Quandaries.* New York: Harper, 1946.

KELLY, GEORGE A. *A Theory of Personality.* New York: Norton, 1963.

KUBEY, ROBERT, and MIHALY CSIKSZENTMIHALYI. *Television and the Quality of Life: How Viewing Shapes Everyday Experience.* Hillsdale, NJ: Lawrence Erlbaum, 1990, 168.

LOFTUS, GEOFFREY R., and ELIZABETH F. LOFTUS. *Mind at Play: The Psychology of Video Games.* New York: Basic Books, 1983.

LITTLEJOHN, STEPHEN W. *Theories of Human Communication.* Belmont, CA: Wadsworth, 1988.

LUFT, JOSEPH. *Of Human Interaction.* Palo Alto, CA: Mayfield, 1969.

O'KEEFE, GARRETT J., and KATHLEEN REID-NASH. "Socializing Functions." In *Handbook of Communication Science.* Ed. by Charles R. Berger and Steven H. Chaffee. Newbury Park, CA: Sage, 1987, pp. 419–445.

PECK, M. SCOTT. *The Road Less Traveled.* New York: Simon & Schuster, 1979.

PELLETIER, KENNETH R. *Mind as Healer, Mind as Slayer.* New York: Delacorte, 1977.

RUBEN, BRENT D. "General Systems Theory: An Approach to Human Communication." In *Interdisciplinary Approaches to Human Communication.* Ed. by Richard W. Budd and Brent D. Ruben. New Brunswick, NJ: Transaction, 1979, 95–118.

RUBEN, BRENT D., and JOHN Y. KIM, eds. *General Systems Theory and Human Communication.* Rochelle Park, NJ: Hayden, 1975.

SCHNEIDER, CY. *Children's Television: How It Works Its Influence on Children.* Lincolnwood, IL: NTC Books, 1989.

SCHRODER, HAROLD M., MICHAEL J. DRIVER, and SIEGFRIED STREUFERT. *Human Information Processing.* (New York: Holt, 1967).

SEYLE, HANS. *The Stress of Life.* Rev. ed. New York: McGraw-Hill, 1976.

SHANDS, HARLEY C. *Thinking and Psychotherapy.* Cambridge, MA: Harvard University Press, 1960.

TAYLOR, ROBERT S. *Value-Added Processes in Information Systems.* Norwood, NJ: Ablex, 1986.

THAYER, LEE. *Communication and Communication Systems.* Homewood, IL: Richard D. Irwin, 1968.

WARTELLA, ELLEN, and BYRON REEVES. "Communication and Children" *In Handbook of Communication Science.* Ed. by Charles R. Berger and Steven H. Chaffee. Newbury Park, CA: Sage; 1987, 619–650.

WARTELLA, ELLEN, and BYRON REEVES. "Historical Trends in Research on Children and Media: 1900–1960." *Journal of Communication,* Vol. 35, 1985, 118–133.

VICKERS, GEOFFREY. "The Multivalued Choice." In *Communication Concepts and Perspectives.* Ed. by Lee Thayer (New York: Spartan Books, 1967)

10

Relationships

For months you have wanted to get together to try to work things out. You think he feels the same way. What's needed is calm and rational conversation. You want to make clear how much the relationship matters and to try to recapture what's been lost. Minutes into the encounter, another argument begins. He thinks he's right; you are convinced you're right. He yells; you yell back even louder, as each of you tries—in vain—to get one another to understand.

Participation in relationships with friends, family members, lovers, roommates, siblings, employers, and peers is basic to life. Situations like the one above are, unfortunately, not all that uncommon. They remind us that productive relationships are as challenging to develop and maintain as they are important to us.

Communication is the basic ingredient in social life, and an understanding of the process can be a very powerful tool for fostering positive and productive relationships of all kinds.

The concepts of *communication* and of *relationship* are intertwined in several basic ways. First, as we have seen, one of the most fundamental outcomes of human communication is the development of social systems; and no such systems are more central to our lives than relationships. Second, our relationships—with parents, relatives, friends, and colleagues—are essential to our learning, growth, and development. Third, it is in relationships of one sort or another that most of our purposeful communication activities take place.

Interpersonal Communication and Relationships

What is a *relationship*? Sometimes the term *relationship* is used as a way of talking about a friendship we regard as particularly significant. In recent years the term has also come to be used in a somewhat more specialized way, to refer to a particular type of friendship—a sexually intimate arrangement or agreement between two people. *Relationship* is also used more generally to refer to other one-to-one social units, such as those composed of a teacher and student, husband and wife, parent and child, employer and employee, or doctor and patient.

Although most people agree that friendships, sexually intimate arrangements, or other social groupings qualify as relationships, few people would use this term to describe passengers riding on an elevator or strangers passing on a crowded street. From the point of view of communication, however, these also can be thought of as relationships.

In the most basic sense, a relationship is formed whenever reciprocal message processing occurs: that is, when two or more individuals mutually take account of one another's verbal or nonverbal behavior, as shown in Figure 10–1. This reciprocal message processing, which we can term *interpersonal communication*, is the means through which relationships of all types are initiated, develop, grow, and deteriorate.

One of the simplest relationships is that created by people passing one another on a crowded sidewalk. In order for two individuals to negotiate past each other without bumping, each must process a number of messages relative to the other's presence, location, direction, and rate of movement. They must use the resulting information to guide their action in order to pass without colliding. In this situation all the essential elements of any relationship are in operation.

A somewhat more complex example is provided by people riding on an elevator, as depicted in Figure 10–2. When alone in an elevator, most of us stand to the rear, often in the center. Typically, as a second person

X_A - Words, actions, appearance, etc., created by A

X_B - Words, actions, appearance, etc., created by B

⟶ - Indicates messages being created

⟵ - - ⟶ - Indicates messages being noted

FIGURE 10–1 *Interpersonal Communication.* A relationship is formed when reciprocal message processing occurs—when two or more individuals take account of one another's verbal or nonverbal behavior.

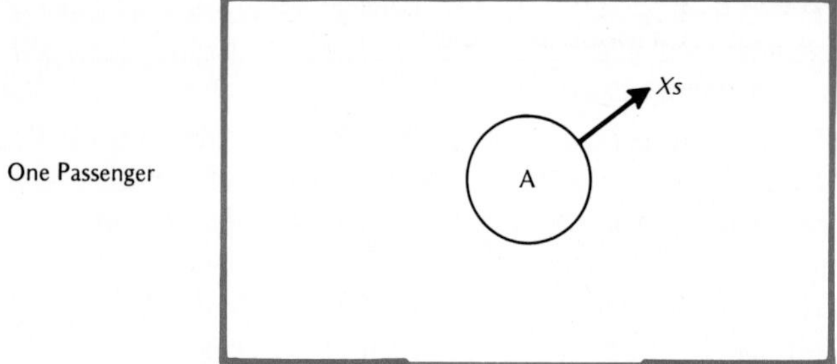

FIGURE 10–2 In a very basic sense, a relationship is formed among passengers on an elevator as the individuals adjust their behavior relative to one another, based on an awareness of one another's presence.

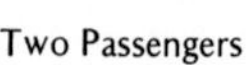

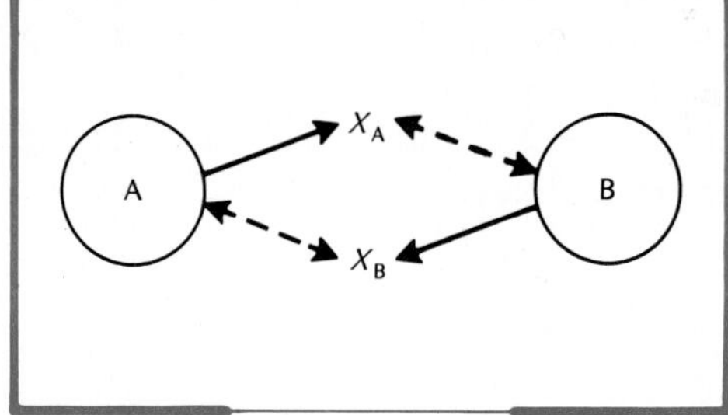

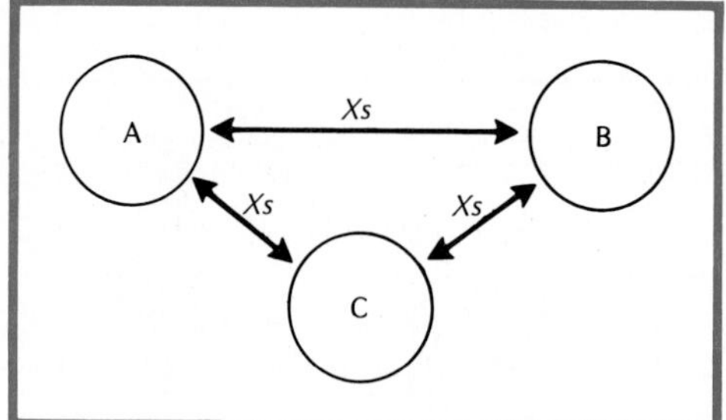

boards, we move to one corner or another, leaving the remaining corner for the newly arriving passenger. In so doing, we initiate a simple relationship as we take note of and adjust our behavior—movements, gestures, and position—relative to one another. With little conscious awareness, reciprocal message processing and mutual influence have taken place, as we define and redefine the territory available for our use.

As a third person enters the elevator, further adjustments are likely to occur as the social unit shifts from a two-person relationship to one composed of three individuals. Readjustments of this kind provide observable evidence that reciprocal message processing is taking place and that a relationship has been formed.

Whether our point of reference is strangers passing on the street or an intimate, enduring friendship, the basic dynamics involved in the formation and evolution of relationships are quite similar. In each circumstance, the individuals enter the relationship behaving toward the other persons on the basis of the personal theories and representations acquired through previous experience. As relationships develop, a mutual influence occurs as the individuals adopt or create *joint,* or *relational,* communication *rules.* These rules guide, shape, and, in a sense govern the particular social unit from its initiation through the various stages of development to its eventual termination, in much the same ways as personal representations guide an individual's behavior.

In the case of strangers passing on the street, the information-processing rules the individuals use are relatively simple; and the relationship itself is short-lived. By contrast, intimate relationships between persons who have lived or worked together for many years can be exceptionally complex.

We are unaware of many of the relationships of which we are a part. Very often, we are taking account of and being taken account of, influencing and being influenced, without awareness or intention.

Types of Relationships

In this chapter, the primary focus of our discussion will be upon those relationships of which we are aware and which we intentionally form and maintain. Relationships of this kind can be classified in terms of number of factors, including the number of persons involved, the purpose of the relationship, its duration, and the level of intimacy attained.

DYADIC AND TRIADIC RELATIONSHIPS

The vast majority of our relationships are *dyads*—two person units. As children, our first contacts with others are dyadic, and it is not until we reach the age of six to twelve years that we are able to engage in conversation with several persons at the same time.[1] In our adult years each of us is a member of a large number of different dyads.

As William Wilmot notes in *Dyadic Communication,* each of the many dyads in which we participate is unique in a number of respects.[2]

1. Every dyadic relationship fulfills particular ends. The functions served by a teacher-student dyad, for instance, are generally quite different from those of a husband-wife relationship; and both are

distinct from those served by doctor-patient or employee-employer relationships.

2. Each involves different facets of the individuals who participate in them. The demands placed on an individual as a student in a teacher-student relationship are different from those placed on that same person as a husband in a husband-wife relationship or as a supervisor in a work relationship. No two dyads in which we participate make precisely the same demands or present the same opportunities.
3. In any dyad, unique language patterns and communication patterns develop that differentiate that relationship from others. Slang and "in-phrases" among friends, terms of fondness between lovers, and ritualized greetings among colleagues at work are the result of these ongoing communication dynamics within relationships.

Although the majority of the relationships in which we participate involve two persons, we also often find ourselves in social units composed of three or four persons.

Triads—three-person relationships—differ from dyads in several respects, particularly in their complexity. In dyads, reciprocal message processing takes place between two persons. With triads, there are six possible message-processing pairings: person 1 with person 2, person 1 with person 3, person 2 with person 3, persons 1 and 2 with person 3, persons 1 and 3 with person 2, and persons 2 and 3 with person 1.[3]

FIGURE 10–3

Beyond the increased complexity resulting from more possible pairings, triads and quadrads differ from dyads in several additional respects. One of these is intimacy. While it is possible for members of triads or quadrads to develop very close relationships, there is generally a greater potential for intimacy when interaction is limited exclusively to two individuals.

Secondly, in relationships of more than two persons, differences of opinion can be resolved by "voting" to determine the "majority opinion." In dyads, negotiation is the only means of decision making available. A further distinction is that triads and quadrads have somewhat more stability than dyads. When only two persons are involved in a relationship, either party has the power to destroy the unit by withdrawal. In triads, and larger social units, the withdrawal of one party may have a marked impact on the unit, but it will not necessarily lead to its termination.

Finally, it is rare that triads operate such that all parties are equally and evenly involved. Typically, at any point in time, two members of the relationship are closer to one another or in greater agreement than the other party or parties. The result is often the formation of coalitions, struggles for "leadership," and sometimes open conflict. Because of this, some authors have argued that there is actually no such thing as a

FIGURE 10–4

triadic or quadratic relationship, but rather that such units are better thought of as a dyad plus one, or two dyads.[4]

TASK AND SOCIAL RELATIONSHIPS

In addition to thinking about relationships in terms of the number of persons involved, one can also look at the primary purpose for their formation. Many relationships are developed for the purpose of *coordinated action*—completion of a task or project that one individual could not manage alone. A simple example of this type of relationship is one person holding on to a board while another person saws off a piece.

The relationships created between a taxi driver and passenger, or between a newspaper carrier and a subscriber, provide other illustrations of two individuals working together to accomplish a specific task.[5] Social units, composed of colleagues at work, employer and employee, leader and follower, doctor and patient, teacher and student, therapist and patient, are additional examples of *task relationships* that play a major role in our lives.

In some situations, accomplishing a task is of secondary importance, or perhaps of no significance whatsoever. In such circumstances, what can be termed *personally- or socially-oriented goals* take precedence. Making a new acquaintance, having a drink with an old friend, and spending time chatting periodically with a co-worker during lunch serve a number of important functions, even though they are not essential to the completion of a task. *Social relationships* can provide a means of diversion, recreation, intimacy, or companionship. They may also be a way of avoiding isolation or loneliness, confirming our own sense of worth, giving and receiving affection, or comparing our views and opinions to those held by others.[6]

Individuals may be willing to devote more or less time, energy, and commitment to a relationship, depending upon whether they see it as essentially task or socially oriented. As a result, the communication patterns that develop will often vary substantially depending upon how the members regard their purpose for participating in a given relationship in the first place.

SHORT- AND LONG-TERM RELATIONSHIPS

Longevity is another factor which has a significant bearing on the nature of relationships. Most of us are engaged in at least several *long-term relationships* with members of our immediate families, relatives,

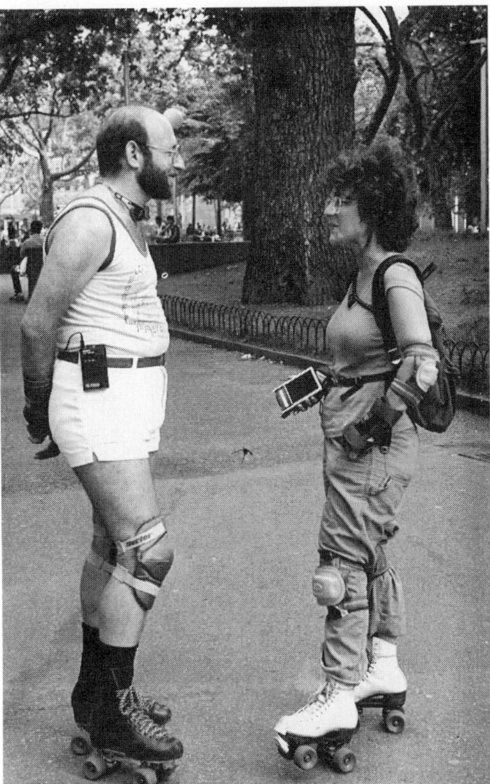

FIGURE 10–5

lovers, and friends. We also participate in the formation and/or maintenance of any number of *transitory relationships*—an exchange of smiles and glances while walking down a corridor, a wave and hello to a familiar face in the apartment complex, or an exchange of pleasantries with a clerk at the shopping mall.

Between these two extremes are relationships of varying duration. In general, the older a relationship, the more the investment one has made in it, and the greater the investment one is willing to make in order to preserve it. A substantial investment in long-term relationships leads to a willingness to maintain them at costs greater than those we would pay in a newly-formed relationship.

With short-term relationships there is little history, generally fewer personal consequences should the relationship not progress, and relatively little personal involvement. In such circumstances, we are far less locked into particular identities, and much less constrained by past actions and the images others may have of us. In many instances, short-term relationships can be attractive and functional precisely because they are seen as allowing greater personal flexibility and requiring less investment, commitment, and follow-through. See Figure 10–6.

CASUAL AND INTIMATE RELATIONSHIPS

Relationships can also be characterized in terms of their "depth" or level of intimacy. At one extreme are relationships between acquaintances. At the other extreme are relationships between intimates. Casual relationships between friends and colleagues fall near the center between these two extremes.

In general, relationships between acquaintances are characterized by impersonal and ritualized communication patterns. The following exchange of pleasantries is typical of such relationships:

ERIC: "Hello. How are you?"
PAM: "Fine, thanks, and you?"
ERIC: "Good."
PAM: "It's a beautiful day today, isn't it?"
ERIC: "Sure is."
PAM: "How's the family?"
ERIC: "Everyone is fine. How's yours?"
And so on.

Disclosure. The specifics of the exchange are impersonal and ritualized in the sense that either person could—and probably would—make the same remarks to anyone. There is little that suggests the uniqueness of the relationship to either individual. Further, in such a conversation, there is a lack of *self-disclosure, other-disclosure,* or *topical disclo-*

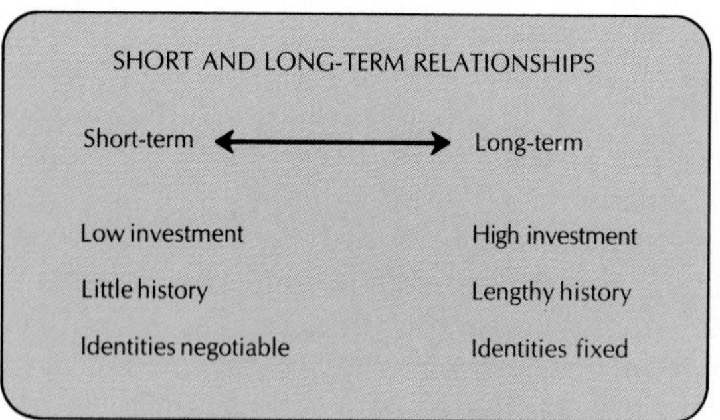

FIGURE 10–6

sure.[7] That is, neither person is disclosing much information as to his or her own opinions or beliefs at other than a surface level, and there is an obvious absence of personal feeling being expressed.

In more intimate relationships, individuals may share some of their private concerns about life, death, illness, and their feelings about other persons and themselves. An exchange between persons who have attained greater intimacy would contrast markedly with the previous exchange:

ERIC: "Hello. How are you?"
PAM: "Not that great, to be honest."
ERIC: "What's the matter?"
PAM: "I went for my routine physical last week, and the doctor found a tumor."
ERIC: "How serious is it?"
PAM: "They don't know yet. The test results aren't back, but I'm scared to death."
ERIC: "I don't blame you. It scares me even hearing about it. Is it something you want to talk about?"
PAM: "I really think I need to, if it's O.K."
ERIC: "Of course it's O.K. . . . "
And so on.

Contrasted with the earlier example, this exchange is neither ritualized nor impersonal. A high degree of topical-disclosure, other-disclosure, and self-disclosure is involved. Further, the interaction is distinctive. It seems unlikely that either person would be participating in precisely the same kind of discussion with many other individuals, which suggests the uniqueness of this relationship.

A good deal of research has been conducted on self-disclosure. Findings include:[8]

- Disclosure increases with increased intimacy.
- Disclosure increases when rewarded.
- Disclosure increases with the need to reduce uncertainty in a relationship.
- Disclosure tends to be reciprocated.
- Women tend to disclose more than men.
- Women disclose more with individuals they like.
- Men disclose more with individuals they trust.
- Disclosure is regulated by rules of appropriateness.

- Attraction is related to positive disclosure but not to negative disclosure.
- Negative disclosure occurs with greater frequency in highly intimate settings than in less intimate ones.
- Relationship satisfaction is greatest when there is moderate—rather than a great deal of or very little—disclosure.

Relationships of different levels of intimacy have varying values for us. As Erving Goffman and other writers have noted, the ritualized exchanges that characterize casual acquaintances permit us to maintain contact with a large number of individuals with a minimum of effort and conscious attention. Such exchanges are a way of saying: "Hello, I see you. It seems to me it is worth acknowledging you. I want you to know that. I hope you feel the same way, too." Ritualized conversation is also important because it is generally the first step in the development of closer relationships.

Intimate relationships, by contrast, require a substantial investment of time and effort. They can, however, provide opportunities for personal and social growth that may well be impossible to derive in any other way. They afford a context of trust in which individuals can express themselves candidly, be reacted to with a greater degree of continuity and honesty than in other relationships, and openly explore and apply the insights gained over a period of time.

Even more basic functions served by intimate relationships are the apparent medical aspects. In his book, *The Broken Heart: The Medical Consequences of Loneliness,* James Lynch cites research that indicates that the absence of intimate relationships can have negative medical consequences. Those studies have shown that a continual state of loneliness, the absence or death of parents during the early years of childhood, or the loss of a loved one are significant factors contributing to the likelihood of premature death. This work vividly underscores the critical role of intimate relationships in our lives.[9]

DATING, LOVE, AND MARITAL RELATIONSHIPS

Communication obviously plays a very important role in dating, love, and marital relationships.[10] The initial attraction and encounters that lead to dating, love, and marriage relationships begin as casual contacts and develop through stages of increasing intimacy.

As Edwin Thomas explains:

FIGURE 10–7 Nonverbal cues provide information about the nature of relationships.

> Talking is one of the primary activities marital partners engage in together and most couples spend enormous amounts of time talking to each other. Communication between marital partners is vitally important for individual well-being and mutual harmony. It reflects difficulties and strengths in the marriage and in other areas of life and sets the stage for future marital satisfaction or discord.[11]

Communication researcher Michael Beatty points out that early in the development of dating and love relationships, couples often overlook or avoid discussions of potential problems and conflicts.[12] They may assume that conversing about problems and the expression of conflict or anger will necessarily be destructive. As difficulties become great, pressure for addressing issues in one way or another mounts. Couples lacking a tradition of disclosure and openness in dealing with one another and their relationship may decide that breaking up is the only logical alternative.

On the other hand, couples who are willing and able to converse with one another about their relationship, its evolution, and its problems may achieve more satisfying and effective relationships because:

Partners will be able to anticipate or deal with potential problems at an early stage.

Partners will have the benefit of knowing how each other perceives and feels about the relationship and its development and each other's contribution to it.

Partners will have the opportunity to work together to meet challenges and solve problems.

Conversation about the relationship will provide an additional source of intimacy and commonness between partners.

The Evolution of Relationships

Whether relationships are dyads or triads, task or socially oriented, short- or long-term, casual or intimate, the dynamics by which they are initiated, develop, and eventually deteriorate and terminate are quite similar in terms of communication.

STAGE ONE: INITIATION

The initial stage in the formation of any relationship involves **social initiation** or **encounter.**[13] In this phase, two or several individuals take note of and adjust to one another's behavior. Often the initial messages to which the individuals adjust are nonverbal—a smile, glance, handshake, movement, or appearance. Should the relationship continue, progressive reciprocity of message processing occurs. One person notices the other's actions, position, appearance, and gestures. The second person reacts, and those reactions are noted and reacted to by the first person, whose reactions are acted on by the second person, and so on. Except in the most fleeting relationships, such as passengers on an elevator, language comes to play an important role as the individuals move beyond first impressions.

During the early stages of a relationship, the individuals involved operate in terms of the personal theories and representations and communication habits they "bring with them" from previous experiences. As interpersonal communication progresses, each begins to acquire some knowledge of the other's maps and ways of sensing, making sense of, acting, and reacting. Gradually, through combination, recombination, blend, mutation, compromise, and unspoken negotiation, the joint rules by which their particular relationship will operate begin to emerge.

STAGE TWO: EXPLORATION

The second stage of relational development picks up shortly after the initial encounter, as the individuals begin exploring potentials of the other person and the possibility of further pursuing the relationship. In this phase the individuals gather information about the other person's maps, style, motives, interests, and values. This knowledge serves as the basis for assessing the merits of continuing the relationship.

FIGURE 10–8

STAGE THREE: INTENSIFICATION

If the relationship progresses, it moves into a third phase, which Mark Knapp has labeled the *intensifying* stage.[14] In reaching this level, the individuals have arrived at a decision—which they may or may not verbalize—that they wish the relationship to continue. As the relationship progresses, the individuals involved acquire a good deal of knowledge of one another and, at the same time, create a number of joint rules, a shared language, and characteristic relational rituals. A relationship may stall at this stage, may deteriorate, or may continue to develop.

STAGE FOUR: FORMALIZATION

Should the relationship progress further, some formal, symbolic acknowledgement binding the individuals to one another is common. In

FIGURE 10–9 Relationship stages are reflected in nonverbal as well as verbal behavior patterns.

the case of a love relationship, the formal bonding may take the form of engagement or wedding rings. With an individual being hired for a job, the employee and employer may sign a contract. Where two persons are entering a business partnership, the relationship may be formalized by ratifying legal agreements.

During this stage, the individuals advance in their joint creation of relational rules, including the development of shared symbols and preferred and characteristic patterns of conversing. The meanings of these verbal and nonverbal behaviors become standardized. Over time, the relationhip develops a distinctiveness that distinguishes it in subtle and not-so-subtle ways from the many other relationships in which the individuals have been involved.

STAGE FIVE: REDEFINITION

With the passage of time, the individuals inevitably grow and develop, creating pressure for change on the other individual or individuals in

FIGURE 10–10 *Symbols and Rituals of Bonding.*

the relationship, as well as upon the relationship itself. As a consequence, a need for redefining some of the joint rules of the relationship often arises. There are many classic illustrations of these types of situations: perhaps a teenager no longer wants to be so closely supervised by his or her parents, or an employee wants more latitude on the job than when first hired. In each instance, changes in the individuals place strains on their relationships and on the accepted and often difficult-to-change rules and patterns that have developed to date.

Sometimes the needed redefinition is a very gradual, natural, and easily manageable part of the evolution of a relationship. In other instances, when change is too rapid or extreme, or resistance too great, a deterioration process begins.

STAGE SIX: DETERIORATION

Initially, the deterioration may go unnoticed, as parties in a relationship begin more and more to "go their own ways" physically and symbolically. Things that once were shared no longer are. Words or gestures that once mattered no longer do. Once-glowing prospects for the future at a particular job become blurred and faded. Rules that grew naturally in a love relationship during its development now seem more like shackles and imposed statutes to be followed with resignation.

Once the deterioration process has reached this point, it is quite likely that the relationship is headed for dissolution, as the behaviors of each person come to make less and less difference to the actions and reactions of the other. Physical separation and the dissolution of any remaining legal or contractual obligations are the final steps in the often painful process of terminating a relationship.

Communication researcher Steve Duck has identified four phases in the dissolution process, which can be summarized as follows:[15]

"Self-Talk" Phase

- Focus on partner's behavior
- Evaluating their own contribution and adequacy in the relationship
- Emphasizing negatives of the relationship
- Considering withdrawal
- Identifying positive aspects of alternative relationships

Interpersonal Communication Phase

- Deciding to confront the problem openly
- Confronting

- Negotiating and discussing
- Exploring possibilities for repair and reconciliation
- Assessing costs of withdrawal or reduced intimacy
- Separating

Group and Social Communication Phase

- Agreeing with partner as to how to relate to one another following dissolution of relationship
- Initiating gossip/discussion in social groups
- Constructing and telling face-saving and blame-placing stories and accounts of what happened
- Considering and dealing with effects on social groups

"Grave Dressing" and Public Communication Phase

- "Rebounding"
- Replaying, analyzing, and moralizing—postmortem replay of events
- Distributing one's own version of break-up story publicly

Relationships do not necessarily move through these stages in an orderly way. They may stall in any one stage, back up and go forward again, or stop at one point for an extended period of time.

Relational Patterns

As relationships evolve, characteristic communication patterns develop. These relational patterns are the result of joint rules that have developed between the persons involved. In this section, we will briefly consider four of the most common of these communication patterns: (1) supportive and defensive climates; (2) dependencies and counter-dependencies; (3) progressive and regressive spirals; and (4) self-fulfilling and self-defeating prophecies.[16]

SUPPORTIVE AND DEFENSIVE CLIMATES

"I appreciate how supportive you were last night when I was feeling down."

"Must you criticize and judge everything I do?"

"I wish you would be more supportive."

"It seems as though you find fault with me no matter what I say or do."

"You're being so defensive!"

The orientations of individuals within relationships and their patterns of communicating with one another create a climate of communication. Climates and individual behaviors can be characterized along a continuum from highly *supportive* to highly *defensive.* Each statement above is a comment on how supportive or defensive the speaker perceives another person—and the relationship overall—to be at a particular point in time.

Researcher Jack Gibb has identified a number of communication behaviors that create and maintain defensive climates within relationships:[17]

- Evaluation—judging other's behavior
- Control—striving to control or manage other's behavior
- Strategy—planning techniques, hidden agenda, and moves to use in relationships, as you might in a chess game
- Neutrality—remaining aloof and remote from others' feelings and concerns
- Superiority—seeing and expressing yourself as more worthy than others
- Certainty—assuming and acting as though you are certain in your knowledge and perceptions

In contrast, the following behaviors are seen as contributing to a supportive climate:

- Description—describing rather than judging or evaluating other's behavior
- Problem Orientation—focusing on specific problems to be solved
- Spontaneity—dealing with situations as they develop, without a hidden agenda or "master plan"
- Empathy—looking at things from the other person's viewpoint
- Equality—seeing and presenting yourself as equal to others
- Provisionalism—maintaining a degree of uncertainty and tentativeness in your thoughts and beliefs

DEPENDENCIES AND COUNTERDEPENDENCIES

The dynamics of dependency and counterdependency is prevalent in many relationships at various points in time. What we can term a *dependency relationship* exists when one individual in a relationship who is highly dependent on another for support, money, job, leadership, guidance, or whatever generalizes this dependency to other facets of the relationship.

The classic example of this kind of relational dynamic is that which develops between children and their parents or, in some cases, between therapists and their patients.[18] In both instances, one individual has particular needs or goals that are being met by the other individual or individuals in the relationship. The dependent pattern may become more generalized, so that one person comes to rely on the other in a broad range of circumstances that are unrelated to the original basis for dependency. When this occurs, a dynamic is set in motion that can have far-reaching impact and consequences for the individuals as well as the relationship. Whether people are discussing politics, sex, or religion, whether they are trying to decide where to eat or where to live, the dependent person comes to take cues from the other, on whom he or she has learned to rely, as the following conversation might suggest:

ALICE: "I think we should go to McDonald's for lunch. How does that sound?"
JENNY: "Fine."
ALICE: "Come to think about it, McDonald's is likely to be busy at this hour. How about the Corner Grill?"
JENNY: "Sure, that sounds great."

In other relationships, or in the same relationship at other points in time, the dependency is in the opposite direction. In these circumstances, one individual relates to the other not as a dependent but, instead, as a *counterdependent.* Where the dependent individual complies with the other person in the relationship across a broad range of topics, the counterdependent person characteristically disagrees, as the following scenario illustrates:

ALICE: "I think we should go to McDonald's for lunch. How does that sound?"
JENNY: "I'm tired of McDonald's."
ALICE: "How about the Corner Grill?"
JENNY: "That's no better. I was thinking of a place we could have a drink and relax."

ALICE: "What about The Attic?"

JENNY: "It's really not worth all this time deciding. Let's just go to McDonald's and be done with it."

In the first circumstance, we can assume that whatever Alice suggested, Jenny would go along. In the second, it seems likely that whatever Alice suggested, Jenny would disagree.

As dependencies and counterdependencies become a habitual way of relating, they guide, shape, and often overshadow the specific content of conversation. Eventually, at the extreme, the content of what the individuals say comes to have little impact on the dynamics. When person A says "yes," person B agrees. Or, When A says "no," B consistently disagrees.

PROGRESSIVE AND REGRESSIVE SPIRALS

When the actions and reactions of individuals in a relationship are consistent with their goals and needs, the relationship progresses on a positive tone with continual increases in the level of harmony and satisfaction. This circumstance can be termed a *progressive spiral.* In progressive spirals, the reciprocal message processing of the interactants leads to a sense of "positiveness" in their experiences. The satisfaction each person derives builds on itself, and the result is a relationship that is a source of growing pleasure and value for the participants.

The opposite kind of pattern can also develop, in which each exchange contributes to a progressive decrease in satisfaction and harmony. In these circumstances—*regressive spirals*—the result is increasing discomfort, distance, frustration, and dissatisfaction for the parties involved. Perhaps the simplest example of this latter type of spiral is provided by an argument:

ANN: "Would you try to remember to take out the garbage tomorrow morning on your way to work?"

MIKE: "You know I get really sick of your nagging all the damn time!"

ANN: "If you were a little more reliable and a little less defensive, we might not need to have these same discussions over and over again."

MIKE: "You're hardly the one to lecture about memory or defensiveness. If you remembered half the things you've committed to do, we would have fewer arguments. And it's your defensiveness, not mine, that causes all of our problems. . . . "

Like dependencies, spirals often take on a "life of their own," fueled by the momentum they themselves create. What begins as a request to take out the garbage can easily become still another in a string of provocations in a relationship where regressive spirals are common. And, by contrast, "Hi, how are you?" can initiate a very positive chain of events in a relationship characterized by frequent progressive spirals.

Over time, the spirals that characterize any relationship alternate between progressive and regressive, as a reflection of the inevitable phases that characterize any social unit. However, in order for a relationship to maintain strength, momentum, and continuity, the progressive phases must outweigh and/or outlast the regressive periods.

SELF-FULFILLING AND SELF-DEFEATING PROPHECIES

Another pattern that often develops in relationships has to do with our own expectations. It is often the case that what we expect to happen will happen, or at the least what we expect to happen will influence what actually occurs. If someone expects, for example, to do poorly in an interview for a new job, that expectation alone is enough to set in motion a process that helps to fulfill a prophecy, or prediction. If someone expects not to get the job, the approach to the interview situation may well be negative. This negative outlook is reflected in what is said and done, with the result that the interviewer may be convinced that the candidate is not appropriate for the position.

The reverse circumstance is also possible. When an individual feels well-qualified for a particular job, this expectation can provide the energy and commitment needed to prepare for the interview and to respond competently. As a result, the chances of being selected for the position are greatly increased.

In a wide range of situations, the expectations we have about ourselves and others influence the outcomes of our interactions and contribute to long-term relational patterns. In relationships, as in so many other facets of human activity, our own effort, commitment, and attitude play a major role in the outcomes that are realized.

Factors That Influence Patterns

We have looked at the role communication plays in the evolution of relationships and the patterns that develop within them. In this section, we will focus on the factors that influence these patterns. A number of elements have an impact on the interpersonal communication dynamics that take place within relationships. Particularly important are stage and context of interaction, interpersonal needs, and style, power, and conflict.

STAGE OF RELATIONSHIP AND CONTEXT

Communication patterns in a relationship vary greatly from one stage to another. Naturally, individuals meeting each other for the first time interact in a different manner than they would had they lived together for several years. The nature of interpersonal patterns also varies depending upon the context in which conversation is taking place. People meeting in a grocery store are quite likely to act and react differently to one another than if they were interacting in a bar or at a business meeting. Together, these two factors account for much of the variation in the patterns of communication within relationships.

INTERPERSONAL NEEDS AND STYLES

Beyond the rather direct and obvious impact of stage and context, the interpersonal needs and styles of the individuals involved represent other influences on communication within relationships.

Often noted as especially important in this way are the *interpersonal needs* for *affection, inclusion,* and *control.* William Schutz has suggested that our desires relative to giving and receiving affection, being included in the activities of others and including them in ours, and controlling other people and being controlled by them are very basic to our orientations to social relations of all kinds.[19]

We each develop our own specific needs relative to control, affection, and inclusion, as we do in other areas. The particular profile of needs we ourselves have, and how these match with those of other persons, can be a major determinant of the relational patterns that result. For instance, we could expect that one person with high needs for control and another with similarly strong needs to be controlled would function well together. The former would fall comfortably into a dominant leadership role, while the latter would be very willing to follow. If, on the other hand, two persons who work or live together have similarly high (or low) needs for control, one might predict a good deal of conflict (or a lack of decisiveness) within the relationship.

Interpersonal *style* also plays a key role in shaping the communication patterns that emerge in relationships. As discussed earlier, some people are more comfortable operating in an outgoing, highly verbal manner in their dealings with others, while others characteristically adopt a more passive and restrained interpersonal style, due either to preference or apprehension about speaking in social situations. Those who use a more outgoing style deal with their thoughts and feelings in a forthright, assertive manner.[20] If they want something, they ask for it. If they feel angry, they let others know. If they feel taken advantage of, they say so. If they don't want to comply with a request, they have little trouble saying "no!" In contrast to what might be termed a "machine-gun style" of interpersonal communication, the more passive "marshmallow style" involves "absorbing" the verbal and nonverbal messages of others, giving the outward appearance of acceptance, congeniality, and even encouragement, regardless of one's thoughts or feelings.[21] For any of several reasons, people who are prone to use the marshmallow style, often "hold onto" and "bottle up" thoughts, opinions, and feelings. If they are angry, it is seldom apparent from what is said. If they disagree, they seldom say so. If they feel taken advantage of, they may allow the situation to continue rather than confront it openly.

Though few of us use either style exclusively, we often favor one approach over the other in the majority of our dealings with people; and, depending upon the style of the people with whom we are in relationships, this factor alone can become a primary influence in shaping our interactions and our relationships, as is suggested in the following conversation:

TOM: "Georgia, you wouldn't mind taking me home tonight after work, would you? I know I impose on you a lot, but Mary needed the car again today, and I know you're the kind of person who doesn't mind helping out now and then."

GEORGIA: "Well, if you have no other way, I . . . "

TOM: "Hey thanks, Georgia. I was sure I could count on you. How are things anyway? Really busy, I'll bet. Well, listen, I'd better get back to work. I'll meet you by your car, at 5:00. Thanks again."

Tom's *machine-gun style,* in combination with Georgia's *marshmallow style,* will no doubt be critical factors in defining most, if not all, of the interactions that take place between them.

POWER

Interpersonal communication within relationships is also shaped by the distribution of power. Where one individual is employed by the other, for instance, the relationship is *asymmetrical,* or uneven, in terms of the actual power each has in the job situation.[22] The employer can exercise more control over that facet of their relationship—so long as the other person does not quit—simply as a consequence of the uneven control over resources and decision making.

There are many similar situations where asymmetries affect the interpersonal communication. The relationship between a therapist and a patient, a teacher and a student, a parent and a child, or a supervisor and supervisee are among the most common examples. In each, one member of the relationship has control over certain facets of the other's life, a circumstance that generally has a substantial impact on the interpersonal communication patterns that develop.

In peer-peer, colleague-colleague, or other relationships of this type, there is the potential for symmetry. Where this possibility exists, interpersonal communication creates rather than perpetuates any dependencies that result.

CONFLICT

The presence of *conflict*—"an incompatibility of interest between two or more persons giving rise to struggles between them"—can have a major impact on communication dynamics.[23] Communication researcher Alan Sillars suggests that when people are involved in conflict situations they develop their own personal theories to explain the situation. These theories, in turn, have a great influence on how interactants deal with one another.

Sillers finds that there are three general communication strategies used in conflict resolution:[24]

- Passive-indirect methods: avoiding the conflict-producing situation and people
- Distributive methods: maximizing one's own gain and the other's losses
- Integrative methods: achieving mutually positive outcomes for individuals and the relationship

Implications and Applications: Interpersonal Competence

• Being competent in interpersonal communication involves applying your understanding of communication and interpersonal relationships to everyday life. The goal is to use your knowledge to increase your interpersonal satisfaction and effectiveness from your own perspective, as well as from the perspective of those with whom you interact.[25]

• Self-awareness in relationships can contribute to interpersonal communication competence. Psychologist Carl Rogers offers the following personal observations on therapeutic relationships, which can be applied in many other types of relationships as well:[26]

In my relationships with persons I have found that it does not help, in the long run, to act as though I were something that I am not.

I find I am more effective when I can listen acceptingly to myself and can be myself.

I have found it of enormous value when I can permit myself to understand another person.

I have found it enriching to open channels whereby others can communicate their feelings, their private perceptual worlds, to me.

I have found it highly rewarding when I can accept another person.

The more I am open to the realities in me and in the other person, the less do I find myself wishing to rush in to "fix things."

Life, as its best, is a flowing, changing process in which nothing is fixed.

• Verbal and nonverbal communication are very important to interpersonal communication competence.

Empathy and respect for others' opinions, knowledge, and perspective generally enhances communication

The message others get is the one that matters.

If your communication style is highly verbal, "take charge," and "machine-gun-like" develop the ability, also, to be less talkative, to follow, and to listen. There are many interpersonal situations in which this flexibility is very valuable.

If your communication style is low-verbal, "follow along," and "marshmallow-like" acquire the skill to be more verbal, to take charge, and to be a "machine gun" when the situation requires it.

• Listening, observing, and interpreting are vital to communication competence in relationships. Every person reacts to a situation in his or her own way; some people are more interpersonally sensitive than others. The following guidelines can be helpful:[27]

Set listening, observing, and interpreting objectives. Before you go into a situation, plan your message receiving.

Try not to be distracted by an emotion-arousing word, phrase, or action.

Adapt to the situation.

Practice your listening, observation, and interpretation skills.

Listen to and observe the total person. Attend to both the verbal and nonverbal channels

Strive to interpret messages according to the other person's codes and meanings, not your own.

Be aware of gender-based differences in communication.

• One of the benefits of studying communication is its value for analyzing your own relationships and the communication behaviors of your acquaintances, friends, family, colleagues, and intimates. This knowledge can sometimes be productively shared with others to help them better understand their own communication in relationships. Sharing interpersonal perspectives effectively requires sensitivity:

Describe rather than criticize.

Be specific and avoid generalizations.

Focus comments on communication behaviors that the other person could change.

Select a time and place for discussions of relationships that is appropriate and meets the needs of all parties.

Strive to make the discussion and suggestions you may have for others constructive, not destructive.[28]

Summary

In this chapter, we have examined the relationship between communication and relationships. We have also discussed a number of ways of thinking about and characterizing relationships, and explored common communication patterns that can occur. Communication plays a central role in the development and evolution of all human relationships. Relationships also provide perhaps the most important context in which we attempt to use our communication abilities to achieve particular goals and meet particular needs.

In the most general sense, a relationship exists whenever there is reciprocal message processing—when two or more individuals are reacting to one another's verbal and nonverbal messages. It is by means of interpersonal communication that relationships are initiated, develop, grow, or deteriorate.

Intentionally-established relationships can be considered from several perspectives: whether they are dyadic or triadic; whether they are task-oriented or social in purpose; whether they are short- or long-term; whether they are casual or intimate. We also have discussed dating, love, and marital relationships.

Relationships progress through a series of relatively predictable stages, beginning from an initial social encounter, progressing to stages of increasing interaction and joint rule creation. Many relationships involve some formalized acknowledgement of their status, such as marriage or a legal business contract. A relationship may stall in one of these stages, back up and go forward again, or stop and remain in one stage for an extended period of time.

Over time, communication patterns develop in relationships. Often these dynamics take the form of defensiveness or supportiveness, dependencies or counterdependencies, progressive or regressive spirals, or self-fulfilling or self-defeating prophecies. These dynamics can have a far more significant impact on the form and development patterns of relationships than does the content of interaction.

A number of factors, such as stage and context, interpersonal needs and style, distribution of power, and the presence of conflict play a role in facilitating the development of particular patterns.

Notes

1. The discussion of dyads and triads draws upon the excellent summary of work on this topic provided by William Wilmot in *Dyadic Communication* (Reading, MA.: Addison-Wesley, 1979), pp. 14–30.

2. Wilmot, 1979, pp. 14–15.

3. William M. Kephart, "A Quantitative Analysis of Intra-Group Relationships," *American Journal of Sociology,* Vol. 55, 1950, pp. 544–549.

4. Wilmot, 1979, p. 21.

5. Fred Davis, "The Cabdriver and His Fare: Facets of a Fleeting Relationship," In *Interpersonal Dynamics.* Ed. by Warren G. Bennis, David E. Berlew, Edgar H. Schein, and Fred I. Steele (Homewood, IL: Dorsey, 1973), pp. 417–426.

6. See Michael D. Scott and William G. Powers, *Interpersonal Communication: A Question of Needs* (Boston, Houghton Mifflin, 1978), for a useful discussion of the role of needs in interpersonal communication and relational development.

7. See Joseph Luft, *Of Human Interaction* (Palo Alto, CA: National Press Books, 1969); Sidney M. Jourard, *The Transparent Self* (Princeton, NJ: Van Nostrand, 1964); and Stella Ting-Toomey, "Gossip as a Communication Construct." Paper presented at the Annual Conference of the Western Speech Communication Association. Los Angeles, February, 1979.

8. Based on summary provided by Stephen W. Littlejohn, *Theories of Human Communication, Third ed.* (Belmont, CA: Wadsworth, 1989), p. 161, adapted from Shirley J. Gilbert, "Empirical and Theoretical Extensions of Self-Disclosure," in *Explorations in Interpersonal Communication.* Ed by Gerald R. Miller (Beverly Hills: Sage, 1976), pp. 197–216.

9. James J. Lynch, *The Broken Heart: The Medical Consequences of Loneliness* (New York: Basic Books, 1979).

10. See extensive discussion of dating and marriage, summarized in this section, in Michael J. Beatty, *Romantic Dialogue: Communication in Dating and Marriage* (Englewood, CO: Morton, 1986).

11. Edwin J. Thomas, *Marital Communication and Decision-Making* (New York: Free Press, 1977), p. 1.

12. Beatty, 1986, pp. 68–77.

13. The discussion of stages of development of relationships draws on the work of Mark L. Knapp in *Social Intercourse: From Greeting to Goodbye* (Boston: Allyn & Bacon, 1978), and Murray S. Davis, *Intimate Relations* (New York: Free Press, 1973).

14. Knapp, 1978, pp. 19–21.

15. Based on Steve Duck, *Personal Relationships 4: Dissolving Personal Relationships,* "A Topography of Relationship Disagreement and Dissolution," (New York: Academic Press, 1982).

16. See discussion of spirals and prophecies in Wilmot, 1979, pp. 121–129,

and in Paul Watzlawick, Janet H. Beavin, and Don D. Jackson, *Pragmatics of Human Communication* (New York: Norton, 1967), pp. 51–54.

17. Jack R. Gibb, "Defensive Communication," *Journal of Communication*, Vol. 11, Sept. 1961, p. 41. Also see discussion of supportiveness-defensiveness in Steven A. Beebe and John T. Masterson, *Family Talk: Interpersonal Communication in the Family* (New York: Random House), 1986, pp. 145–150.

18. See Robert R. Carkhuff and Bernard G. Berenson, *Beyond Counseling and Therapy* (New York: Holt, 1967).

19. William Schultz, *The Interpersonal Underworld* (Palo Alto, CA: Science and Behavior Books, 1968).

20. See Colleen Kelley, "Assertion Theory," in *The 1976 Annual Handbook for Group Facilitators.* Ed. by J. William Pfeiffer and John E. Jones (La Jolla, CA: University Associates, 1976); Sharon and Gordon Bowers, *Asserting Yourself* (Reading, MA: Addison-Wesley, 1976); and Colleen Kelley, *Assertion Training* (La Jolla, CA: University Associates, 1979).

21. Brent D. Ruben, "The Machine Gun and the Marshmallow: Some Thoughts on the Concept of Communication Effectiveness." Paper presented at the annual conference of the Western Speech Association (Honolulu: November, 1972), and Brent D. Ruben "Communication, Stress, and Assertiveness: An Interpersonal Problem-Solving Model," in *The 1982 Annual Handbook for Group Facilitators.* Ed. by J. William Pfeiffer and John E. Jones, (La Jolla, CA: University Associates, 1982).

22. Watzlawick and Colleagues, 1967, pp. 67–71.

23. Herbert W. Simons, "The Carrot and Stick as Handmaidens of Persuasion in Conflict Situations," in *Perspectives on Communication in Social Conflict.* Ed. by Gerald R. Miller and Herbert W. Simons (Englewood Cliffs, NJ: Prentice Hall, 1974), pp. 177–178. See also review of definitions and approaches to conflict in Brent D. Ruben, "Communication and Conflict: A System-Theoretic Perspective," *The Quarterly Journal of Speech,* Vol 64, 1978, pp. 202–210.

24. Alan L. Sillars, "Attributions and Communication in Roommate Conflicts," *Communication Monographs,* Vol. 47, 1980, p. 180–200.

25. See discussion of communication competence in Brian H. Spitzberg and William R. Cupach, *Interpersonal Communication Competence* (Beverly Hills: Sage, 1984). Also see discussion in Littlejohn, p. 182.

26. Carl Rogers, *On Becoming a Person: A Therapist's View of Psychotherapy* (Boston: Houghton Mifflin, 1970), pp. 15–27.

27. Adapted from Beebee and Masterson, 1986, pp. 182–183.

28. Based on Beebee and Masterson, 1986, 217–219; Gibb, 1961.

References and Suggested Readings

BALES, ROBERT F. *Personality and Interpersonal Behavior.* New York: Holt, 1970.

BEATTY, MICHAEL J. *Romantic Dialogue: Communication in Dating and Marriage.* Englewood, CO: Morton, 1986.

BEEBE, STEVEN A., and JOHN T. MASTERSON. *Family Talk: Interpersonal Communication in the Family.* New York: Random House, 1986.

BENNIS, WARREN G., DAVID E. BERLEW, EDGAR H. SCHEIN, and FRED I. STEELE, eds. *Interpersonal Dynamics.* Third Ed. Homewood, IL: Dorsey, 1973.

BERGER, PETER L., and THOMAS LUCKMANN. *The Social Construction of Reality.* Garden City, NY: Doubleday, 1967.

BLUMER, HERBERT. *Symbolic Interactionism.* Englewood Cliffs, NJ: Prentice Hall, 1969.

BOWERS, SHARON and GORDON. *Asserting Yourself.* Reading, MA: Addison-Wesley, 1976.

CARKHUFF, ROBERT R., and BERNARD G. BERENSON. *Beyond Counseling and Therapy.* New York: Holt, 1967.

DAVIS, MURRAY S. *Intimate Relations.* New York: Free Press, 1973.

DEETZ, STANLEY A., and SHERYL L. STEVENSON. *Managing Interpersonal Communication.* New York: Harper & Row, 1986.

DUCK, STEVE. *Personal Relationships 4: Dissolving Personal Relationships.* New York: Academic Press, 1982.

EAKINS, BARBARA W., and R. GENE EAKINS. *Sex Differences in Human Communication.* Boston: Houghton Mifflin, 1978.

GIBB, JACK R. "Defensive Communication." *Journal of Communication,* Vol. 2, 1961, 141–148.

GILBERT, SHIRLEY J. "Empirical and Theoretical Extensions of Self-Disclosure." In *Explorations in Interpersonal Communication.* Ed by Gerald R. Miller. Beverly Hills: Sage, 1976, 197–216.

GOFFMAN, ERVING. *Interaction Ritual.* Garden City, NY: Doubleday, 1967.

———. *The Presentation of Self in Everyday Life.* Garden City, NY: Doubleday, 1959.

JOURARD, SIDNEY M. *The Transparent Self.* Princeton, NJ: Van Nostrand, 1964.

KELLEY, COLLEEN. "Assertion Theory." In *The 1976 Annual Handbook for Group Facilitators.* Ed. by J. William Pfeiffer and John E. Jones. La Jolla, CA: University Associates, 1976.

KEPHART, WILLIAM M. "A Quantitative Analysis of Intra-Group Relationships." *American Journal of Sociology,* Vol. 55, 1950, 544–549.

KNAPP, MARK L. *Social Intercourse: From Greeting to Goodbye.* Boston: Allyn & Bacon, 1978.

LEVINSON, DANIEL J. *The Seasons of a Man's Life.* New York: Ballantine, 1978.

LITTLEJOHN, STEPHEN W. *Theories of Human Communication. Third Ed.* Belmont, CA: Wadsworth, 1989.

LUFT, JOSEPH. *Of Human Interaction.* Palo Alto, CA: National Press Books, 1969.

LYNCH, JAMES J. *The Broken Heart: The Medical Consequences of Loneliness.* New York: Basic, 1977.

MORRIS, DESMOND. *Intimate Behaviour.* New York: Holt, 1961.

PFEIFFER, J. WILLIAM, and JOHN E. JONES, eds. *The 1976 Annual Handbook for Group Facilitators.* La Jolla, CA: University Associates, 1976.

PHILLIPS, GERALD M., and NANCY J. METZGER. *Intimate Communication.* Boston: Allyn & Bacon, 1976.

ROGERS, CARL. *On Becoming a Person: A Therapist's View of Psychotherapy.* Boston: Houghton-Mifflin, 1970.

RUBEN, BRENT D. "Machine Guns and Marshmallows: Thoughts on the Concept of Communication Effectiveness." Unpublished paper presented at the Western Speech Communication Association, Honolulu, 1972.

———. "Communication, Stress, and Assertiveness: An Interpersonal Problem-Solving Model." In *The 1982 Handbook for Group Facilitators.* Ed. by J. William Pfeiffer and John E. Jones. La Jolla, CA: University Associates, 1982.

———. "Communication and Conflict: A System-Theoretic Perspective," *The Quarterly Journal of Speech,* Vol. 64, 1978, 202–210.

RUESCH, JURGEN, and GREGORY BATESON. *Communication—The Social Matrix of Psychiatry.* New York: Norton, 1951.

SCHUTZ, WILLIAM. *The Interpersonal Underworld.* Palo Alto, CA: Science and Behavior Books, 1968.

SCOTT, MICHAEL D., and WILLIAM G. POWERS. *Interpersonal Communication: A Question of Needs.* Boston: Houghton Mifflin, 1978.

SILLERS, ALAN L. "Attributions and Communications in Roommate Conflicts," *Communication Monographs,* Vol. 47, 1980, p. 180–200.

SIMONS, HERBERT W. "The Carrot and Stick as Handmaidens of Persuasion in Conflict Situations," *Perspectives on Communication in Social Conflict.* Ed. by Gerald R. Miller and Herbert W. Simons. Englewood Cliffs, NJ: Prentice Hall, 1974.

SOMMER, ROBERT. "Further Studies of Small Group Ecology." *Sociometry,* Vol. 28, 1965, 337–348.

SPITZBERG, BRIAN H., and WILLIAM R. CUPACH. *Interpersonal Communication Competence.* Beverly Hills: Sage, 1984.

STEWART, JOHN, ed. *Bridges Not Walls.* Fourth Ed. Reading, MA: Addison-Wesley, 1986.

THOMAS, EDWIN J. *Marital Communication and Decision-Making.* New York: Free Press, 1977.

TING-TOOMEY, STELLA. "Gossip as a Communication Construct." Unpublished paper presented at the Annual Conference of the Western Speech Communication Association. Los Angeles, February, 1979.

WATZLAWICK, PAUL, JANET H. BEAVIN, and DON D. JACKSON. *Pragmatics of Human Communication.* New York: Norton, 1967.

WILMOT, WILLIAM W. *Dyadic Communication.* Third Ed. Reading, MA: Addison-Wesley.

11

Groups

Groups: Fiction and Fact

Why People Join Groups

Types of Groups

Task and Social Dimensions: Productivity and Morale

Contrived and Emergent Groups

Group Development

Group Communication Networks

Stages of Development

Group Culture: Symbols, Rules, and Codes

Decision Making

Consensus

Compromise

Majority Vote

Decision by Leader

Arbitration

Roles and Responsibilities

Task-Oriented Roles

Group-Building and Support Roles

Individualistic Roles

Leadership

Functions of Leadership

Approaches to Leadership

Followership and Membership Issues

Cohesiveness

Symptoms of Too Little Cohesiveness: Boredom and Indifference

Symptoms of Too Much Cohesiveness: The Group Think Syndrome

Conflict in Groups

Implications and Applications: Groups in Action

Each of us spends great quantities of time in groups of various kinds—working at our jobs, participating in clubs and associations, attending community or religious functions, and taking part in social activities. As members of families, peer groups, clubs, religious groups, and other groups, we are selectively exposed to the world around us. As we grow from infancy to adulthood, the groups in which we participate generate a wide range of demands and opportunities for us; and, in the process of adjusting them, we develop, change, and grow.

As with relationships, groups are created and maintained by people engaged in reciprocal message processing. As we shall see, the communication process makes groups possible and is essential to every facet of group functioning.

Groups differ from relationships in terms of the number of people involved, the resources available for decision making, and the complexity of the communication dynamics that result. The presence of the additional individuals and more complex communication dynamics is, on the one hand, a very positive characteristic of groups. See Table 11–1 With increased size comes additional people to address issues, undertake projects, and solve problems. On the other hand, the larger size also leads to problems associated with agreeing on goals, ensuring that information is available to all group members and not only members in the group decision-making process, defining roles and responsibilities, providing appropriate leadership, creating cohesiveness, and avoiding undue pressure on individuals toward conformity.

Groups: Fiction and Fact

A decision about this year's group project has to be made. The board—of which you are a newly-elected member—has proposed a service project to help homeless people in the community. A meeting of the group is scheduled to approve the recommendation and begin the planning process.

The group has a fairly simple and straightforward agenda. A decision has to be made, and a recommendation is at hand. You envision a brief meeting of the group at which members will share information and perspectives and begin planning together to achieve the common goal.

The meeting is scheduled at what is supposed to be a good time for everyone. Eleven members of the group are present at the designated starting

TABLE 11–1 Characteristics of Groups: Consequences of Size

Benefits	Costs
Additional Members to Assist with Activities	Effort Needed to Develop Consensus on Goals
	Effort Needed to Keep Members Informed
Additional Members to Participate in Decision Making	Effort Needed to Include Members
	Effort Needed to Counteract Pressures Toward Conformity
Additional Resources for Problem Solving	Effort Needed for Leadership

time. One member arrives fifteen minutes later. Six people are absent, and no one is sure why.

As discussion proceeds, it becomes clear that five of the members present are in agreement with the proposed project.

Three members in attendance are opposed to the idea. (Two don't like the idea, and the third—an unsuccessul candidate for board membership during the last election—doesn't feel the board sought enough input from members in arriving at its recommendation). Of those not present, two people are reportedly opposed to the idea, but no one seems to know the reasons for their disapproval.

The other three members in attendance haven't spoken; one looks angry, one bored, and a third seems to be working on an unrelated writing assignment of some kind while others are engaged in discussion.

Unfortunately, the realities of group life often do not match our expectations.[1] In the abstract we tend to think of groups as collections of active, supportive, and enthusiastic people, working together rationally and unemotionally to pursue shared goals. In fact, groups are composed of individuals with varying motivations, emotional makeup and attachments, perspectives, and needs who come together to negotiate a framework for communication that permits collective action. While this goal seems to be reasonable and rational, the process by which individuals pursue it may not be.

Why People Join Groups

Most basically people join groups to pursue individual needs in a social context. Groups assist individuals in meeting a number of goals, including: socializing and companionship, support for personal development or change, spiritual growth, and economic gain. See Figure 11–1. A number of factors go into individual decisions as to which groups to join, among them:[2]

Attractiveness of group's members—physical, social, and task attractiveness

Attractiveness of group's activities and goals

Attractiveness of being a member of a particular group—personal, social, symbolic, occupational, or economic benefits

Types of Groups

TASK AND SOCIAL DIMENSIONS: PRODUCTIVITY AND MORALE

Groups are created to serve a number of goals. Often, the primary objective is *productivity*—the completion of a task or job. Examples are or-

FIGURE 11–1

ganizing a party, building a house, or carrying out community service projects. We can distinguish several types of task-oriented groups:[3]

- Duplicated activity group. Each member does the same job. Examples: All members plant trees or prepare letters for mailing.
- Assembly line group. Each member works on a different part of the task. Examples: Some members dig holes, others plant trees, and others water and clean up; or some members fold letters, others affix stamps, and others stuff and mail.
- Judgmental, problem-solving and decision-making group. Members of group identify and choose among possible answers, strategies, or options. Examples: A group decides how many and what kind of trees to plant, and plans the planting process.

There are also groups in which the primary goal is to create positive *morale*—and to facilitate members achieving personal- or socially-oriented goals, such as interpersonal support, encouragement, and diversion. Social clubs and discussion groups are examples.

To a greater or lesser extent, most groups serve a combination of task-, personally-, and socially-oriented goals. Even in what might seem to be a rigidly task-oriented group, such as a work group on an industrial assembly line where productivity is the primary measure of success, good morale is also important. This is especially the case if members of a task group will need to work together for some period of time. In such cases, good morale may enhance productivity; and, conversely, poor morale can undermine it. Within groups whose goals are primarily social, task orientation can also be essential, even in decision making as to where to meet, what projects to undertake, where to eat, or what movies to attend. Most groups—such as families, service clubs, or religious or professional groups— require a fairly even balance between concern for productivity and morale. Task orientation is necessary to carry out group activities; personal and social orientation are necessary to encourage full participation and to foster positive feelings by members toward the group and one another.

CONTRIVED AND EMERGENT GROUPS

Some groups are *emergent.* Such groups form naturally out of spontaneous activities of individuals. Acquaintances who become friends and begin to go places and do things with one another provide an example of an emergent group.

More often, groups are *contrived*—purposely formed for specific purposes.[4] Contrived groups typically have specific, stated goals or objectives, such as to serve the community, to share professional interests, to make a profit, to help members quit smoking, or to advance a political candidate. Sometimes, groups that are initially emergent shift to contrived, such as when acquaintances decide to form a club or business group.

Group Development

GROUP COMMUNICATION NETWORKS

In a two-person relationship, there is the possibility of only one reciprocal communication linkage. With three interactants, there are six possible message-processing pairs: person 1 with person 2, person 1 with person 3, person 2 with person 3, person 1 and 2 with person 3, person 1 and 3 with person 2, and persons 2 and 3 with person 1. When we consider the possible interpersonal linkages in a group of four members, there are twenty-five potential communication relationships! The addition of just one more person creates the potential for nineteen additional communication linkages.[5]

In groups that are emergent, reciprocal message-processing linkages—*networks*—develop naturally, often spontaneously. Networks begin to form as individuals meet and get to know one another. With the passage of time, the network becomes well-developed as all mem-

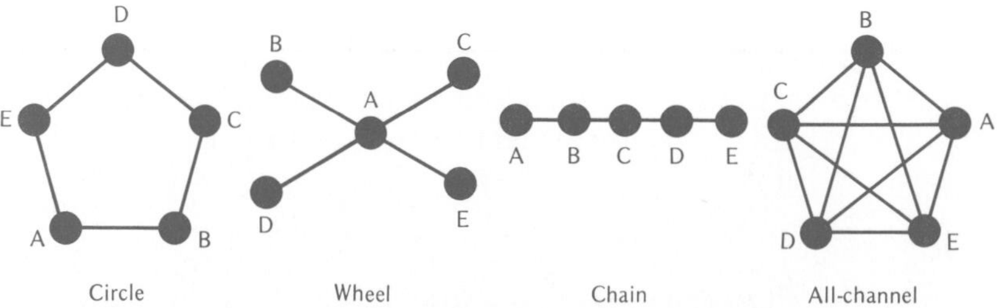

FIGURE 11–2 The development of linkages in a group is marked by the emergence of networks that connect individuals to one another and define the unit. A group need not progress through all phases but may move from a stage of high integration to stages of lower integration and back again periodically.

bers of the group participate in interaction. Theoretically, as shown in Figure 11–2, the network will evolve to include all group members, at least minimally.[6]

In actual practice, a number of possible patterns of linkage are possible, as shown in Figure 11–3. In the *circle* network, each group member interacts with two other people. Person A interacts with Person B and Person E, Person B with Person A and Person C, and so on. The *wheel* configuration describes a situation in which all messages flow through one individual—Person A. Person A interacts directly with all members of the group, but none of the others interact directly with one another. In a *chain,* members interact in a serial, straight-line manner. The *all-channel* pattern denotes a network in which each member of a group sends messages to, and receives messages from, every other member. In any group, some linkages in networks are utilized more and others less; some people become central to the network, others peripheral; still others may become isolated from others in the network. And, clearly, patterns change over time.

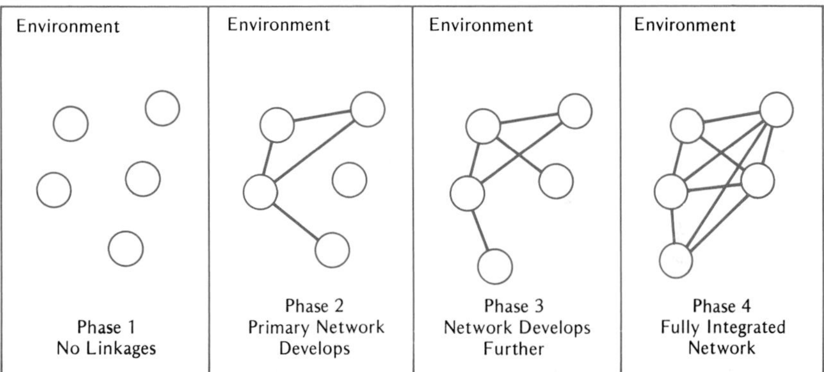

FIGURE 11–3 In studies of common group communication networks, such as those shown here, centralized networks (like the "wheel") contributed to rapid performance, but the error rate was high. Low centralization (such as provided in the "circle") was found to be associated with a high degree of individual satisfaction. Researchers also noted that being in a key position in a network, one requiring that information be channeled through one individual, led to information "overload."

Source: Harold J. Leavitt, "Some Effects of Certain Communication Patterns on Group Performance," *Journal of Abnormal and Social Psychology*, 46, 1951, pp. 38–50; M. E. Shaw, "Some Effects of Unequal Distribution of Information Upon Group Performance in Various Communication Nets," *Journal of Abnormal and Social Psychology*, **49,** 1954, pp. 547–553.

Stages of Development

Studies of the development of task-oriented groups suggest that they move through the following phases:[7]

1. Orientation phase
2. Conflict phase
3. Emergence phase
4. Reinforcement phase

The first stage consists of getting acquainted, expressing initial points of view, and forming linkages relative to the task at hand. In the early stages of the emergence of groups, the content of discussion tends to focus on "small talk," such as the weather, composition of the group, the setting, circumstances that brought the individuals together, goals of the group, and so on.

As the group proceeds, groups are generally characterized by the delineation of roles and responsibilities; the expression of differing points of view leads to polarization. Gradually, accommodations are made among members and subgroups with differing view points, as the group begins to take on an identity of its own. As the group's project nears completion, cooperation among individuals in the network increases, as does support for—and reinforcement of—the group's solution.[8]

A number of factors influence the dynamics of groups as they evolve. Among these are: the amount of structure within the group; the time available to the group for completion of the task; the group size; the group members' attitudes and feelings about the task, topic, and one another; and the nature of the task.[9] The following task characteristics are particularly important:[10]

- Task difficulty—amount of effort required to complete the job
- Solution multiplicity—number of reasonable alternatives available to solve the problem
- Intrinsic interest—interest generated by the task itself
- Cooperation requirements—degree to which cooperation by group members is necessary to complete the task

- Familiarity—extent to which the group has had experience with a particular task

Group Culture: Symbols, Rules, and Codes

As networks develop, symbols, rules, and codes of various types emerge and become standardized through communication, as shown in Figure 11–4. The process creates what we might think of as the group's *culture.* Some aspects of the culture develop naturally, as with slang phrases among members of a club or social group, or informal "dress codes" of a peer group. In other instances, symbols, rules, and codes result from systematic efforts by members of a group. In such cases, symbols and rules are created to give the group an identity, to differentiate it from others, or to identify or differentiate a particular group from a larger unit of which it is a part. The decorated jackets of street gangs serve this function as do the crests, handshakes, or "secret words" of fraternities and sororities. See Figure 11–4.

Cultures play a pervasive role in the dynamics of groups. They provide members of the group with a sense of individual and collective identity and contribute at the same time to the development of order, structure, and cohesiveness in the overall operation of the system.

Decision Making

One of the major activities of all task-oriented groups is decision making. Decisions range from simple and straightforward questions such as when to hold a meeting, to more complex and entangled questions about group policy and activities. Rules that guide decision making in small informal groups emerge naturally over time as members spend time with one another. In larger, more structured groups, decision-making sessions are generally convened and given a specific name—*meetings.* During meetings, the behaviors of individuals follow a number of reasonably well-defined rules, some emerging spontaneously, with others following group traditions, formalized bylaws, or parliamentary procedure.

There are a number of methods by which groups can make decisions,

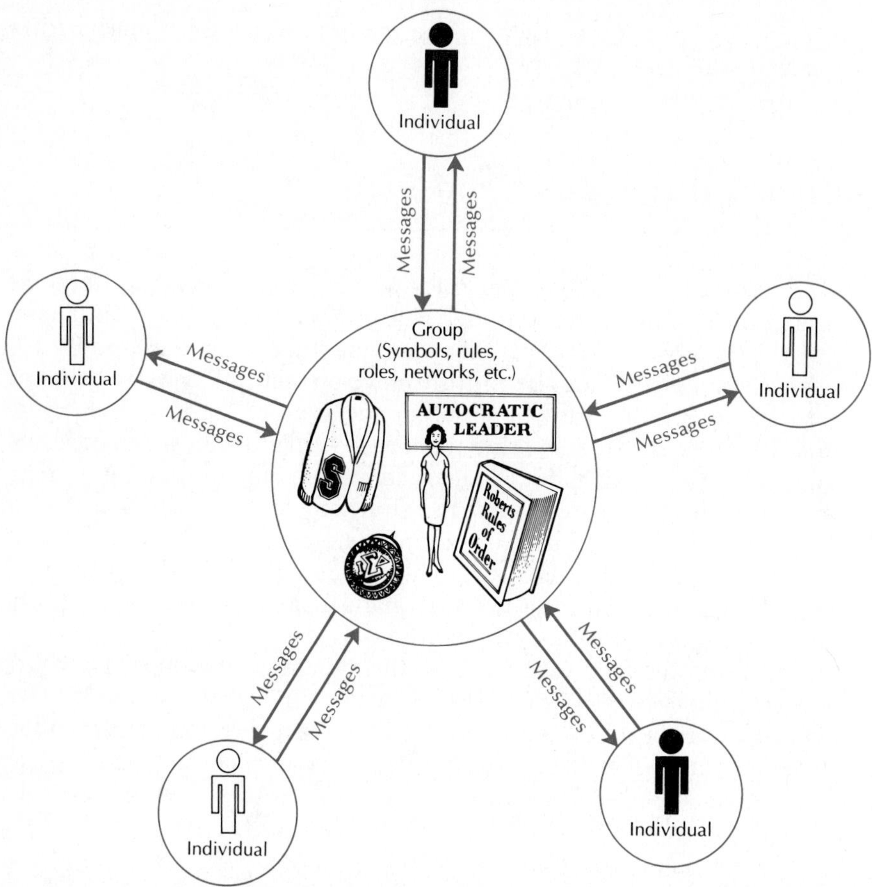

FIGURE 11–4 Through their verbal and nonverbal behavior individuals collectively create the groups to which they belong and the cultures, symbols, rules, jargon, and other conventions characteristic of each. Once created, the culture of the group "acts back upon" its members. Over time, individuals are greatly influenced by the group, and in turn individuals influence the group.

among them: consensus, compromise, majority vote, decision by leader, and arbitration.[11]

CONSENSUS

Consensus refers to a process which requires that a group arrive at a collective decision with which all members genuinely agree. For example, through discussion, it becomes apparent that every member of a club likes the idea of doing a service project for homeless senior citizens, and the group decides to undertake this kind of project.

COMPROMISE

Compromise is a process of negotiation and give-and-take to arrive at a position that takes account of—but may not be completely consistent with—the preferences of individual members. For example, some members of a club want to do a service project for senior citizens, while others favor a project for the homeless. Through discussion, the group decides to undertake a project for homeless seniors.

MAJORITY VOTE

Voting is a method for arriving at group decisions mathematically. A decision is made when it is supported by a majority of members. For example, four members want to do a project for senior citizens; six want to do something for the homeless. The decision is in favor of a homeless project six to four.

DECISION BY LEADER

Leader decision making involves the imposition of a resolution by a group's leader. In this instance, it is a decision by proclamation. For example, the group is unable to meet because of bad weather, and a decision is made by the club president that this year the group will do a service project for senior citizens.

ARBITRATION

Agreement through a process of formal negotiation between parties unable to reach a decision by other means is termed *arbitration*. For example, two subgroups exist within the club. One is determined to do a project for seniors, while the other insists that something should be done for community homeless. Members of each group have very strong personal convictions about the matter. Discussion and a trial vote reveals that there is a five to five split, with no one willing to change his or her position. An imposed decision risks permanently alienating members.

The chairman of the local community service coordinating the organization is invited to the next meeting to help the group reach a decision. More often than not, arbitration would be used in conflicts between, rather than within, groups—for instance, a deadlock between labor and management over terms of a contract.

Roles and Responsibilities

In small informal groups, member roles and responsibilities develop primarily as the result of informal, often unverbalized, agreements, as illustrated in Figure 11–5. In larger, more formal groups, individual roles and responsibilities may be made explicit. In clubs, for instance, the responsibilities and duties of officers, committee members, and other positions are generally detailed in written bylaws or a constitution.

In a now classic article on group roles, Benne and Sheats outlined three types of roles that develop in groups over the course of time:[12] (1) roles related to the completion of the task, (2) roles related to building

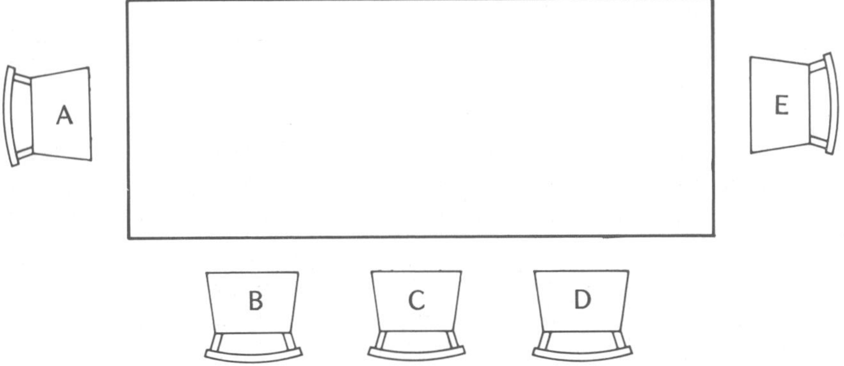

FIGURE 11–5 Studies of seating patterns in groups and communication behavior suggest that people who sit in position A, C, and E are more vocal contributors to discussion than persons at positions B or D. Often, more dominant personalities tend to choose the high participation positions, while others who prefer to avoid high levels of participation, avoid them.

Source: A. Hare and Robert Bales, "Seating Position and Small Group Interaction," *Sociometry*, **26,** 1963, pp. 480–486, and Mark L. Knapp, *Essentials of Nonverbal Communication* (New York: Holt Rinehart & Winston, 1980), p. 88.

and supporting the group, and (3) individualistic roles. Within each of these broad categories, a number of specific roles are identified.

TASK ROLES

- **initiator-contributor**—suggests or proposes new ideas or changed ways of regarding the group problem or goal.
- **information-seeker**—asks for clarification of suggestions made in terms of their factual adequacy, for authoritative information and facts pertinent to the problem being discussed.
- **opinion-seeker**—asks for a clarification of the values pertinent to what the group is undertaking, of values involved in a suggestion made, or of values in alternative suggestions.
- **information-giver**—offers facts or generalizations which are "authoritative" or relates his or her own pertinent experience to the group problem.
- **opinion-giver**—states his or her belief or opinion pertinent to a suggestion made, or to alternative suggestions.
- **elaborator**—spells outs suggestions in terms of examples, offers a rationale for suggestions previously made, and tries to deduce how an idea or suggestion would work out if adopted by the group.
- **coordinator**—shows or clarifies the relationships among various ideas and suggestions, tries to pull ideas and suggestions together, or tries to coordinate the activities of various members of subgroups.
- **orienter**—defines the position of the group with respect to its goals by summarizing what has occurred, points to departures from agreed upon directions or goals, or raises questions about the direction the group discussion is taking.
- **evaluator-critic**—subjects the accomplishment of the group to some standard or set of standards of group functioning in the context of the group task.
- **energizer**—prods the group to action or decision, attempts to stimulate or arouse the group to "greater" or "higher quality" activity.
- **procedural-technician**—expedites group movement by doing things for the group—performing routine tasks, e.g., distributing materials, or manipulating objects for the group, e.g., rearranging the seating.
- **recorder**—writes down suggestions, makes a record of group decisions, or writes down the product of discussion.

GROUP BUILDING AND SUPPORT ROLES

- **encourager**—praises, agrees with, and accepts the contribution of others.
- **harmonizer**—mediates the differences between other members, attempts to reconcile disagreements, relieves tension in conflict situations through jesting, and so on.
- **compromiser**—operates from within a conflict in which his or her ideas or position is involved.
- **gatekeeper/expediter**—attempts to keep communication channels open by encouraging or facilitating the participation of others or by regulating the flow of communication.
- **standard setter**—expresses standards for the group to attempt to achieve in its functioning or applies standards in evaluating the quality of group processes.
- **group observer**—keeps records of various aspects of group process and feeds such data with proposed interpretations into the group's evaluation of its own procedures.
- **follower**—goes along with the movement of the group, more or less passively accepting the ideas of others, serving as an audience in group discussion and decision making.

INDIVIDUALISTIC ROLES

- **aggressor**—may work in many ways—deflating the status of others, expressing disapproval of the values, acts or feelings of others, attacking the group or the problem it is working on, joking aggressively, showing envy toward another's contribution by trying to take credit for it, etc.
- **blocker**—tends to be negativistic and stubbornly resistant, disagreeing and opposing without or beyond reason, and attempting to maintain or bring back an issue after the group has rejected it.
- **recognition seeker**—works in various ways to call attention to himself or herself, whether through boasting, reporting on personal achievements, acting in unusual ways, struggling to prevent being placed in an "inferior" position, etc.
- **self-confessor**—uses the audience opportunity the group setting provides to express personal, nongroup-oriented "feeling," "insight," "ideology," etc.

- **dominator**—tries to assert authority or superiority in manipulating the group or certain members of the group.
- **help seeker**—attempts to call forth "sympathy" responses from other group members or from the whole group.
- **special interest pleader**—speaks for the "small business man," "the grass roots" community, the "housewife," "labor," etc., usually cloaking his or her own prejudices or biases in the stereotype which best fits his or her individual need.

Leadership

No doubt the role that receives the most attention in discussion of groups is that of the leader. The basic role of a leader is to coordinate the activities of individuals so that they contribute to the overall goals and general adaptability of the group.

In groups of two, three, or four individuals, patterns of leadership are almost totally the result of the needs, preferences, and communication styles of the individuals involved. Leadership may well be a subtle, even unnoticeable, aspect of the group's operation. In larger groups, leadership is an essential, formalized, and often highly visible element in the day-to-day and long-run functioning of the group. In either case, the role involves the design, implementation, and/or supervision of procedures, policies, or mechanisms necessary to bringing about the desired coordination of the individuals and activities of the group.

FUNCTIONS OF LEADERSHIP

The basic functions of leadership fall into two categories: (1) group maintenance functions, and (2) group achievement functions. A comprehensive synthesis of these functions is provided by Baird and Weinberg.[13] They list:

Group Maintenance Functions

- Promoting participation
- Regulating interaction
- Promoting need satisfaction
- Promoting cooperation

- Arbitrating conflict
- protecting individual rights
- providing exemplary behavior
- assuming responsibility for group failure
- promoting group development

Group Achievement Functions

- Informing
- Planning
- Orienting
- Integrating
- Representing
- Coordinating
- Clarifying
- Evaluating
- Stimulating

APPROACHES TO LEADERSHIP

Leadership has to do with the exercise of control within a group. There are any number of ways this control can be exercised, and a variety of points of view as to what constitutes good leadership.[14]

Good-Leaders-Are-Born Approach. The traditional view of leadership holds that leadership is a *trait*—an ability one inherits. In this perspective, "good leaders are born not made." The assumption is that leadership qualities are inherent within one's personality. It follows that either we possess, or do not possess, these qualities. According to this approach, the challenge of leadership involves finding people who have "the right stuff."

One-Best-Style Approach. Another approach views leadership as a matter of style. Control over decision making can be wholly centralized or can be totally diffused among members of a group. Where the former exists, the leadership style may be characterized as *autocratic*. The autocratic leader uses authority to direct group activities. Typically, this type of leader tightly controls information, assigns members to roles and responsibilities, and has formal systems of accountability. When authority is shared, the leadership style is described as *democratic*. This style involves members of the group in decision making and involves a more open sharing of information. Moreover, roles and responsibilities are determined, at least in part, by the group. A third approach to leadership—*laissez-faire*—is a "hands-off" style, in which no authority is exercised by the leader. From the perspective of the "one-best style" approach, the challenge of leadership is determining whether the autocratic, democratic, or laissez-faire style of leadership is most effective.

Based on studies comparing leadership styles and their effects, it was first thought that the democratic style was superior in terms of its impact on group productivity and morale. However, further research confirmed that some groups functioned very well with more authoritarian leadership. Examples are military groups, surgical units, and sporting teams. A reasonable conclusion is that there is no one ideal leadership style for all groups and circumstances; rather, the appropriateness of a particular style depends upon the nature and purpose of the group.[15]

Contextual Approach. The contextual approach views leadership as the result of individual abilities (inherited plus learned), the purposes of the group, pressures put on the group from outside, and the way members in the group talk, work, or relate to one another.[16]

Bormann and Bormann offer the following description of this approach to leadership:

> The contextual view recognized that some people learn to play the game of being leader and that they tend to have certain opening moves they use in starting the game whenever they join a new work group. To some extent, the way they try to be leader depends upon what they think about the group. They do not approach the squad at basic training in the army with the same expectations they display toward a peer discussion group. . . . Such an explanation provides a more complete view of leadership than does either the trait approach or the one-best-style approach. It includes the idea that leaders are to some extent born, but it also suggests that potential leaders can acquire skills and improve talents.[17]

FOLLOWERSHIP AND MEMBERSHIP ISSUES

For the individual, leadership is an important element that differentiates the involvement in a group from participation in relationships. In relationships, each individual has a direct hand in creating and controlling the system, its culture, communication patterns, rules, and roles. This is not often the case with groups, since we are usually initiated into—rather than initiating—them.

Becoming a participant in any group involves an initiation into the culture and communication patterns of the unit. Our training for membership in groups begins during our earliest years. As a child in a family of three or four individuals, for instance, a good deal of compromise, accommodation, and fitting in is required. The child must learn the family's rules as to what to do, when to do it, what to say, and where to say it.

Later, as the child seeks to attain membership in various other groups, a similar process operates. Entry into certain clubs, fraternal orders, and religious groups makes this process of fitting in a very explicit part of the initiation of a new member into the unit. Even in those groups where there is no formal apprenticeship, internship, or trial period, the individual must come to terms with the group's rules and realities in order to be accepted and to function effectively as a member.

Thus, in those instances in which one's role requires *adjustment* to the situation rather than the *creation* of that situation, the initial function of communication is identifying and fitting oneself to the ongoing rules and structures made by others. This generally means that becoming a member of a group is a less active, less creative, more accommodating—and for some a more frustrating—process than becoming part of a relationship.

Cohesiveness

Cohesiveness refers to group loyalty.[18] A cohesive group is one in which members have a "team spirit" and are committed to the group's well being. As Ernest and Nancy Bormann note in *Effective Small Group Communication,* the essence of the concept of cohesiveness is aptly reflected in the motto of Alexandre Dumas's *Three Musketeers:* "All for one and one for all."

The relationship between communication, cohesiveness, and performance is important in any group. It is through communication that cohesiveness—or the lack of it—is fostered. Moreover, the presence or absence of cohesiveness influences the patterns and quality of communication within a group. When present, cohesiveness also encourages task and social dimensions of productivity and good morale:[19]

- Cohesive task groups are more productive. They do more work because members work cooperatively, distribute the work load well, and use time efficiently.
- Cohesive groups have higher morale because their members value and feel a part of the group. Members pay attention to, appreciate,

spend time and effort with one another, and share success as well as failure.

- Cohesive groups have efficient and effective communication because channels are open. Members are present, receptive, and committed to ensuring the communication necessary to promote productivity and high morale.

SYMPTOMS OF TOO LITTLE COHESIVENESS: BOREDOM AND INDIFFERENCE

There are a number of symptoms and consequences of low cohesiveness.[20] These include a lack of member involvement, the absence of enthusiasm, and minimal question asking. Meetings are quiet, even boring, with members behaving in a polite but apathetic manner. Even important decisions are handled routinely, and the prevailing sentiment is best expressed as, "Let's get this over with."

SYMPTOMS OF TOO MUCH COHESIVENESS: THE GROUPTHINK SYNDROME

Cohesiveness and loyalty to the group can have a down side. Scholar Irving L. Janis explains in *Victims of Groupthink* that decision-making groups can actually be *too* cohesive.[21] Within highly cohesive groups, pressure to agree with the group can become very powerful. A *norm*, or accepted standard, of avoiding disagreement may develop. The group can be so cohesive and team-oriented that opinions that contradict the majority view may go unverbalized and/or be inadvertently overlooked. The *Groupthink Syndrome* occurs because members place so much value on loyalty and being a team player. One of the characteristics of groupthink that makes it particularly troublesome is that the process often occurs without the awareness of the participants.

Groupthink Warning Signs. The presence of certain factors signals the potential for groupthink. These include:[22]

- Overestimation of the group's power and morality: assuming the group is not accountable to others and that it is pursuing the morally correct course of action
- Closed-mindedness: ignoring or distorting alternative view points
- Pressures toward conformity: subtle and not-so-subtle influence to-

ward agreement among group members and lack of willingness to acknowledge or discuss differences of opinion

Consequences of groupthink may include: an incomplete survey of alternatives and options, failure to examine risks of preferred choices, failure to reappraise initially-rejected alternatives, poor information search, selective bias in processing information at hand, and failure to work out contingency plans.[23]

Conflict in Groups

At various stages in the development of any group, conflict is inevitable. The conflict may have to do with disagreements over a group's goals, member roles or responsibilities, decision making, resource allocation, group dynamics, relationships among particular individuals, or any of a number of other factors.

Conflict is not inherently a problem. In fact, while the experiencing of conflict is generally unpleasant, we know that without conflict, quality, diversity, growth, and excellence may be diminished for individuals, relationships, or groups. Thus, the goal is not necessarily to eliminate conflict. Rather, the objective in any situation should be to better understand conflict, to be able to identify its origins, to be able to determine its potential for making a positive contribution, and to be able to resolve or manage it productively.

A number of approaches have been developed to analyze and resolve conflict within groups. One interesting approach classifies conflict based on two dimensions:[24]

- Assertiveness—behaviors intended to satisfy one's own concerns; and
- Cooperativeness—behaviors intended to satisfy the concerns of others.

Considered in combination, these two dimensions describe five different styles of conflict.[25] See Figure 11–6.

1. Competitive style: high in assertiveness and low in cooperativeness. Example: the tough competitor who desires to defeat others—a "fight orientation."
2. Accommodative style: low in assertiveness and high in cooperative-

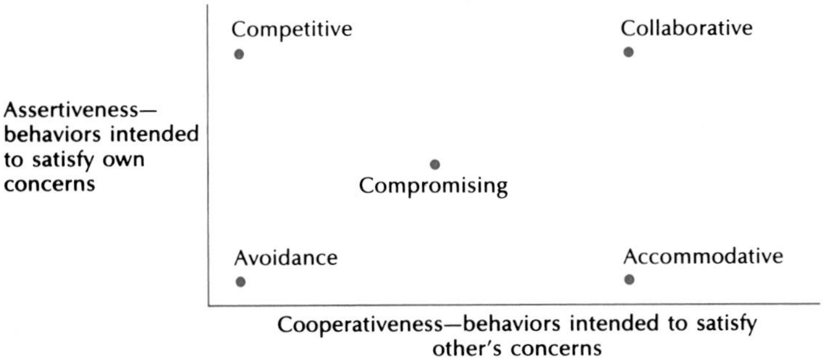

Competitive
Collaborative
Assertiveness—behaviors intended to satisfy own concerns
Compromising
Avoidance
Accommodative
Cooperativeness—behaviors intended to satisfy other's concerns

FIGURE 11–6 *Five Conflict-Management Styles and Their Relationships.*
Source: From Thomas L. Ruble and Kenneth W. Thomas, "Support for a Two-Dimensional Model of Conflict Behavior," in *Organizational Behavior and Human Performance, 16,* 143–155, 1976. Copyright 1976 by Academic Press, Inc.

ness. Example: the easygoing, undemanding, and supportive follower.

3. Avoiding style: low in assertiveness, low in cooperativeness. Example: the low-profile, indifferent, group isolate—a "flight orientation."
4. Collaborative style: high in assertiveness, high in cooperativeness. Example: the active, integrative problem solver.
5. Compromising style: moderate in assertiveness, moderate in cooperativeness. Example: the "meet-you-half-way," "give-up-something-to-keep-something" approach.

This framework is useful for understanding origins of conflict within groups. Moreover, it suggests how certain styles and strategies can be helpful in resolving and managing conflict.

Implications and Applications: Groups in Action

• Groups are complex social systems made up of individuals who bring their own unique orientations—perspectives, goals, needs, values, experiences, styles, and motivations—to group membership.

• Groups are successful to the extent that the diverse orientations of members can be coordinated, channeled, and/or focused.

• Success has two dimensions: productivity and morale. From the perspective of productivity, a group is successful when the job is done. In terms of morale, a group is successful when people feel satisfied. Sometimes these two outcomes go together in groups; sometimes they do not. For instance, taking time to focus on members' personal and social needs which will contribute to good morale is time taken away from work on completing a task. However, if a group is to work together on more than a single task, effort spent to foster positive morale in the short-run often is rewarded by contributing to increased productivity in the longer term. And, even in the short-run, poor morale can have major consequences in terms of productivity.

• The communication dynamics and networks that emerge within a group often by accident frequently take on a life of their own. Once particular cliques or subgroups form, for instance, they are often self-perpetuating.

• The way in which new members are initiated into groups is a critical aspect of group development. The kind of orientation new members receive, and the place they initially occupy in group communication networks, may have long-term consequences for the new members' thoughts about, and actions toward, the group.

• Every group has its own culture and its unique symbols, rules, and codes. These serve to contribute to the group's identity and provide a basis for commonness among members.

• Often without the intention of group members, cultures support and encourage some kinds of behavior—for instance, cooperativeness, aggressiveness, service, or racial or gender bias—while discouraging others. By analyzing communication patterns and practices, one can become aware of the implicit values and behaviors that are endorsed and encouraged by particular group cultures. This knowledge can be put to good use by individual members and the group as a whole to evaluate and refine goals and operations.

• Decision making is the central activity of groups. When we think about quality decision making, we think in terms of *what* decision is made. *How* decisions are made, however, is often as important. Issues related to the "how" of decision making have to do with the *process* a group goes through in deciding. Issues related to the "what" have to do with the *product* of group decision making. Various decision-making methods are available; and each has pluses and minuses in terms of the quality of the process and product. A decision made by a knowledgeable leader for the group may be a better decision than one less informed members would reach through discussion and compromise. However, discussion and compromise are likely to result in better feelings and greater commitment to the decision by members, because they play a more active part in the process. Ideally, decision making should be undertaken in a way that provides the best of both a process- and product-orientation.

• Roles evolve within groups. Some members more often play task-oriented roles, and some play more personally- and socially-oriented roles. Each type of role has an impact on the dynamics of the group. It can be important to be aware of what roles are being played, and by whom. For instance, in a group decision-making session, it may become apparent that everyone who is active in the discussion is very task-oriented. This may suggest the need for someone in the group to adopt a maintenance or support role to ensure that less vocal members who may have important insights or fundamental disagreements are encouraged and allowed to speak.

• Cohesiveness is an important element of successful groups in terms of performance, morale, and effective communication. Techniques that foster group cohesiveness include:[26]

Increasing the amount of communication between members

Giving a group an identity and emphasizing it: talking about the group as a group

Building a group tradition—dates, special occasions

Emphasizing teamwork and striving to increase the attractiveness of the group participation

Encouraging the group to recognize good work

Setting clear, attainable group goals

Providing rewards for the group

Treating members like people worthy of respect and dignity, not like parts in a machine

• Extreme pressure toward group loyalty and being "team players," can stifle dissent and critique—both of which can play essential parts in creativity and quality decision making. The techniques that can be used to lessen the likelihood of the groupthink syndrome include:[27]

Leaders can encourage members to be critical.

Leaders can avoid stating their own preferences and expectations at the outset.

Members of the group can discuss the group's deliberations with trusted associates outside the group and report back to the group on reactions.

Experts can be periodically invited to meetings and should be encouraged to challenge the views of group members.

A member who is articulate and knowledgeable can be appointed to the role of devil's advocate, with the task of looking for alternatives, questioning the group's direction, and assuring that possible objections are considered.

Leaders can allocate time during each meeting to review minority, opposing, or alternative points of view.

• Conflict is an inevitable, and not necessarily a negative, aspect of group life. It is important to learn to recognize the potentially positive functions of conflict for the individual and for the group as a whole. Learning to understand and manage conflict, rather than striving always to eliminate or suppress it, can be productive.

Summary

We spend a great deal of time in groups of various kinds—working at our jobs, participating in clubs and associations, attending community or religious functions, and taking part in social activities. The groups in which we participate over the course of our lifetime create a wide range of demands and opportunities for us; and, in the process of adjusting to these, we develop, change, and grow.

As with relationships, groups are created and maintained by people engaged in reciprocal message processing. Groups differ from relationships in terms of the number of people involved, available resources, and complexity. Groups are created to serve a number of goals and purposes. Some groups serve primarily task-oriented functions and emphasize performance. Others stress personally- or socially-oriented functions and morale. Most groups are concerned with both types of goals. Groups may be contrived or emergent. In small social units, group communication networks evolve naturally. In larger and more formalized groups, networks are often purposefully established to regulate the flow of information.

Groups move through a series of stages as they evolve. The dynamics involved depend on a number of factors, including the difficulty of their tasks, the number of alternative solutions, and the interest created by the tasks. Groups develop a culture—their own symbols, rules, and codes.

The major activity of groups is decision making, and a number of methods are available for doing this. Roles and responsibilities also are central to the functioning of groups. In smaller groups, roles and definitions of responsibility evolve naturally. Some roles are related to task completion. Others have to do with group building and support; still others are individualistic. In larger, more structured groups, roles and responsibilities are often formal rather than informal, created rather than natural, explicit rather than implicit. Leadership is basic to groups of all kinds.

Cohesiveness is an important factor in group functioning. It is important for productivity, morale, and effective communication. The groupthink syndrome occurs when members—often unknowingly—become preoccupied with maintaining cohesiveness within a group. Conflict is an inevitable, and often productive, aspect of group functioning.

Notes

1. See discussion of "realistic" and "unrealistic" views of groups in Ernest G. Bormann and Nancy C. Bormann, *Effective Small Group Communication, 4th ed.* (Edina, MN: Burgess, 1988), pp. 2–4.

2. Gerald L. Wilson and Michael S. Hanna, *Groups in Context: Leadership and Participation in Small Groups* (New York: Random House, 1986), pp. 110–114; and Bormann and Bormann, 1988, pp. 64–72.

3. Based on distinctions suggested in Charles Pavitt and Ellen Curtis, *Small Group Discussion: A Theoretical Approach* (Scottsdale, AZ: Gorsuch Scarisbrick, 1990), pp. 27–29.

4. See Lee Thayer, *Communication and Communication Systems* (Homewood, IL: Irwin, 1968) p. 188–190.

5. A formula for computing the number of such linkages has been provided by William M. Kephart in "A Quantitative Analysis of Intra-Group Relationships." *American Journal of Sociology,* Vol. 55, 1950, pp. 544–549.

$$PR = \frac{3^{N} + -2^{N+1} + +1}{2}$$

Note: PR is the number of potential relationships, and N is the number of persons involved.

6. See Richard W. Budd, "Encounter Groups: An Approach to Human Communication," in *Approaches to Human Communication.* Ed. by Richard W. Budd and Brent D. Ruben (Rochelle Park, NJ: Hayden-Spartan, 1972), especially pp. 83–88; and Gerald Egan, *Encounter: Group Processes for Interpersonal Growth* (Belmont, CA: Brooks/Cole, 1970) pp. 69–71.

7. B. Aubrey Fisher, "Decision Emergence: Phases in Group Decision-Making," *Speech Monographs* Vol. 37, 1970, pp. 53–66, and *Small Group Decision Making* (New York: McGraw-Hill, 1974).

8. See Fisher, 1970, and discussion in Stephen W. Littlejohn, *Theories of Human Communication* (Columbus: Merrill, 1989) pp. 222–224.

9. Wilson and Hanna, 1986, pp. 27–30.

10. Marvin E. Shaw, "Scaling Group Tasks: A Method for Dimensional Anal-

ysis," *JSAS Catalog of Selected Documents in Psychology,* Vol. 8, 1973, M.S. 294. See discussion in Wilson and Hanna, 1986, pp. 28–29.

11. Based on Wilson and Hanna, 1986, pp. 68–71.

12. Kenneth Benne and Paul Sheats, "Functional Roles of Group Members," *Journal of Social Issues,* Vol. 4, 1948, pp. 41–49.

13. John E. Baird, Jr., and Sanford B. Weinberg, *Group Communication,* 2d ed. (Dubuque, IA: Brown, 1981) p. 215.

14. Based on discussion by Bormann and Bormann, 1988, pp. 127–130.

15. Bormann and Bormann, 1988, p. 129.

16. Bormann and Bormann, 1988, p. 129.

17. Bormann and Bormann, 1988, p. 129.

18. Bormann and Bormann, 1988, p. 55.

19. Based on Bormann and Bormann, 1988, p. 55.

20. Bormann and Bormann, 1988, pp. 56–57.

21. Irving Janis, *Victims of Groupthink: A Psychological Study of Foreign Decisions and Fiascos,* (Boston: Houghton Mifflin, 1967). See discussion in Littlejohn, 1988, pp. 208–210.

22. Wilson and Hanna, 1986, pp. 197–198; based on Janis, 1967.

23. Wilson and Hanna, 1986, p. 198; based on Janis, 1967.

24. T. L. Ruble and K. W. Thomas, "Support for a Two-Dimensional Model of Conflict Behavior," *Organizational Behavior and Human Performance,* Vol. 16, 1976, pp. 143–155. See discussion in J. P. Folger and M. S. Poole, *Working Through Conflict* (Glenview, IL: Scott, Foresman, 1984), pp. 40–41.

25. Ruble and Thomas, 1976; Folger and Pool, 1984, p. 41.

26. Bormann and Bormann, 1988, pp. 74–76; See also Pavitt and Curtis, p. 97.

27. Janis, 1967; See discussion in Littlejohn, 1988, pp. 209–210.

References and Suggested Readings

ARONSON, ELLIOT. *The Social Animal.* San Francisco: Freeman, 1972.

BAIRD, JOHN E., JR., and SANFORD B. WEINBERG. *Group Communication.* Dubuque, IA: Brown, 1981.

BALES, ROBERT F. *Personality and Interpersonal Behavior.* New York: Holt, 1970.

BEEBE, STEVEN A., and JOHN T. MASTERSON. *Family Talk: Interpersonal Communication in the Family.* New York: Random House, 1986.

BENNE, KENNETH, and PAUL SHEATS. "Functional Roles of Group Members," *Journal of Social Issues.* Vol. 4, 1948, 41–49.

BERNE, ERIC. *The Structure and Dynamics of Organizations and Groups.* New York: Grove, 1963.

BLUMER, HERBERT, *Symbolic Interactionism.* Englewood Cliffs, NJ: Prentice Hall, 1969.

BORMAN, ERNEST G., and NANCY C. BORMANN. *Effective Small Group Communication.* Fourth Ed. Edina, MN: Burgess, 1988.

BUDD, RICHARD W., "Encounter Groups: An Approach to Human Communication." In *Approaches to Human Communication.* Ed. by Richard W. Budd and Brent D. Ruben. Rochelle Park, NJ: Hayden, 1972, 75–96.

CAMPBELL, JAMES H., and JOHN S. MICHELSON. "Organic Communication Systems." In *General Systems Theory and Human Communication.* Ed. by Brent D. Ruben and John Y. Kim. Rochelle Park, NJ: Hayden, 1975, 207–221. Reprinted by Transaction Books, New Brunswick, NJ: 1988.

DUNCAN, HUGH D. *Symbols in Society.* New York: Oxford University Press, 1968.

EGAN, GERALD. *Encounter: Group Processes for Interpersonal Growth.* Belmont, CA: Books/Cole, 1970.

FISHER, B. AUBREY. "Decision Emergence: Phases in Group Decision-Making." *Speech Monographs*, Vol. 37, 1970.

———. *Small Group Decision Making.* New York: McGraw-Hill, 1974.

FOLGER, J., P. FOLGER, and M. S. POOLE. *Working Through Conflict.* Glenview, IL: Scott, Foresman, 1984, 40–41.

GALVIN, KATHLEEN M., and BERNARD J. BROMMEL. *Family Communication: Cohesion and Change.* Glenview, IL: Scott, Foresman, 1982.

HOMANS, GEORGE C. *The Human Group.* New York: Harcourt, 1950.

———. *Social Behavior.* New York: Harcourt, 1961.

JANIS, IRVING. *Victims of Groupthink: A Psychological Study of Foreign Decisions and Fiascos.* Boston: Houghton Mifflin, 1967.

LEAVITT, HAROLD J. "Some Effects of Certain Communication Patterns on Group Performance." *Journal of Abnormal and Social Psychology.* Vol. 46, 1951, 38–50.

LEWIN, KURT. "Group Decision and Social Change." In *Readings in Social Psychology.* Ed. by Theodore Newcomb and Eugene L. Hartley. New York: Holt, 1958.

PAVITT, CHARLES, and ELLEN CURTIS. *Small Group Discussion: A Theoretical Approach.* Scottsdale, AZ: Gorsuch Scarisbrick, 1990.

PHILLIPS, GERALD M. *Communication and the Small Group.* Indianapolis, IN: Bobbs-Merrill, 1973.

ROGERS, EVERETT M., and D. LAWRENCE KINCAID. *Communication Networks.* New York: Free Press, 1981.

RUBEN, BRENT D., and JOHN Y. KIM, eds. *General Systems Theory and Human Communication.* Rochelle Park. NJ: Hayden, 1975. Reprinted by Transaction Books: New Brunswick, NJ, 1988.

RUBLE, T. L., and K. W. Thomas. "Support for a Two-Dimensional Model of Conflict Behavior." *Organizational Behavior and Human Performance.* Vol. 16, 1976, 143–155.

SHAW, MARVIN E., "Scaling Group Tasks: A Method for Dimensional Analysis." *JSAS Catalog of Selected Documents in Psychology.* Vol. 8, 1973, M.S. 294.

TANNENBAUM, ROBERT, and WARREN H. SCHMIDT. "How to Choose a Leadership Pattern." *Harvard Business Review*, May-June, 1973.

THAYER, Lee. *Communication and Communication Systems.* Homewood, IL: Irwin, 1968.

WILSON, GERALD L. and MICHAEL S. HANNA. *Groups in Context.* New York: Random House, 1986.

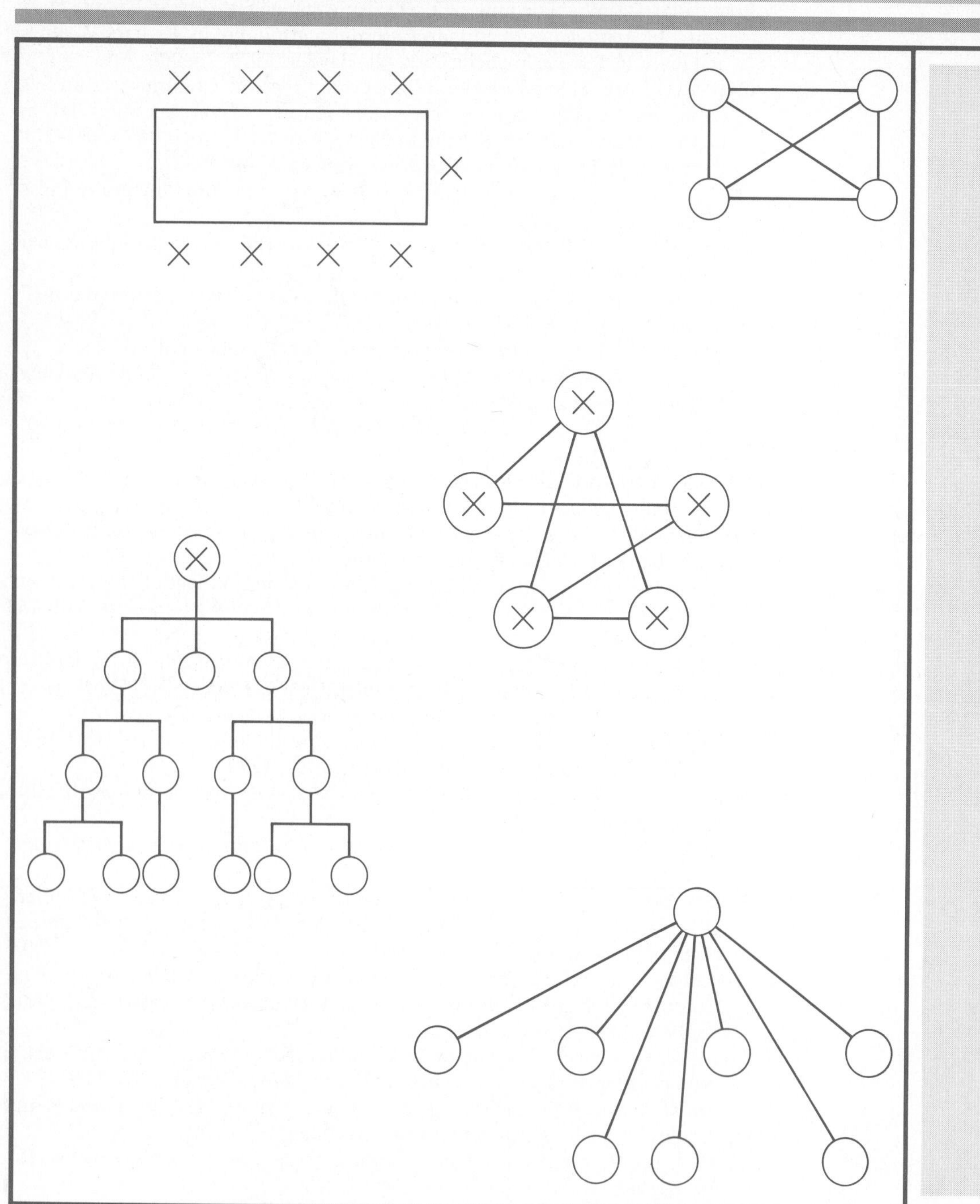

12

Organizations

Communication and Organizations

We spend a good deal of time in organizations during our lifetimes—attending school, working, and participating in professional, religious, political, health, civic, and other organizations. We look to these organizations for fulfillment of our physical, psychological, social, spiritual, political, and economic needs.

While organizations come in many different shapes and sizes, all have a good deal in common in terms of communication. Like relationships and groups, organizations are systems—social systems, to be more precise. Communication is necessary for the emergence of any such system. It is communication that makes possible the coordination of activity by several individuals without which, any form of social organization would be impossible.

Communication is also essential to the day-to-day functioning of organizations. It is through communication that members of organizations: (1) define goals, (2) delineate the roles and responsibilities of members, (3) control operations, (4) establish information networks, and (5) develop the culture and climate, all of which guide the behavior of members. In the sections that follow, we will examine each of these organizational activities and their relationship to communication.

Organizational Goals

A *goal* is the objective a system is designed to achieve. It is the benchmark against which the effectiveness, success, viability, and adaptability of the system can be assessed. In human systems, communication plays an important role in setting goals, in monitoring progress toward them, and, where appropriate, in periodic goal redefinition.

Some organizations are formed with the primary goal of manufacturing and marketing consumer goods—producing automobiles, computers, or bread, for instance. For other organizations, the "product" is a service. Hospitals, schools, or libraries are examples of this type of organization.

As with any system, the survival and growth of an organization depend upon the availability of adequate resources. Organizations provide goods and services, while in exchange they typically receive financial

The Wall Street Journal celebrated its 100th anniversary with a series of articles on the future, including a sampling of opinions from world business leaders who were asked to list the skills needed by future managers. The hypothetical "typical" manager in the year 2010 was projected to be a liberal arts undergraduate with joint degrees in business and communication. It is projected that even the leaders of large companies will be generalists with backgrounds in several disciplines.

The skills projected to be most needed by managers in the next century include:

- Interpersonal and human relations skills, and the ability to handle greater cultural diversity.
- The capability to work as a member of a team.
- The ability to create information and move it electronically for quick access and use.
- Familiarity with computers and computerized communication and information systems.

BOX 12–1 *Communication Skills Are Essential for Management .*

Sources: Amanda Bennett, "The Chief Executives in Year 2000 Will be Experienced Abroad," *The Wall Street Journal,* Feb. 27, 1989, pp. 1, A-9; Carol Hymowitz, "A Day in the Life of Tomorrow's Manager," *The Wall Street Journal,* March 20, 1989, p. B-1.

compensation. For organizations, the process of exchanging products or services for resources is parallel in importance to the oxygen-carbon dioxide exchanges for individual systems.

The presence of productivity goals is not a unique characteristic of organizations. As we have seen, relationships and groups also may be task-oriented. The distinguishing characteristic of organizational goals is to be found in the *origin* and *clarity* of the goals. In relationships and small, informal groups, the goals for the enterprise typically emerge as the system evolves. With organizations, goals are contrived—consciously set. This is not to say that initial organizational goals may not evolve. They can and often do. Through major reorganizations, goal reformulation, and more subtle evolutionary processes, goals may change over time.

Roles and Responsibilities

In any organization, the completion of the product- or service-oriented task requires a *division of labor*—the partitioning of the larger tasks into small parts, and the delineation of roles. As previously discussed, a *role* is a set of behaviors—a job to be done, a position to be filled, or a function to be carried out.

In relationships and groups, the roles individuals play—and their responsibilities to others in the social unit—generally evolve out of the interaction between members as the unit develops. In these instances, the process of role delineation is informal, as in gangs or tribes. In organizations, the division of labor and role definition is highly formalized.

The formalization of roles has several aspects:

1. specification of roles themselves;
2. establishment of a process of selecting people to fill these roles;
3. determination of responsibilities associated with the roles; and
4. development of procedures for moving from one role to another.

Each of these aspects is clearly and formally delineated in the form of "job titles," "hiring policies," "job descriptions," and "promotion and termination procedures."

Fundamental aspects of role relationships—the ways in which roles are related to one another—are also formalized in most organizations. Formal organization charts, such as those shown in Figure 12–1, portray these relationships. They indicate a **chain of command** and **reporting lines**—who reports to whom.

Organizational Control

MANAGEMENT FUNCTIONS

Other basic considerations in the design and day-to-day functioning of an organization that directly involve communication have to do with *control.* Organizational systems need a mechanism for planning, decision making, financial oversight, monitoring the activities of the organization, coordinating activities of its component parts, evaluating the organization's functioning in comparison with other organizations and the environment, and so on. These are typically termed *management functions.*

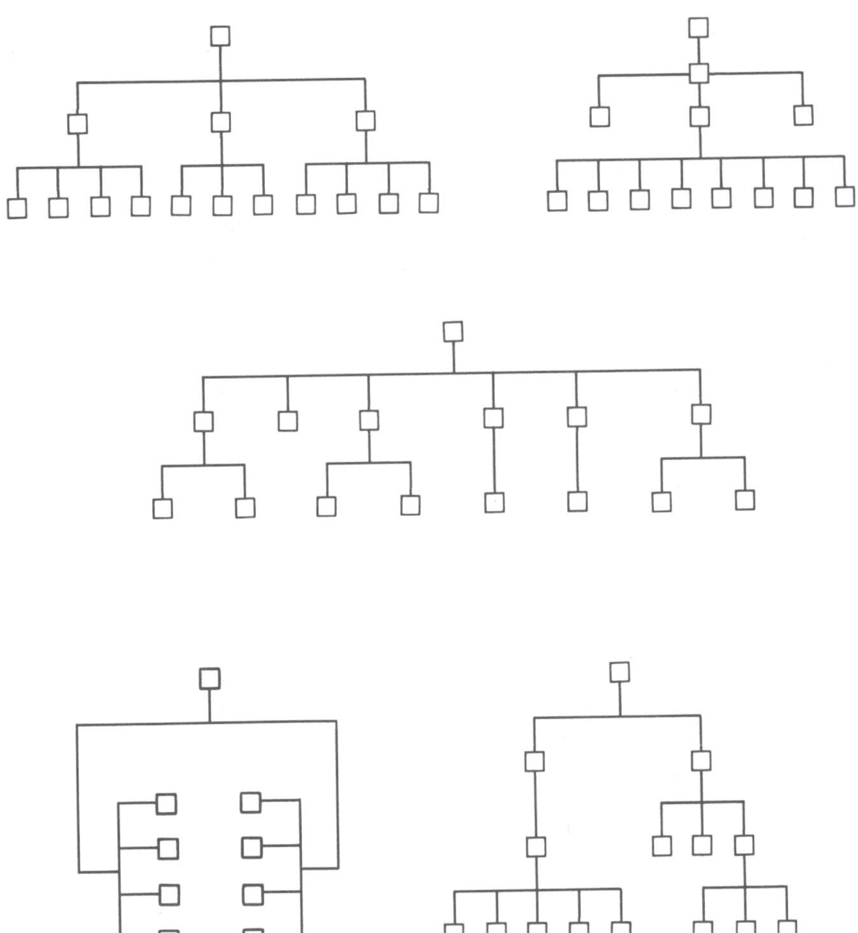

FIGURE 12–1 *Organizational Structures.*

Source: Everett M. Rogers and Rehka Agarwala-Rogers, *Communication in Organizations* (New York: Free Press, 1976), and Henry Mintzberg, *Structures in Fives: Designing Effective Organizations* (Englewood Cliffs, NJ: Prentice Hall, 1983).

In organizations, management is an essential, formalized, and highly visible element in the day-to-day and long-run functioning of the unit. Like group leadership functions, management functions may be very centralized, or authority can be diffused in varying degrees among members of the organization, providing for what is termed *participatory management.*

Memo	The Grapevine
Telephones	Intercom
Newsletters	Lectures
Electronic Mail	Manuals
Business Luncheons	Bulletins
Videotape Presentations	Booklets
Training Sessions	Directory of Employees
Conferences	Guest Speakers
Speeches	Annual Reports
Paging Systems	Announcement Flyers
Meetings	Paycheck Stub Messages
Grievance Interviews	Audiotapes
Family Picnics/Events	Charts And Graphs
Workshops	Posters
Ad Reprints	Suggestion Box
Exhibits and Displays	Teleconferences
Slide Presentations	Committees
Daily Interpersonal Contact	Social Get-Togethers
FAX	Counseling Interviews

BOX 12–2 *A Sampling of Organizational Communication Channels.*

Source: Adapted from R. Wayne Pace, *Organizational Communication,* Englewood Cliffs, NJ: Prentice Hall, 1983, pp. 45–56.

HUMAN NATURE AND ORGANIZATIONAL COMMUNICATION

To a large extent, the orientation that is taken relative to management depends upon the prevailing views of human nature within an organization. Traditionally scholars have identified three main schools of thought regarding human nature.[1] Each of the three suggests a set of principles and assumptions about how individuals behave in organizations, and each has its own implications regarding the functions management and communication should serve.

THE SCIENTIFIC MANAGEMENT SCHOOL

In this view, humans in organizations are seen as being motivated primarily by a desire for money and material rewards. By implication, maximum productivity is presumed to be achievable by employees who are clear on what they are to do and to whom they are responsible, and who are rewarded appropriately.

A clear and specific organizational structure, job specialization, fair rewards, defined rules, and distinct lines of responsibility and authority are regarded as basic. The purpose of communication is to provide information to employees that will clarify the tasks they are to perform and to reward them monetarily, according to their accomplishments.

THE HUMAN RELATIONS SCHOOL

This view provides a less mechanistic approach to human behavior in organizations. Humans are seen as being motivated by social, as well as economic, goals. Humans are thought to be most highly motivated when they are socially involved with colleagues and when they have been involved in making decisions that affect them.

In this school of thought, communication is seen as a means to facilitate social interaction and participation in organizational decision making. Achieving this objective is regarded as the primary function of management.

THE SYSTEMS SCHOOL

As we have seen in previous discussions, the systems perspective views individuals, relationships, groups, and organizations as interacting with and dependent upon one another and their environment. Human behavior in organizations is seen as being shaped by the organization—its goals, roles, rules, culture, climate, networks, and so on. Simultaneously, organizations are seen as being influenced by the individuals, relationships, and groups that compose them.

Communication is viewed as the process through which organizations emerge and evolve and the basis upon which individuals, relationships, groups, and organizations relate to their surroundings and to one another. Communication also serves in decision making and control of the system as a whole in its efforts to adapt to its environment. In this perspective, management functions emphasize the need for effective communication and information systems to facilitate interaction, coordination, and adaptability.

Reviewing the scientific management, human relations, and systems schools of thought is a useful way to highlight differences between concepts of human behavior in organizations and implications for management and communication functions. Clearly none of the three perspectives is "right" or "wrong." They provide broad frameworks for thinking about management and communication and serve as a backdrop for more specific approaches to management practice.

Communication Networks

NETWORK FUNCTIONS

As with relationships and groups, organizations have their origins in *communication networks*— reciprocal message processing linkages. From the perspective of an organization, the functions of communication networks include:

1. providing the means for coordinating the activities of individuals, relationships, groups and other subunits within the organization;
2. providing mechanisms for directing the activities of the organization as a whole;
3. facilitating the exchange of information within the organization; and
4. ensuring the flow of information between the organization and the external environment in which it exists.

NETWORK SIZE

One important differentiating characteristic of organizations is size. We have seen in previous discussions that an increase in the number of individuals in a social unit dramatically increases the number of reciprocal communication linkages that are possible and necessary to connect the persons involved. This is a problem of major proportion within large organizations.

In small groups, little needs to be done to formalize communication networking. People can generally talk to whom they wish, about what they wish. When the group gets together, whatever happens, happens. In organizations, given the incredibly large number of potential two-person linkages, formalization of face-to-face and mediated communication networks is essential. See Figure 12–2.

INTERNAL NETWORKS: MESSAGE FLOWS WITHIN ORGANIZATIONS

Downward Message Flows. Generally speaking, formalized lines of information that flow within organizations correspond closely with the lines of authority. The most familiar pattern of formalized information

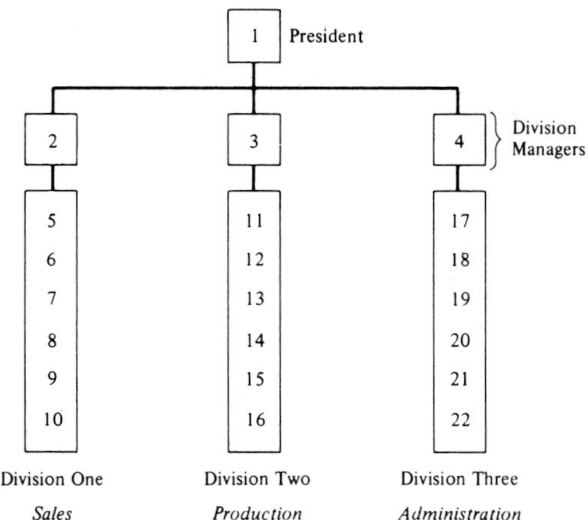

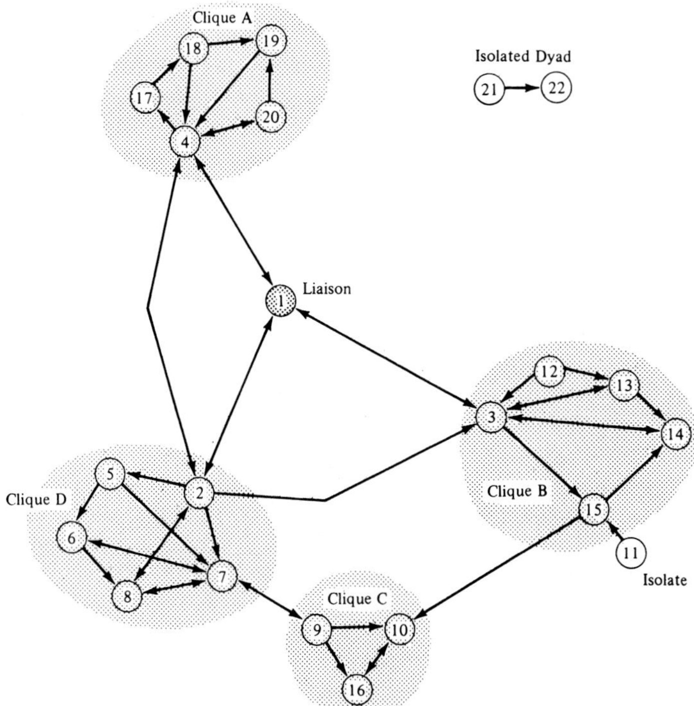

FIGURE 12–2 The chart at the top depicts the *formal organization* and *chain of command* within a typical company. The drawing underneath illustrates the *communication network* among members of the company. Within the company, there are four *cliques*—subsystems of individuals who interact with one another relatively more than with others. There is also an *isolate* (11), an *isolated dyad* (21 and 22), and a *liaison* (1)—an individual interlinking various cliques.

Source: Communication in Organizations by Everett M. Rogers and Rehka Agarwala-Rogers. Copyright © 1976 by The Free Press, a Division of Macmillan Publishing Co., Inc. By permission.

flow is from management to employees—from a superior to a subordinate.

In such circumstances, messages flow "downward" from persons in positions of relatively greater authority to others in the organization who report to them—directly or through others. Messages transmitted downward generally serve one or more of the following functions:[2]

1. specifying a task to be performed;
2. providing instructions about how to perform a task;
3. providing information about the reason for a particular task that needs to be performed;
4. providing information about organizational policies or practices;
5. providing information about an employee's performance; and/or
6. providing information about the organization and its mission.

Upward Message Flows. Messages channeled from subordinates to superiors—from individuals in organizational groups, departments, or divisions to persons occupying managerial roles—represent what is called an *upward message flow.* Upward communication has several functions, including:[3]

1. providing input for decision making;
2. advising about subordinates' information needs;
3. providing information regarding subordinates' level of receptivity to information, satisfaction, and morale;
4. providing a potentially constructive outlet for grievances and complaints;
5. allowing superiors to assess the effects of previous downward communication; and
6. helping subordinates cope with problems and facilitating their involvement.

Horizontal Networks. What are often termed *horizontal communication networks* refer to linkages that connect individuals at the same level of authority within an organizational group, department, or division. Functions of horizontal information sharing include:[4]

1. coordinating planning and execution of tasks;
2. providing for collective problem solving;

3. facilitating common understanding;
4. resolving differences; and
5. developing supportive and productive work relationships.

Informal Networks. Aside from the formalized, intentionally designed linkages, other *informal,* or *emergent, networks* inevitably develop among individuals and subunits in any group or organization. These informal networks—which include *the grapevine*—serve to link individuals to one another in much the same way as do formal networks. Unlike their formalized counterparts, however, informal linkages come into being primarily because of the personal and social needs of the members.

Sometimes *informal communication networks* correspond closely in structure to the formal systems. For instance, a supervisor and his or her subordinate may regularly have lunch together and discuss personal and professional matters. Often, as depicted in Figure 12–2, formal and informal networks are very different. A shipping clerk may ride to work with a secretary to the Vice President for Operations, for instance. In any case, informal networks established between workers in different departments, at after-hours get-togethers, at the tennis court, or on the way to and from work, are important channels within any group or organization. These networks have a substantial impact on both the content and flow of messages in the more formalized networks.

Informal networks:[5]

1. are generally face-to-face;
2. are less constrained by organizational and political restraints;
3. move messages rapidly;
4. tend to be more the result of the situation than the people or their roles;
5. tend to develop more often within organizational workgroups, departments, or divisions than between them; and
6. generally transmit information that is accurate, though often somewhat incomplete, leading to misinterpretation.

EXTERNAL NETWORKS: RELATING TO OTHER ORGANIZATIONS AND PUBLICS

Inflow: Research and Surveillance. All groups and organizations depend on various constituencies, stakeholders, or *publics,* in the larger environment for their survival. Voluntary groups rely on contributors, business organizations on consumers and the government, hospitals on patients and physicians, advertising agencies on their clients and the public, newspapers on their subscribers and advertisers, and so on. *External networks* connect the organization with these publics and to the larger environment.

External networks also enable the system to gather information from the environment. Through market research, monitoring and analysis of various information sources, and direct surveillance of competitors and other environmental factors, organizations receive information necessary to identify and respond appropriately to environmental change, threat, opportunity, or challenge.

Outflow: Advertising, Marketing, and Public Relations. External networks are also used to provide external publics with information that members of the group or organization think desirable, proper, or necessary. The terms *advertising, marketing,* and *public relations* refer to activities that involve the transmission of messages into the environment with the aim of informing and systematically influencing these publics.

MEDIATED COMMUNICATION NETWORKS

In many organizations, face-to-face interaction between members on a regular basis may be impossible due to the large number of people involved or to physical separation. Therefore, in most enterprises, mediated communication is essential. The traditions of the mail and telephone are now supplemented by FAX, teleconferences, on-line computer systems, electronic mail, voice-messaging systems, and many other new communication media.

ORGANIZATIONAL COMMUNICATION NETWORKS IN ACTION

In the ongoing dynamics of organization communication, networks seldom operate in the straightforward, rational, predictable manner one might infer from a description of possible types of networks and directions of message flow. In actuality, the functioning of communication networks is exceptionally complex, often unpredictable, sometimes uncontrollable, and frequently chaotic. See Figure 12–3.

In any organization, messages are being sent simultaneously in a va-

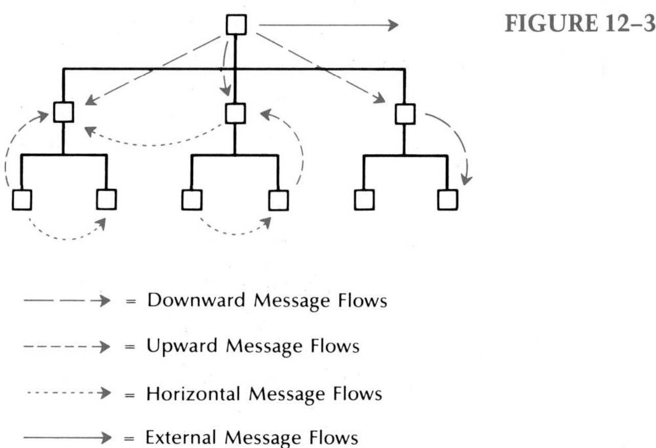

FIGURE 12–3

riety of directions. In such circumstances, "breaks" in the network, distortion, contradiction, and confusion inevitably occur—they are more the rule than the exception. And, as in other communication situations, the message a manager or a subordinate thinks he or she is sending in a memo or through face-to-face conversation is often quite different than the message others receive. Furthermore, the sheer size of an organizational network and the distance between the top and bottom levels of the hierarchy intensify problems. Distance generally increases the likelihood of message loss, distortion, and the likelihood of distrust and suspicion.

The difficulties associated with information flow in organizations are described—in the extreme case—by Osmo Wiio:[6]

- If communication can fail, it will.
- If a message can be understood in different ways, it will be understood in just the way that does the most harm.
- There is always somebody who knows better than you what you meant by your message.
- The more communication there is, the more difficult it is for communication to succeed.

Clearly, the complexity of organization networks and that of the communication process combine to make organizational communication one of the most challenging contexts for those interested in studying or applying an understanding of the nature of communication and its impact on human behavior.

Organizational Culture

As interaction takes place through the networks of any organization, verbal and nonverbal behavior patterns develop and become standardized. Over time, they become important social realities for the organization—what can be termed the organization's *culture*. An *organizational culture,* is the sum of its symbols, events, traditions, standardized verbal and nonverbal behavior patterns, "folk tales," rules, and rituals that give the organization its character or "personality." See Figure 12–4.

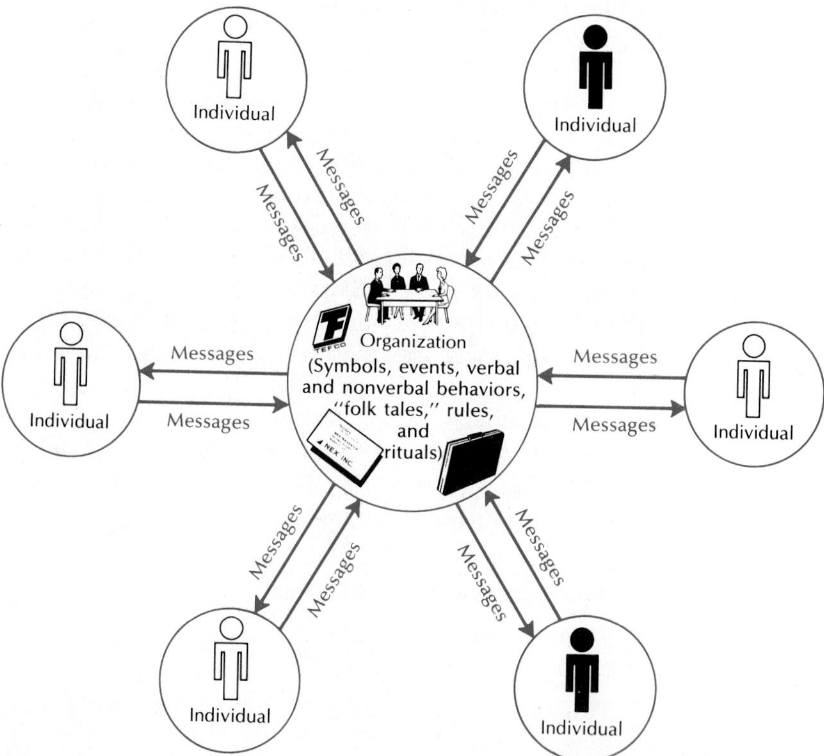

FIGURE 12–4 *Organizational Culture.* Through their verbal and nonverbal behavior individuals collectively create the organizations to which they belong and the symbols, events, standardized verbal and nonverbal behavior patterns, "folk tales," rules, rituals, and other conventions characteristic of each. To become a member of an ongoing organization, the individual must adapt to the culture of the organization.

ORIGINS OF ORGANIZATIONAL CULTURES

Organizational cultures grow out of the communication activities of individual members. Though organizational cultures are the products of human communication, they take on an objective quality and "act back on" individuals within an organization as depicted in Figure 12–4.

Symbols are one important element of the culture of many organizations. Trademarks, buildings, office furnishings, and uniforms are examples of symbols that are often a visible facet of an organization's culture. See Figures 12–5 and 12–6. Sometimes organizational symbols develop naturally, as with informal dress codes among employees of a company. In other instances, symbols—trademarks or slogans, for instance—are purposefully developed and actively promoted.

Space is another important organizational symbol. In many organizations, rules are developed for use in allocating space to employees, such that the location, size, and decor of an employee's office or workspace reflect his or her position. Larger, more elaborately furnished and decorated offices go to individuals of a higher rank within the organization. Lesser officials may have smaller, modestly decorated offices; persons at still lower levels may have no private workspace, separated from one another by portable partitions or bookcases and file cabinets. For reasons that may make little sense to an "outsider," carpeting in a vacated office might be ripped up and thrown away, rather than being left for a new occupant whose rank within the organization would not "call for" carpeted floors. These actions are regarded as necessary to preserve the culture. Variations are substantial from one organization to the next, as suggested in Figure 12–7.

Events like "the annual picnic," "the senior prom," "the annual Christmas party," or "the management retreat" also contribute to and reflect an organization's culture. They serve much the same functions for the culture of the organization as do birthdays, anniversaries, and reunions for individuals, relationships, and families.

The language used to talk about an organization is also a reflection of, and at the same time an influence on, its culture. An organization in which people talk about promotions in terms of military language like "fighting one's way to the top" is likely to have quite a different culture than one where promotions are described in terms of "members of a family working together to help one another succeed." One framework distinguishes between corporations based upon whether their cultures are like academies, clubs, fortresses, or baseball teams, based on the language used by its employees.[7]

Organizational "folk tales" or "stories" are another important facet of an organization's culture. Most organizations have a collection of "fa-

FIGURE 12–5 Business cards are personal, portable symbols of organizational affiliation.

vorite" stories about notorious past and present personnel, organization achievements or failures, and memorable moments in the life of the organization. An illustration: "Did anyone tell you about the fellow a few years back who tried to bargain his way to a higher salary by boasting to management of an offer from another company. They wished him luck in his new position, and asked him how soon he would be leaving." Or: "Did you hear what happened when management learned that a vice president was having an affair with a secretary?" Implicit in these stories are statements about organizational values, ethics, management practices, and other facets of life in the organization. Through stories and storytelling, organizational cultures are transmitted from one generation of employees to another.

FUNCTIONS OF ORGANIZATIONAL CULTURES

Organizational cultures play a central and pervasive role in the dynamics of organizations of all kinds, and they serve many important com-

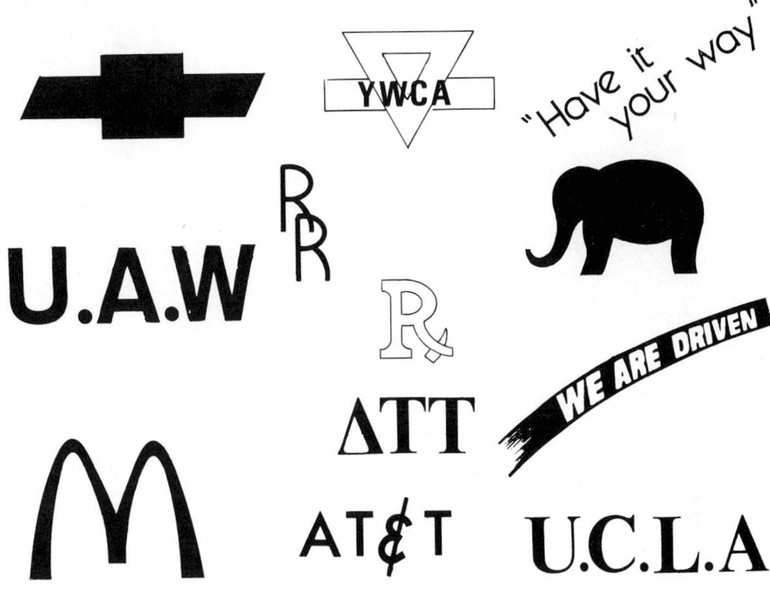

FIGURE 12–6 *Organizational Symbols.*

munication functions for those who create and participate in them, including:

1. providing people within these units with a sense of individual and collective identity;
2. contributing to the establishment of structure and control;
3. aiding with the socialization of members to the customs and traditions of the organization; and
4. fostering cohesiveness among members of the organization.

ASSIMILATION, SOCIALIZATION, AND INNOVATION IN ORGANIZATIONS

Becoming a member of an organization requires an initiation into the culture through processes referred to as *socialization* and *assimilation*. Even in organizations with no formal apprenticeship or internship, the individual must come to terms with the organization's culture to be ac-

FIGURE 12–7 *Offices.*
Source: "Presidentes Municipales," A photo-essay of mayors of Mexican cities and their offices by Richard Tichich, in *Studies in Visual Communication*, Vol. 6, 3, Fall 1980, pp. 76–83. By permission.

cepted and function effectively as a member. The formal communication networks play a role in this process, but informal networks are even more essential to "learning the ropes."

Within an open system—an individual, relationship, group, organization, or society—there is a tension between influences that contribute to cultural stability and continuity and those that contribute to cultural innovation and change. Stability within organizations is fostered when members of the unit carry cultural traditions forward with them in time. Innovation and change call for departures from tradition. Sometimes innovations are introduced intentionally. At other times, change happens by accident because of the way individuals cope with and internalize the culture of the organization. Cultural continuity and cultural innovation are equally necessary to the survival and prosperity of organizations over time.

Organizational Climate

Climate is another aspect of organizations in which communication plays a direct role and one which is closely related to culture. An

FIGURE 12–7 *(continued).*

organization's *climate* is the atmosphere or tone members of the organization experience as they go about their daily routines. Climates are created through communication. In turn, climates influence organizational members and are perpetuated through organizational communication processes. Even as consumers, we may have a sense that not all organizations—department stores, hospitals, or schools, for instance—"feel the same" although their product or service may be similar. Often, differences in the "feeling we get" are a reflection of differences in the organizational climates, which were created and maintained through communication.

In very general terms, we can talk about climates being "positive" or "negative." Positive—supportive—climates have been described as having the following characteristics:[8]

1. supportiveness of superior-subordinate communication;
2. perceived quality and accuracy of downward communication;
3. perceived openness of the superior-subordinate relationship;
4. opportunities and degree of influence of upward communication; and
5. perceived reliability of information from subordinates and coworkers.

FIGURE 12–7 *(continued).*

Studies show that where supportive climates exist, job satisfaction is high and productivity may improve as well.[9] Generally speaking, a positive climate and high levels of satisfaction will be reflected in the positive treatment of clients and consumers, as well as colleagues.

Organizational climates, whether "positive" or "negative," are self-perpetuating. Individuals tend to be attracted to—and selected to participate in—organizations in which members share their values, needs, attitudes, and expectations. Individuals with incompatible orientations are less likely to stay or be retained, if they do initially affiliate themselves.

Implications and Applications: Organizations and Their Publics

- Organizations have multiple constituents, or publics; and communication is the means through which the needs and expectations of these individuals and groups are identified and addressed.
- In many respects, an organizations' most important constituents

FIGURE 12–7 *(continued).*

are internal. Each staff member, work group, or division has a contribution to make to the organization as a whole. Moreover, these constituents have needs and expectations—financial, informational, and social needs, for instance—which must be accommodated and coordinated if the unit is to perform efficiently and effectively.

- Organizations also have a number of external publics—customers and suppliers, for example—upon whom the viability of the organization depends.

- Organizational quality can be evaluated based on:[10]

Technical quality—the adequacy of the products and services, and technical skills of staff. For example: clinical skills of hospital staff, or clerical skills of college secretarial personnel.

Administrative quality—the adequacy of management policies, procedures, practices, and staff. For example: billing systems in hospitals, or course registration systems in colleges.

Relationship quality—the adequacy of the interpersonal communication and relationship building skills of staff. For example: physician interpersonal skills for relating to patients, or college receptionist relationship skills in dealing with students or visitors.

• When internal publics evaluate an organization, they typically base their judgments on technical or administrative factors. "Insider" assessments of the quality of a college, for example, are generally based on an evaluation of administration, research, teaching, and service, using academic and technical criteria. External publics often take technical quality for granted, or are unable to assess it. In the case of a college, for instance, students, parents, and members of the public at large are typically unable to make or understand assessments based on administrative practices or faculty research. Instead, their images are often based on what they can more easily see and comprehend, such as the quality of faculty and staff interpersonal communication and relationships.[11]

• The image of an organization with its external publics is influenced by mediated communication (news coverage, advertising, public relations initiatives, and so on) and especially by face-to-face contact with representatives of the organization. Thus, the preoccupied college receptionist who seems indifferent to a student's problem, or the faculty member who is unavailable to meet with a student, unknowingly and unintentionally provide the basis for stories that may be told and retold to friends, parents, and acquaintances. From this perspective, every contact between an employee and a "constituent" is an encounter that either contributes to or detracts from the perception—and the reality—of organizational quality.[12] Interactions between representatives of an organization and its external publics are critical communication links that are vital to the continued viability of any organization.

Summary

Communication, as we have seen, is as essential to the emergence of organizations as it is for the development of individuals, relationships, and groups. Without message processing even the simplest coordination between individuals would be impossible. In small organizations with a dozen persons and large enterprises of several thousand persons, communication is critical to defining goals, delineating individual roles and responsibilities, controlling the organization's operations, establishing networks, and creating the organization's culture and climate.

A goal is the objective a system is designed to achieve. It is the benchmark against which the effectiveness, success, viability, and adaptability of the system can be assessed. Organizations are formed with product- or service-oriented goals. A division of labor and a delineation of roles are needed to achieve these goals. A role is a set of defined behaviors—a job to be done, a position to be filled, or a function to be carried out. Relationships between roles are indicated by reporting lines and formal organizational structure.

Organizational systems need a control mechanism for planning, decision making, financial oversight, monitoring operations, coordinating activities, and evaluating organizational functioning. These are management functions. The way in which they are carried out in an organization depends upon the prevailing view of the nature of human behavior in organizations. The scientific management, human relations, and systems views provide three ways of thinking about organizational behavior, management, and communication functions.

Communication networks serve important functions within organizations. Formal message flow through networks in an organization may be downward, upward, or horizontal. Informal networks are also basic to organizations. External networks link an organization to its environment. Face-to-face networks in organizations are increasingly supplemented by mediated communication. In the ongoing dynamics of organizational communication, networks seldom operate in the straightforward, rational, and predictable manner suggested by descriptions of the types of networks and the direction of message flow.

Organizational cultures emerge over time as a result of interactions among organization members. An organization's culture is the sum of its symbols, events, standardized verbal and nonverbal behavior patterns, "folk tales," rules, and rituals that give the organization a character or personality.

Communication also results in the creation of organizational climates. A climate is the atmosphere or tone experienced by members of an organization as they go about their daily routines.

Notes

1. See discussion in Everett M. Rogers and Rekha Agarwala-Rogers, *Communication in Organizations* (New York: Free Press, 1976); Gerald M. Goldhaber, *Organization Communication,* 4th ed. (Dubuque IA: Brown, 1986); and R. Wayne Pace, *Organizational Communication* (Englewood Cliffs, NJ: Prentice Hall, 1983).

2. An excellent research summary and discussion of information flow is provided in Pace, 1983, Chapter 5. Values of downward information flow based on

the work of Daniel Katz and Robert Kahn, *The Social Psychology of Organization* (New York: Wiley, 1966), are discussed on pp. 39–41.

3. Pace, 1983, p. 47.

4. See Pace, 1983, p. 53.

5. See discussion and summary of research by William L. Davis and J. Regis O'Connor, "Serial Transmission of Information: A Study of the Grapevine," *Journal of Applied Communication*, Vol. **5**, 1977, pp. 61–72, and discussion in Pace, 1983, pp. 57–58.

6. Osmo Wiio, *Wiio's Laws—and Some Others* (Espoo, Finland: Weling-Goos, 1978), laws 1.2, 2, 3, and 4.

7. Carol Hymowitz, "Which Corporate Culture Fits You?" *The Wall Street Journal*, July 17, 1989, p. B1.

8. An excellent discussion of the organizational climate concept and current research is provided by Raymond L. Falcione, Raymond L. and Elyse A. Kaplan in "Organizational Climate, Communication and Culture." In *Communication Yearbook 8*. Ed. by Robert N. Bostrom (Beverly Hills: Sage, 1984) pp. 285–300. See also discussions of climate and its impact on customer relations and on perceptions of organization quality in Karl Albrecht and Ron Zemke, *Service America! Doing Business in the New Economy* (Homewood, IL: Dow Jones/Irwin, 1985); and Wendy Leebov, *Service Excellence: The Customer Relations Strategy for Health Care* (Chicago: American Hospital Association, 1988).

9. Falcione and Kaplan, 1984, pp. 295–296.

10. Brent D. Ruben, "Quality of Care: Insights from Patients, the Social Literature, and the Pet Shop," 1990. Unpublished paper presented at the Mid-Atlantic College Health Association, Silver Springs, PA, Oct. 1990.

11. Brent D. Ruben, "The Health Caregiver-Patient Relationship: Pathology, Etiology, Treatment." In *Communication and Health: Systems and Applications*. Ed. by E. B. Ray & L. Donohew (NJ: Lawrence Erlbaum, 1990) pp. 51–68; Ruben, 1991; Brent D. Ruben and June C. Bowman, "Patient Satisfaction: Critical Issues in the Theory and Design of Patient Relations Training," *Journal of Healthcare Education and Training*, Vol. 1, No. 1, 1986, pp. 1–5; and B. D. Ruben, D. Christensen and N. Guttman, *College Health Service: A Qualitative Analysis of the Patient Perspective*. Unpublished Report, 1990.

12. Albrecht and Zemke, 1985; Wendy Leebov, *Service Excellence: The Customer Relations Strategy for Health Care*. Chicago: American Hospital Association, 1988.

References and Suggested Readings

ALBRECHT, KARL, and RON ZEMKE. *Service America! Doing Business in the New Economy*. Homewood, IL: Dow Jones/Irwin, 1985.

ALLEN, THOMAS J. *Managing the Flow of Technology.* Cambridge, MA: M.I.T. Press, 1977.

ARGYRIS, CHRIS. *Understanding Organizational Behavior.* Homewood, IL: Dorsey, 1960.

BARNARD, CHESTER I. *The Functions of the Executive.* Cambridge, MA: Harvard University Press, 1938.

BERRIEN, KENNETH F. *General and Social Systems.* New Brunswick, NJ: Rutgers University Press, 1968.

BOTAN, CARL, and HAZELTON, V., (eds.), *Public Relations Theory.* Hillsdale, NJ: Lawrence Erlbaum Associates, 1989.

BUCKLEY, WALTER. *Sociology and Modern Systems Theory.* Englewood Cliffs, NJ: Prentice Hall, 1967.

CRANE, DIANA. *Invisible Colleges.* Chicago: University of Chicago Press, 1972.

DAVIS, WILLIAM L., and J. REGIS O'CONNOR. "Serial Transmission of Information: A Study of the Grapevine." *Journal of Applied Communication,* Vol. **5.** 1977, 61–72.

DEETZ, STANLEY. *Democracy in an Age of Corporate Colonization: Developments in Communication and the Politics of Everyday Life.* Albany: SUNY Press, 1991.

DEETZ, STANLEY, and DENNIS MUMBY. "Metaphors, Information , and Power." In *Information and Behavior: Volume 1.* Ed. by Brent D. Ruben. New Brunswick, NJ: Transaction, 1985, 369–387.

DOWNS, CAL W., and TONY HAIN. "Productivity and Communication." In *Communication Yearbook* 5. Ed. by Michael Burgoon. New Brunswick, NJ: Transaction-International Communication Association, 1982, 435–454.

EISENGERG, ABNÉ, M. *Understanding Communication in Business and the Professions.* New York: Macmillan, 1978.

FALCIONE, RAYMOND L., and ELYSE A KAPLAN. "Organizational Climate, Communication and Culture." In *Communication Yearbook 8.* Ed. by Robert N. Bostrom. Beverly Hills: Sage, 1984, 285–309.

GOLDHABER, GERALD M. *Organizational Communication.* Fourth Ed. Dubuque, IA: Brown, 1986.

GRUNIG, JAMES E., and TODD HUNT. *Managing Public Relations.* Second Ed. New York: Holt, Rinehart, Winston, 1992.

HARRISON, MICHAEL I. *Diagnosing Organizations: Methods, Models and Processes.* Newbury Park, CA: Sage, 1987.

JABLIN, FRED M. "Organizational Communication Theory and Research: An Overview of Communication Climate and Network Research." In *Communication Yearbook 4.* Ed. by Dan Nimmo. New Brunswick, NJ: Transaction-International Communication Association, 1981, 327–348.

KATZ, DANIEL, and ROBERT KAHN. *The Social Psychology of Organization.* New York: Wiley, 1966.

KELLY, LYNNE, LINDA C. LEDERMAN, and GERALD PHILLIPS. *Communicating in the Workplace. A Guide to Business and Professional Speaking.* New York: Harper & Row, 1989.

KREPS, GARY L. *Organizational Communication.* White Plains, NY: Longman, 1986.

LEEBOV, WENDY. *Service Excellence: The Customer Relations Strategy for Health Care.* Chicago: American Hospital Association, 1988.

LIKERT, RENSIS. *The Human Organization.* New York: McGraw-Hill, 1967.

MCGREGOR, DOUGLAS. *The Human Side of Enterprise.* New York: McGraw-Hill, 1960.

MAYO, ELTON. *The Human Problems of an Industrial Civilization.* New York: Macmillan, 1933.

MORGAN, GARETH. *Images of Organization.* Newbury Park, CA: Sage, 1986.

MINTZBERG, HENRY. *Structure in Fives. Designing Effective Organizations.* Englewood Cliffs, NJ: Prentice Hall, 1983.

MUMBY, DENNIS K. *Communication and Power in Organizations: Discourse, Ideology, and Domination.* Norwood, NJ: Ablex, 1988.

PACE, R. WAYNE. *Organizational Communication.* Englewood Cliffs, NJ: Prentice Hall, 1983.

ROGERS, EVERETT M., and D. LAWRENCE KINCAID. *Communication Networks.* New York: Free Press, 1981.

ROGERS, EVERETT M., and REKHA AGARWALA-ROGERS. *Communication in Organizations.* New York: Free Press, 1976.

———"The Health Caregiver-Patient Relationship: Pathology, Etiology, Treatment." In *Communication and Health: Systems and Applications.* Ed. by E. B. Ray & L. Donohew. NJ: Lawrence Erlbaum, 1990. 51–68.

RUBEN, BRENT D., and JUNE C. BOWMAN. "Patient Satisfaction: Critical Issues in the Theory and Design of Patient Relations Training." *Journal of Healthcare Education and Training.* Vol. 1, No. 1, 1986, 1–5.

RUBEN, BRENT D., and JOHN Y. KIM, eds. *General Systems Theory and Human Communication.* Rochelle Park, NJ: Hayden, 1975.

SCHOCKLEY-ZALABAK, PAMELA. *Fundamentals of Organizational Communication.* Second Ed. New York: Longman, 1991.

SEILER, WILLIAM J., E. SCOTT BAUDHUIN, and L. DAVID SCHUELKE. *Communication in Business and Professional Organizations.* Reading, MA: Addison-Wesley, 1982.

SIMON, HERBERT A. *Administrative Behavior.* New York: Macmillan, 1947.

SMITH, RONALD L., GARY M. RICHETTO, and JOSEPH P. ZIMA. "Organizational Behavior." In *Approaches to Human Communication.* Ed. by Richard W. Budd and Brent D. Ruben. New York: Spartan, 1972, 269–289.

STEWART, LEA P., ALAN D. STEWART, SHERYL A. FRIEDLEY, and PAMELA J. COOPER. *Communication Between Sexes: Sex Differences and Sex-role Stereotypes.* Second Ed. Scottsdale, AZ: Gorsuch Scarisbrick, 1990.

THAYER, LEE. *Communication and Communication Systems.* Homewood, IL: Irwin, 1968.

———. "Communication and Organizational Theory." In *Human Communication Theory.* Ed. by Frank E. X. Dance. New York: Holt, 1967.

VINCENT, DAVID R. *The Information-Based Corporation.* Homewood, IL: Dow Jones/Irwin, 1990.

WIIO, OSMO. *Wiio's Laws—and Some Others.* Espoo, Finland: Weling-Goos, 1978.

YATES, JOANNE. *Control Through Communication: The Rise of System in American Management.* Baltimore: The Johns Hopkins Press, 1989.

13

Cultures and Societies

A Case Study: The Culture of the Nacirema

> Nacirema culture is characterized by a highly developed market economy which has evolved a rich natural habitat. While much of the people's time is devoted to economic pursuits, a large part of the fruits of these labors and a considerable portion of the day are spent in ritual activity. The focus of this activity is the human body. . . .
>
> The fundamental belief underlying the whole system appears to be that the human body is ugly. . . . Every household has one or more shrines . . . The more powerful individuals in the society have several shrines in their house; and, in fact, the opulence of a house is often referred to in terms of the number of such ritual centers it possesses. . . .
>
> . . . the rituals associated with it are not family ceremonies but are private and secret. . . . The focal point of the shrine is a box or chest built into the wall. In this chest are kept the many charms and magical potions without which no native believes he (or she) could live. . . .
>
> Beneath the charm-box is a small font. Each day every member of the family in succession enters the shrine room, bows his (or her) head before the charm-box, mingles different sorts of holy waters in the font and proceeds with a brief rite of ablution. The holy waters are secured from the Water Temple of the community, where the priests conduct elaborate ceremonies to make the liquid ritually pure. . . .
>
> Our review of the ritual life of the Nacirema has certainly shown them to be a magic-ridden people. It is hard to understand how they have managed to exist so long under the burdens which they have imposed upon themselves.[1]

If these "magic-ridden people" and strange culture seem even remotely familiar, it may be because they are us! "Nacirema" is "American" spelled backwards. In this brief excerpt from his classic article, anthropologist Horace Miner pokes fun at American culture and our preoccupation with bathrooms and body rituals.

The Nature of Culture

"Culture," like "communication," is a familiar term to most people. Partly because of this familiarity, there are a number of different ways the term is used. The most common use of "culture" is as a synonym for country or nation. If we come across several persons conversing in a language other than English, or notice a woman wearing a veil over her face, we may well say they are from another culture, meaning another country.

At other times, the term is used to refer to desired qualities or attributes. For instance, someone who uses "street language," is sloppy in his or her eating habits, or lacks a knowledge of the arts, may be described as uncultured—meaning unrefined, uneducated, or unsophisticated.

To those who study human behavior, "culture" has a more precise usage. It is not regarded as something one has or does not have, nor is it something which is thought of as being positive or negative. In fact, culture is not some *thing* at all, in the sense that an object can be touched, physically examined, or located on a map. Rather, it is an idea or a concept, which E. B. Tylor in 1871 described as having to do with "that complex whole which includes knowledge, belief, art, morals, law, custom, and any other capabilities and habits acquired by man as a member of society."[2] From the point of view of communication, *culture* can be defined as the complex combination of common symbols, knowledge, folklore conventions, language, message-processing patterns, rules, rituals, habits, life styles, and attitudes that link and give a common identity to a particular group of people at a particular point in time.

The Relationship between Communication and Culture

Let's examine the concept of culture and its relationship to communication in more detail: First, it is helpful to remind ourselves that all social systems—relationships, groups, organizations, and societies—develop and maintain cultures.[3] And they do so through communication.

In each relationship, for instance, a *relational culture* emerges naturally over time. Couples have "our songs," dates of special significance, unique terms of endearment, and shorthand verbal and nonverbal codes—such as cryptic (to others) verbal references to events they shared, or a roll of the eyes. Each of these has a particular meaning and significance for the couple involved, because of their shared history of reciprocal message processing.

The same process occurs in groups and organizations, though a larger number of people are involved. As communication networks emerge and evolve, shared patterns and realities are created in families, clubs, prison communities, social groups, educational institutions, business organizations, and government agencies. In each, as we have seen, particular words or phrases, "war stories," approaches to leadership, norms of behavior, or conventions of dress emerge as a result of communication and mutual adaptation of the members.

Societies, about which we have more to say later, are larger and more complex social systems, yet the same communication dynamics are at work. The symbols of a society are perhaps the most visible signs of culture. Of these, spoken and written language are the most pervasive. Coins and currency are other basic symbol systems of any society. The flags of countries are another example.

As illustrated in Figure 13–1, flags of any one society are distinctive. Yet, if we analyze them in terms of physical characteristics such as their form, overall size, composition, and weight, most are really quite similar. Composed of pieces of cloth that vary from one another in little more than color, flags play important symbolic roles in human affairs. They mark territories, represent particular geographic locations, symbolize political or religious ideologies, and provide a symbol of commonality and unity for the residents of the territories they symbolize. For these reasons, burning or in any other way defiling the national flag is punishable by law in some countries. It is the cultural significance of such symbols that also explains why revolutionary changes in government of a territory are sometimes accompanied by a change of flag.

There are also many other significant symbols in the culture of any society—heroes and heroines, leaders, monuments, buildings, songs, events, and places. See Figure 13–2 on pp. 416–17. For us, George Washington, Martin Luther King, the Capitol Building, Old Glory, The Star Spangled Banner, The Statue of Liberty, Gettysburg, and a more contemporary event, Desert Storm, have important symbolic value. Shared verbal and nonverbal communication patterns, orientations toward religion, politics, sex roles, courtship, child rearing, race, and other facets of social life also become a part of the culture of any society.

Within societies, as in other social systems, communication allows individuals to create, share, and perpetuate culture by their activities. See Figure 13–3 on p. 418.

Cultures—whether of relationships, groups, organizations, or societies—serve several common functions related to communication:

- linking individuals to one another;
- providing the basis for a common identity; and
- creating a context for interaction and negotiation among members.

As is apparent by this point, the relationship between culture and communication is an intimate one. Cultures are the byproduct of communi-

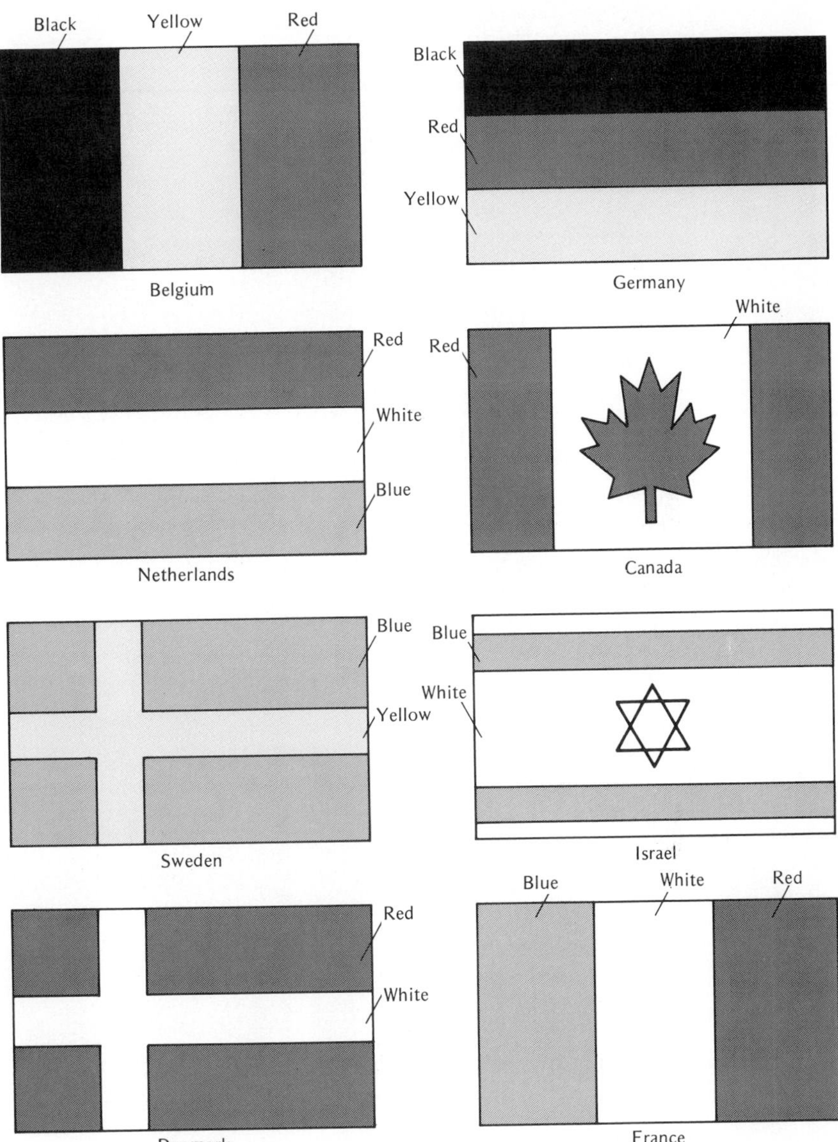

FIGURE 13–1 Flags are societal symbols.

FIGURE 13–2 A variety of verbal and nonverbal message sources provide the visible traces of culture that confront individuals within societies.

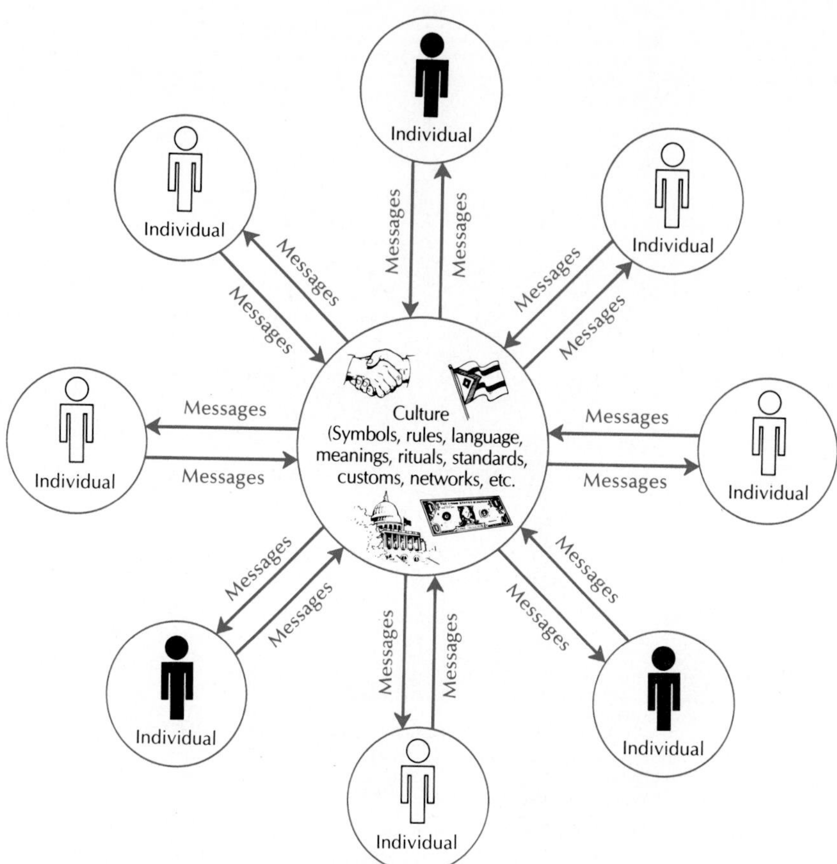

FIGURE 13–3 The relationship between the individual and culture is mutually influencing and reciprocally defining. Culture is created and perpetuated through the communication activities of individuals. Collectively, their behaviors provide the realities—symbols, rules, language, standards, customs, etc.,—with which each individual must adapt in order to be part of the unit.

cation activities in relationships, groups, organizations, and societies. Were it not for our human capacity for symbolic language, we would be unable to develop a common culture. And, without communication and communication media it would be impossible to pass along the elements of our culture from one place to another and from one generation to the next. At the same time, our individual ways of sensing, making sense of, and acting are developed as we adapt to the cultural demands and opportunities we encounter over the course of our lifetimes.

As much as it is accurate to say that culture is defined, shaped, transmitted, and learned through communication, the reverse is equally correct.[4] In effect, then, there is a reciprocally-influencing, or reciprocally-defining, relationship between human communication and culture. Through communication we shape our cultures; and, in turn, our cultures shape our communication patterns.[5]

Characteristics of Culture

The idea of culture and its relationship to communication can be made clearer by discussing the following common characteristics of cultures: (1) Cultures are complex and multifaceted; (2) cultures are invisible; (3) cultures are subjective; and (4) cultures change over time.

CULTURES ARE COMPLEX AND MULTIFACETED

The complexities of culture are most apparent, and potentially most problematic in terms of communication, at the level of societies. Here, language differences are often involved, along with fundamental issues such as social customs, family life, clothing, eating habits, class structure, political orientations, religion, customs, economic philosophies, beliefs, and value systems.[6]

Cultural elements do not exist in isolation from one another but, instead, influence one another in a number of subtle ways. For example, values of a societal culture have an impact on economics and vice versa; and both influence and are influenced by social customs, religion, and family life. Consider this illustration: The tendency toward large families in some cultures is explained not only by custom but also by economics, religion, health, and the level of technology. Where infant mortality is high due to disease and poor health conditions, a couple must have many children in order to be certain to have enough healthy children to farm and help with other duties necessary to the survival of the family unit. In North America, the decreasing size of families is also influenced by many of these same cultural factors, including economics, customs, available technology, social conditions, and evolving gender attitudes.

If we examine the verbal and nonverbal communication patterns in any culture, the same pattern of complexity and association is apparent. Greeting forms, gestures, conversational topics and formats, dress, language habits, courtship practices, eye-contact preferences, uses of space, orientations toward time, male-female roles, orientations toward elders, and attitudes toward work all influence and are, in turn, influenced by a variety of cultural dimensions such as religion and economics.

In Saudi Arabia, for example, gender differences are very pronounced. Women traditionally wear dark robes (abayah) and veils (hijab) in public. Men do not approach women to initiate interaction in a social setting, nor do they look directly at a woman or do anything else that might be interpreted as a sign of interest. These gender role differences extend to other social settings as well. For instance, it is quite normal for a Saudi male to invite a married man to dinner at his home with the expectation that the guest will not bring his wife. Even in those situations in which a couple is invited, the wife may be met at the door by the host's wife and entertained in a separate area of the home, leaving the men to dine alone. Many restaurants have separate entrances and special areas where women and children are expected to dine.

These traditional Saudi customs, objectionable as they may at first seem to a North American, must be understood in relation to the entire Arabic culture. They are the tip of what can be thought of as the "cultural iceberg."[7] In the case of the Arabic culture, the Islamic religion and tradition prescribe a very different role for women than for men. Saudi women are treated as they are because of a long-standing concern for protecting them from the harsh realities of life. For this same historical reason, the traditional dress of the Saudi women is designed to conceal and protect her from invasions of privacy that are regarded as rude and inappropriate. Similarly, while troublesome to many foreigners, the practice of polygamy, which is permitted by Saudi law and religion, has the intent of ensuring that no woman will be forced to live alone or to fend for herself.

Yet another example of the way in which facets of culture and communication are influential is apparent in business situations in Saudi Arabia. Saudis place great value on family, friends, and relationships. As a result, in Saudi business dealings, a substantial amount of time is spent discussing family, friends, and "how things are going." In fact, two businessmen meeting one another for the first time might devote their initial meeting to discussing only these topics, engaged totally in what *we* think of as "small talk." Only after the Saudi feels he knows and trusts the other person does he feel disposed to talk business—what *he* is more apt to regard as "small talk." From the perspective of North American culture, where a great premium is placed upon efficiency and problem solving in business affairs, the Saudi business communication behavior may well be frustrating and difficult to comprehend.[8] In a culture like Saudi Arabia, where a high premium is placed on supportive and socially-oriented communication, the highly taskoriented, "time-is-money" style of North Americans is generally not appreciated or effective. In fact, such styles are met with suspicion, distrust, and even hostility.

While every culture is unique in many respects, it is also possible to classify them based on certain similarities and differences. In an effort to categorize cultures based on communication, noted communication and culture scholar Edward Hall distinguishes between cultures which are high and low context and monochronic and polychronic in their orientations to time.[9]

High and Low Context Cultures. Hall defines *context* as "information that surrounds an event; it is inextricably bound up with the meaning of that event."[10] He indicates that cultures of the world—and the communication practices of individuals within those cultures—range from *high* to *low context.*

> A high context (HC) . . . message is one in which *most* of the information is already in the person, while very little is in the coded, explicit, transmitted part of the message. A low context (LC) communication is just the opposite; i.e., the mass of the information is vested in the explicit code. Twins who have grown up together can and do communicate more economically (HC) than two lawyers in a courtroom during a trial (LC), a mathematician programming a computer, two politicians drafting legislation, two administrators writing a regulation.[11]

In Japanese, Arab, and Mediterranean cultures there is extensive overlapping of personal, social, and work relationships. Because of these overlapping communication networks, these are high-context cultures; and, therefore, many everyday communication activities do not require much background information. The people who work together spend so much time together socially and in family activities that they are very well-informed about many aspects of one another's lives. Thus, when they converse, much can be taken for granted because of the rich communicative history of their relationships. Hall contrasts such cultures with low-context peoples, such as Americans, Germans, Swiss, Scandinavians, and other northern Europeans, who tend to compartmentalize their personal relations, work relationships, and other aspects of their lives.[12] Interactants from high- or low-context cultures have few problems interacting with one another. However, conversations across context types can become quite problematic, as when a North American and a Saudi meet for the first time to do business.

Monochronic and Polychronic Time. Time—a dimension of importance in many communication situations—is particularly vital to understanding cultures and differences between them. Hall distinguishes between two orientations to time: monochronic and polychronic. *Monochronic time* describes the orientation of people who pay attention to, and do, only one thing at a time. *Polychronic* refers to people who attend to and do many things at once.

> In monochronic cultures, time is experienced and used in a linear way-comparable to a road extending from the past into the future. Monochronic time is divided quite naturally into segments; it is scheduled and compartmentalized, making it possible for a person to concentrate on one thing at a time. In a monochronic system, the schedule may take priority above all else and be treated as sacred and unalterable.
>
> Monochronic time is perceived as being almost tangible: People talk about it as though it were money, as something that can be "spent," "saved," "wasted," and "lost."[13]

Whereas scheduling, time management, and the compartmentalization of personal and work-related activities are important in monochronic cultures, people in polychronic cultures want to keep current on everything simultaneously. Life in the United States—especially business life—clearly exemplifies the monochronic orientation, which is also a part of the cultures of Switzerland, Germany, and Scandinavia. In contrast are time-flexible Mediterranean cultures.[14]

Differences between high- and low-context and monochronic and polychronic cultures are useful for characterizing cultures and also help to explain some of the problems that occur in intercultural communication, a topic we will discuss in more detail later. Figure 13–5 on pp. 426–28 provides a listing of other dimensions that are useful to characterizing and distinguishing between societal cultures.

CULTURES ARE INVISIBLE

Most of what characterizes culture of a relationship, group, organization, or society is as invisible to the individuals it envelops as the air that surrounds them. The case of the Nacirema at the opening of this chapter illustrates the point well. Our culture is so subtle and pervasive that it simply goes unnoticed. It's there now, it's been there as long as anyone can remember, and few of us have reason to think much about it.

In most parts of North America, we take the English language for granted, as we do a number of nonverbal conventions. For instance, business associates in our culture think little about the familiar two-or three-pump handshake greeting, intermittent eye glances, and two and one-half to four feet space separating interactants when they first meet. In a similar way, we take for granted our relational, group, and organizational cultures. The romantic glances and expressive touch between intimates and the conventions of dress and jargon in our various groups and organizations become natural behaviors to the persons involved.

Sometimes we do become aware of the existence and nature of our cultures. When this occurs, it generally happens in one of three ways: (1) violation of a cultural convention, (2) cross-cultural contact, or (3) scholarly analysis.

1. *Violation of a Cultural Convention.* When someone within our culture violates taken-for-granted cultural practices or standards, it tends to attract our attention. In the case of the customary handshake ritual, for instance, we think little about it unless our expectations are violated. If, when meeting an individual for the first time, he or she takes hold of our hand with a very limp or exceptionally overpowering grip, we are likely to take note. Our reaction would be even more pronounced if an individual we were meeting were to pump our hand four, five, six, or seven times, and only then reluctantly let go. And imagine our response if someone reached out to shake hands in the middle of a long conversation! We have a similar reaction when a new acquaintance stares incessantly, or stands only one or two feet from us during casual conversation. As with so many other facets of our lives, we have been learning the cultural conventions for greeting and conversing with one another since we were children; and we generally think nothing about these conventions unless or until they are violated.

The same process occurs in relational cultures. Perhaps the most striking example happens when one individual in an intimate relationship "senses that something is wrong" because the other person doesn't look at his or her partner "in the way he or she is used to," or no longer seems to "joke around" in the accustomed way. When our expectations are violated, we realize at some level of awareness that we have acquired a number of patterns, customs, habits, and meanings which we simply take for granted.

2. *Cross-Cultural Contact.* The second way in which we can be alerted to the presence and impact of our culture is when we encounter people from another culture and observe major differences between

their behavior and our own. To the Saudi, men kissing one another on the cheek as a greeting goes unnoticed, while this same behavior startles and often upsets the European. The Japanese habit of closing the eyes when concentrating on a question may be quite traumatic to the Canadian businessman who has no idea how to interpret the action. Similarly, the "street language" of an urban youth may be shocking to one raised in a wealthy suburb, whose verbal and nonverbal behavior, in turn, may also seem strange to urban residents.

Without our necessarily being aware of it, these circumstances afford us some of our only opportunities to observe the subtle and pervasive influence our own cultures and subcultures have upon us. In either of these two kinds of circumstances, we know intuitively that "something is wrong" and that we feel somewhat uncomfortable, though we may not know exactly what is troubling us.

3. *Scholarly Analysis.* The third way we can become aware of our culture is through studying our own or others' descriptions of it. Figure 13–4, presenting the results of research comparing Japanese and American male and female perceptions of ideal qualities in a mate, provides

In the United States

According to Males	*According to Females*
1. Sex Appeal	1. Sex Appeal
2. Respect	2. Affectionate
3. Affectionate	3. Respect
4. Supportive	4. Intelligent
5. Friendship	5. Friendship
6. Intelligent	6. Supportive
7. Attractive	7. Attractive

In Japan

According to Males	*According to Females*
1. Common Values	1. Sound Health
2. Easy to Talk to	2. Honest
3. Sound Health	3. Easy to Talk to
4. Intelligent	4. Common Values
5. Affectionate	5. Intelligent
6. Honest	6. Affectionate
7. Handles Money Well	7. Handles Money Well

FIGURE 13–4 *Ranking Qualities of the Ideal Mate in the U.S. and Japan.*

Source: Donald Cushman and Tsukasa Nishida. "Mate Selection in the United States and Japan." Unpublished manuscript, 1984.

one illustration. Figure 13–5, providing overview descriptions of several cultures, also stimulates this kind of cultural awareness.

CULTURES ARE SUBJECTIVE

Because we have grown up with and take our cultures so much for granted, we are largely unaware of their subjective nature. To the people involved, aspects of culture are rational and make perfect sense, though they may not to "outsiders." We may easily come to assume that things are the way they should be—one wife for one husband, intermittent glances during casual conversation, waving to an acquaintance and so on.

An excellent example of this kind of assumption making is provided by colors. Obviously, red is red, and orange is orange. And, we all know that red is *not* orange, right? Not necessarily, as illustrated in Figure 13–6 on p. 429. The taken-for-granted language people use to describe color and the ways they categorize and perceive color around them may vary considerably from one culture to another. In Western cultures and language communities, we divide the color spectrum into six more or less distinct categories—red, orange, yellow, green, blue, and purple. What we seldom think about is that these divisions are arbitrary, as are their labels. They are the result of the historical influence of European culture in the western world. People in certain other language communities divide the color spectrum differently. The Shona of Rhodesia and the Bassa of Liberia, for instance, have fewer categories. The Shona divide the spectrum into four parts, which are pronounced *cipsuka, cicena, citema* and *cipsuka. Cipsuka* appears two times, because it refers to colors at both the red and purple ends of the spectrum. The Bassa use two major categories—*ziza* and *hui.*[15]

Examples such as these help to remind us that the cultural patterns, codes, and realities we take for granted are not necessarily "true" or "right." A more theoretically appropriate view is that our cultures are the way they are because we and our ancestors created them in particular ways. We have come to accept their correctness in the same way that other persons have come to accept the rightness of their cultures—through communication.

CULTURES CHANGE OVER TIME

Cultures and subcultures do not exist in a vacuum. We carry the influence of these cultures with us as we participate in any number of rela-

Country	Topic	Custom
China	Greetings	A nod or a slight bow will usually suffice when greeting someone, but a handshake is also acceptable. The Chinese tend to be quite formal when introducing visitors and use the full title of their guests. Nonetheless, the Chinese often avoid identifying themselves precisely. Chinese names consist of a one syllable family name followed by a one-or-two-syllable given name. Addressing Chinese by their family name without a title is not polite; thus, Chen Yunpo should be addressed as Mr. Chen.
	Visiting	Guests should be prompt, or even a little early. The guest should make the first move to leave. Guests are expected to conduct themselves with restraint, and to refrain from loud, boisterous speech and actions. Valuable gifts are usually not accepted from strangers. The Chinese enjoy discussing many interesting topics, including the differences between China and the West. In any situation, however, it is best to avoid belittling remarks about Chinese society or its leaders.
	Eating	When invited to a home for dinner, it is polite to sample every dish served. Chopsticks are used for all meals and should be placed neatly on the table when one has finished eating. The food is placed in the center of the table. It is customary to hold the bowl close to the mouth when eating rice. Any bones, seeds, etc., should be placed on the table or in special dishes, not in the rice bowl. When dining at a restaurant, the host will pay the bill. Business is generally not discussed during meals. It is impolite to drink alone; therefore, toasts are usually offered to the people sitting nearby or to the whole table. At formal banquets, guests should have a short, friendly speech prepared to respond to what their host says. Nondrinkers may toast with water, juice, or soft drinks. Tipping is seen by some as something a superior does to an inferior, and, hence is sometimes regarded as an insult.
	Personal Appearance	Visitors to China can dress informally and comfortably for most occasions. Women should not wear shorts or halter tops. The Chinese wear little or no makeup or jewelry. Most of them—men and women alike—wear bulky jackets and trousers. Some women, however, are beginning to wear skirts, blouses, and dresses or brightly colored blouses under their tunics.
	Gestures	The Chinese do not like to be touched by people they do not know. A smile is preferred over a pat on the back or similar gesture. It is especially inadvisable to exhibit physical familiarity with older people or people with important positions. The Chinese use their open hand to point rather than one finger, and they beckon to someone with the palm of the hand facing down.
	Dating and Marriage Customs	Chinese customs stress moral purity. Premarital sex and public displays of affection are discouraged. Due to the enormous population, effective family planning is a major goal of the government. Traditionally, the Chinese have had large families, but present law dictates that each couple may have only 1 child.
Japan	Greetings	A bow is the traditional greeting. Upon meeting, Japanese will often bow to each other. Guests should try to bow as low and as long as the other person is bowing, but not lower. This signifies humility. Western-style handshakes are also becoming increasingly popular. The Japanese are quite formal in introductions and at social events. They always use the name and title of their guests. It is polite to reciprocate this custom. The use of first names without a title is reserved for family and friends.
	Visiting	Shoes should be removed before stepping from the enclosed porch into a Japanese-style home. Western-style buildings, however, may be entered with shoes on. After shoes are removed, they are placed together pointing toward the outdoors. Slippers should also be removed before entering rooms with the immaculate straw mat floors (*tatami*). Japanese traditionally emphasize modesty and reserve. When offered tea or fruit, one should express a slight hesitation to accept it. It is also advisable to deny compliments graciously. Guests should avoid excessive compliments to the host on items of decor; otherwise the host may feel obligated to give the items as gifts. When visiting, it is customary for guests to take a gift (usually fruit or cakes) to their host. Gifts should be given and accepted with both hands and a slight bow. The Japanese like to discuss their country and its accomplishments.
	Eating	Eating while walking on the street exhibits poor taste. Snack foods are sold at street stands, but it is appropriate to stay at the stand until finished eating. The Japanese typically eat from their bowl while holding it at chest level instead of bending down to it on the table. Knives and forks are almost always available for the visitor who is not skilled with chopsticks.

FIGURE 13–5

Japan	**Personal Appearance**	Conformity, even in appearance, is one of the distinct characteristics of Japanese people. The general rule is to act in a manner similar to, or in harmony with, the crowd. Men wear suits and ties in public; women wear modest and clean dresses. It is advisable to avoid colors that are conspicuous. The accepted style of clothing is usually European rather than American. During the summer months (from June to August) men generally do not wear their coats. Handkerchiefs are usually carried.
	Gestures	It is impolite to yawn in public. A person should sit erect placing both feet on the floor. Legs can be crossed with one knee directly over the other or they can be crossed at the ankles. Beckoning is done with the palm down instead of up, and pointing is done with the entire hand. Shaking one hand from side to side with the palm forward means no. Laughter does not necessarily signify joy or amusement; it can also be a sign of embarrassment or distress. The mouth should be covered when using a toothpick or yawning. Also, it is best to avoid chewing gum in public. It is not uncommon to see members of the same sex strolling hand in hand.
	Dating and Marriage Customs	In Japan, dating is a recent phenomenon. Young people begin dating at age seventeen or eighteen. Movies and dining out are favorite dating activities. Marriage age averages about twenty-five to twenty-seven for men and slightly younger for women. Traditionally, elderly friends of the family arranged the marriages, but now the individual couples decide.
USSR	**Greetings**	When meeting a stranger, a Soviet will offer to shake hands and simply state his or her name. A Soviet usually prefers to be direct and informal, rather than to recite a polite phrase. Visitors should also keep greetings brief. Hellos and goodbyes among relatives and older people often include hugging and the traditional greeting of three kisses on the cheek.
	Visiting	As in many European nations, it is common (but not required) for houseguests to bring flowers or liquor. Other appropriate gifts include chewing gum for children, popular records, American cigarettes, American jeans, jewelry, books, neckties, or shaving equipment. A much nicer present for a special person is an inexpensive pocket calculator or a small bottle of perfume. As in most countries, however, gifts that are given to suggest the superiority of another country are not appreciated. It is a serious crime for tourists to sell anything to Soviet citizens, including used clothing. It is also against the law to bring in dissident literature, to export undeclared art objects, or to exchange money with private individuals. Officially, tipping is not expected. However, waitresses and taxi drivers often keep the change unless asked to return it. In conversation, one should avoid dwelling on negative aspects of Soviet history and society (the horrors of Stalinism, present problems with alcoholism, long lines, etc.).
	Eating	The continental style of eating, with the fork in the left hand and knife in the right, is the most common. Hands are kept above the table and not in the lap. When dining in a restaurant, guests should wait to be seated by the manager ("administrator"). A polite way to call the waitress is with a slight nod of the head. Any problems concerning the bill should be settled with the manager. After 8:00 p.m., in almost every restaurant, an orchestra plays music while the guests dance.
	Personal Appearance	Women do not wear as much make-up and jewelry as is commonly worn in the U.S. Urban clothing styles are basically like those in any western European city, but men's fashions are more conservative than in the U.S.
	Gestures	Approval is expressed by the thumbs up sign. Visitors should avoid shaking the raised fist, or using the American OK sign with the index finger pressed to the thumb tip, since these gestures are considered vulgar. Visitors should not sit with one ankle on the other knee or with legs far apart.
	Dating and Marriage Customs	Despite official exhortations against premarital sex, the Soviet rate of promiscuity is comparable to that in the West. Wedding "palaces" established by the government are common, but some young people also choose to be married in a church. The government now officially encourages moderately large families, but inadequate housing and low wages generally discourage families from having more than one child. The average family size is about 3.7 people (3.1 in U.S.).

FIGURE 13–5 *(continued).*

Puerto Rico	**Greetings**	Usually people shake hands when greeting, although close friends often embrace after a long absence. Women often greet each other by grasping shoulders and kissing each other on the cheek. People stand very close when talking, and those of the same sex often touch each other with their hands. Moving away, even slightly, may be considered an insult.
	Visiting	Visits are relaxed and the whole family participates. Items of decor should be complimented carefully; otherwise, the host may feel obliged to give them to the guest. Gifts are given freely and unwrapped immediately. Guests usually decline a few times on ceremony before accepting anything.
	Eating	The atmosphere at mealtime is very relaxed, although both hands should remain above the table. Bread is often used to push food onto the fork. Guests should not leave directly after the meal but should relax and enjoy some conversation with the host. Food bought at a street stand should be eaten there. Fifteen percent is an appropriate tip in restaurants.
	Personal Appearance	Lightweight, casual clothes are generally worn, but too much informality in dress may be offensive. Formal dress is expected at parties and social gatherings.
	Gestures	Beckoning is done with the palm down instead of up. Wiggling the nose can mean "what's going on?"' People often point with puckered lips. Small items should always be handed to people, not thrown. A waiter in a Spanish restaurant may be summoned by making a "psst" sound. Puerto Ricans interrupt each other freely and are not upset at interruptions. Peers tease each other, but in formal situations joking is expected to stop. Those with authority are expected to use it wisely. Commenting in a low voice while others are talking is not usually considered offensive. Men often smile and stare at women, but it is considered improper for a woman to smile indiscriminately at strangers.

FIGURE 13–5 *Comparing Cultures: Culturegrams.* *

The David M. Kennedy Center for International Studies has produced a series of about one hundred *Culturegrams* that contain a variety of information about countries around the world. More information can be obtained by writing to: Brigham Young University, David M. Kennedy Center for International Studies, Publication Services, 280 HRCB, Provo, UT 84602.

Source: "How to Map a People," Provo, UT: Brigham Young University, David M. Kennedy Center for International Studies, 1976. By permission.

tionships, groups, or organizations. As we as individuals change, we provide an impetus for the change of cultures of which we are a part. In this sense we are each agents of cultural change.

In addition to natural, evolutionary cultural developments that inevitably occur, other cultural changes occur in a more intentional revolutionary way. In recent years, for example, concerned African-Americans, Hispanics, women, gays and lesbians, and handicapped individuals have focused attention on the discriminatory conventions and practices that have become a part of our society's culture. See Box 13–1. Efforts by members of these groups have not only accelerated and directed cultural developments within the society as a whole but have undoubtedly had an impact on the cultures of relationships, groups, and organizations, as well.

ENGLISH:

red	orange	yellow	green	blue	purple

SHONA:

cipsuka	cicena	citema	cipsuka

BASSA:

ziza	hui

FIGURE 13–6

Source: Word Play: What Happens When People Talk, Peter Farb. Copyright © 1979 by Alfred A. Knopf, Inc. By permission.

I have just returned from a two-week lecture tour of India. Fascinating place; so many things are different. For example, the men walk through the streets holding hands. Not just fathers and their little sons: young men, old men, friends, brothers—they all hold hands. And they don't just *hold* hands. Their fingers twine around each other as if they were lovers—only they're not. It's just the way men walk around in India.

What you *don't* see in India is men and women holding hands or putting their arms around each other. But presumably the Indians are mating, as there are now 850 million of them. You just don't see displays of affection between men and women in public (or women and women as in the Latin world) only between men and men.

Naturally, India made me think of Rutgers, where a photo of the public display of affection between two men last fall sent half the community into orbit, with many expressing their outrage in this newspaper. A few weeks after that historic picture in the *Targum* I noticed another picture—this time of a man and woman kissing—but not a soul wrote into the newspaper about it one way or the other.

Mind you, I'm not claiming any moral superiority on the homophobia front. I'm as cowed by guilt-association as the next guy. I have gay friends who are terrific people, but I have yet to support them by marching in a Gay Pride parade. I even worry about what people think about me being so affectionate with my sons.

Recently, I had to see my son Jeffrey off at Newark Airport. Jeffrey is full-grown, but he and I remain physically affectionate with each other. When we say goodbye we kiss each other. But usually we do this in private.

We kissed each other goodbye at airport security and Jeffrey headed for his flight. Then I turned around and saw these people looking at me. Actually, maybe they weren't looking at me, I was just afraid they were looking at me. I imagined them thinking: "Here's this middle-aged guy saying goodbye to his young lover at Newark Airport."

The truth is, I'll never know what, if anything, those people were thinking, will I? But I do know what *I* was thinking. And I'm not particularly proud of it.

BOX 13–1

Source: Michael A. Rockland, Professor of American Studies at Rutgers University. Reprinted from "Off the Banks," *The* (Rutgers University) *Daily Targum*, Feb. 1, 1991, p6. By permission of the author.

The Role of Mediated Communication

Many institutions within society contribute to the creation, perpetuation, and evolution of culture. Families play a very basic part in this process, as do churches, schools, organizations, the government and the business community. Mediated communication also plays an indispensable role.

Mediated communication extends our creating, duplicating, and storing capabilities. Our technology broadens the pool of messages available in common to individuals. Some of these mediated messages relate to our relational, group, and organizational cultures. Telephone calls and photographs serve this purpose for relationships, in much the same way that printed constitutions, badges, and emblems serve this function for groups. Brochures, newsletters, and video products, similarly, contribute to the culture of organizations.

At the societal level, the cultural contribution of mediated communication is immense. Mass media institutions such as newspapers, radio, television, books, and film have long played a fundamental role in packaging and transmitting cultural information, as do libraries and museums.[16]

News, entertainment, sports, and advertising programming tell us stories about people and how they live. They provide insights into how people think, and they portray the consequences of particular behaviors. Often in very subtle ways, they provide lessons about friendship, family life, war, crime, politics, music, art, religion, politics, economics, styles of dress, gender roles, sexuality, life styles, morality, and economics. They contribute to the visibility, currency, and legitimacy of the topics they address, whether the topic is sex, violence, drugs, or racial issues.

For example, the television program "Who's the Boss?" makes a direct and forceful statement about gender roles by reversing stereotypes. Angela, the head of the house, is the tough-minded, independent, detached, no-nonsense professional. Tony, on the other hand, is the supportive, dependent, cuddly, "I'm-here-whenever-you-need me" housekeeper, exemplifying characteristics more frequently associated with the "traditional woman" stereotype. Soap operas and call-in shows like Dr. Ruth also have implicit cultural messages. With their emphasis on interpersonal intrigue, entanglements, and intimate dialogue, they reinforce the idea that intimate conversation and self-disclosure are appropriate ways to cope with personal and social problems.

Advertising also contributes to our cultural information base. Ads promote our market-based economic system and urge us to become consumers. Encouraging consumption is a universal theme in advertising. Rarely, however, is the message, "We want you all to get out there and buy all kinds of things and services," made explicit. But the message is powerful, nonetheless. College students are a prime target for these campaigns. Direct mailings and "take an application" posters urge students "to establish your credit now" and reassure them that the bank will "say yes," when the application is submitted. The implicit economics lesson is a simple one: It is important to be a consumer; it is necessary to establish credit—the sooner the better—and it is good to buy on credit.

Sporting events provide another interesting illustration of the ways in which mediated, especially mass, communication can serve as a carrier of cultural messages. Dan Nimmo and James Combs in *Mediated Political Realities* discuss how sports programming provides a number of lessons which prepare viewers for political participation in society. Sporting events—particularly when distributed by mass media—are presented as suspense-filled contests with hero and villains. They present a story of the "triumph of justice or the intervention of fortune . . . heroic deeds and untimely errors, dramatic climaxes, and the euphoria of the victors along with the gloom of the vanquished."[17]

Even video games provide implicit cultural messages:

> Trees, people, houses, animals, and other cars buzz back and forth across the road in front of your metallic red Porsche 944, as you screech around the turns. Suddenly a bike pulls out in front of you and you are forced to swerve off the road into a ditch, where your car crashes into a brick wall and blows up.[18]

Is this a problem? Not if the press of a button brings you back to the start of the track in your same shiny Porsche. This is exactly how things work in the world of video gaming. One of the strongest messages of video games is immortality and the possibility of redoing what went wrong without consequence.[19] Home video games come equipped with a "reset" button that allows the player to have a fresh start at any time without consequence. Inserting a quarter in a coinoperated machine accomplishes the same goal. In some games the character on the screen merely needs to swallow a "power pill" to be granted a few additional lives. If one is involved in a particular situation which is displeasing, the touch of a button wipes the trouble away. Obviously, these lessons can be a problem if applied to real-life situations:

> It is much easier to rid oneself of a Teenage Mutant Ninja Turtle with no regrets, than it is to delete a lover or "reset" a relationship. The turtle is much more forgiving and will have no regrets about playing the same game again with no recollection of the previous interaction.
>
> Many video games offers the consumers a pause control. When a player desires to take a break from a particular game and to return later, the touch of a button makes this possible. When the individual returns, hours or days later, he or she will find the game patiently waiting at the same place it was when stopped, another luxury unfortunately absent in everyday encounters.[20]

Mass communication often plays a role in giving commercial value to, and often helping to sell, particular cultural symbols. Media play a major role in the commercialization of celebrities, brand names, art objects, music, and other elements of culture. This is especially obvious in areas in which the popularity of particular individuals, achieved through mass communication, has given them their name, and anything associated with them great value. One example is endorsement of clothes or other sporting gear by sports figures. Not only people, but also fictional characters, are commercialized through mass communication, as with Big Bird, Miss Piggy, E.T., or Mickey Mouse. So, too, mass communication is essential in the commercialization of places, among them Disney World, Central Park, Fort Lauderdale, Las Vegas, New York, and Paris.

Mediated messages are a kind of cultural mirror, combining with the messages of face-to-face communication to provide a menu and an agenda of concerns, issues, values, personalities, and themes that occupy a central role in the symbolic environment to which individuals must adapt. In this way, mediated communication plays a fundamental role in the socialization process of the individual and in so doing contributes at the same time to the stability and order of social systems.[21]

Cultural Adaptation

Adapting to a culture is a matter of learning, of developing appropriate personal representations, maps, and images of the cultures created by the relationships, groups, organizations, and society of which we are members.

Most of the learning is natural and inevitable. We would learn to speak our native language, for example, whether we were ever formally taught it or not. We absorb cultures—become Americans, Swiss, Tanzanians—with virtually no effort or awareness on our part that it is happening. Even less obviously, we adapt to and absorb the cultures of relationships, groups, and organizations in which we become involved. We become "a corporate person," "a salesman," "a Protestant," or "masculine" with very little effort on our part, as we "take on" the cultural conventions of our gender, friends, family, ethnic group, profession, and society. Cultural adaptation also involves persuasion, as with the education provided by family, church, and school aimed at providing the knowledge, values, and rules that others deem necessary.

Because we tend so easily and so thoroughly to adapt to our own cultures, it is often a difficult and stressful matter to readjust to others. Newly retired, divorced, or widowed people, for instance, often find the adjustment to their new situation extremely difficult. Adjusting to the subculture of a prison often presents the same problems; and, once this adjustment has taken place, readjustment to the culture of the "outside world" upon release can be even more difficult.

These kinds of adjustments represent what has been called *culture shock.*[22] Initially, culture shock was thought to be a *disease*—a malady contracted by persons who were suddenly transplanted from one geographic locale to another. Symptoms associated with the illness were noted to include frustration, anger, anxiety, feelings of helplessness, overwhelming loneliness, and excessive fears of being robbed, cheated, or eating dangerous food.[23] As the following story indicates, the turbulence that goes with the experience of physical relocation can apparently be as traumatic for animals as well as humans:

> In the spring of 1972, the United States and China exchanged gifts of animals as gesture of goodwill between countries. The Chinese pandas, Hsing-Hsing and Ling-Ling, quickly adjusted to the National Zoo in Washington, D.C. After a few days, they were in excellent health, standing on their heads and wiggling their rumps. Milton and Matilda, the two musk oxen sent to Peking, did not make a healthy adjustment to the Peking Zoo—they suffered from postnasal drip and a skin condition that caused them to shed their hair. . . .[24]

The explanation provided by Dr. Theodore Reed, director of the National Zoo, who accompanied the oxen to Peking, was that their runny noses and other symptoms were the result of culture shock and the rigors of travel—"hearing Chinese spoken instead of English, seeing new faces, new uniforms, new surroundings, and eating Chinese hay and grain."[25] Within several months, Milton and Matilda recovered, as a result of antibiotics and what Reed termed "tender loving care."

As one might predict even from this brief story, the medical view of cultural adjustment has broadened in recent years to include an emphasis on psychology, sociology, and especially, communication. In fact, in his classic book *Silent Language* Edward Hall described culture shock as "simply the removal or distortion of the familiar cues one encounters at home and the substitute of them by other cues which are strange."[26]

STAGES OF CULTURAL ADAPTATION

There have been numerous attempts to describe and delineate the stages of cultural adaptation.[27] These writings suggest that there are generally four phases, as shown in Figure 13–7.

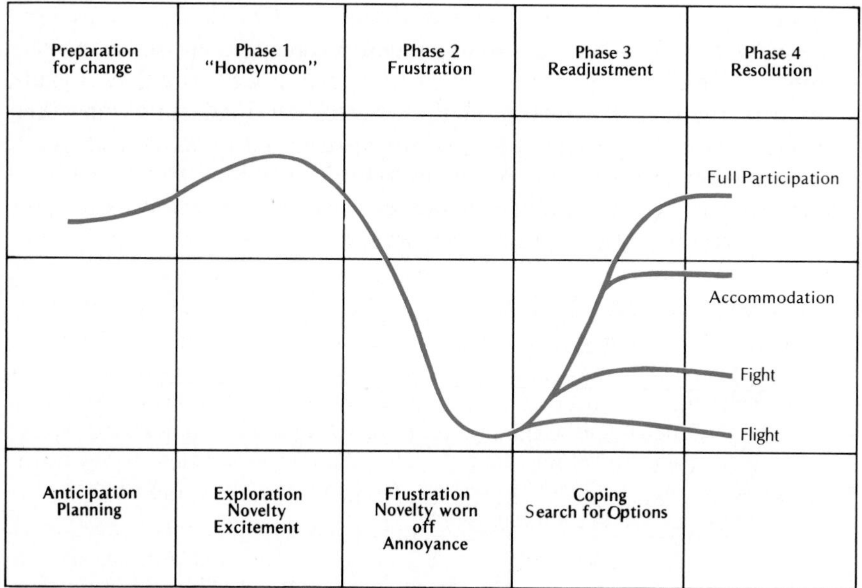

FIGURE 13–7 *Stages of Adaptation in a New Environment.*

Source: Based on review of literature on stages of adaptation presented in *Adaptation to a New Environment,* by Daniel J. Kealey (Ottawa, Canada: Canadian International Agency, Briefing Centre, 1978).

1. Phase 1 is a "honeymoon" period during which individuals adjusting to a new culture are excited by the novelty of the people and new surroundings or situations.
2. Phase 2 is a period in which fascination and novelty often turn into frustration, anxiety, and even hostility, as the realities of life in an unfamiliar environment or circumstance become more apparent.
3. Phase 3 marks the beginning of the readjustment process, as individuals begin to develop ways of coping with their frustrations and the challenge of the new situation.
4. In phase 4, the readjustment continues. During this period, several outcomes are possible. Many individuals regain their balance and comfort level, developing meaningful relations and an appreciation of the new culture. Other individuals are unable fully to accept the new culture but find a way to cope with it adequately for their purposes. A third response is simply to find a way to "survive," though with substantial personal discomfort and strain. Some are unable to reach even this level of adjustment and find their only alternative is to retreat from the situation.

When an individual is adjusting to the culture of a new society thousands of miles from home, where the geography, climate, rituals, customs, lifestyles and languages are unfamiliar, with no companions and no prospect of returning to one's home country for several years, cultural adaptation may be a very intense and stressful experience.

The same dynamics of adaptation occur in situations that are more common and familiar. Any time we end one intimate relationship, start a new job, move in with new roommates, join a sorority or fraternity, or move from one culture or subculture to another, we are likely to go through stages of adaptation on some level, as the adjustment to new people, new expectations, new symbols and, often, new cultural realities take place.

Often, the initial enthusiasm in a new job, relationship, organization, or community gives way to frustration, disappointment, and even some degree of depression, as it becomes apparent that the new situation is not all we have hoped it would be. Gradually, we begin to adapt, as we revise our expectations downward, develop new understanding, and apply the skills necessary to cope with the new relationship, group, organization, or circumstance. In some instances, we adjust fully. In others, we give the appearance of fitting in but never really become comfortable. Sometimes we may be unable to continue and may decide to withdraw.

Intercultural Communication

Whenever we interact with someone from another culture, we are engaged in *intercultural communication.* Given our definition of culture, this means that every communication situation involving people who don't know one another well is intercultural to some degree. In any communication situation, each person brings unique symbols, meanings, and patterns that reflect the many cultures of which they have been a part over the course of their lifetime. And, as we meet new people, we are in the process of negotiating the beginnings of a new relationship and relational culture.

From the first moments of contact between two individuals, for example, they begin a process of intercultural communication, mutual exploration, and accommodation. At the instant we take notice of a person, we don't know whether we have similar knowledge levels, backgrounds, orientations toward time, political philosophies, gestural patterns, greeting forms, religious orientations, or even a common language capability. We may not be certain whether we share a common flag, race, or nationality. And we don't know whether or not we have had similar experiences in previous relationships, groups, or organizations.

We use communication to reduce our uncertainty about the situation and the person or persons involved.[28] We study their appearance, dress, adornments, posture, and walk. We listen to them speak, and we talk to them. Gradually, we begin to acquire information that helps us to determine what we have in common and where we differ. As the process continues, the pool of common information available to us grows steadily, and with it the possibilities for adjusting to and shaping the relationship, group, or organization of which we are becoming a part.

Societies—Complex Cultural and Communication Systems

A *society* is a complex social system composed of a large number of diverse, geographically dispersed, and mutually dependent individuals, groups, and organizations in pursuit of interrelated goals. Societies are created, defined, and maintained through communication.

NATIONAL AND INTERNATIONAL NETWORKS

Two types of communication networks are basic to the functioning of a society: (1) national networks, and (2) international networks. *National networks* are the pathways *within* a society that connect individuals, groups and organizations to one another. See Figure 13–8. The functions served by these networks include:

1. providing the means through which information is conveyed among members of a society;
2. facilitating the coordination of often diverse activities of individuals, groups, and organizations within a society; and
3. supplying the channel through which collective decisions are made and implemented.

In a democratic society, many of the critical linkages in the national network will be provided by individuals elected or chosen to represent a

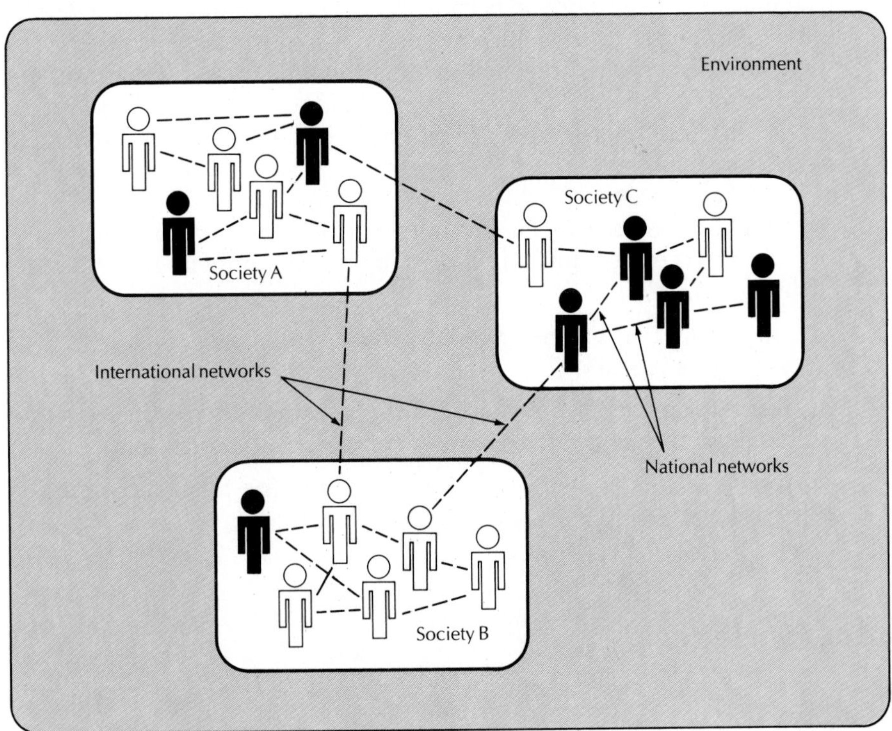

FIGURE 13–8 *National and International Networks.*

particular group or organization. Members of a community select individuals to represent their concerns and point of view to other groups at a regional or state level. At a still higher level, representatives from regions, states, and other groups and organizations join to pool information, discuss common concerns, set priorities, and make decisions for the society as a whole.

This process of collaboration and collective decision making results in the creation of recommendations, policies, and laws. Information about these deliberations and their outcomes is then distributed to members of the society using a variety of pathways. News and public affairs media programming, political campaigning, government publications, and other mass communication channels operate in combination with interpersonal communication. Collectively, these national networks create what Karl Deutsch termed the "nerves of government."[29]

Besides the national networks, so essential to the functioning of a society, *international networks* are also extremely important. These *transnational networks* are linkages *between* societies.

Interpersonal contact by tourists, foreign service personnel, and representatives to the United Nations and other international agencies plays an important role in linking societies to one another. Other pathways are those created through international news and entertainment programming, international banking transactions, governmental propaganda, and intelligence operations. Functions served by international networks include:

1. providing societies access to information necessary to identify and adapt to the needs and challenges of the environment and the world community;
2. supplying the means through which information is conveyed among societies;
3. facilitating the identification and coordination of often diverse needs, activities, and perspectives of various societies; and
4. providing the pathways through which international collaboration is possible.

Information Societies

An **information society** is one in which communication and information play a central role. More specifically, information societies have the following characteristics:[30]

1. Information is regarded as an economic commodity.
2. Information technology is widely diffused.
3. Many messages and channels operate.
4. Individuals, groups, and organizations are highly interconnected.
5. A large information work force exists.
6. Scientific knowledge is highly valued.

The United States, Japan, Sweden, England and a number of other countries fit the general definition, whereas Mexico, Iran, Turkey, and Nigeria do not. In information societies, communication and information media, products, and services are important economically and socially, and at least half of the society's labor force is engaged in information-related work.[31] Further, in these countries, the number of communication and information workers has increased steadily over the past hundred years, compared to those working in noninformation jobs.[32]

ECONOMICS OF THE INFORMATION AGE

In information societies, communication media, products, and services—for example, direct broadcast satellites, VCRs, videocassetes, television sets, CDs, computers, computer programs, and telephone systems—are commodities that must be bought and paid for. Even with economies resulting from large-scale production, they can be expensive. Beyond the cost of technology itself are the costs associated with its use. Often the one-time cost of buying equipment, for example, is small compared to the costs of continued purchase of software and maintenance.

Obviously enough, the economic benefits go to individuals, organizations, and societies who can afford *to buy and use* communication media, products, and services and to individuals, organizations, and societies who have these commodities *to sell.*

International Communication: The Global Village

A number of popular and scholarly writers have pointed optimistically to a future in which citizens of the world would be linked together in what we might think of as a "world community" or "global village." The image is of a massive network in which individuals in all societies would be united through communication—"an information world," as an extension of today's growing number of information societies.

The events of Operation Desert Shield and Operation Desert Storm have vividly demonstrated that something approaching a global village has already become a reality. Cable News Network (CNN) is available in ninety countries, and the world (and its diplomatic and military leaders) watched as the air attacks on Iraq and Kuwait were broadcast live. Today newspapers are printed and distributed at various geographic sites via satellite; and the international distribution of books, videotapes, records, and cassettes are realities of life in the 1990s. MTV—the music station—is also an international medium. In fact, it is available in more homes (sixty million) abroad than in the U.S. (fifty million). MTV says that about 10 percent of their revenue comes from foreign countries, an amount which has doubled in recent months. Estimates call for foreign revenues to account for 15 to 20 percent of the total MTV income in the period ahead.[33]

One example of the influential role of communication is East-West relations. There is little question that increased face-to-face interaction along with mediated communication have facilitated information flow and understanding between the U.S. and Soviet citizens, through increasing exposure to one another's leaders, cultures and perspectives. At times, the impact of this increased exposure has been to highlight areas of difference and dispute. In other instances, similarities and common objectives have been clarified. In so doing, communication has led to an increase in levels of East-West familiarity, predictability, and understanding. A number of what Edward Hall terms "fast" and "slow" messages operate on an ongoing basis to increase familiarity between cultures and societies.[34] See Figure 13–9.

THE OTHER SIDE OF THE COIN

With a recognition that something approaching a global village is indeed a possibility, come new questions as to whether a global village is really what everyone wanted. Indeed, some are suggesting now that the barriers that could be broken with communication technology may be quite important to maintain.

Although most of us would probably regard cultural change as desirable, not all people share this view. To some, the intrusion of messages from other cultures is negatively valued. Detractors contend that communication across cultural boundaries can contribute to a "melting pot" effect, and fear that valued distinctions between cultures or socie-

Fast Messages	**Slow Messages**
Prose	Poetry
Headlines	Books
A communiqué	An Ambassador
Propaganda	Art
Cartoons	Etchings
Television	Print
Easy familiarity	Deep relationships

FIGURE 13–9 *Examples of Fast and Slow Messages.*
Source: Selected examples from Edward T. Hall and Mildred Reed Hall, *Understanding Cultural Differences: Germans, French, and Americans,* Yarmouth, ME: Intercultural Press, 1989, p. 5

ties often become blurred in the process. To those who see this melting down of differences as threatening the distinctiveness of a particular relationship, group, organization, culture, or society, intercultural communication and change may be actively resisted.

It is also argued that economic dependency on countries that produce communication hardware also has implications for dependency on these same providers for content and programming—CDs, computer programs, content of television shows, for instance. Many are concerned because they see North American culture linked to our communication products and services. For a less industrialized country, the prospect of enabling its citizens to be linked to the world community in order to have access to U.S. prime time television—HBO, MTV, or the Playboy Channel—raises some obvious questions. Can a culture hope to preserve its identity, political or ideological integrity, or its traditional values when its citizenry is plugged into "Dallas," "The Simpsons," or "Rambo"? Concerned about precisely these issues, French television and movie producers have demanded that a quota be placed on the broadcast of U.S. television programs. The goal is to ensure that at least 60 percent of Europe's television shows are created in Europe. The French concern—shared to a greater or lesser extent in other European countries—is to limit American "cultural imperialism" by placing quotas on the invasion of U.S. programs, especially popular shows like "Dallas," "Miami Vice," and "L.A. Law."[35] If mass communication products from the U.S., Japan, and other industrialized countries are widely consumed throughout the world, these societies may have an inevitable—if unintended—cross-cultural impact.

This potential for economic and cultural control raises a fundamental question that will be at the core of discussions in the 1990s: Is it possible for an individual, organization, or society to be dependent on others economically and technologically but be uninfluenced by their cultural messages? Or does control of communication media, products, and services imply cultural influence and dependency? Clearly, the challenge is to reap the benefits of global communication without unnecessarily sacrificing individual and cultural integrity and independence in the process.

Another important issue has to do with the nature of communication as it relates to increasingly optimistic predictions about improvements in international cooperation and understanding. While we can think of examples in which communication seems to have contributed to improved relations, we can think of counter examples, as well. Certainly, the confrontation between the U.S. and other coalition forces and Iraq did not occur without numerous attempts to send messages back and forth. While one could question the quality and effectiveness of the message sending and receiving, certainly communication was not absent.

Examples such as this remind us that more communication media, networks, messages, and services, alone, provide no guarantee of improved international understanding or cooperation. The capability of communication and the sharing of a common symbolic environment do not automatically lead to shared or converging ways of thinking or behaving, common value orientations or similar information processing patterns for the individuals involved. In all fundamental respects, a war, an argument, or a divorce, are as much a product of communication as are peaceful coexistence, a reconciliation, or a marriage. Occasionally, "negative" outcomes develop because of a lack of a common base of information or reciprocal message processing. More often, however, these results occur because of the *presence* rather than *absence* of communication. As we know, even when two individuals are confronted by the same messages, their ways of selecting, attaching meaning and significance, and retaining information may inhibit—or even preclude—the chance for mutual understanding, agreement, or convergence. The problem of human rights in many countries of the world does not seem to be the result of a "breakdown" in reciprocal message processing. Virtually all of us have access to messages relative to the problems of human rights and some "awareness" of the problem. But access to and awareness of messages are not necessarily good predictors of whether and how the messages will be used—"message sent" does not equal "message received."

In the short run, at least the presence of communication and commonly available messages are not necessarily more likely to produce convergence than divergence, love than hate, understanding than misunderstanding, peace than war. In the long run, we can speculate that the ever-increasing pool of shared "fast" and "slow" messages—along with common needs and goals—will lead to an increasingly predictable and shared world culture. And, while simply increasing the number of communication situations provides no guarantee of improved world relationships, efforts to improve our individual communication skills, such as listening, empathy, and respect, can certainly help to bridge the gap.

Implications and Applications: Intercultural Relations and Understanding

- Each relationship, group, organization, and society has a culture that is to some extent unique.

- As we engage in communication, we are at the same time contributing to the creation or maintenance of the cultures of our relationships, groups, organizations, and/or societies. Each time you behave in a culturally-consistent manner—adhere to the usual practices of a group, follow conventional patterns of dress or speech at work, or use a traditional greeting or gesture—you help to reinforce and perpetuate that culture.

- Cultures are so basic to our lives that we take them for granted, as with the air that surrounds us.

- We tend to assume our own cultural practices are correct; and contrasting cultures are often regarded as *wrong* rather than simply *different.*

- Mediated communication contributes to the processes of creating, maintaining, and changing cultures. News and entertainment programs portray particular cultural images—about male and female roles, for example—and these images become a part of the culture to which we must adapt. Even sporting events and video games reflect and promote certain cultural themes.

- When we move from one locale, relationship, or job to another, we go through a process of adaptation as we learn to fit ourselves with the new culture. Depending upon the degree of difference between the previous and new circumstances—and our own expectations and adaptability—we may experience "culture shock."

• Every communication situation is somewhat intercultural in the sense that no two people have precisely the same cultural backgrounds. The greater the difference in cultural backgrounds, the greater the communication challenge and the less likely that "message sent" will equal "message received." However, some situations in which we assume there are no major cultural differences—for instance, all parties were raised in the United States and speak English as their first language—can still present major intercultural challenges as a result of differing family, religious, ethnic, occupational, or geographic influences.

• Potentially important components of intercultural communication competence are:[36]

Respect for people whose behaviors and cultures differ from our own.

Knowledge of the cultures involved.

Willingness to acquire knowledge of others' cultures.

Empathy for others' situations.

Sensitivity to cultural differences in language, conversational rules, and nonverbal behavior.

A nonjudgmental approach to different cultural patterns.

Tolerance for new and ambiguous situations.

The capacity to balance task- and support-role orientation.

Self-awareness.

Summary

From the point of view of communication, culture can be defined as the complex combination of common symbols, knowledge, folklore conventions, language, message-processing patterns, rules, rituals, habits, lifestyles, and attitudes that link and give a common identity to a particular group of people at a particular time.

All social systems—relationships, groups, organizations, and societies—develop and maintain cultures through communication. The symbols of a society are among the most visible signs of culture. Of these, spoken and written language are the most pervasive. Cultures link individuals to one another, provide the basis for a common identity, and create a context for interaction and negotiation among members. The relationship between culture and communication is reciprocally-defining: Through communication we shape our cultures; and in turn, our cultures shape our communication patterns.

Cultures are complex and multifaceted, invisible, and subjective; and cultures change over time. We become aware of cultures through violations of cultural conventions, cross-cultural contact, and scholarly analysis.

Mediated communication plays an important role in the creation and maintenance of cultures. By extending our capacity to create, duplicate, and store messages, our technology broadens the pool of information available in common to individuals in relationships, groups, organizations, and societies. The cultural information base of a society consists of news, information, and entertainment programming. Mediated messages are a kind of cultural mirror, combining with the messages of face-to-face communication to provide an agenda of concerns, issues, values, personalities, and themes that occupy a central role in the symbolic environment to which individuals must adapt.

Adapting to a culture is a natural process of developing appropriate personal theories, representations, maps, and images of the cultures of which we are members. Because we adapt to our own cultures so easily and thoroughly, it is frequently a difficult and stressful matter to readjust to others, often resulting in what has been termed "culture shock."

We are engaged in intercultural communication when we interact with people from other cultures. Every communication situation involving someone we don't know well is intercultural to some degree. As we meet new people, we negotiate the beginnings of new relationships and new relational cultures.

A society is a complex social system composed of a large number of diverse, geographically dispersed, and mutually-dependent individuals, groups, and organizations in pursuit of common goals. Societies are created, defined, and maintained through communication among the individuals who compose them. Societies operate by means of national and international networks. These networks provide the means through which information is conveyed among members of a society, facilitate the coordination of diverse activities within a society, and supply the channel through which collective decisions are made and implemented. An information society is one in which communication and information play a central role economically and socially, as in for example, the United States, Japan, Sweden, and England.

Many writers have pointed optimistically to a future in which citizens of the world would be linked together in a global village. As this seems to be an increasingly likely possibility, concerns are being expressed that the intrusion of messages from other cultures can be destructive, economically and socially. Moreover, the availability of common messages among members of different societies does not assure common understanding, acceptance, or peace. However, the ever-increasing pool of shared environmental information—along with new common needs and goals—seems likely to lead to a more predictable and shared world culture than the one guiding relations between countries of the world today. The increasing number of communication situations alone provides no guarantee of improved world relationships, but efforts to improve our individual communication skills can help to bridge the gap.

Notes

1. Excerpted from Horace Miner, "Body Ritual among the Nacirema," *American Anthropologist,* Vol 58, No. 3, June, 1956, pp. 503–507.
2. E. B. Tylor, quoted in Marvin E. Wolfgang and Franco Ferracuti, *The Subculture of Violence* (New York: Tavistock 1967), p. 95.
3. See Lee Thayer, *Communication and Communication Systems* (Homewood, IL: Irwin, 1968), p. 47.
4. See Edward Hall, *The Silent Language* (New York: Doubleday, 1959), pp. 50–52.
5. An acknowledgment for this phraseology is due to Marshall McLuhan and the well-known adage of his time: "We shape our tools and thereafter our tools shape us."
6. See *How to Map a People* (Provo, UT: Brigham Young University, David M. Kennedy Center for International Studies, 1976).
7. For the phrase "cultural iceberg" I am indebted to the writings of Donald Timkulu, "The Cultural Iceberg" (Ottawa, Canada: Canadian International Development Agency, Briefing Center), 1980.
8. See Alison Lanier, *Saudi Arabia* (New York: Overseas Briefing Associates, 1978), especially Sections II and V.
9. Edward T. Hall, *Beyond Culture* (Garden City, NY: Anchor Press/Doubleday, 1979); and Edward T. Hall and Mildred Reed Hall, *Understanding Cultural Differences: Germans, French, and Americans* (Yarmouth, ME: Intercultural Press, 1989).
10. Hall and Hall, 1989, p. 6.
11. Hall, 1976, p. 91.
12. Hall and Hall, 1989, pp. 6–7.
13. Hall and Hall, 1989, p. 13.
14. Hall and Hall, 1989, p. 14.

15. Peter Farb, *Word Play: What Happens When People Talk* (New York: Knopf, 1979).

16. See Todd Hunt and Brent D. Ruben, *Mass Communication: Producers and Consumers* (New York: HarperCollins, 1992); Richard W. Budd and Brent D. Ruben, eds. *Beyond Media: New Approaches to Mass Communication,* 2nd ed. (New Brunswick, NJ: Transaction, 1988); and Herbert Schiller, *Culture, Inc.: The Corporate Takeover of Public Expression* (New York: Oxford University Press, 1989), especially Chapter 2, "The Corporation and the Production of Culture," for a more detailed discussion of mass communication and mass production and distribution of culture.

17. A summary of a more lengthy discussion provided by Dan Nimmo and James E. Combs, *Mediated Political Realities* (New York: Longman, 1983). See Chapter 6 "Fantasies of the Arena: Popular Sports and Politics."

18. Robbi L. Ruben, "Lessons of Videogaming," Unpublished paper, Rutgers University, November, 1989.

19. R. Ruben, 1989.

20. R. Ruben, 1989.

21. See "Socialization and Concepts of Social Reality," in *Television and Behavior: Ten Years of Scientific Progress and Implications for the Eighties. Volume 1: Summary Report* (Rockville, MD: National Institute of Mental Health, 1982), pp. 54–66; Hugh D. Duncan, *Communication and Social Order* (London: Oxford University Press, 1962); and Hugh D. Duncan, *Symbols in Society* (New York: Oxford University Press, 1968), especially Parts II and III.

22. Kalvero Oberg, "Culture Shock and the Problem of Adjustment to New Cultural Environments," Unpublished paper, Washington, DC: Department of State, Foreign Service Institute, 1958.

23. *Guidelines for United States Navy Overseas Diplomacy* (Washington, DC: Department of Navy,) p. 33.

24. *Guidelines for United States Navy,* p. 33.

25. *Guidelines for United States Navy,* p. 33.

26. Hall, 1959, p. 199.

27. See Young Y. Kim, *Communication and Cross-Cultural Adaptation* (Clevedon, England: Multilingual Matters, 1988). Excellent summaries of writing and research in the area of cultural adaptation are also provided by Marjorie H. Klein, " Adaptation to New Cultural Environments," in *Overview of Intercultural Education, Training and Research. Volume I: Theory.* Ed. by David S. Hoopes, Paul B. Pedersen, and George W. Renwick (Washington, DC: Society for Intercultural Education, Training and Research, 1977) pp. 50–56; David Reed Barker, in "Culture Shock and Anthropological Fieldwork," Paper presented at the conference for the Society for Intercultural Education, Training and Research, Mount Pocono, PA., 1980; and by Daniel J. Kealey in *Adaptation to a New Environment* (Ottawa, Canada: Canadian International Development Agency, Briefing Centre, 1978).

28. William B. Gudykunst and Young Yun Kim, *Communicating with Strangers: An Approach to Intercultural Communication* (New York: Random House, 1984), pp. 23–24.

29. Karl Deutsch, *The Nerves of Government* (New York: Free Press, 1966).

30. Jorge Reina Schement and Leah Lievrouw, eds., *Competing Visions, Complex Realities: Social Aspects of the Information Society* (Norwood, NJ: Ablex, 1987).

31. Jerry L. Salvaggio, "The Telecommunications Revolution: Are We Up to the Challenge." In *Telecommunications: Issues and Choices for Society.* Ed. by Jerry L. Salvaggio (New York: Oxford University Press, 1983), pp. 148–153.

32. Marc U. Porat, *The Information Economy: Definition and Measurement (OT Special Publication 77-12), Volumes 1–9* (Washington, DC: Department of Commerce/Office of Telecommunication, Government Printing Office, 1977).

33. Bill Carter, "MTV's International Beat Brings a Sound of Dollars," *The New York Times,* May 7, 1990, p. D 8.

34. Hall and Hall, 1990, p. 5.

35. Philip Revzin, "La Boob Tube: Europe Complains About U.S. Shows," *The Wall Street-Journal,* October 16, 1989, p. 1–10.

36. Based on summary of research and discussions in Gudykunst and Kim, 1984; Young Y. Kim, *Communication and Cross-Cultural Adaptation* (Clevedon, England: Multilingual matters, 1988); Brent D. Ruben and Daniel J. Kealey, "Behavioral Assessment of Communication Competency and the Prediction of Cross-Cultural Adaptation," *International Journal of Intercultural Relations,* Vol. 3, No. 1 (Spring, 1979), pp. 15–48; Brent D. Ruben, "Human Communication and Cross-Cultural Effectiveness," *International and Intercultural Communication Annual,* Vol. 4, 1978, pp. 95–105; and others. See "References and Suggested Readings."

References and Suggested Readings

ALMANEY, A. J., and A. J. ALWAN. *Communication with Arabs: A Handbook for the Business Executive.* Prospect Heights, IL: Waveland, 1982.

BARNLUND, DEAN C. *Communicative Styles of Japanese and Americans: Images and Realities.* Belmont, CA: Wadsworth, 1989.

BERGER, ARTHUR ASA. *Signs in Contemporary Culture: An Introduction to Semiotics.* Salem, WI: Sheffield, 1989.

BERGER, PETER L., "Sociology of Knowledge." In *Interdisciplinary Approaches to Human Communication.* Second Ed. Ed. by Richard W. Budd and Brent D. Ruben. New Brunswick, NJ: Transaction, 1988.

BERGER, PETER L., and THOMAS LUCKMANN. *The Social Construction of Reality.* Garden City, NY: Doubleday, 1966.

BERRIEN, F. KENNETH. *General and Social Systems.* New Brunswick, NJ: Rutgers University Press, 1968.

BLUMER, HERBERT. "Symbolic Interaction." In *Interdisciplinary Approaches to*

Human Communication. Second Ed. Ed. by Richard W. Budd, and Brent D. Ruben. New Brunswick, NJ: Transaction, 1987.

———. *Symbolic Interactionism.* Englewood Cliffs, NJ: Prentice Hall, 1969.

BOSTAIN, JAMES. "How to Read a Foreigner Like a Book." Parts I and II. Videotape. Produced by the Canadian International Development Agency, Briefing Centre, Hull, Quebec, 1977.

BRISLIN, RICHARD W. *Cross-Cultural Encounters.* New York: Pergamon, 1981.

BRISLIN, RICHARD W., KENNETH CUSHNER, CRAIG CHERRIE, and MAHEALANI YONG. *Intercultural Interactions: A Practical Guide.* Beverly Hills, CA: Sage, 1986.

BROWN, RICHARD H. *Society as Text: Essays on Rhetoric, Reason, and Reality.* Chicago: University of Chicago Press, 1987.

BUCKLEY, WALTER. *Sociology and Modern Systems Theory.* Englewood Cliffs, NJ: Prentice Hall, 1967.

BUDD, RICHARD W., and BRENT D. RUBEN. *Beyond Media.* Second Ed. New Brunswick, NJ: Transaction, 1988.

———. *Interdisciplinary Approaches to Human Communication.* New Brunswick, NJ: Transaction, 1987.

CAREY, JAMES. "The Mass Media and Critical Theory: An American View." In *Communication Yearbook 6.* Ed. by Michael Burgoon. Beverly Hills: Sage, 1982, 18–33.

CHERRY, COLIN. *World Communication.* New York: Wiley, 1971.

CULTUREGRAM SERIES. Provo, UT: Brigham Young University, David M. Kennedy Center for International Studies, Publication Services, 1990.

CUSHMAN, DONALD P., and DUDLEY D. CAHN, JR. "Cross-Cultural Communication and Interpersonal Relationships." In *Bridges Not Walls,* Fourth Ed. Ed. by John Stewart. New York: Random House, 1986, 324–333.

DEETZ, STANLEY. *Democracy in an Age of Corporate Colonization: Developments in Communication and the Politics of Everyday Life.* Albany: SUNY Press, 1991.

DOUGLAS, MARY, ed. *Rules and Meanings.* New York: Penguin, 1972.

DUETSCH, KARL W. *The Nerves of Government.* New York: Free Press, 1966.

DUNCAN, HUGH D. *Communication and Social Order.* London: Oxford University Press, 1962.

———. *Symbols in Society.* New York: Oxford University Press, 1968.

———. *Symbols and Social Theory.* New York: Oxford University Press, 1969.

ELLINGSWORTH, HUBER W. "Conceptualizing Intercultural Communication." In *Communication Yearbook 1.* Ed. by Brent D. Ruben. New Brunswick, NJ: Transaction-International Communication Association, 1977, 99–106.

FARB, PETER. *Word Play: What Happens When People Talk.* New York: Knopf, 1979.

FERSH, SEYMOUR, ed. *Learning about Peoples and Cultures.* Evanston, IL: McDougal, Littell, 1974.

FISHER, WALTER R. *Human Communication as Narration: Toward a Philosophy of Reason, Value, and Action.* Columbia, SC: University of South Carolina Press, 1987.

FISKE, JOHN. *Television Culture.* London: Routledge, 1987.

FRANK, LAWRENCE. "Cultural Organization." In *General Systems Theory and Human Communication.* Ed. by Brent D. Ruben and John Y. Kim. Rochelle Park, NJ: Hayden, 1975, 128–135.

FURNHAM, ADRIAN and STEPHEN BOCHNER. *Culture Shock.* London: Metheun, 1986.

GEERTZ, CLIFFORD. *The Interpretation of Cultures.* New York: Basic Books, 1973.

GERARD, R. W. "A Biologist's View of Society." *General Systems, Vol. 1, 1956.*

GIDDENS, ANTHONY. *The Constitution of Society: Outline of the Theory of Structuration.* Berkeley: University of California Press, 1984.

GUDYKUNST, WILLIAM, and YOUNG KIM. *Communicating with Strangers.* Reading, MA: Addison-Wesley, 1984.

Guidelines for United States Navy Overseas Diplomacy. Washington, DC: Department of Navy.

GUMPERT, GARY. *Talking Tombstones and Other Tales of the Media Age.* New York: Oxford University Press, 1987.

HALL, EDWARD T. *Beyond Culture.* Garden City, NY: Doubleday, 1979.

———. *The Silent Language.* Garden City, NY: Doubleday, 1959.

HALL, EDWARD T., and MILDRED REED HALL. *Understanding Cultural Differences: Germans, French, and Americans.* Yarmouth, ME: Intercultural Press, 1989.

HALL, STUART. "Ideology and Communication Theory." *In Rethinking Communication. Volume 1: Paradigm Dialogues.* Ed. by Brenda Dervin, Lawrence Grossberg, Barbara J. O'Keefe, and Ellen Wartella. Newbury Park: Sage, 1989, 40–52.

HALL, STUART, CHAS CRITCHER, TONY JEFFERSON, JOHN CLARKE, and BRIAN ROBERTS. *Policing the Crisis: Mugging, the State, and Law and Order.* London: Macmillan, 1978.

HOLZNER, BURKART. *Reality Construction in Society.* Cambridge, MA: Schenkman, 1968.

How to Map a People. Brigham Young University, David M. Kennedy Center for International Studies, 1976.

HUNT, TODD, and BRENT D. RUBEN. *Mass Communication: Producers and Consumers.* New York: HarperCollins, 1992.

KEALEY, DANIEL J. *Adaptation to a New Environment.* Ottawa, Canada: Canadian International Development Agency, Briefing Centre, 1978.

KIM, YOUNG YUN. *Communication and Cross-Cultural Adaptation.* Clevedon, England: Multilingual Matters, 1988.

KIM, YOUNG Y., and BRENT D. RUBEN. "Intercultural Transformation: A Systems Theory." *International and Intercultural Communication Annual.* Vol. 12, 1988, 299–321.

KLEIN, MARJORIE H. "Adaptation to New Cultural Environments." In *Overview of Intercultural Education, Training and Research. Volume I: Theory.* Ed. by David S. Hoopes. Paul B. Pedersen, and George W. Renwick, Washington, DC: Society for Intercultural Education, Training and Research, 1977.

LANIER, ALISON. *Saudi Arabia.* New York: Overseas Briefing Associates, 1978.

LASZLO, EWIN. *The Systems View of the World.* New York: Braziller, 1972.

———, ed. *The World System.* New York: Braziller, 1973.

LEISS, WILLIAM, STEPHEN KLINE, and SUT JHALLY. *Social Communication in Advertising.* Second Ed. Scarborough, Ontario: Nelson Canada, 1985.

LEVINE ROBERT A. *Culture, Behavior, and Personality.* Chicago: Aldine, 1973.

LIPPMAN, WALTER. *Public Opinion.* New York: Free Press, 1922.

MARUYAMA, MAGORAH. "Metaorganization of Information." *Cybernetica,* Vol. 4, 1965.

MEAD, GEORGE HERBERT. *Mind, Self and Society.* Chicago: University of Chicago, 1934.

MERRITT, RICHARD L. "Transmission of Values Across National Boundaries." In *Communication in International Politics.* Ed. by Richard L. Merritt. Urbana, IL: University of Illinois Press, 1972.

MINER, HORACE. "Body Ritual Among the Nacirema." *American Anthropologist.* Vol 58, No. 3, June, 1956.

MONANE, JOSEPH H. *A Sociology of Human Systems.* New York: Appleton-Century-Crofts, 1967.

MORRIS, DESMOND. *Manwatching.* New York: Abrams, 1977.

NIMMO, DAN, and JAMES E. COMBS. *Mediated Political Realities.* New York: Longman, 1983.

POOL, ITHIEL DE SOLA. *Technologies of Freedom.* Cambridge, MA: Harvard University Press, 1983.

POOL, ITHIEL DE SOLA, HIROSHI INOSE, NOZOMU TAKASAKI, and ROGER HURWITZ. *Communication Flows.* Amsterdam: North-Holland, 1984.

POOL, ITHIEL DE SOLA, RICHARD E. PORTER, and NEMI C. JAIN. *Understanding Intercultural Communication.* Belmont, CA: Wadsworth, 1981.

PORAT, MARC U. *The Information Economy: Definition and Measurement. (OT Special Publication 77-12), Volumes 1–9.* Washington, DC: Department of Commerce/Office of Telecommunication, Government Printing Office, 1977.

RIVERS, WILLIAM L. *The Adversaries.* Boston: Beacon Press, 1970.

RUBEN, BRENT D. "Cross-Cultural Communication Competence: Traditions and Issues for the Future." *International Journal of Intercultural Relations.* Vol. 13, No. 3, 1989.

———. "Human Communication and Cross-Cultural Effectiveness." *International and Intercultural Communication Annual.* Vol. 4, 1978, 95–105.

RUBEN, BRENT D., and DANIEL J. KEALEY. "Behavioral Assessment of Communication Competency and the Prediction of Cross-Cultural Adaptation." *International Journal of Intercultural Relations.* Vol. 3, No. 1, Spring 1979, 15–48.

RUBEN, BRENT D., and JOHN Y. KIM, eds. *General Systems Theory and Human Communication.* Rochelle Park, NJ: Hayden, 1975.

SALVAGGIO, JERRY L. "The Telecommunications Revolution: Are We Up to the Challenge." In *Telecommunications: Issues and Choices for Society.* Ed. by Jerry L. Salvaggio. New York: Oxford University Press, 1983, 148–153.

SARBAUGH, L. E. *Intercultural Communication.* Second Ed. New Brunswick, NJ: Transaction, 1987.

SCHILLER, HERBERT I. *Mass Communications and American Empire.* New York: Kelley, 1969.

———. *Culture, Inc.: The Corporate Takeover of Public Expression.* New York: Oxford University Press, 1989.

SHAHN, BEN. *The Shape of Content.* Cambridge, MA: Harvard University Press, 1967.

SIEBERT, FREDERICK, S., THEODORE PETERSON, and WILBUR SCHRAMM. *Four Theories of the Press.* Urbana, IL: University of Illinois Press, 1956.

SINGER, MARSHALL R. *Intercultural Communication.* Englewood Cliffs, NJ: Prentice Hall, 1987.

SMITH, ANTHONY. *The Geopolitics of Information: How Western Culture Dominates the World.* New York: Oxford University Press, 1980.

SMITH, ALFRED G., ed. *Communication and Culture.* New York: Holt, 1966.

STARK, WARNER, ed. *The Sociology of Knowledge.* London: Routledge and Kegan Paul, 1958.

"Socialization and Concepts of Social Reality." In *Television and Behavior: Ten Years of Scientific Progress and Implications for the Eighties. Volume 1: Summary Report.* Rockville, MD: National Institute of Mental Health, 1982.

STEWART, JOHN, ed. *Bridges Not Walls.* Fourth Ed. New York: Random House, 1986.

THAYER, LEE. *Communication and Communication Systems.* Homewood, IL: Irwin, 1968.

———. "On the Mass Media and Mass Communication: Notes Toward a Theory." In *Beyond Media: New Approaches to Mass Communication. Second Ed.* Ed. by Richard W. Budd and Brent D. Ruben. New Brunswick, NJ: Transaction, 1988, 52–83.

VICKERS, GEOFFREY. *Value Systems and Social Process.* New York: Basic, 1968.

WILSON, JOAN, and MARGARET OMAR. "A Self-Taught Guide to Cultural Learning." Revised in *Human Communication Handbook: Simulations and Games: Volume 2,* Rochelle Park, NJ: Hayden, 1978, 116–121.

WILSON, STAN LE ROY. *Mass Media/Mass Culture: An Introduction.* New York: Random House, 1989.

Index

Name Index

Subject Index